misassessment, miscategorization, misplacement, and misinstruction of multi-cultural learners with and without exceptionalities. For researchers and scholars, this book presents important opportunities to ask and answer questions critical to building the fields of general and special education.

ACKNOWLEDGMENTS

Invited to contribute chapters to *Multicultural Special Education: Culturally Responsive Teaching* are well-known scholars and educators. Many of them are nationally or internationally renowned in the fields of psychology, education, counseling, health care, and speech and language pathology. Without these scholars and educators, this book would not be successful.

I am grateful to the reviewers of this book for making critical suggestions that have buttressed its quality: Beverly Argus-Calvo, University of Texas, El Paso; Mary Curtis, University of Texas, Brownsville; Jozi De Leon, New Mexico State University; Bruce Mitchell, Eastern Washington University; Robert W. Ortiz, California State University, Fresno; Mary Ann Prater, Brigham Young University; Melanie S. Reid, Metropolitan State College of Denver; and Robin M. Smith, State University of New York at New Paltz. My special thanks go to Luciana Ugrina of the Word Processing Department of the School of Education, the University of Wisconsin–Milwaukee for her dedication to quality service. I want to especially acknowledge Allyson Sharp of Merrill/Prentice Hall for her intense support in creating this book. Finally, books of this nature are only successful with the dedicated support of family members and friends. My heartfelt thanks go especially to my wife, Pauline, and my children, Charles II, Gina, Kristen, and Alicia for their patience, love, and kindness throughout this book project.

F. E. O.

Discover the Merrill
Resources for Special Education Website

Technology is a constantly growing and changing aspect of our field that is creating a need for new content and resources. To address this emerging need, Merrill Education has developed an online learning environment for students, teachers, and professors alike to complement our products—the *Merrill Resources for Special Education* Website. This content-rich website provides additional resources specific to this book's topic and will help you—professors, classroom teachers, and students—augment your teaching, learning, and professional development.

Our goal with this initiative is to build on and enhance what our products already offer. For this reason, the content for our user-friendly website is organized by topic and provides teachers, professors, and students with a variety of meaningful resources all in one location. With this website, we bring together the best of what Merrill has to offer: text resources, video clips, web links, tutorials, and a wide variety of information on topics of interest to general and special educators alike. Rich content, applications, and competencies further enhance the learning process.

The *Merrill Resources for Special Education* Website includes:

- Video clips specific to each topic, with questions to help you evaluate the content and make crucial theory-to-practice connections.
- Thought-provoking critical analysis questions that students can answer and turn in for evaluation or that can serve as basis for class discussions and lectures.
- Access to a wide variety of resources related to classroom strategies and methods, including lesson planning and classroom management.
- Information on all the most current relevant topics related to special and general education, including CEC and Praxis™ standards, IEPs, portfolios, and professional development.
- Extensive web resources and overviews on each topic addressed on the website.
- A search feature to help access specific information quickly.

To take advantage of these and other resources, please visit the *Merrill Resources for Special Education* Website at

http://www.prenhall.com/obiakor

About the Author

Festus E. Obiakor, Ph.D., is Professor in the Department of Exceptional Education, University of Wisconsin–Milwaukee. His graduate degrees are from Texas Christian University and New Mexico State University. Dr. Obiakor is a teacher, scholar, and consultant. His specific areas of interest include self-concept development, multicultural psychology and special education, comparative/international education, and educational reform/program evaluation. Dr. Obiakor has written more than 150 academic publications, including books, chapters, articles, and commentaries. For two consecutive years (1990 and 1991), he was the recipient of the University of Tennessee at Chattanooga School of Education Outstanding Research and Scholarship Award; in 1992, he was honored with the University of Tennessee at Chattanooga Horace J. Traylor Minority Leadership Award; in 1993 and 2001, he was the recipient of the Dedicated Service Award of the National Black Caucus of Special Educators, Council for Exceptional Children; in 1995, he received the Emporia State University Presidential Award for Distinguished Service to Diversity; and in 1996, 2000, 2002, and 2005, he was listed in *Who's Who Among America's Teachers*. He has served as Distinguished Visiting Professor/Scholar at Frostburg State University, Hendrix College, Indiana University of Pennsylvania, Portland State University, the University of Georgia, Eastern Illinois University, Marquette University, West Virginia University, Hampton University, Illinois State University, Brigham Young University, Tennessee State University, and Morgan State University. Additionally, Dr. Obiakor is on the editorial board of many scholarly publications, including *Teacher Education and Special Education, Multicultural Learning and Teaching,* and *Multiple Voices*—he currently serves as Associate Editor and Co-Editor of these journals, respectively. In his teachings, writings, workshops, and presentations, he has continued to prescribe multidimensional methods of assessment, divergent teaching techniques, and a comprehensive support model to connect the self, the family, the school, and the community in providing learning opportunities and choices for *all* students.

List of Contributors

Patricia Addison
Director of Special Education
Fairfax County Public Schools
Fairfax, Virginia

Bob Algozzine
Professor
Department of Educational Administration
University of North Carolina at Charlotte
Charlotte, North Carolina

Jeffrey P. Bakken
Professor
Department of Special Education
College of Education
Illinois State University
Normal, Illinois

Sandra Burkhardt
Professor
Department of Counseling Psychology
St. Xavier University
Chicago, Illinois

Kathleen M. Chinn
Associate Professor
Department of Special Education and
  Communication Disorders
New Mexico State University
Las Cruces, New Mexico

Bertina H. Combes
Associate Professor and Program Coordinator
Department of Special Education
College of Education
University of North Texas
Denton, Texas

Vera I. Daniels
Professor
Department of Special Education
College of Education
Southern University
Baton Rouge, Louisiana

Elizabeth A. Dooley
Professor and Head
Department of Educational Theory and
  Practice
College of Human Resources and Education
West Virginia University
Morgantown, West Virginia

Barbara J. Dray
Doctoral Candidate
Department of Special Education
University of Texas at Austin
Austin, Texas

Beth A. Durodoye
Associate Professor
Department of Counseling, Educational
  Psychology, and Adult and Higher Education
College of Education and Human
  Development
University of Texas at San Antonio
San Antonio, Texas

Tina Taylor Dyches
Associate Professor
Department of Counseling Psychology and
  Special Education
College of Education
Brigham Young University
Provo, Utah

C. Jonah Eleweke
Special Needs Education Program Assistant
Grant McEwan College
City Center Campus
Edmonton, Alberta
Canada

Alice Farling
Assistant Superintendent
Department of Special Services
Fairfax County Public Schools
Fairfax, Virginia

Joan Fleitas
Associate Professor
School of Nursing
Lehman College
City University of New York
Bronx, New York

Shernaz B. Garcia
Associate Professor and Graduate Advisor
Department of Special Education
College of Education
University of Texas at Austin
Austin, Texas

Mark B. Goor
Professor and Associate Dean
College of Education
George Mason University
Fairfax, Virginia

Patrick A. Grant
Professor
Department of Special Education
Slippery Rock, University of Pennsylvania
Slippery Rock, Pennsylvania

Eric J. López
Assistant Professor
Department of Special Education and
  Communication Disorder
New Mexico State University
Las Cruces, New Mexico

Martha Scott Lue
Professor
Department of Educational Studies
College of Education
University of Central Florida
Orlando, Florida

Angela Stephens McIntosh
Assistant Professor
Department of Special Education
College of Education
San Diego State University
San Diego, California

Arletha J. McSwain
Professor and Head
Department of Early Childhood
Norfolk State University
Norfolk, Virginia

Sunday O. Obi
Associate Professor
Division of Education and Human Services
Kentucky State University
Frankfurt, Kentucky

Alba A. Ortiz
President's Chair for Education and Academic
  Excellence
Department of Special Education
College of Education
University of Texas at Austin
Austin, Texas

Howard P. Parette
Endowed Professor of Assistive Technology
Department of Special Education
College of Education
Illinois State University
Normal, Illinois

James M. Patton
Professor
Department of Special Education
College of Education
College of William and Mary
Williamsburg, Virginia

Loretta P. Prater
Professor and Dean
College of Health and Human Services
Southeast Missouri State University
Cape Girardeau, Missouri

Anthony Rotatori
Professor
Department of Counseling Psychology
St. Xavier University
Chicago, Illinois

Robert Rueda
Professor
School of Education
University of Southern California
Los Angeles, California

Spencer J. Salend
Professor
Department of Special Education
College of Education
State University of New York–New Paltz
New Paltz, New York

Wendy Sapp
Educational Consultant
Visual Impairment Educational Service
5030 Village Drive
Cohutta, Georgia

Janice Morgan Taylor
Staff Coordinator
CCC—Speech Pathology
Orange County Public Schools
Orlando, Florida

Shandra R. Terrell
Director
Teaching/Learning Center
College of Veterinary Medicine, Nursing, and
  Allied Health
Tuskegee University
Tuskegee, Alabama

Cheryl A. Utley
Associate Research Professor
Juniper Gardens Children's Project
University of Kansas
Kansas City, Kansas

Eugene C. Valles
Associate Professor and Chair
Department of Special Education
College of Education
San Diego State University
San Diego, California

Lynn K. Wilder
Associate Professor
Department of Counseling Psychology and
  Special Education
College of Education
Brigham Young University
Provo, Utah

James R. Yates
John L. & Elizabeth G.H. Centennial Professor
  in Education
Department of Educational Administration
University of Texas at Austin
Austin, Texas

Brief Contents

Part III   *Lifespan Issues and Multicultural Special Education   195*

Part IV   *Future Perspectives of Multicultural Special Education   247*

Contents

CHAPTER
5

Working with Multicultural Learners with Cognitive Disabilities   64
Festus E. Obiakor and Cheryl A. Utley

CHAPTER
6

Working with Multicultural Learners with Learning Disabilities   78
Patrick A. Grant and Sunday O. Obi

CHAPTER
7

Working with Multicultural Learners with Behavioral Problems   96
Cheryl A. Utley and Spencer J. Salend

CHAPTER
8

Working with Multicultural Learners with Gifts and Talents   110
Vera I. Daniels

Part III   *Lifespan Issues and Multicultural Special Education*   *195*

CHAPTER **14**   *Early Childhood Multicultural Special Education*   *196*
Arletha J. McSwain and James M. Patton

CHAPTER **15**   *Multicultural Special Education Transition Programming*   *206*
Bertina H. Combes and Beth A. Durodoye

CHAPTER 19

CHAPTER 20

Note: Every effort has been made to provide accurate and current Internet information in this book. However, the Internet and information posted on it are constantly changing, and it is inevitable that some of the Internet addresses listed in this textbook will change.

Part I

Foundations of Multicultural Special Education

Chapter 1

Multicultural Special Education in Today's Schools

Festus E. Obiakor

Chapter Outline

Thinking About Multicultural Special Education

Juan was a 10-year-old Latino student who had lived in the United States for 5 years. He attended a "good" school where the focus was on making higher test scores. Although his family spoke primarily Spanish in the home, Juan spoke moderate English. Peers frequently ridiculed his English—they felt he was not "smart" because of his slight accent—and he had difficulty relating to them. Classmates consistently used negative words to describe him. On one occasion, the teacher noted that "Juan does not get along with his peers." Juan's parents had tried working with the classroom teacher; however, she appeared not to understand their concerns regarding their son. Juan was referred by this teacher for standardized testing for behavior disorders. Meanwhile, the teacher was taking a "multicultural learning and teaching in special education" course at a nearby university for self-improvement. In this course, she began to learn new ideas and techniques on working with culturally diverse students.

Since Juan was referred for assessment, his official day of assessment was scheduled by the school psychologist. The night before Juan's assessment, his dog was hit by a car and killed. He therefore was in poor spirits, yet he was assessed as scheduled. On the testing date, the school psychologist, who spoke no Spanish, was late because of car problems on the way to school. The tests were administered in her small office, a place unfamiliar to Juan. His test scores were compared to white norms. In the end, he was labeled "behavior disordered" and was to be placed in the special education program.

Surprisingly, Juan's teacher scheduled a meeting with both the parents and the school psychologist to inform them about her opinion regarding Juan's intended placement. She did not agree with the placement because she had learned so much in her university course that she could use to support Juan in her class. She even noted that "variables such as cultural differences, academic background, ability to speak and understand English, negative peer behavior, her lack of understanding, emotional concerns over losing the pet, and the examiner's demeanor were not considered in the identification and assessment of behavior disorders for Juan." This was a pleasant surprise for the parents and a shock to the school psychologist. Before long, Juan's parents and the teacher began to get along, and he started to make remarkable progress in school as she made some modifications and adaptations. Juan's teacher hired a bilingual paraprofessional for her class. She was so good at responding to her students' learning styles that her principal began to use her to help other teachers in her school and district.

- What lessons can be learned from Juan's case?
- How can more teachers like Juan's be produced in education?

It is not uncommon to see multicultural learners in today's public schools. According to the National Center for Education Statistics (2001), public school enrollments for 2000–2001 showed a national student population of 67% Anglo American (white), 17% African American, 16% Hispanic (Latino), 4% Asian/Pacific Islander, and 1% American Indian/Alaska Native. However, with regard to special education, the racial/ethnic placement composition of students was 43% Anglo American (white), 20% African American, 14% Hispanic (Latino), 2% Asian/Pacific Islander, and 1% American Indian/Alaska Native (U.S. Department of Education, 2001). Interestingly, even with this increase in student diversity, "the cultural gap between the current school age population and the teaching pool is widely recognized" (Kozleski, Sobel, & Taylor, 2003, p. 75). In other words, the changing student demography in general and special education programs has not truly reflected changes in the teaching force. It is no surprise that there is sometimes a disconnect between what multicultural learners bring to the classroom and what their white peers and teachers bring to the classroom.

Juan's case demonstrates traditional teaching-learning situations in which some multicultural learners find themselves when teachers are unprepared or ill prepared. To a large measure, it reveals unintended consequences associated with the current selection process for special education, which sometimes leads to misidentification, misassessment, miscategorization, misplacement, and misinstruction or misintervention. But a bigger positive picture is revealed in this case; that is, the teacher decided to take advantage of a "multicultural learning and teaching in special education" course offered at a nearby university. This teacher decided to shift her power and paradigm. Although the initial goal in the classroom was to assist Juan, the unintended consequence was ultimate exclusion from the general education environment. Because of the teacher's education, she changed this course of action. She did not want Juan to be entangled with school programs that appear to downplay his strengths while highlighting his supposed weaknesses (Baca & Cervantes, 2004; Banks, 2002; Guinier, 2002; Henze, Katz, Norte, Sather, & Walker, 2002; Obiakor & Ford, 2002). To effectively discuss Juan's case and provide the rationale for multicultural special education (the main focus of this text), it is important to analyze his classroom/school experiences within the contexts of the selection process for special education (i.e., identification, assessment, categorization, placement, and instruction).

THE IDENTIFICATION OF JUAN

Is it possible that Juan's classroom situation warranted his teacher's attention? Initially, his situation was unclear to the teacher, not because she was not a good person, but because she was unaware of some conflicting issues in Juan's education. She came to the realization that he had a linguistic difference and not a linguistic deficiency, as his classmates might have initially assumed. Clearly, the initial identification of Juan as a problem student set the stage for further legally mandated activities not routinely addressed in regular education classrooms. Once a student has been identified as having an educational problem, the laws (e.g., the 1975 Education for All Handicapped Children Act, the 1990 Individuals with Disabilities Education Act, or its reauthorization in 1997) mandate that teachers employ several interventions before the testing phase is set in motion. Initially, Juan's teacher did not seem to empower his parents or engage them in any form of due process collaboration needed to enhance a successful learning experience for him. Before Juan was recommended for assessment, multiple sources of information (e.g., classroom observations of how Juan interacted with his classmates or how he performed in classroom activities) should have been employed.

Grossman (2002) and Sbarra and Pianta (2001) agreed that some teachers judge ethnic minority and poor students' behaviors as more deviant than those of white children. They also noted that these perceptions are due to teachers' cultural biases. Interestingly, parents trust and rely on general and special educators to detect various disabilities; however, some teachers play on the subjective nature of the current system and abuse the initial referral process by selectively excluding those whom they deem as different (Skrtic, 2003; Utley & Obiakor, 2001). As demonstrated in Juan's case, his teacher shifted her paradigm after taking a course on multicultural learning and teaching. She reversed the circle of failure into which Juan was heading. She began to view his parents as equal partners (Fletcher & Bos, 1999).

THE ASSESSMENT OF JUAN

The key terms in education today are *accountability* and *evidence-based practices* (see the National Research Council's 2002 report and the 2001 No Child Left Behind Act). Assessment is not only a part of accountability; it is also an integral part of the teaching-learning process. However, there are historical problems with the reliability and validity of the tools used to assess multicultural learners (Guinier, 2002; Karp, 2002; Karr & Schwenn, 1999; Obiakor, 1999; Obiakor, Beachum, & Harris, 2005; Skrtic, 2003). In Juan's case, the reasons for referral were unclear. He seemed to have been initially referred for assessment because he could not get along with his peers. Clearly, many variables appeared to have been intertwined in his assessment situation. However, in the end the teacher was able to identify these variables because of her new knowledge.

In their works, Grossman (2002) and Karr and Schwenn (1999) suggested that a more comprehensive, holistic model of assessment must be used to avoid miscategorizing students. Multiple voices and multiple information sources (e.g., parents and community members) in Juan's school and home environments would have been beneficial to him before and during the assessment. Apparently, the teacher's new knowledge would help her to make Juan's future assessments (a) instructionally related, (b) operational and functional, (c) authentic and realistic, (d) multidimensional and nondiscriminatory, (e) nonjudgmental and meaningful, (f) responsive to interindividual and intraindividual differences, (g) consultative and collaborative, and (h) germane to culture, race, environment, and language

(Langdon, 2002; Obiakor, 2001, 2003). As a result, Juan's assessment would be measurable, devoid of emotions, and used for making goal-directed decisions in school programs.

THE CATEGORIZATION OF JUAN

Did Juan deserve to be initially categorized as having behavior disorders because he could not get along with classmates who made fun of his linguistic difference? His classroom problem presents the traditional ambiguity regarding criteria for categorical labeling in general and special education. Biased general and special education professionals sometimes predict an ominous doom for some multicultural learners who fail to conform to their individual standards (Grossman, 2002; Guinier, 2002; Obiakor & Beachum, 2005; Rothenberg, 2002; Weiss, 2002; Wise, 2002). In the end, Juan's teacher acknowledged that words and labels are needed to classify students, but that they make victims of students and affect students' self-empowerment. As Hobbs (1975) pointed out

> Categories and labels are powerful instruments for social regulation and control, and they are often employed for obscure, covert, or hurtful purposes: to degrade people, to deny their access to opportunity, to exclude "undesirables" whose presence in some way offends, disturbs familiar custom, or demands extraordinary effort. (p. 11)

Invariably, categories and labels negatively force students to overestimate or underestimate themselves. In addition, they force students to internalize the self-fulfilling prophecy (i.e., when individuals act according to their assigned labels). Trends like these cannot be reversed unless teachers take courses to reeducate themselves. Ysseldyke, Algozzine, and Thurlow (2000) agreed that

> Despite a presumed need for them, labels are an unfortunate by-product of a system that attaches money to acts, thus resulting in classifications and categories. Labels are often irrelevant to the instructional needs of students. Furthermore, labels become real attributes that prevent meaningful understanding of actual individual learning needs. By causing some to believe that students labeled as having mental retardation cannot perform certain tasks, the act of classifying condemns these students to a life of lesser expectations and performance. Labels require official sanction. Resources diverted to the process of identifying and classifying students are extensive. Time and money spent on labeling are time and money not spent on teaching. Time spent being labeled is time not spent on being taught or learning. (p. 11)

THE PLACEMENT OF JUAN

In some cases, placements assist general and special education professionals in designing appropriate programs for persons with special needs. In Juan's case, he would have been placed in an environment that would have diminished his potential. Initially, it seemed that the goal was to exclude him from the regular classroom. Clearly, he was tracked for exclusion! Juan's teacher found out later that he needed her support in the regular classroom. According to Ysseldyke et al. (2000), "placement issues have a broader base than just those individuals with disabilities. The jump from special education segregation to teaching (in grouping) students by their implied level is not a huge leap, and the effects of tracking have been noted repeatedly" (p. 135).

Apparently, Juan's teacher reversed the negative trend for her student. Her focus shifted to his needs and not to his racial and cultural identities. She understood that where a student like Juan is placed reflects how much value he is assumed to have. Critical to education today are issues of the overrepresentation of culturally diverse learners in special education programs (e.g., programs for students with emotional/behavioral disorders) and the underrepresentation of these students in programs for students with gifts and talents (Artiles, 1998; Cartledge, Tillman, & Talbert-Johnson, 2001; Coutinho, Oswald, & Forness, 2002; Ford, 1998; Obiakor et al., 2002, 2004; Skiba, Simmons, Ritter, Kohler, & Wu, 2003). Following are important placement principles for general and special education professionals:

- Race and culture can matter in the placement of students.
- Placements must be based on students' needs and not on racial and cultural identities.
- Language difference should never be misconstrued as a lack of intelligence.
- Empathy is an important ingredient of good placement.
- Good placements are usually the least restrictive environments.
- Differences are not deficits.
- Students are best served when their due process rights are respected.
- Appropriate inclusion reduces biased exclusion of students in classroom activities.
- Prejudicial placements have devastating effects on students.
- The unique differences students bring to the classroom must be valued.

THE INSTRUCTION OF JUAN

Initially, Juan was not expressing his full potential in class. Later on, the teacher shifted her instructional paradigm. To improve her teaching, she decided to take a multiculturally focused course. She did not want to dwell on past assumptions—she wanted to be an effective teacher for Juan. She understood the importance of creating effective instructional environments that promote academic productivity and appropriate social behaviors for an increasingly diverse student population. It appears that Juan's potential will be optimized as the teacher takes advantage of a broad range of strategies useful in designing, implementing, and evaluating instruction. He will have opportunities to learn new skills and take part in new activities. Other instructional strategies for Juan should include (see De La Paz, 1999; Obiakor, Utley, & Rotatori, 2003; Orlich, Harder, Callahan, & Gibson, 2001):

- Believing in a holistic view of his instruction (i.e., valuing the kind of instruction that uses multiple variables)
- Having equity as a big picture in his classroom (i.e., incorporating human respect in classroom activities)
- Monitoring his success (i.e., finding out if learning is occurring)
- Engaging him and his classmates in small-group discussion and cooperative learning (i.e., enhancing collaboration and consultation in classroom activities)
- Sequencing and organizing his instruction (i.e., trying to manipulate learning environments)
- Engaging him in higher level thinking (i.e., practicing critical thinking)
- Having adequate goals, standards, and outcomes for his instruction (i.e., making sure instruction responds to individual needs)
- Understanding his classroom and school milieu (i.e., moving beyond acceptance to acclimatization in classroom and school activities)
- Managing his classroom environment (i.e., making sure classrooms are not disruptive)
- Providing him with positive school outcomes (i.e., making sure school is rewarding)

Appropriate instruction is not totally divorced from the identification, assessment, categorization, and placement of students. For Juan, interaction with his peers in the classroom initially led to some negative learning-teaching processes. However, his teacher was able to change his classroom circumstances. For instruction to be appropriate for students like Juan, general and special education teachers must

- know each student,
- learn the facts about each student when they are in doubt,
- challenge the thinking of each student,
- use resources and persons to assist each student,
- build each student's self-concepts,
- teach each student with different techniques,
- make the right choices based on "new" knowledge of each student,
- continue to learn how to help each student to grow.

It is important that these teachers follow the example presented by Juan's teacher by (a) educating themselves about things they do not know; (b) using creative ideas to develop classroom interactions; (c) creating an atmosphere that welcomes parents, students, and staff; (d) being knowledgeable about different teaching modes; and (e) putting individual students in a positive learning environment.

MAKING MULTICULTURAL SPECIAL EDUCATION FUNCTIONAL

Imagine how boring life would be if society had one skin color, one race, one gender, one religion, one language, one culture, and one nation. In fact, imagine how boring it would be if everyone ate the same food, drove the same brand of car, wore the same clothes, built the same style of house, and danced to the same music (Obiakor, 2003). Differences and divisions have always existed among human beings; however, how these differences and divisions are valued and incorporated in inclusive school programs appears to be challenging (Arthur, 2000; Banks, 2002; Boykin, 2000; Guinier, 2002; Karp, 2002; Rothenberg, 2002; Weiss, 2002; Wise, 2002).

Looking back at Juan's case, we see a strong relationship between students' languages or cultures and how they are treated in general and special education. Juan's teacher later recognized that and so should other educational professionals and service providers. It is critical that general and special educators understand multicultural education, how language valuing or devaluing affects special education, and how all these variables are tied to multicultural special education.

Understanding Multicultural Education

Multicultural education is not just the study of exotic groups; it is also an inevitable force worthy of complementing major theoretical frameworks like humanistic education, behavioristic education, and cognitive education approaches (Smith, Richards, MacGranley, & Obiakor, 2004). It is no wonder that multicultural education is infused into existing educational, psychological, counseling, and sociological programs. Earlier in his classic work, Dewey (1958) acknowledged that "education must have the tendency, if it is education, to form attitudes" (p. 56). His views have since been corroborated by many scholars and educators (see Banks, 2002; Guinier, 2002; Karp, 2002; Obiakor, 2003; Rothenberg, 2002; Sparks, 1999; Utley & Obiakor, 2001; Weiss, 2002; Wise, 2002) who have incessantly noted the need for the nation's citizens to develop cultural, linguistic, and ethnic valuing to revamp school and societal thinking. In more ways than one, multicultural education taps into the human resources of *all* Americans and ascertains that educational and vocational options and opportunities are provided for all.

Clearly, multicultural education has an equalizing effect on traditional general and special education because it aims at maximizing the fullest potential of *all* learners, in spite of cultural and linguistic differences, national origins, and socioeconomic backgrounds (Brantlinger & Roy-Campbell, 2001; Gollnick & Chinn, 2002; Smith et al., 2004). Whether students are in general or special education programs, multicultural education inspires teachers and service providers to

- value students' cultures, languages, national origins, and socioeconomic backgrounds by welcoming them in school programs;
- stimulate students intellectually by providing them with more novel ideas;

- assist students in maximizing their full potential by understanding their strengths and weaknesses;
- create nurturing environments for students by empowering them;
- collaborate and consult with students' parents by regarding them as equal partners;
- provide support mechanisms for students' growth and development by playing many roles in their lives.

Language Valuing/Devaluing and Special Education

Language is an integral part of classroom instruction, just as it is an integral part of culture. For many multicultural learners (e.g., Latinos), "language is a complex and unique characteristic of their culture. Hispanic Americans exhibit variants in terms of native language use, bilingualism, or English language proficiency" (Delgado & Rogers-Adkinson, 1999, p. 57). Clearly, general and special educators must understand the linguistic skills of their students to evaluate the type or extent of educational provisions (Baca & Cervantes, 2004). Going back to Juan's case, he was proficient in Spanish and was learning to be proficient in English, the language of instruction. He was a bilingual student or English-language learner (ELL) who functioned in a monolingual classroom environment. According to Delgado and Rogers-Adkinson, "many Hispanic American (Latino) students come to school with different experiences than the majority of children. Several factors that may influence the child's performance in the classroom must be considered before formal assessment is initiated" (p. 62).

In many schools, students come with different cultural languages. These languages conflict with the official Standard English used in classroom instruction. Some African American children, for example, speak *Ebonics* as they interact in the classroom (Smitherman, 2001; Williams, 1975). Although this language is a non–Standard English, many experienced teachers have been able to utilize it in classroom instruction without diluting their focus on helping students master official Standard English (Craig & Washington, 2000). For instance, rap music or hip-hop music has a strong poetic or Ebonic influence that psychologically engages urban, suburban, or rural youth in today's changing society. Consequently, labeling students who use Ebonics as having a linguistic deficiency can lead to academic disengagement and behavior problems. In the long run, when these behavior problems are inappropriately addressed, students drop out of school and begin displaying antisocial behaviors and practicing criminal activities (e.g., drug dealing) that eventually land them in jail. Put another way, language and cultural valuing enhance academic engagement, student retention and graduation, and productive life.

In a related fashion, many students in urban schools come from immigrant Chinese, Japanese, Korean, or Hmong families where the language spoken at home is different from the language spoken in the school (Chang, Lai, & Shimizu, 1999). As a result, there are missed learning opportunities for Asian and Pacific

American students, especially when school practices are fragmented. Chang et al. addressed the "model minority" syndrome or "model student" myth (i.e., the assumption that all Asian and Pacific American students are brilliant, talented, and gifted) as a critical problem in general and special education. They argued that instead of making unwarranted assumptions about these learners, it is important for teachers and service providers to (a) take advantage of students' prior knowledge, (b) identify knowledge of students' multiple abilities, (c) use multifaceted teaching techniques, and (d) utilize parents/guardians as learning resources. Similarly, there are African Americans who have immigrated willingly to the United States from African and Caribbean nations (e.g., Nigeria and Jamaica). These immigrants speak different languages (e.g., Igbo and Patua) at home and speak Standard English outside their homes. However, they sometimes speak Standard English with heavy accents (Arthur, 2000; Obiakor & Grant, 2002). In many cases, children of these immigrants experience prejudice in school programs because of their linguistic differences, cultural backgrounds, and national origins. Interestingly, many of these children excel academically despite their differences.

MULTICULTURAL SPECIAL EDUCATION: THE REALITY OF CHANGE

Multicultural special education represents a realistic view of change as an integral part of general education. It guarantees respect for multicultural education, general education, special education, and bilingual education. In addition, it highlights the positive relationship between important educational, noneducational, and societal variables in the teaching-learning process. A few years ago, Winzer and Mazurek (1998) acknowledged that

> Special education can no longer be concerned solely with the nature of a disabling condition and appropriate intervention strategies tailored for a particular disability. With the composition of the school-age population shifting to encompass more students from culturally diverse backgrounds, bilingual homes, and economically disadvantaged families, the need for special services in the schools increases, and special educators must consider a broader range of characteristics that specifically include (but are certainly not restricted to) cultural and linguistic difference. Today and in the future, schools must develop programs, teaching methods, and resources to teach a diverse body and improve special education service delivery for exceptional learners from a wide variety of cultural and linguistic backgrounds. (p. 1)

An analysis of Winzer and Mazurek's statement reveals why general and special educators and multicultural and bilingual educators have the similar mission of helping *all* learners to optimize their potential. In other words, multicultural special education encompasses educational programming that helps *all* learners who are at risk of suffering misidentification, misassessment, miscategorization, misplacement, and misinstruction because of their racial, cultural, and linguistic differences.

Looking back at Juan's case, there is every indication that his teacher, even with the best intentions, lacked the initial necessary knowledge needed to work with multicultural learners. However, this teacher began to seek new knowledge to help her students. She went beyond seeking the knowledge; she actually implemented the knowledge. With new education and preparation, the teacher could

- focus on how *all* students, including Juan, can be treated *equitably* without losing the intended *quality*;
- respect Juan's linguistic difference while motivating him to learn the second language;
- learn that linguistic difference does not mean linguistic deficit;
- infuse social justice and mutual respect for *all* students in her class;
- focus on well-planned cooperative learning among Juan and his classmates;
- empower Juan's parents to participate as equal partners in her class;
- reverse Juan's negative experiences in her class;
- utilize a bilingual paraprofessional or a translator in Juan's instruction, which led to *all* students benefiting from the presence of a bilingual teacher;
- utilize not just Juan's parents but also members of the Latino community in her interactions with Juan;
- learn that behavior disorder does not occur in isolation; for instance, Juan's interaction with his classmates became an ultimate interest of the teacher.

Based on the aforementioned ideas garnered from Juan's classroom experiences, it is reasonable to conclude the following:

- Special education works when it is connected to a free and appropriate public education (FAPE) for all learners, including those from multicultural backgrounds. Legally, *all* learners must receive free education appropriate to their needs.
- Special education works when multicultural learners are not misidentified. Legally, *all* learners must be identified and referred without prejudice.
- Special education works when multicultural learners are not discriminately assessed. Legally, assessments must be nondiscriminatory to *all* learners.
- Special education works when multicultural learners are afforded procedural safeguards, including due process procedures. Legally, the civil rights of *all* learners must be protected.
- Special education works when parents of multicultural learners are empowered and treated as equal partners. Legally, parents and guardians of *all* learners must be contacted by the school during the special education process.
- Special education works when confidentiality of information is maintained for multicultural learners. Legally, information about *all* learners must be kept confidential and not openly discussed in places such as faculty lounges.
- Special education works when multicultural learners are educated in least restrictive environments. Legally, indiscriminate inclusion or exclusion of *all* learners must be avoided.

- Special education works when individualized education plans (IEPS) are based on (a) multicultural learners' needs, (b) the collaboration and consultation of team members, and (c) culturally responsive strategies. Legally, a team of professionals and the parents must work together to address programmatic needs of *all* learners.
- Special education works when accountability does not discriminate against multicultural learners. Legally, schools must be accountable for the education of *all* learners.
- Special education works when it is not connected to illusory conclusions and prejudicial expectations that demean multicultural learners. Legally, acceptable categories must be used to work with *all* learners.

A Culturally Responsive Educator

1. Understands that people grow, demographics change, societies develop, and paradigms shift.
2. Knows the self and evaluates his or her knowledge base before working with multicultural learners.
3. Uses assessments for the right reasons (i.e., to find out how and what students are learning in the classroom without labeling or getting rid of them).
4. Shows willingness to manipulate classroom environments in culturally sensitive ways.
5. Utilizes special education to adequately identify, assess, categorize, place, and instruct multicultural learners.
6. Sees "goodness" in students in spite of their racial, cultural, linguistic, and socioeconomic backgrounds.
7. Continues to learn to develop the pedagogical power that inspires multicultural learners.
8. Respects human differences and values personal idiosyncrasies.
9. Incorporates emotional intelligence, learning styles, and cultural backgrounds in teaching multicultural learners.
10. Exposes multicultural learners to positive collaborations and consultations among students, families, schools, communities, and governments.

Conclusion

This chapter exposed the importance of multicultural special education in educating *all* learners in today's schools. Students like Juan deserve the kind of educational environment that gives them the opportunity to grow. In addition, they deserve general and special education teachers who understand the relationship between language, culture, and learning. The issue is not whether Juan's teacher was good or bad; the issue is whether she was well prepared for the complexities of today's multicultural classrooms. Special education is needed to maximize the fullest potential of learners with exceptionalities. Although there are legal obligations involved in working with these learners, the focus must be on doing what is right for *all* learners. Clearly, special education must be valued as an important educational phenomenon. However, it works when general and special educators nurture different human intelligences; challenge their own perspectives, just as Juan's teacher did; and incorporate multicultural voices as they resolve traditional problems confronting students like Juan in their educational programs.

Discussion Questions

1. Evaluate how Juan's race and culture influenced his identification process in the class.
2. Briefly explain why Juan's linguistic difference does not mean linguistic deficit.
3. In your own words, define multicultural special education.
4. Briefly explain why general and special education professionals should shift their paradigms.
5. How could you become a more culturally responsive educator like Juan's teacher?

References

Arthur, J. A. (2000). *Invisible sojourners: African immigrant diaspora in the United States.* Westport, CT: Praeger.

Artiles, A. J. (1998, Spring). The dilemma of difference: Enriching the disproportionality discourse with theory and context. *The Journal of Special Education, 32,* 32–36.

Baca, L. M., & Cervantes, H. T. (2004). *The bilingual special education interface* (4th ed.). Upper Saddle River, NJ: Merrill/Prentice Hall.

Banks, J. A. (2002). *An introduction to multicultural education* (3rd ed.). Boston: Allyn & Bacon.

Boykin, A. W. (2000). Talent development, cultural deep structure, and school reform: Implications for African immersion initiatives. In D. S. Pollard & C. S Ajirotutu (Eds.), *African-centered schooling in theory and practice* (pp. 143–161). Westport, CT: Bergin & Garvey.

Brantlinger, E. A., & Roy-Campbell, Z. (2001). Dispelling myths and stereotypes confronting multicultural learners with mild disabilities: Perspectives for school reform. In C. A. Utley & F. E. Obiakor (Eds.), *Special education, multicultural education, and school reform: Components of quality education for learners with mild disabilities* (pp. 30–52). Springfield, IL: Charles C Thomas.

Cartledge, G., Tillman, L. C., & Talbert-Johnson, C. (2001). Professional ethics within the context of student discipline and diversity. *Teacher Education and Special Education, 24,* 25–37.

Chang, J., Lai, A., & Shimizu, W. (1999). Educating the Asian-Pacific exceptional English-language learners. In F. E. Obiakor, J. O. Schwenn, & A. F. Rotatori (Eds.), *Advances in special education: Multicultural education for learners with exceptionalities* (pp. 33–51). Stamford, CT: JAI Press.

Coutinho, M. Z., Oswald, D. P., & Forness, S. R. (2002). Gender and socio-demographic factors and the disproportionate identification of culturally and linguistically diverse students with emotional disturbance. *Behavioral Disorders, 27,* 109–125.

Craig, H. K., & Washington, J. A. (2000, April). An assessment battery for identifying language impairments in African American children. *Journal of Speech, Language, and Hearing Research, 43,* 366–379.

De La Paz, S. (1999). Self-regulated strategy instruction in regular education settings: Improving outcomes for students with and without learning disabilities. *Learning Disabilities Research & Practice, 14,* 92–106.

Delgado, B. M., & Rogers-Adkinson, D. (1999). Educating the Hispanic American exceptional learner. In F. E. Obiakor, J. O. Schwenn, & A. F. Rotatori (Eds.), *Advances in special education: Multicultural education for learners with exceptionalities* (pp. 53–71). Stamford, CT: JAI Press.

Dewey, J. (1958). *Philosophy of education.* Ames, IA: Littlefield, Adams.

Education for All Handicapped Children Act (1975), Pub. L. No. 94–142.

Fletcher, T. V., & Bos, C. S. (1999). *Helping individuals with disabilities and their families: Mexican and U.S. perspectives.* Tempe, AZ: Bilingual Press.

Ford, D. Y. (1998, Spring). The underrepresentation of minority students in gifted education: Problems and promises in recruitment and retention. *The Journal of Special Education, 32,* 4–14.

Gollnick, D. M., & Chinn, P. C. (2002). *Multicultural education in a pluralistic society* (6th ed.). Columbus, OH: Merrill/Prentice Hall.

Grossman, H. (2002). *Ending discrimination in special education* (2nd ed.). Springfield, IL: Charles C Thomas.

Guinier, L. (2002, Summer). Race, testing and the miner's canary. *Rethinking Schools, 16,* 13, 23.

Henze, R., Katz, A., Norte, E., Sather, S. E., & Walker, E. (2002). *Leading for diversity: How school leaders promote positive interethnic relations.* Thousand Oaks, CA: Corwin Press.

Hobbs, N. (1975). *The futures of children: Categories, labels, and their consequences.* San Francisco: Jossey-Bass.

Individuals with Disabilities Education Act Amendments (1990), Pub. L. No. 101–476.

Individuals with Disabilities Education Act Amendments (1997), Pub. L. No. 105–117.

Karp, S. (2002, Summer). Let them eat tests. *Rethinking Schools, 16,* 3–4, 23.

Karr, S., & Schwenn, J. O. (1999). Multimethod assessment of multicultural learners. In F. E. Obiakor, J. O. Schwenn, & A. F. Rotatori (Eds.), *Advances in special education: Multicultural education for learners with exceptionalities* (pp. 105–119). Stamford, CT: JAI Press.

Kozleski, E. B., Sobel, D., & Taylor, S. V. (2003, September). Embracing and building culturally responsive practices. *Multiple Voices, 6,* 73–87.

Langdon, H. W. (2002, August). Factors affecting special education services for English-language learners with suspected language-learning disabilities. *Multiple Voices, 5,* 66–82.

National Center for Education Statistics (2001). *Digest of educational statistics.* Washington, DC: U.S. Government Printing Office.

National Research Council (2002). *Minority students in special and gifted education.* Washington, DC: National Academic Press.

No Child Left Behind Act (2001), Pub. L. No. 107–110.

Obiakor, F. E. (1999). Teacher expectations of minority exceptional learners: Impact on "accuracy" of self-concepts. *Exceptional Children, 66,* 39–53.

Obiakor, F. E. (2001). *It even happens in "good" schools: Responding to cultural diversity in today's classrooms.* Thousand Oaks, CA: Corwin Press.

Obiakor, F. E. (2003). *The eight-step approach to multicultural learning and teaching* (2nd ed.). Dubuque, IA: Kendall/Hunt.

Obiakor, F. E., Algozzine, B., Thurlow, M., Gwalla-Ogisi, N., Enwefa, S., Enwefa, R., et al. (2002). *Addressing the issue of disproportionate representation: Identification and assessment of culturally diverse students with emotional or behavioral disorders.* Arlington, VA: Council for Children with Behavioral Disorders, the Council for Exceptional Children.

Obiakor, F. E., & Beachum, F. D. (2005, Winter). Developing self-empowerment in African American students using the comprehensive support model. *The Journal of Negro Education, 74,* 18–29.

Obiakor, F. E., Beachum, F. D., & Harris, M. (2005, March). Restrictiveness and race in special education: Practicalizing the laws. *Learning Disabilities: A Contemporary Journal, 3,* 52–55.

Obiakor, F. E., Enwefa, S., Utley, C., Obi, S. O., Gwalla-Ogisi, N., & Enwefa, R. (2004). *Serving culturally and linguistically diverse students with emotional and behavioral disorders.* Arlington, VA: Council for Children with Behavioral Disorders, the Council for Exceptional Children.

Obiakor, F. E., & Ford, B. A. (2002). *Creating successful learning environments for African American learners with exceptionalities.* Thousand Oaks, CA: Corwin Press.

Obiakor, F. E., & Grant, P. A. (2002). *Foreign-born African Americans: Silenced voices in the discourse on race.* Huntington, NY: Nova Science.

Obiakor, F. E., Utley, C. A., & Rotatori, A. F. (2003). *Effective education for learners with exceptionalities.* Oxford, England: Elsevier Science/JAI Press.

Orlich, D. C., Harder, R. J., Callahan, R. C., & Gibson, H. W. (2001). *Teaching strategies: A guide to better instruction* (6th ed.). Boston: Houghton Mifflin.

Rothenberg, P. S. (2002). *White privilege: Essential readings on the other side of racism.* New York: Worth.

Sbarra, D. A., & Pianta, R. C. (2001). Teacher ratings of behavior among African American and Caucasian children during the first two years of school. *Psychology in the Schools, 38,* 229–238.

Skiba, R. J., Simmons, A. B., Ritter, S., Kohler, K. R., & Wu, T. C. (2003, September). The psychology of disproportionality: Minority placement in context. *Minority Voices, 6,* 27–40.

Skrtic, T. M. (2003, September). An organization analysis of the overrepresentation of peer and minority students in special education. *Multiple Voices, 6,* 41–57.

Smith, T. B., Richards, P. S., MacGranley, H., & Obiakor, F. E. (2004). Practicing multiculturalism: An introduction. In T. B. Smith (Ed.), *Practicing multiculturalism: Affirming diversity in counseling and psychology* (pp. 3–16). Boston: Allyn & Bacon.

Smitherman, G. (2001). *Talkin that talk: Language, culture, and education in African America.* New York: Routledge.

Sparks, S. (1999). Educating the Native American learner. In F. E. Obiakor, J. O. Schwenn, & A. F. Rotatori (Eds.), *Advances in special education: Multicultural education for learners with exceptionalities* (pp. 73–90). Stamford, CT: JAI Press.

U.S. Department of Education (2001). *23rd annual report to Congress on the implementation of the Individuals With Disabilities Education Act.* Washington, DC: Author.

Utley, C. A., & Obiakor, F. E. (2001). *Special education, multicultural education, and school reform: Components of quality education for learners with mild disabilities.* Springfield, IL: Charles C Thomas.

Weiss, D. (2002, Summer). Confronting white privilege. *Rethinking Schools, 16,* 14, 22.

Williams, R. (1975). *Ebonics: The true language of Black folks.* St. Louis, MO: R. W. Associates.

Winzer, M. A., & Mazurek, K. (1998). *Special education in multicultural contexts.* Upper Saddle River, NJ: Merrill/Prentice Hall.

Wise, T. (2002, Summer). Membership has its privileges. *Rethinking Schools, 16,* 15.

Ysseldyke, J. E., Algozzine, B., & Thurlow, M. L. (2000). *Critical issues in special education* (3rd ed.). Boston: Houghton Mifflin.

Chapter 2

Bilingualism and Special Education

Shernaz B. García and Barbara J. Dray

Chapter Outline

Thinking About Multicultural Special Education

One day in her deaf accent I heard Rosa say "abuelita" in Spanish. I couldn't believe it, it was so clear. She spoke it so naturally, even better than English. Inside I was angry, you know, thinking, "If only we had taught her Spanish" and "What sacrifice we went through 'in her best interest'." Or in what the doctors deemed to be "in her best interest." Really, I do not blame them, I truly believe they were doing the "right" thing; they just didn't know any better. We didn't know any better.

Comments like this from Rosa's father and family members of other students in the class really helped Ms. Webster realize the challenges that English-language learners (ELLs) and their families face when they enter the public school system. She was Rosa's special education teacher that year, and the first one who spoke Spanish. When she first began teaching, her students mostly came from Spanish-speaking homes. Before long, more than 10 different languages were represented at the school! That changed things, even for bilingual teachers like Ms. Webster. She had to quickly learn how to work with all the other language groups to make sure that she was doing the "right" thing. She began to realize that it was important for teachers, as educators, to "know better." It was not easy to tell if ELL students were struggling because they did not speak English, or because they had a learning disability. And then there was the issue of assessment! The school's evaluation teams were scrambling to locate community members to serve as interpreters. Until she met Rosa's family, Ms. Webster used to believe students with disabilities would be confused if the school used two languages. It took her a long time to sort these things out, to discover what was best for Rosa and her family; and not everyone agreed with her. Some teachers believed using the native language interfered with learning English, and they would not allow other languages to be spoken in their classrooms.

Even though she knew she couldn't possibly learn all the languages spoken by the students in her classroom, Ms. Webster tried to learn as much as possible from her students and their families and began to incorporate their varied cultures and languages into her teaching. The classroom walls were decorated with pictures of people and places that were familiar and represented her students' experiences. She posted items such as photographs and artifacts that students brought from home in the "Sharing Our World" corner. She made sure that the library and learning centers included materials both in English and in students' home languages, including books on tape. Community and family volunteers were invited to share family stories, poems, songs, and literature native to their culture, which Ms. Webster would turn into books for children to use as they practiced language skills. An interpreter who was proficient in American Sign Language shadowed Rosa as Ms. Webster taught. Ms. Webster met daily *with the interpreter to go over lesson plans, key vocabulary, and goals and objectives for activities. The interpreter then used this information to assist Rosa in understanding and fully participating in lessons. As well, Ms. Webster used a lot of hands-on activities, visuals, manipulatives, and other supports to make the material comprehensible to all students, but especially the ELLs in her classroom. Through the years, Ms. Webster learned that these types of strategies worked really well and were needed in addition to the special education modifications she was using. Equally important, she realized that maintaining high expectations, respecting and valuing families' culture, and encouraging the development of the home language (even those she didn't speak) allowed her students to become more confident, successful learners.*

- *What new demographic changes call for teaching-learning changes in Rosa's school?*
- *How can teachers and service providers help Rosa to maximize her educational potential?*

In spite of steady increases in the number of students in U.S. public schools who come from homes where languages other than English are spoken, teachers like Ms. Webster represent a small number of educators who are bilingual and who understand the complexity of educating ELLs with disabilities. Even bilingual teachers face challenges because many of today's classrooms include children from many different language groups. Although it is not realistic to expect teachers to become proficient in all these languages, they need to be qualified to teach ELLs; that is, they must know how to modify curriculum and instruction so that their ELLs can learn the academic content while they are simultaneously learning English. According to a recent report by Zehler, Fleischman, Hopstock, Pendzick, and Stephenson (2003), only about 14% of teachers who serve ELLs with disabilities are fluent in a language spoken by their students, and an even smaller number are certified to teach ELLs. Only 11.4% of special education teachers in this study were certified in English as a second language (ESL), and a mere 2.3% held bilingual education certification. This means that the majority of general and special educators are not adequately prepared by their teacher education programs to educate ELL students, especially those with special education needs. This chapter aims at reversing this trend. It is important to note that the term *ELL* represents those learners from homes where English is not the native language, who are still in the process of acquiring English as a second language when they enter school, and who therefore cannot function successfully in school without the support of the native language and/or English as a second language instruction. In many cases, the terms *limited English proficient (LEP)* and *language minority* have traditionally been used to describe this population. The term *LEP* is used when the focus is specifically on the language proficiency of students being discussed; the use of the term *language minority* usually reflects their status in U.S. society as speakers of a nondominant language or nonstandard dialect of English. For purposes of clarity, the term *ELL* is used throughout this chapter.

Although disproportionate representation of students from certain racial/ethnic groups in special education has been a concern for more than 30 years, the focus on children and youth who are also ELLs with special needs is much more recent. The Office of Civil Rights only began to compile data on the number of ELL students in special education in 1994 for selected disability categories. But these statistics are not yet available by language group or by language proficiency. Nationally aggregated data indicate that ELLs are more likely to be underrepresented in special education (e.g., Zehler et al., 2003), raising questions about some students who may have disabilities but whose special needs are unrecognized and therefore unmet (McCray & García, 2002). Moreover, underrepresentation does not eliminate concerns about accurate identification and placement: Even when schools are not overidentifying ELLs with special needs, there is the issue of whether the right students are identified, given the existing shortages of bilingual personnel and materials, tests, and other resources. For example, if tested by monolingual speech-language pathologists, Spanish-speaking students are at risk of being identified with speech-language impairments on the basis of substitution of letter sounds such as *b/v*, *sh/ch*, and *s/z*, when, in fact, these are characteristics of their status as native Spanish speakers (Ortiz, García, Maldonado-Colón, & Wheeler, 1986).

Many ELLs enter school with social, cultural, and linguistic experiences that are quite different from those expected in the classroom. They are typically taught by teachers who are not members of their own communities; who are unfamiliar with students' culturally based ways of interacting, thinking, and behaving; and who are likely to teach from their own cultural frames of reference using methods and approaches that have been validated mainly for students from the mainstream, dominant culture (Delpit, 1995; García & Guerra, 2004; Hollins, 1996). In other words, there is a greater likelihood that some students will become "curriculum casualties" (Hargis, as cited in Gickling & Thompson, 1985) because the school culture is not responsive to their learning differences. It is important to note that cultural or linguistic differences in and of themselves do not automatically result in academic failure, and that culture is the context for teaching and learning for *all* students, not just students from racial, ethnic, and linguistically different communities. Rather, educational risk and underachievement for certain groups of multicultural learners reflects the sociopolitical status of their communities in the larger society and the failure of the educational system to provide equitable opportunities for educational success (Cummins, 1986; Heller, Holtzman, & Messick, 1982; Ogbu, 1994).

Efforts to improve educational opportunities for ELLs must therefore begin with an examination of the educational system and the larger societal context in which schools operate, because educators and schools tend to mirror these broader values, beliefs, and attitudes toward language and culture, resulting in a tendency to look for the causes of failure within students, families, and communities rather than to question the adequacy of the classroom learning environment (García & Guerra, 2004). In this context, appropriate identification of a disability requires that educators and related professionals must first rule out that the child's difficulties were primarily the result of inadequate instruction in general education (García & Ortiz, 1989; Heller et al., 1982; Ortiz, 2002). This point is particularly important for students who are identified as having mild to moderate learning disabilities, emotional/behavioral disorders, speech-language impairments, or developmental delays/cognitive impairments, as these categories have historically been associated with a higher incidence of inappropriate labeling and placement for students from multicultural backgrounds (see Harry, 1994; Heller et al., 1982; Mercer, 1973).

REFERRALS OF ELLs

Recognition that students' underachievement can result from the educational system's failure to adequately address their instructional needs leads to a focus on preventing school underachievement and failure through high-quality, culturally and linguistically responsive educational experiences for *all* students. Such programs require a positive school climate in which (a) educators share responsibility for educating *all* students, (b) an array of general education services and programs is available to accommodate diverse learners, and (c) schools establish collaborative relationships with families. Finally, there must be ongoing professional development activities to ensure that teachers and administrators have opportunities to develop their expertise related to effective practices for multicultural learners (García & Ortiz, 2004). In all these efforts, culture and language must be viewed as resources and funds of knowledge (Moll, Amanti, Neff, & Gonzalez, 1992) rather than "deficits" that disrupt the instructional process.

Prevention efforts must be accompanied by early intervention for struggling learners. Traditionally referred to as *prereferral intervention*, early intervention involves the use of diagnostic/prescriptive teaching approaches in general education and the implementation of problem-solving support systems to ensure that teachers and students are provided the resources to ensure successful teaching and learning (García & Ortiz, 2004; Ortiz, 2002). Early intervention ensures that teachers and their students who are experiencing academic or behavioral difficulties receive immediate attention. Once students fall more than a year behind, this achievement gap becomes difficult to close, even with the best remedial interventions (Slavin & Madden, 1989). During early intervention, teachers are expected to

- reteach concepts using significantly different approaches,
- gather classroom data (i.e., observation and work samples) about students' sociocultural and linguistic skills in the native language and in English,
- use the language data gathered to determine how each language may influence student progress,
- systematically document student progress and use the data to modify instruction.

When these efforts are not successful, teachers need access to school-based support systems for further problem solving before a referral to special education is considered (e.g., teams of general education teachers, multidisciplinary teams, teacher support teams, student success teams, or child study teams). Teachers like Ms. Webster are an excellent resource for such teams because they possess important background knowledge to understand students' language and culture, and they are familiar with instructional approaches that are effective with ELLs. As García and Ortiz (2004), Leung (1996), and Salend and Salinas (2003) pointed out, these teachers should play an active role in

- identifying any cultural or linguistic factors contributing to students' difficulties,
- brainstorming appropriate interventions,
- providing feedback through peer observations,
- modeling ESL techniques,
- serving as peer coaches and cultural informants for teachers who are still acquiring these skills.

Students' failure to respond to team-based interventions cannot be attributed to a disability unless these remedial approaches take into account their sociocultural, linguistic, and racial/ethnic characteristics and life experiences. Teams also have the responsibility for monitoring the progress of alternate interventions and documenting the results of these efforts, so that there is adequate data to support and validate any referrals that result. Implementing these steps ensures that only ELLs who are likely to have a disability will be referred for assessment, and that others will receive alternate interventions and supports they need within general education. In addition, it ensures that teachers receive instructional support and the professional development they need to successfully respond to similar situations in the future. It is only when these avenues have been exhausted that a referral to special education is considered appropriate.

ASSESSMENT AND ELIGIBILITY CONSIDERATIONS

A comprehensive individual evaluation is the next step when students are referred for special education services. The primary purpose of this initial assessment is to determine eligibility and to plan an appropriate, specialized educational program (i.e., whether the student qualifies for special education services, and if so, the kind of special education services needed). Many factors can contribute to cultural and linguistic bias in the assessment process, even when referrals have been validated through the problem-solving process. A critical shortage of bilingual evaluators (e.g., school psychologists, speech-language pathologists, educational diagnosticians, and hearing and vision specialists), as well as the limited availability or nonexistence of tests and materials in students' languages exacerbate the problem. In instances where students do have a disability, such bias also contributes to underestimating a child's level of functioning and potential, leading to more restrictive placements and services, thereby denying access to the least restrictive environment. Clearly, the failure to address culture and language ignores students' background knowledge and life experiences, and fails to encourage alternative culturally relevant perspectives about disability, intelligence, giftedness, and education (García & Dominguez, 1997).

To be effective for ELLs, assessment practices ought to reflect an advocacy orientation (Cummins, 1986; Leung, 1996). With this approach, a major goal of assessment will be to change the instructional program to better suit the student, rather than to find a "cause" of the "problem" within the student. As a result, instructional plans strategically recognize the student's existing strengths and resilience, and utilize these qualities to develop new skills and help the student to be successful at school. Following are specific strategies that are likely to improve the quality of assessment practices for ELLs (see Dao, 1991; Jitendra, Rohena-Diaz, & Nolet, 1998; Leung, 1996; Lopez-Reyna & Bay, 1997; Ortiz, 1997; Ortiz & García, 1990; Salend & Salinas, 2003):

- Gathering student data from a variety of sources, including educationally relevant cultural and linguistic information from home and community (e.g., immigrant/migrant/refugee experiences, level of acculturation, emotional states including acculturation stress, prior educational history, and language(s) spoken in the home and community)
- Using results of a current language assessment to determine the language(s) in which the student will be evaluated, including measures of the student's language proficiency in the native language/dialect and English, and language dominance across a variety of formal and informal settings for social-interpersonal as well as cognitive/academic tasks
- Supplementing formal, standardized testing with informal assessment techniques and data sources, student-centered procedures, dynamic, curriculum-based assessment approaches, and portfolios of student work
- Ensuring that the membership of multidisciplinary teams includes family/community members, professionals fluent in the student's language and culture, and educators trained in assessing second-language learners and designing educational programs appropriate for students' language development as well as academic needs
- Using trained interpreters who are neutral and understand their role in the process
- Triangulating or cross-validating information across data sources, time, and settings
- Considering the student's educational history and the adequacy of the general education program for ELLs, in terms of developing English proficiency as well as attaining academic goals

In summary, ELLs are more likely to be accurately identified if (a) there is evidence of a disability in both languages; (b) the influence of the primary language and English proficiency and sociocultural background on test performance were adequately considered and accounted for; (c) the data suggest that the student has not responded to interventions that have been used successfully with other peers from similar or comparable sociocultural and linguistic backgrounds; (d) the interpretation of test results takes into account any adaptations that were made to formal, standardized assessment procedures; and (e) the final determination of a disability involves family members and takes into account their culturally based views about disability and their cultural norms or expectations for academic performance and behavior. In a nutshell, the results of prereferral problem solving as well as the assessment must provide substantial evidence that the student's poor performance does not reflect primarily a lack of opportunity to learn; the impact of culture, language, or social class; or inadequate instruction in the general education program. If it is then determined that the student is eligible for special education services, decisions about instructional placements and services must be equally responsive to his or her sociocultural and linguistic characteristics and learning needs.

CREATING OPTIMAL LEARNING EXPERIENCES FOR ELLs

In spite of the complexity surrounding language policy in the United States, for educators the central questions about language development are primarily pedagogical. How do educators best work with ELLs, given the variety of their sociocultural experiences and levels of native and second-language proficiency? How can this be achieved without sacrificing children's socioemotional well-being and positive identity development (Fillmore, 2000; Hernández-Sheets & Hollins, 1999)? In schools where a significant number of students are ELLs, bilingual and ESL instruction can no longer be relegated to the bilingual/ESL program; *all* teachers who work with ELL populations must know how to adapt their instructional methods and materials to the language proficiency levels of their students (Obiakor & Smith, 2005). These skills are also necessary when working with ELLs who have just exited from ELL programs because they will continue to need language supports as they transition to general education classrooms where instruction is entirely in English at levels targeted for native speakers. Moreover, in multilingual classrooms, even bilingual teachers like Ms. Webster rely primarily on ELL strategies for those students whose languages they do not speak. In these instances, academic instruction must be provided using strategies that will make new concepts comprehensible to ELLs without watering down the content or lowering standards. Creating successful learning experiences for ELLs requires that educators (a) understand how children acquire their first and second language, (b) recognize the educational implications of bilingualism and second-language acquisition, and (c) make instruction comprehensible for English learners.

As students advance through school, language use becomes more abstract. On academic English assessments, ELLs who are in their third year of second-language acquisition generally score one standard deviation below native English speakers because they are still acquiring the second language. As a result, ELLs must constantly catch up to a moving target: native English speakers who continue to acquire new content-area knowledge (Cummins, 2000). What may appear to be academic deficits may actually be a result of the second-language acquisition process. When children have opportunities to explore and use their own language, they are more likely to gain phonemic awareness and other oral language skills needed to acquire reading skills (National Association for the Education of Young Children, 1996). Additionally, learning foundational skills and knowledge in their native language as they are acquiring English promotes the likelihood of becoming proficient readers and writers in English (Thomas & Collier, 2002). Students who receive instruction in content areas in their native language have a higher probability of acquiring a second language and demonstrating academic proficiency in the second language (Cummins, 2000; Thomas & Collier, 2002). Based on these findings, Thomas and Collier suggested that it takes a minimum of 4 years of second-language instruction for an ELL to reach grade-level performance. In contrast, ELLs who do not have prior instruction in their native language and receive English-only instruction take at least 7 to 10 years to acquire English language skills that reflect the age and grade-level norms of native English peers (Collier, 1995).

Because ELLs' cognitive functioning may be higher than their ability to function in English, decisions about the language(s) of instruction should be based on a variety of data sources about the student's language characteristics (Ortiz & García, 1990). Moreover, because children's language is continuously developing and changing, it is essential to make sure that these language data are current; that is, no more than 6 months old (Ortiz, 1997). Following are types of language data that are necessary for instructional planning (Ortiz & García, 1990; Ortiz, 1997):

- A measure of the student's language proficiency in each language (i.e., the extent to which there is mastery over the various aspects of language use). It is important to have measures of proficiency in both languages even if instruction can only be provided in English, so that the student's performance in English can be appropriately interpreted.
- Information about the student's language dominance (i.e., the language in which the student is more proficient, and/or which language is preferred in the respective settings in which he or she is to be taught). In some cases, students may prefer English although it is their weaker language, because they realize it is the language valued most at school, because they may not feel comfortable using their native language, and/or because they are with others who do not speak their native language.
- Information about the level of acquisition of the surface structures of the language (syntax, grammar, and vocabulary) as well as functional language use (pragmatics)
- Receptive as well as expressive language skills in each language. It is not uncommon for ELLs to have higher levels of receptive language compared to the language they are able to produce. For example, in homes where Vietnamese is the language of the grandparents and older family members, but English is used by the younger members of the family, it is possible that children understand much higher levels of Vietnamese than they are able to speak and therefore have acquired important knowledge in this language, which may not be demonstrated in English.

Even though the nature and severity of a disability can be expected to affect a student's ability to become proficient in both languages, having a disability does not mean that children cannot learn a second language or that their native language should not be supported (Cummins, 1984). Children with special needs who are ELLs are entitled to receive native-language support and/or ESL instruction and should receive both to the extent necessary for them to achieve their individualized educational goals. In cases where only one language is feasible, the choice of language of instruction should consider sociocultural contexts, family preferences, and other factors to ensure that children will continue to function in their homes and communities (García & Malkin, 1993; Obiakor & Smith, 2005; Ortiz, 1997). If instruction is provided in English, careful attention is required to make sure that ELL strategies are used and that instruction is modified for the student's levels of performance related to the language as well as the disability (Cloud, 1990). At a very minimum, the home language should be promoted and encouraged within the classroom so that the student feels valued (Obiakor & Smith, 2005). There are many ways in which native language development can be supported even when teachers are monolingual English speakers (Fillmore, 2000; García & Malkin, 1993; Ortiz, 1997). Some examples are

- using paraprofessionals who can provide native language support,
- involving parents and other community members as tutors or volunteers,
- collaborating with the student's bilingual education teacher or other bilingual resources available in the school or district,
- using bilingual students as peer tutors,
- encouraging parents and families to use the native language at home, including reading, and engaging children in a variety of topics and language experiences,
- making available a variety of materials in the student's language, including library books, audiotapes, and videos to promote language development as well as reinforce academic concepts being taught in the classroom.

MAKING INSTRUCTION COMPREHENSIBLE FOR ELLs IN GENERAL AND SPECIAL EDUCATION: WHAT MS. WEBSTER DID

Whether ELLs are being taught in dual-language classrooms or receiving all their instruction in English, their educational goals are twofold: to learn the academic content expected of all students while at the same time acquiring English as a second language. When students are required to do both simultaneously because teachers cannot provide native language instruction, it is critical that English instruction be comprehensible. Making a lesson comprehensible requires teachers to rely less on the language (oral and written) of the texts and to support students' ability to follow the lesson by using a variety of multisensory aids and supplementary materials, and by modifying the language level and scope of assignments. Ms. Webster found it helpful to systematically incorporate a variety of these and other supports into her teaching when working with ELLs with special needs. She worked with the basic components of an approach called *sheltered instruction* (Echevarria & Graves, 1998) and made sure that her instruction was sensitive to her students' culture-, language- and disability-related educational needs (Cloud, 1990). Sheltered instruction is distinct in its emphasis on providing comprehensible input and careful modification of the core curriculum to align objectives and key concepts to be taught within students' linguistic reach. This also helps to create a sense of belonging for students, enhances their motivation to learn, and reduces anxiety and tension associated with learning and functioning in the second language (Diaz-Rico, 2004; Echevarria & Graves, 1998).

An important aspect of Ms. Webster's instruction was her use of *scaffolding* techniques that supported her students' ability to participate meaningfully in instructional activities and to demonstrate their learning. As with scaffolds used in building construction, instructional scaffolds provide temporary supports while students are learning language, vocabulary, or a new skill by building on what they already know or are able to do, moving from a lower to a higher level of language use, and building on language and literacy skills already acquired (Jiménez, Gersten, & Rivera, 1996; Santamaría, Fletcher, & Bos, 2002). Overall, she paid careful attention to four components of instruction (i.e., lesson preparation, comprehensibility, lesson delivery, and interaction) discussed in the following paragraphs.

Lesson Preparation

Lesson planning is an important part of the teaching-learning process. Ms. Webster made sure that each lesson contained age- and developmentally appropriate concepts and vocabulary, and tried to gather as many supplementary aids to contextualize the lesson as she could (e.g., visuals, manipulatives, models, videos). She also reviewed assignments and texts to identify sections that needed to be outlined, rewritten, or paraphrased within the linguistic reach and ability level of her students. As a special educator, she considered modifications required to individualize instruction for the students' ability levels, which involved modifying the text, instructional objectives, and planning to teach prerequisite skills, study skills, or other learning strategies. Finally, she made sure to include real-life activities that were meaningful to her students and relevant to their interests and sociocultural backgrounds. Inviting family and community members to contribute to classroom activities helped her to personalize the learning experience and communicated that she valued them as resources and strengths. In large measure, these activities provided access to native language support for students who needed it and were sources of relevant cultural information for the lesson.

Comprehensibility

When Ms. Webster delivered instruction, whether in groups or individually, she paid careful attention to her speech, making sure to repeat key vocabulary so that students were exposed more than once to new terms and phrases. She also used gestures, facial expressions, and/or body language to support verbal messages as appropriate. Because she was bilingual in Spanish, she introduced new content in her Spanish-speaking students' primary language when necessary. When using English with them and with students from other language groups, she made sure to speak slowly and pronounce words clearly in a natural way. In addition, she made sure to give LEP students adequate response time (e.g., waiting 5 seconds) before she repeated, rephrased, and/or asked another student for assistance.

Lesson Delivery

As Ms. Webster presented new concepts, she made sure that she introduced and taught key vocabulary and new words first, so that the linguistic demands of the lesson would be manageable for students. Additionally, she taught concepts by using a variety of approaches (e.g., modeling, demonstration, visuals, simulations) and linked new information to prior learning and students' experiences. Sometimes, she expanded a student's ideas by taking what he or she said and rephrasing it in a new way, modeling more complex grammar or vocabulary. New information or tasks were made accessible through peer tutoring or assistance from her instructional aide (*mediated scaffolds*). For some students, a task was adjusted by reducing the amount of information generated independently (*task scaffold*). Advanced organizers such as story maps, paragraph frames, and sentence starters were used that provided less and less support over time (*materials scaffold*). Equally important, all students had opportunities to use higher order thinking skills such as predicting, problem solving, evaluating, and synthesizing so that her ELLs were held to the same high standards and expectations as her native English-speaking students.

Interaction

Ms. Webster's lessons typically involved activities that required students to interact with her and with one another. Students were encouraged to elaborate their answers, to expand, explain, justify, or support their responses, because she recognized that these opportunities to interact and engage in meaningful dialogue with native English speakers would ultimately increase their social and academic language proficiency in English. In addition, these interactions provided ELL students and those with disabilities with language development opportunities that entailed using complex language, expressing ideas, and arguing positions, compared with teacher-dominated classroom discourse (Echevarria & Graves, 1998).

A Culturally Responsive Educator

1. Encourages students to develop high levels of proficiency in their home language or dialect because the educator understands the important role of the primary language in students' cognitive development as well as second-language learning.

2. Uses a variety of strategies to adjust linguistic demands of the classroom to match students' language development level without lowering academic standards and expectations.

3. Creates a linguistically responsive learning environment in which students have meaningful opportunities to learn the second language/dialect as well as the academic content.

4. Collaborates with professionals across general, bilingual education/ESL, and special education to share effective strategies and compare student performance across settings.

5. Teaches the whole child, knowing that ELLs can experience culture shock when learning a second language/dialect or culture, which requires sensitivity to emotional, psychological, and intellectual needs.

6. Understands that sociopolitical factors affect language policies in schools and society, but remains focused on the educational implications of bilingualism and second-language acquisition.

7. Takes time to consider issues from perspectives of students, families, and their world and builds on their sociocultural and linguistic experiences.

8. Makes sure that parents of ELLs have access to teachers and other school personnel by providing information in the native language and/or the use of interpreters.

9. Finds ways to become familiar with and get involved with the communities in which students live.

10. Is reflective about his or her teaching practices and actively seeks opportunities to increase, update, and validate knowledge and skills related to working with ELLs in general and special education.

Conclusion

Although the educational rights of ELLs have been established legally and through the courts for more than 30 years, and in spite of educational reforms targeted at improving their academic performance, they continue to experience lower levels of educational success when compared to their white, monolingual, native English-speaking peers (Berman, Chambliss, & Geiser, 1999; National Center for Education Statistics, 1998; Rubanova & Mortenson, 2002). Students and families who have been the targets of school reform have often been excluded from discussions about how to close achievement gaps (Jones, 1995), and explanations as well as solutions for these disparities have often centered around deficit views of their sociocultural, linguistic, and racial/ethnic experiences (Valencia, Valenzuela, Sloan, & Foley, 2001). Of particular relevance to the discussion in this chapter are questionable placements of ELLs in special education as well as inadequate or inappropriate special education services for them. In contrast, educators who adopt a sociocultural perspective of teaching and learning understand that ELLs can be successful in school if the structure of schooling is responsive to their linguistic and sociocultural characteristics (García & Guerra, 2004; Owens, 2005). If educators work closely with multicultural families and communities to build on their strengths to promote resilience and, ultimately, create positive learning environments, all ELLs will have equitable opportunities to be successful in school.

Discussion Questions

1. Explain ways that classroom teachers can help ELLs feel welcome in the classroom.
2. Discuss how school-based early intervention and problem-solving systems can reduce the number of inappropriate referrals of ELLs to special education.
3. Summarize why it is important for teachers to provide culturally relevant instruction to ELLs.
4. Placing yourself in the role of a teacher like Ms. Webster, imagine that you have been asked to make a presentation during the next faculty meeting for teachers who work with ELLs at your school. Identify three or four key concepts that you want to share, and explain why you think they are important.
5. Describe two steps that you can take that you think will make you a linguistically responsive practitioner in your own preparation as an education professional.

References

Berman, P., Chambliss, and Geiser, K. D. (1999). *Making the case for a focus on equity in school reform*. Berkeley, CA: RRP International. Retrieved April 5, 2003, from www.rppintl.com/HPLC/Equity_FINAL.pdf

Cloud, N. (1990). Planning and implementing an ESL program. In A. Carrasquillo & R. Baecher (Eds.), *Teaching the bilingual special education student* (pp. 106–131). Norwood, NJ: Ablex.

Collier, V. P. (1995, Fall). *Acquiring a second language for school: Directions in language and education series* (Vol. 1, No. 4). Washington, DC: National Clearinghouse for Bilingual Education.

Cummins, J. (1984). *Bilingualism and special education: Issues in assessment and pedagogy.* Clevedon, England: Multilingual Matters.

Cummins, J. (1986). Empowering language minority students. *Harvard Educational Review, 56*, 18–36.

Cummins, J. (2000). *Language, power, and pedagogy: Bilingual children in the crossfire.* Tonawanda, NY: Multilingual Matters.

Dao, M. (1991). Designing assessment procedures for educationally at-risk Southeast Asian-American students. *Journal of Learning Disabilities, 24*(10), 594–601, 629.

Delpit, L. (1995). Language diversity and learning. In *Other people's children: Culture conflict in the classroom* (pp. 48–69). New York: The New Press.

Diaz-Rico, L. T. (2004). *Teaching English learners: Strategies and methods.* Boston: Allyn & Bacon.

Echevarria, J., & Graves, A. (1998). *Sheltered content instruction: Teaching English-language learners with diverse abilities.* Needham Heights, MA: Allyn & Bacon.

Fillmore, L. W. (2000). Loss of family languages: Should educators be concerned? *Theory into Practice, 39*(4), 203–210.

García, S. B., & Dominguez, L. (1997). Cultural contexts which influence learning and academic performance. *Child and Adolescent Psychiatric Clinics of North America, 6,* 621–655.

García, S. B., & Guerra, P. L. (2004). Deconstructing deficit thinking: Working with educators to create more equitable learning environments. *Education and Urban Society, 36*(2), 150–168.

García, S. B., & Malkin, D. H. (1993). Toward defining programs and services for culturally and linguistically diverse learners in special education. *Teaching Exceptional Children, 26*(1), 52–58.

García, S. B., & Ortiz, A. A. (1989). *Preventing inappropriate referrals of language minority students to special education* (New Focus Series, No. 5). Wheaton, MD: National Clearinghouse for Bilingual Education.

García, S. B., & Ortiz, A. A. (2004). *Preventing disproportionate representation: Culturally and linguistically responsive pre-referral interventions.* Denver, CO: National Center for Culturally Responsive Educational Systems. Available from www.nccrest.org/publications.html

Gickling, E. E., & Thompson, V. P. (1985). A personal view of curriculum-based assessment. *Exceptional Children, 52,* 205–218.

Harry, B. (1994). *The disproportionate representation of minority students in special education: Theories and recommendations: Final report.* Alexandria, VA: Project FORUM, National Association of State Directors of Special Education.

Heller, K. A., Holtzman, W. H., & Messick, S. (1982). *Placing children in special education: A strategy for equity.* Washington, DC: National Academy Press.

Hernández-Sheets, R., & Hollins, E. (Eds.). (1999). *Racial and ethnic identity in school practices.* Hillsdale, NJ: Erlbaum.

Hollins, E. (1996). *Culture in school learning: Revealing the deep meaning.* Mahwah, NJ: Erlbaum.

Jiménez, R. T., Gersten, R., & Rivera, A. (1996). Conversations with a Chicana teacher: Supporting students' transition from native to English language instruction. *The Elementary School Journal, 96,* 333–341.

Jitendra, A. K., Rohena-Diaz, E., & Nolet, V. (1998). A dynamic curriculum-based language assessment: Planning instruction for special needs students who are linguistically diverse. *Preventing School Failure, 42*(4), 182–185.

Jones, T. G. (1995). A framework for investigating minority group influence in urban school reform. *Urban Education, 29,* 375–395.

Leung, B. P. (1996). Quality assessment practices in a diverse society. *Teaching Exceptional Children, 28,* 42–45.

Lopez-Reyna, N. A., & Bay, M. (1997). Enriching assessment: Using varied assessments for diverse learners. *Teaching Exceptional Children, 29*(4), 33–37.

McCray, A. D., & García, S. B. (2002). The stories we must tell: Developing a research agenda for multicultural and bilingual special education. *International Journal of Qualitative Studies in Education, 15,* 599–612.

Mercer, J. R. (1973). *Labeling the mentally retarded.* Berkeley: University of California Press.

Moll, L. C., Amanti, C., Neff, D., & Gonzalez, N. (1992). Funds of knowledge for teaching: Using a qualitative approach to connect homes and classrooms. *Theory into Practice, 31*(1), 132–141.

National Association for the Education of Young Children. (1996, January). NAEYC Position Statement: Responding to linguistic and cultural diversity—Recommendations for effective early childhood education. *Young Children*, pp. 4–12.

National Center for Education Statistics. (1998). *Dropout rates in the United States: 1996.* Washington, DC: U.S. Department of Education, Office of Educational Research and Development, National Center for Education Statistics.

Obiakor, F. E., & Smith, D. J. (2005). Understanding the power of words in multicultural education and interaction. In R. Hoosain & F. Salili (Eds.), *Language in multicultural education* (pp. 77–92). Greenwich, CT: Information Age.

Ogbu, J. (1994). From cultural differences to differences in cultural frame of reference. In P. M. Greenfield & R. R. Cocking (Eds.), *Cross-cultural roots of minority child development* (pp. 365–392). Hillsdale, NJ: Erlbaum.

Ortiz, A. A. (1997). Learning disabilities occurring concomitantly with linguistic differences. *Journal of Learning Disabilities, 30,* 321–332.

Ortiz, A. A. (2002). Prevention of school failure and early intervention for English-language learners. In A. J. Artiles & A. A. Ortiz (Eds.), *English-language learners with special education needs: Identification, assessment, and instruction* (pp. 31–48). Washington, DC: Center for Applied Linguistics and Delta Systems.

Ortiz, A. A., & García, S. B. (1990). Using language assessment data for language and instructional planning for exceptional bilingual students. In A. L. Carrasquillo & R. E. Baecher (Eds.), *Teaching the bilingual special education student* (pp. 25–47). Norwood, NJ: Ablex.

Ortiz, A. A., García, S. B., Maldonado-Colón, E., Wheeler , D. (1986). *Characteristics of Hispanic limited English proficient students in programs for the speech and language handicapped: Implications for policy, practice and research.* Austin: The University of Texas at Austin, Department of Special Education, Handicapped Minority Research Institute on Language Proficiency. (ERIC Document Reproduction Service No. ED 292 280)

Owens, R. E. (2005). *Language development: An introduction* (6th ed.). Boston: Allyn & Bacon.

Rubanova, N., & Mortenson, T. (2002). *Public high school graduate rates by state: 1981 to 1999.* Postsecondary Education Opportunity. Retrieved April 6, 2003, from www.postsecondary.org/ti/ti_24.asp

Salend, S. J., & Salinas, A. (2003). Language differences or learning difficulties: The work of the multidisciplinary team. *Teaching Exceptional Children, 35*(4), 36–43.

Santamaría, L. J., Fletcher, T. V., & Bos, C. S. (2002). Effective pedagogy for English-language learners in inclusive classrooms. In A. J. Artiles & A. A. Ortiz (Eds.), *English-language learners with special education needs: Identification, assessment, and instruction* (pp. 133–157). Washington, DC: Center for Applied Linguistics.

Slavin, R. E., & Madden, N. A. (1989). What works for students at risk: A research synthesis. *Educational Leadership, 46*(5), 4–13.

Thomas, W. P., & Collier, V. P. (2002). *A national study of school effectiveness for language minority students' long-term academic achievement.* Center for Research on Education, Diversity, and Excellence. Available from www.crede.ucsc.edu/research/llaa/1.1_final.html

Valencia, R., Valenzuela, A., Sloan, K., & Foley, D. E. (2001). Let's treat the cause, not the symptoms: Equity and accountability in Texas revisited. *Phi Delta Kappan, 83,* 318–321, 326.

Zehler, A. M., Fleischman, H. L., Hopstock, P. J., Pendzick, M. L., & Stephenson, T. G. (2003). *Descriptive study of services to LEP students and LEP students with disabilities [Special Topic Report #4]: Findings on special education LEP students.* Arlington, VA: Development Associates.

Chapter 3

Litigation and Legislation: Impact on Multicultural Special Education

Elizabeth A. Dooley

Chapter Outline

Thinking About Multicultural Special Education

Steven was a 12-year-old African American who attended Love Lace Elementary School. He was diagnosed at age 7 with near-average to above-average intelligence and a specific learning disability in mathematics. Before long, his parents and teachers noticed he had increasing difficulty in reading as well as low scores on the state standardized achievement test. Steven's mother stated that she was displeased with his academic progress. Steven had attended this school for the past 5 years with continued grade promotion, even with existing and apparent academic deficiencies and specific subject difficulties. Upon further investigation, his mother strongly believed teachers and staff lowered academic standards for him to aid his success in school.

Steven's mother said that over the past several years, his teachers always reported his good manners and great personality. When she inquired about his standardized test scores and debilitating reading levels, some teachers avoided her questions by referring to Steven's strong communication skills, social maturity, and creative talents. She told the school's administration as well as Steven's teachers that Steven needed more challenging and interesting work because he frequently complained about how bored he was with school. The school's response was that all of their students were treated equally and given appropriate grade-level work. Before long, Steven's mother reviewed his homework and was dismayed to find that her child was doing a book report on a picture book version of Huckleberry Finn *in addition to subtraction and addition ditto puzzles for math. She was completely outraged that this level of work was assigned to him. There was nothing on Steven's IEP that required accommodations for his reading assignments. Moreover, she did not feel that color fill-in math ditto sheets were appropriate for her 12-year-old son.*

Interestingly, in Steven's school, 40% of African American students tested below the 50th percentile on the state standardized achievement test. More specifically, the disaggregated data indicated that 25% of those African American students that tested in the lowest quartile were male, whereas 68% of the white students tested at or above the 50th percentile. In Steven's case, his school failed to make adequate yearly progress (AYP). As a result, the school was placed on probation. When the school was placed on probation, the principal took an active role in the school assessment system and instructional practice. To turn things around, the principal took full advantage of the Individuals with Disabilities Education Act (IDEA) and the No Child Left Behind (NCLB) fundings that were earmarked for professional development activities. Teachers and service providers were given a series of professional development sessions that specifically focused on the instructional needs of students from culturally diverse backgrounds. These professionals received instruction in culturally relevant pedagogy, working with families from ethnically and linguistically diverse backgrounds. In addition to professional development, the principal started after-school tutoring programs. Because of these implemented programs, communication between the parents and teachers improved, teachers became more cognizant of the social and emotional needs of students from diverse backgrounds, and instruction was tailored to the unique characteristics of students from multicultural backgrounds.

Steven participated in the after-school tutoring program, where he received direct instruction in reading and mathematics. Teachers learned that he had an interest in astronomy, and textbooks and supplemental materials on astronomy were presented to him at his readability levels. Math across the curriculum was implemented, and he saw a direct benefit from instruction in math. As a result, Steven was able to see the utility of math in several different contexts. For example, teachers participating in the after-school tutoring program created math problems around the astronomy subject matter. After several months of direct instruction and weekly meetings between the teacher and Steven's mother, Steven's reading comprehension and word recall improved. The success that Steven experienced was a direct benefit of legislation that clearly articulated a vision for all learners and mandated programs and initiatives that brought about changes in student learning.

- *Why do you suppose the No Child Left Behind legislation brought about desirable academic results for Steven?*
- *What can schools do to increase effective, legally required communication between school staff and parents of children from multicultural backgrounds?*

Public schools in the United States are uniquely diverse, and they are urged to provide educational opportunities to students who represent many different demographic entities that may include race, religion, color, gender, national origin, disability, and age (Civil Rights Act of 1964; Education for All Handicapped Children Act of 1975; Individuals with Disabilities Education Act, 1990, 1997, 2004). According to the Twenty-fourth Annual Report to Congress (U.S. Department of Education, 2003), a diverse student body is served under Part C of IDEA. For instance, child count data for children age 6 through 21—with the omission of data from the state of New York—showed that 62.3% of the student population was classified as white; 14.5% were Latino; 19.8% were African American; 1.9% were Asian/Pacific Islander; and 1.58% were American Indian/Alaska Native (U.S. Department of Education, 2003). Often, educational opportunities provided to children vary across demographic groups because teachers and/or administrators typically use demographic variables to (a) dictate educational opportunities made available to students, (b) determine the level and quality of instruction for many children, and (c) define student expectations and educational outcomes (Obiakor, 1999, 2001; Obiakor, Grant, & Dooley, 2002). This subjective approach results in variance in achievement levels across multicultural groups, disability groups, and socioeconomic status. In addition, in many cases this variance results in intentional or unintentional civil rights violations, such as in Steven's case. School districts have been taken to task; and many times, this has resulted in groundbreaking legislation and equitable educational services for *all* learners. This chapter focuses on this ideal and discusses the impact of litigation and legislation on multicultural special education.

LITIGATION AND LEGISLATION: CIVIL RIGHTS CHANNELS

The equal protection clause of the Fourteenth Amendment protects the individual rights of *all* people, including students who come from multicultural backgrounds. According to this Amendment, *all* individuals are guaranteed equal protection under the law. However, equal protection has not always been given to all. Historically, African American students like Steven or students with disabilities have not fully enjoyed equal protection under the law, equal access to opportunities, and equal educational realities. In addition, students with linguistic differences or those who are English-language learners (ELLs) often have met obstacles that prevented them from being successful in school. These inequities have resulted in advocacy, litigation, and legislation. One example is the landmark case of *Brown*, a case that has had tremendous impact on challenging school districts' exclusionary practices. Popularly known as the *Brown v. Board of Education* (in Topeka, Kansas) case of 1954 (S. Ct. 1954), it was the premier precedent-setting litigant case for all civil rights and disabilities legislation. The Supreme Court ruled in *Brown* that separate education was not equal and held the separate-but-equal doctrine (i.e., Jim Crow law) to be inherently unconstitutional. School districts were instructed to desegregate schools with "deliberate speed." In addition, the court ruled that to exclude students like Steven from school was a violation of the equal protection clause of the Fourteenth Amendment (Obiakor & Utley, 2004). By legal mandate, school districts had to come into compliance with the law by allowing all children to attend and to receive an educational benefit from public schooling. Put another way, schools could no longer impose educational inequities upon all children, including those from multicultural backgrounds.

The *Brown* decision significantly affected the Civil Rights Act of 1964, which itself emerged from an era of ill will and distrust. The civil rights movement incited people who were disenfranchised and who, because of Jim Crow laws, were denied access to a public education. Their dissatisfaction led to protests such as demonstrations, marches, and frequent sit-ins. The civil rights movement culminated in the Civil Rights Act of 1964, which protected *all* individuals from discriminatory practices and in large measure provided a remedy for equal protection violations, more specifically, illegal actions such as discrimination and disparate treatments perpetrated upon disenfranchised people (Title VI of the Civil Rights Act of 1964). The Civil Rights Act of 1964 prohibits discrimination on the basis of race, color, or national origin in any program receiving federal funds. Violation of the Civil Rights Act was supposed to result in the withdrawal of federal funding. Surprisingly, not many schools or districts have been penalized in this regard.

In 1998, the U.S. Department of Education revised the Civil Rights Act of 1964. With the revisions, the Department of Education provided schools with specific guidelines regarding the education of multicultural learners. These guidelines were developed to alleviate the persistence of inequities within public education (Dooley & Dooley, 2002). The following were provided as accountability measures:

- **Assignment to classes.**   School districts are not allowed to segregate students on the basis of race, color, or national origin in making classroom assignments. When schools offer courses of study that result in disproportionate numbers based on minority or nonminority status, they must be able to demonstrate valid and nondiscriminatory reasons that such assignments occurred. The U.S. Department of Education, Department of Civil Rights (1998) recognized that valid educational reasons may exist when a class provides specialized instruction to assist ELLs in acquiring language skills.
- **Special education classes for students with disabilities.**   School districts must ensure that students are not misidentified as being disabled and that misclassification does not result in students being inappropriately labeled and placed in special education programs. School districts are required to educate students with disabilities in an integrated setting with nondisabled peers.
- **Classes designed for national origin minority students who are ELLs.** School districts must provide equal educational opportunity to national origin minority students who are ELLs. Therefore, students with limited English should not be assigned to special education because of their lack of English-language skills; and schools should consider allowing enough time for English-language acquisition. Many schools have responded to the needs of ELLs by developing special courses of instruction. These courses should allow students to move into the regular classroom setting in a reasonable period of time.
- **Assignment to ability grouping and tracking.**   Schools should not employ practices such as ability grouping or tracking that result in discrimination on the basis of race, color, or national origin. Ability grouping appears to place students in classes or instructional groups based on their levels of ability or achievement; and tracking appears to place students in different courses of instruction. Ability grouping and tracking may result in disproportionate enrollments of multicultural students in certain classes.
- **Testing, evaluations, and criteria for student assignment.**   School districts must use appropriate criteria, evaluation, and testing methods before assigning students to specialized classes or courses of study. Tests must be designed to assess each student's needs, and they should also serve as valid and reliable measures of student achievement.

DISABILITY LEGISLATION

Brown v. Board of Education and the civil rights movement served as springboards for disabilities litigation and legislation. *Pennsylvania Association for Retarded Children v. Commonwealth of Pennsylvania* (E.D. Pa. 1971) was the premier disabilities litigation. Prior to 1972 in the state of Pennsylvania, students with mental retardation were denied access to the public schools. The federal district court ruled that excluding children with disabilities from public school was unconstitutional. Schools in Pennsylvania were instructed to provide a free education and training appropriate to the child's capacity. Another case, *Mills v. Board of Education of District of Columbia* (1972), addressed the issue of exclusion; and in that case, children with disabilities in the District of Columbia were excluded from schools without due process of law. The court ruled that children had been excluded from attending school and stipulated that the District of Columbia had to provide adequate alternative educational services suited to their needs (Alexander & Alexander, 2003).

The legislation significantly affected by *Pennsylvania Association for Retarded Children v. Commonwealth* and *Mills v. Board of Education* was Public Law 94-142, the Education for All Handicapped Children Act (EAHCA), passed in 1975. This legislation protected the educational rights of children with exceptionalities (i.e., cognitive disabilities, learning disabilities, communication disorders, speech and language disorders, behavior disorders, gifted/talented, visual impairments, hearing impairments/deafness, and physical/health impairments) by ensuring a free and appropriate public education (FAPE). The law was respectively amended or reauthorized in 1986 (P.L. 99-457), 1990 (P.L. 105-17), 1997 (P.L. 101-476), and 2004 (P.L. 108-446). The 1986 law was extended to infants and toddlers by protecting their educational rights and making educational intervention services available to infants, toddlers, and their families; the 1990 law was enacted to provide appropriate education based on students' needs and add new categories (i.e., autism and traumatic brain injury); and the 1997 and 2004 laws focused on more inclusive multicultural approaches to provide individualized educational services and alternative education for those who could not be "normally" served.

Additional legislation banning intentional discrimination and supporting and protecting educational and societal rights (i.e., having access to facilities outside of the public school environment) of students with and without disabilities was enacted between 1970 and 1990. Section 504 of the Vocational Rehabilitation Act of 1973 (P.L. 93-112) protects the rights of students with disabilities and those students with special needs who are not eligible for special education entitlement services but who require and will benefit from additional academic assistance and/or program modifications. Section 504 influenced the enactment of the Americans with Disabilities Act (ADA) of 1990 (P.L. 101-336). The ADA protects the rights of individuals with disabilities in the workplace and allows for greater access to employment, community facilities, and other aspects of local communities, such as public transportation and recreational facilities.

EQUALIZING EDUCATION: IN QUEST OF LEARNERS' RIGHTS

Clearly, civil rights and disability laws have continued to focus on students excluded from a free and appropriate education. Although there have been instances when children have not been denied access, these laws have failed to yield appropriate instructional services to meet their specific needs. For example, in *Lau v. Nichols* (S. Ct. 1974), Chinese students were denied special English instruction because the school district did not have adequate funds. The U.S. Supreme Court ruled that the school's inability to provide methods of bridging the language gap "offended" Title VI of the Civil Rights Act of 1964, 42 W.S.C.A § 2000d, which is viewed as discrimination on the basis of national origin. Furthermore, the court insisted that it was the school's responsibility to provide students with the skills necessary for learning.

Over the years, efforts have been made by politicians and various organizations to eliminate what might be translated into disparate impact, such as the achievement gaps between ethnic groups. The achievement gaps between ethnic groups in academic performance and across socioeconomic standing or across disability groups is pervasive (U.S. Department of Education, 2003). According to data provided by the National Center of Education Statistics (2003), the average score of African American and Latino students in the areas of math and reading is at least 30 points below that of white students. Moreover, in the area of reading, by the time these students reach the twelfth grade, only one in six (approximately 17%) African Americans and one in five Latinos (approximately 20%) can read proficiently. It becomes more disheartening in the area of math, because only 3% of African American and only 4% of Latino students are testing at the proficient level (U.S. Department of Education, 2003). As the U.S. Department of Education stated, 60% of poor fourth graders cannot read at a basic level. The achievement gap that exists in this country spans race, gender, class, disability, and culture. Even though laws have been enacted to change educational inequalities, legislative remedies have not been explicit nor have they included well-documented learner outcomes. One major example of these laws is the No Child Left Behind Act of 2001 (P.L. 107-110).

No Child Left Behind Act of 2001: Impact on Multicultural Learners with Exceptionalities

The No Child Left Behind Act of 2001 (NCLB) speaks to the inefficiencies in the public schools and calls for a radical change. This act is designed to leave no child behind, no matter his or her race, culture, language, ability, or disability. To a large extent, it is designed to improve school achievement and academic proficiency of *all* children regardless of their characteristics. The fundamental principles of the NCLB legislation include (a) stronger accountability for schools and school districts to ensure equal, quality, and efficient educational practices to meet student needs; (b) increased flexibility and local control for local and state educational agencies; (c) increased parental choice, awareness and involvement in the educational decision-making process for their children; and (d) stronger focus on research-based programs that have been proven to work in maximizing the academic success of *all* children. Unlike previous educational legislation, NCLB outlines specific learner goals, objectives, and outcomes to result in greater student achievement and skill proficiency in mathematics and reading (and science beginning in 2005–2006), which are measured by yearly state standardized tests. In addition, NCLB insists that educational opportunities must bring about desirable and reliable educational results regardless of the student's socioeconomic background, race, gender, language, and/or disability.

The NCLB documents its commitment to changing the educational plight of disenfranchised, disabled, and atypical groups in public schools. The demand for highly qualified teachers, added resources and programs for all students with skill deficits or disability, and high learner expectations for all children directly affect the multicultural special education ideology. A major focal point of this legislation is to "meet the educational needs of low-achieving children in our Nation's highest-poverty schools, limited English proficient children, migratory children, children with disabilities, Indian children, neglected or delinquent children, any young children in need of academic assistance" (NCLB, 2001, p. 9). Unfortunately, these groups (i.e., poor, minority, and disabled) historically have not achieved nearly the same success as other children, thus creating the disparities in achievement. According to the Department of Education (2003), the NCLB is designed to change the culture of America's schools by closing the achievement gap, offering more flexibility, giving parents more options, and teaching students based on what produces greater learner outcomes. Under the law's accountability provisions, states must describe how they will close the achievement gap and make sure all students, including those who are disadvantaged, achieve academic proficiency. Schools must produce annual state and school district report cards that provide information to parents and their communities about state and school progress. In addition, schools that do not make progress are required to provide supplemental services, such as free tutoring or after-school assistance; and, if still not making adequate yearly progress after 5 years, to make dramatic changes in the way the school is run (U.S. Department of Education, 2003).

The Council for Exceptional Children (CEC, 2003), the premier national professional organization for special educators, offered its opinion about the NCLB and cites two areas in which the NCLB significantly affects special education. As the CEC noted:

> One of the most significant implications of NCLB in terms of special education policy and practice concern adequate yearly progress (AYP) and the set of graduated accountability measures that follow NCLB when students fail to meet AYP. The law requires schools to show adequate yearly progress towards meeting the goal of 100% proficiency in reading and math for all students, in grades 3 though 8, within 12 years. The performance of students is a desegregation based on a host of identifying factors, including poverty, race, ethnicity, limited English proficient, and disability status. If children with disabilities (grades through 8) within a school fail to make adequate yearly progress toward reaching the 100% proficiency goal in reading and math by 2014, the school will potentially face a host of remedial actions intended to improve performance of students failing to make AYP. Thus, the performance of children with disabilities on statewide and district wide assessments will partly determine whether a school faces possible remedial actions in the future. (p. 7)

Furthermore, those schools that fail to make adequate yearly progress toward statewide proficiency goals will be subject to remedial actions. Remedial actions may consist of, but are not limited to, (a) improvement measures (including technical assistance, public school choice, and supplemental educational services; (b) correctional actions; and (c) restructuring measures.

Another most important piece of the NCLB legislation, according to the Council for Exceptional Children, is the call for highly qualified educators. In order to meet the guidelines for AYP for *all* students to be proficient in the set academic standards, schools must have a highly qualified teaching force (CEC, 2003). The two pieces identified by CEC also affect the schooling of multicultural learners. According to the legislation, all schools must have highly qualified teachers in the classroom by the 2005–2006 academic year. The NCLB Act of 2001 defines the term *highly qualified teacher* as

- the teacher who has obtained full certification or passed the state teacher licensing examination,
- the teacher who was not certified through emergency certification, temporary, or provisional basis,
- the teacher who holds at least a bachelor's degree,
- the teacher who is new to the profession and demonstrated, by passing a rigorous state test, subject knowledge and teaching skill in reading, writing, mathematics, and other areas of the basics.

The NCLB legislation implies a reconditioning of how professionals are prepared to teach in a heterogeneous setting. Yet it does not include discussions about the nature of "highly qualified" with regard to students with disabilities and students from culturally diverse backgrounds. Given the legislation's goals of narrowing achievement gaps and improving the quality of instruction to increase learner outcomes, the need to infuse diversity in current discourse cannot be underestimated. According to the National Association for Multicultural Education (2003), in reference to staff qualifications, multicultural education demands a school staff that is culturally competent and to the greatest extent possible racially, culturally, and linguistically diverse. All staff members must be multiculturally literate and capable of including and embracing families and communities to create an environment that is supportive of multiple perspectives and experiences. Banks (2004) affirmed that equity pedagogy exists when teachers modify their teaching in ways that facilitate the academic achievement of students from diverse racial, cultural, and gender groups.

Clearly, the NCLB challenges schools to use evidence-based instructional techniques. The issue, however, is that an evidence-based technique does not necessarily guarantee civil rights or equal access. There is substantial evidence that when teachers adjust their teaching styles and incorporate strategies that are culturally relevant, students from underrepresented groups show academic gains. Some researchers have found that achievement test scores increased when teachers incorporated teaching strategies that included student cultures and student experiences (Au, 1980; Darling-Hammond, 1995; Utley & Obiakor, 2001). For instance, Darling-Hammond noted that when students of color and low-income students have high quality teachers who are experts in their content areas, pedagogy, and child development, student achievement increases. When teachers are knowledgeable about students' cultures, values, and languages, and when they learn the characteristics of their students, opportunities for student success increase (Delpit, 1995; Ladson-Billings, 1994; Obiakor, 2004). Clearly, all students can be successful in supportive classrooms that respect their civil rights.

MULTICULTURAL SPECIAL EDUCATION: RESPONDING TO CIVIL RIGHTS

Although multicultural education and special education have not been traditionally presented as a single concept, they share the same origin. Both special education and multicultural education emerged out of the civil rights era, a time when multicultural students and those with disabilities were denied equal educational opportunities. Both concepts transform traditional teaching methodology into culturally relevant pedagogy because each concept was in direct response to civil rights litigation and special education litigation. In IDEA (1997), Congress listed concerns about the education of multicultural learners in special education and recommended that greater efforts be employed to minimize their mislabeling. Congress also recommended that greater efforts were needed to decrease high dropout rates among multicultural children with disabilities. With the reauthorization of the Individuals with Disabilities Education Improvement Act (IDEIA) of 2004, H. R. 1350, Congress highlighted the following points concerning culturally and linguistically diverse learners:

(10) (A) The Federal Government must be responsive to the growing needs of an increasingly diverse society.

(B) America's ethnic profile is rapidly changing. In 2000, 1 of every 3 persons in the United States was a member of a minority group or was limited English proficient.

(C) Minority children comprise an increasing percentage of public school students.

(D) With such changing demographics, recruitment efforts for special education personnel should focus on increasing the participation of minorities in the teaching profession in order to provide appropriate role models with sufficient knowledge to address the special education needs of these students.

(11) (A) The limited English proficient population is the fastest growing in our Nation, and the growth is occurring in many parts of our Nation.

(B) Studies have documented apparent discrepancies in the levels of referral and placement of limited English proficient children in special education.

(C) Such discrepancies pose a special challenge for special education in the referral for assessment of, and provision of services for, our Nation's students from non-English language backgrounds.

(12) (A) Greater efforts are needed to prevent the intensification of problems connected with mislabeling and high dropout rates among minority children with disabilities.

(B) More minority children continue to be served in special education than would be expected from the percentage of minority students in the general school population.

(C) African American children are identified as having mental retardation and emotional disturbance at rates greater than their white counterparts.

(D) In the 1998–1999 school year, African American children represented just 14.8 percent of the population aged 6–21, but comprised 20.2 percent of all children with disabilities.

(E) Studies have found that schools with predominately white students and teachers have disproportionately high numbers of their minority students in special education.

(13) (A) As the number of minority students in special education increases, the number of minority teachers and related services personnel produced in colleges and universities continues to decrease.

According to these congressional findings, linguistically and cultural diverse learners continue to experience educational inequities. Multicultural education is not a national mandate by law, but past and present litigation and legislation more than suggest its infusion into general school programming. The mandate comes through laws that were enacted to address the vestiges of racism. The belief in equal opportunity and the belief that education must be accessible and appropriate to *all* children put multicultural special education at the forefront. Multicultural special education ascertains that *all* learners can be educated in an undiscriminatory way, and to a large measure, ascertains that no child can be left behind. The underpinnings of multicultural special education focus on educating *all* children by (a) setting high expectations, (b) using culturally relevant and responsive strategies to work with all students, (c) providing equal access and opportunity, and (d) using best teaching practices that enhance educational experiences for all children. For instance, the IDEA, NCLB, and IDEIA laws support most of the same principles. Yet although they outline guidelines for students from at-risk populations, ELLs, and students who come from historically oppressed or discriminated groups, they have not fully done what they are supposed to do. As a result, general and special education professionals must put these laws into proper practical perspective.

A Culturally Responsive Educator

1. Respects the civil rights of all persons.
2. Understands the impact of litigation in general and special education.
3. Engages in nondiscriminatory identification and referral of students.
4. Is knowledgeable about the laws in special education.
5. Is not afraid to do what is right in the classroom in spite of the threat of lawsuits.
6. Evaluates students in unprejudicial ways.
7. Avoids disproportionate representations in special and gifted education.
8. Continues to learn about new laws and their impact on his or her professional activities.
9. Respects the laws of the land.
10. Works to understand the legal ramifications of special education.

Conclusion

All too often, disparities in education occur because of failure of some professionals in general and special education to have an appreciation or understanding of differences and how diverse characteristics of learners affect learning outcomes. As a result, the civil rights of students are intentionally or unintentionally violated. When this happens, advocacy results in litigation, which in turn results in legislation. Laws must be promulgated to protect students like Steven, and they must require school districts to provide equitable services for all learners, no matter what their racial, cultural, linguistic, or behavioral characteristics. For instance, although the NCLB does not speak specifically about highly qualified teachers as the term relates to the teaching of students with disabilities and the teaching of students from culturally and linguistically diverse backgrounds, national organizations and national accrediting bodies recognize the importance of multicultural education. Directly or indirectly, civil rights legislation and disability legislation support multicultural special education. Legal mandates of civil rights legislation have continued to set clear expectations for public schools. However, these expectations must be transformed into measurable goals and objectives and to a large degree, must stimulate pedagogical applications of multicultural special education. The laws as written or as stated do not alone bring about changes in how all children are taught. Changes are brought about by practitioners who understand the impact that the letter of these laws will have on practice.

Discussion Questions

1. Evaluate two legislative efforts to bring about changes in special education before the 1990s.
2. Explain the concept of civil rights and discuss the legal basis for them.
3. Analyze the common themes across major educational laws.
4. Identify four major ingredients of P.L. 94-142 and some of its amendments.
5. Discuss the role of educational laws in narrowing the achievement gaps between students.

References

Alexander, K., & Alexander, M. D. (2003). *The law of schools, students, and teachers.* St. Paul, MN: West.

Americans with Disabilities Act (1990), Pub. L. No. 101-336, 104 Stat. 327.

Au, K. (1980). Participation structures in a reading class with Hawaiian children. *Anthropology and Education Quarterly, 11*(2), 91–115.

Banks, J. A. (2004). Multicultural education historical development, dimensions, and practice. In J. A. Banks & C. A. M. Banks (Eds.), *Handbook of research on multicultural education* (2nd ed., pp. 3–29). San Francisco: Jossey-Bass.

Brown v. Board of Education of Topeka, Shawnee County, Kansas, 347 U.S. 483, 74 S. Ct. 686, 98 L. Ed. 873, 53 O. O. 326 (1954), Supp. 349 U.S. 294, 75 S. Ct. 753, 99 L. Ed. 1083, 57 O.O. 253 (1955), 197, 199, 200, 201, 206, 208, 214, 411. Title VI. Pub. L. 88-352, Sess. 601 (1964).

Civil Rights Act (1964), Pub. L. No. 88-352, 42 U.S.C. § 2000 et seq.

Council for Exceptional Children (2003). *Implications for special education policy and practice. Title II—Preparing, training, and recruiting high quality teachers and principals.* Arlington, VA: Author.

Darling-Hammond, L. (1995). Inequality and access to knowledge. In J. A. Banks & C. A. M. Banks (Eds.), *Handbook of research on multicultural education* (pp. 465–483). New York: Macmillan.

Delpit, L. (1995). *Other people's children: Cultural conflict in the classroom.* New York: New Press.

Dooley, E. A., & Dooley, K. (2002). Legal foundations of special education for African American learners. In F. E. Obiakor & B. A. Ford (Eds.), *Creating successful learning environments for African American learners with exceptionalities* (pp. 17–25). Thousand Oaks, CA: Corwin Press.

Education for All Handicapped Children Act (1975), Pub. L. No. 94-142.

Education for All Handicapped Children Amendments (1986), Pub. L. No. 99-457.

Individuals with Disabilities Education Act Amendments (1990), Pub. L. No. 101-476.

Individuals with Disabilities Education Act Amendments (1997), Pub. L. No. 105-17.

Individuals with Disabilities Education Improvement Act (2004), 20 U.S.C. 1400 et seq., Pub. L. No. 108-446.

Ladson-Billings, G. (1994). *The dreamkeepers: Successful teachers of African American children.* New York: Jossey-Bass.

Lau v. Nichols, 414 U.S. 563, 94 S. Ct. 786 39 L. Ed.2d 1 (1974), 50.

Mills v. Board of Education of District of Columbia, 348 F. Supp. 866 (D.C.D.C. 1972).

National Association for Multicultural Education (2003). *Resolutions and position papers.* Office of Special Education and Rehabilitative Programs. www.ed.gov/about/offices/list/osers/osep/index.html?src=mr

No Child Left Behind Act (2001), Pub. L. No. 107-110.

Obiakor, F. E. (1999, Fall). Teacher expectations of minority exceptional learners: Impact on "accuracy" of self-concepts. *Exceptional Children, 66,* 39–53.

Obiakor, F. E. (2001). *It even happens in "good" schools: Responding to cultural diversity in today's classrooms.* Thousand Oaks, CA: Corwin Press.

Obiakor, F. E. (2004). Impact of changing demographics on public education for culturally diverse learners with behavior problems: Implications for teacher preparation. In L. M. Bullock & R. A. Gable (Eds.), *Quality personnel preparation in emotional/behavioral disorders: Current perspectives and future directions* (pp. 51–63). Denton, TX: University of North Texas, Institute for Behavioral and Learning Differences.

Obiakor, F. E., Grant, P., & Dooley, E. (2002). *Educating all learners: Refocusing the comprehensive support model.* Springfield, IL: Charles C Thomas.

Obiakor, F. E., & Utley, C. A. (2004). Educating culturally diverse learners with exceptionalities: A critical analysis of the *Brown* case. *Peabody Journal of Education, 79,* 141–156.

Pennsylvania Association for Retarded Children v. Commonwealth of Pennsylvania, 343 F. Supp. 279 (D.C. Pa. 1971).

U.S. Department of Education (2003). *National report card.*

U.S. Department of Education (2003). *Twenty-fourth annual report to Congress on the implementation of the Individuals with Disabilities Education Act.* Washington, DC: U.S. Government Printing Office.

U.S. Department of Education Department of Civil Rights (1998). *Student assignment and Title VI in elementary and secondary schools.* Washington, DC: Author.

Utley, C. A., & Obiakor, F. E. (2001). *Special education, multicultural education, and school reform: Components of quality education for learners with mild disabilities.* Springfield, IL: Charles C Thomas.

Vocational Rehabilitation Act (1973), § 504, 19 U.S.C. § 794.

Part II

Categories of Exceptionalities: Multicultural Perspectives

Chapter 4

Working with Multicultural Learners with Communication Disorders

Martha Scott Lue and Janice Morgan Taylor

Thinking About Multicultural Special Education

Louis, a 12-year-old middle school student of Haitian descent, served as the "interpreter" for his entire family. He was the oldest of 10 siblings and lived with his mom, Bernice. Louis presented a challenge to his teachers. Although he could translate in both English and Haitian Creole, when his teachers gave him written work (in English) to read and explain, he was not able to do that and became very frustrated. He was behind in most of his academic subjects because of his inability to fully understand English. He spoke with a slight accent, and his classmates often made fun of him. Tests performed by the speech language pathologist indicated a slight delay in language, but one that could be remediated with help from his family. The speech pathologist recommended strategies that his parents and family members could use in working with him at home in his natural environment.

Bernice, Louis's mother, worked at a theme park at minimum wage. She spoke very little English. Formal education was not directly encouraged in the family, because Bernice's main priority was to provide for her family here, while at the same time sending money back to those family members in Haiti. The local Community Services coordinator had invited her to participate, free of charge, in the community's English-language learners (ELL) classes. She repeatedly declined because she had no time; she got by with the little English that she knew. Her husband was deported to Haiti because of a criminal offense. Before long, things began to change. The theme park had reached out to her in its recruitment efforts to have more workers of Haitian descent, and she was promoted to supervisor on her shift. Her hours became a bit more flexible and her hourly wage increased; she was able to participate more at the Community Services center. At the center, a family liaison began to recognize some of the needs of the family and also began to hold evening office hours, so working parents could drop in and talk. Things began to work out better for this family.

Jennifer, Louis's homeroom teacher, was in her second year of teaching in this urban school. Jennifer was not certified in education. She was taking certification and ELL endorsement courses, while at the same time studying for her teaching examination. Her frustration with her class grew daily. This reached an unbearable level and she found herself saying, "They just don't see the importance of education. I talk to my middle school students all the time about how much I care about them, and how anxious I am for them to learn. One of the very few times that I see any of their parents is when there is a conflict in the classroom. I am nearly burned out. Don't you feel my dilemma? I'm doing the best that I can, but I just need some help!"

During this time, a local university developed an online certificate program in urban education, and Jennifer was one of the first students to be admitted. On the first *assignment, "acknowledging your own biases," Jennifer admitted that she held many biases toward some of the parents of students in her school because of the way that they "presented themselves." Her relationship with the family members of students in her class began to improve, as did her understanding of some of the students' behaviors in the classroom. She began to seek input from her mentor and principal, both of whom started commenting on how she was appearing more confident in managing classroom behaviors. In the end, she became an exemplary teacher and it was not uncommon to hear her say, "I just want them to know that I care about them, not only now, but what they will be in the future when I'm no longer their teacher." Jennifer and Louis's mother developed an excellent collaborative relationship that helped Louis both in his language skills and in his schoolwork.*

- *How did Louis's parent's condition affect his language learning abilities in school?*
- *What conditions led to positive changes in the collaborative relationships between Louis's teacher and parent?*

The National Center on Educational Statistics (2005) reported that the number of children ages 5 to 17 who spoke a language other than English at home more than doubled between 1979 and 2003. Clearly, language has some influence on education. One's language is personal, interactive, and original. It is an important human characteristic (American Speech-Language-Hearing Association [ASHA], 2001). Delpit (2002) noted that it "embraces us long before we are defined by any other medium of identity" (p. xvii). In addition, it helps to shape one's cultural and personal identity (Gollnick & Chinn, 2002), and to a large extent, demonstrates what separates humans from other beings. It celebrates who people are and from whence they have come. It should come as no surprise, then, that as the nation's schools become more diverse, more challenging issues related to communication, language differences, and language disorders will arise (Kuder, 2003; Manning, 2000; Nieto, 2004; Obiakor & Ford, 2002).

Many forms of human diversity (e.g., race, ethnicity, culture, gender, class, language, and disability) exist. Diversity in the nation's schools continues to evolve (Hodgkinson, 2000/2001; Lord, 2002; Martin & Midgley, 1994; Orfield, 2001). Today's society is in constant change (Roseberry-McKibbin, 2000). Although most students who enter school speak Standard English, there are increasing numbers of students, many of whom are similar to Louis, whose nationality, ethnicity, race, gender, social and economic classification, and language patterns may be different. Often, stigma is attached to youngsters, such as Louis, whose language patterns are different (Gollnick & Chinn, 2002; Heward, 2003). As Heward noted, learners who experience difficulty in absorbing information through listening and reading and who are unable to express themselves in spoken words are almost certain to experience difficulties, not only in their schools, but in their communities as well. He added that this difficulty may have an impact on the individual's ability to form satisfying relationships with others.

This chapter provides a framework for understanding terms and concepts concerning communication, language disorders, and language differences in multicultural learners. It also discusses challenges of demographic change, issues of language differences or language disorders, and Standard English and ELLs. Lastly, it offers recommendations that the teacher, primary caregiver, or service provider must use to facilitate communication and, if needed, remediation.

THE REALITY OF CULTURAL AND LINGUISTIC DIVERSITIES

Diversity is all around. Where one lives, however, determines the level of cultural diversity that one might encounter (Parker, 2005). It is generally agreed that in years to come, general and special educators will be teaching groups of learners who are quite different from those they have taught in the past. The number of students from diverse cultures is expected to grow to 24 million, 37% of the school-age population, by the year 2010. Hodgkinson (2005), however, noted that future population growth in the United States will continue to be uneven, with an increase in students of Latino and Asian descent, and with 10 states each containing 90% of the Latino population and 90% of the Asian population. Further, many of these youngsters will come from more diverse cultural and linguistic backgrounds (ASHA, 2001; Roseberry-McKibbin, 1995). As a result, they will exhibit a wide range of language, learning, and behavioral characteristics that may present challenges to educators (Adger, Wolfram, & Detwyler, 1993; Lue, 2001). Some of these students may be at risk of academic failure and placed in special education settings because they are ELLs who have different behavioral characteristics and different socioeconomic backgrounds (Roseberry-McKibbin, 1995; Thomas, Correa, & Morsink, 2001). Apparently, many multicultural learners with exceptionalities experience general language difficulties (Rodriquez, Parmar, & Signer, 2001).

It is believed if students were distributed evenly across the nation's classrooms, every class of 30 students would include about 10 students from multicultural groups. Of the 10, about 6 would be from language minority families. Two to four of these students would be ELLs, of whom two would be from immigrant families. Of the six language minority students in the class, four would speak Spanish in their native language, and one would speak an Asian language. The other language minority student would speak any one of more than a hundred languages (McLaughlin & McLeod, 1996). A few years ago, the U.S. Department of Census (2000) released preliminary U.S. population figures for the year 2000. As the Department explained, there are slightly more than 281 million persons, an increase of 13.2% in the last decade. The greatest population growth in the nation occurred in the states of Arizona, Georgia, Florida, and Texas, with growth ranging from 23% to 44%.

LANGUAGE DIFFERENCE VERSUS LANGUAGE DISORDER

In view of the diversity in schools, it is important to understand communication in the context of students like Louis. Payne and Taylor (1998) noted that communication is considered to be disordered when it (a) deviates from the standards of the community enough that it interferes with the transmission of messages, (b) stands out as being unusually different, and (c) produces negative feelings within the communicator. Vaughn, Bos, and Schumm (2000) observed that the disorder may either be developmental or acquired through injuries or diseases that affect the brain. Conversely, speech disorders result when the individual's speech is unintelligible, unpleasant, or interferes with communication.

Communication involves languages. How, then, can communication and/or language disorders be explained? There are different kinds of communication disorders. *Articulation disorders,* perhaps the most common speech disorders, result when individuals are not able to produce the various sounds and sound combinations of language at the developmentally appropriate age. A *fluency disorder* occurs when the individual has difficulty with the flow and rate of speech. Two of the most common types of fluency disorders are *stuttering* (an interruption of the forward flow of speech) and *cluttering* (speech that is overly rapid, disorganized, and occasionally filled with unnecessary words and unrelated insertions). A *voice disorder* refers to difficulty with the quality, resonance, pitch, or intensity of one's voice. Students with *language disorders* may have delays in the development of comprehensive or expressive language. When is a language difference, such as Louis's, misinterpreted to mean language disorder?

In a society such as the United States made up of many cultures and languages, each person uses language differently. Hedge (1995) noted that "in order to understand a language, its use, its diversity, and its disorders, it is necessary to understand the broader context of that language" (p. 415). Therefore, it is helpful to understand the important attributes of language (ASHA, 1982). As ASHA pointed out:

- Language evolves within specific historical, social, and cultural contexts.
- Language is rule governed.
- Language learning and use are determined by the interaction of biological, cognitive, psychological, and environmental factors.
- Effective use of language for communication requires a broad understanding of human interactions, including such associated factors as nonverbal cues, motivation, and sociocultural role.

Often, language is described along dimensions such as *form* (phonology, morphology, syntax), *content* (semantics), and *use* (pragmatics). *Phonology* is the system of rules that governs sounds and their combination. Each language has specific sounds, or phonemes, that are characteristic of that language (Bernstein, 1984). A *phoneme* is further defined as the smallest unit of sound in a word that makes a difference in its meaning. *Morphology* is the system of rules for combining sounds into meaningful units, such as words, suffixes, and prefixes. Simply stated, *morphemes* are the smallest linguistic unit with meaning, and they form a bridge between phonology and syntax. *Syntax* refers to the arrangement of words combined by following the rule governance and patterns of the specific language to form meaningful sentences. The content of language is referred to as the *semantics* of the language. The concept of semantics refers to the ability to distinguish word meaning, including multiple meanings and subtle nuances, and to understand the language. The actual use of language within a social context is referred to as *pragmatics.* Moreover, it is the awareness of socially appropriate behaviors in communication interactions. For more information, read Lue (2001) and Heward (2003). In addition, see the Web site of the ASHA (www.asha.org).

ASHA (2001), the national professional, scientific, and credentialing association for speech, language, and hearing professionals, explains that English is composed of many linguistic varieties, which may include Ebonics, Spanish-influenced English, Appalachian English, and Standard English. *Accents,* such as the one exhibited by Louis, are sound differences of spoken languages. They are derived from one's geographic region and the influences of foreign languages. A *dialect,* on the other hand, can be a variation of the form and content of a language (Culatta, Tompkins, & Werts, 2003). Both accents and dialects are types of language differences. A language difference, in and of itself, may not require intervention and remediation; however, those students who are found to be language disordered by a team of professionals will require intervention and remediation. Carmack and Thomas (1990) defined language as being disordered when "it interferes with communication, calls unfavorable attention to itself, or causes its user to be maladjusted" (p. 18). Earlier, ASHA (1982) noted that an individual with a language disorder may have problems in sentence processing and in abstracting information meaningful for storage and retrieval from short- and long-term memory.

A *language difference* is not necessarily a language disorder. Each language contains a variety of forms, called *dialects,* which are a variation of a symbol system and reflect shared regional, social, or cultural and ethnic factors (ASHA, 1982; Turnbull, Turnbull, Shank, Smith, & Leal, 2002). ASHA (1983) further posited that each dialect represents a functional form of English, permitting speakers to communicate adequately, while at the same time maintaining a "symbolic representation of the historical, social, and cultural background of the speakers" (p. 24). Although some dialect speakers may have a speech or language disorder, the dialect itself is not the disorder. However, the presence of a dialect should not necessarily rule out the possibility that a language disorder might exist (Van Riper & Erickson, 1996). A *language disorder* is a problem in understanding or producing meaningful conversation and might involve (a) a serious disruption of the language acquisition process; (b) difficulty with following rules of grammar; (c) the ability to understand or use words in correct context; (d) not choosing appropriate language for different situations; and (e) problems of written or spoken language and/or other symbol systems (see ASHA, 1982). Language disorders may vary in severity, ranging from mild to severe (Polloway, Patton, & Serna, 2001).

Speech-language pathologists, the professionals who treat speech and language disorders, are trained to distinguish between a language difference (e.g., dialect) and a language disorder. In some cases, it might be helpful for them to become familiar with specific rules that underlie the use of particular dialects (Van Riper & Erickson, 1996). How, then, can a classroom teacher or service provider determine when a child's language usage is different or disordered? It is important to note that the way a child speaks is a reflection of his or her culture (Heward, 2003). If a professional is unsure about whether the child has a speech or language problem, he or she might refer the child for testing by a speech, language, or hearing professional. Speech-language pathologists are specially trained to serve as consultants to teachers and other professionals on dialectal variations and modifications.

LANGUAGE DIFFERENCE AND NONSTANDARD VARIETIES OF ENGLISH

Like many youngsters, Louis entered school speaking a "home language." Home languages might include Black English, Spanish/French Creole, Appalachian English, and Hmong. The majority of these youngsters may not have anything "wrong" with their speech and will not require any special educational services. Some, for example, dialect speakers, may face significant barriers as they enter and progress through school (Bountress, 1994; Ovando, 2003). The speech-language pathologist, as in Louis's case, must be instrumental in developing strategies that may assist the student. For some students of African American descent, their language use may not be the "standard" that is usually heard in most middle-class families. Thus, the issue of Standard English should be addressed in classrooms and school programs.

It is apparent that the population that speaks another language or dialect outside of Standard English has increased dramatically. Thus it is important for general and special education teachers to differentiate between typical and atypical phonological development in children who do not speak Standard American English. Should Standard English be taught? Teaching Standard English to multicultural learners is important because they may be at risk for academic failure. Sometimes, however, teachers whose only language is English may feel unqualified to teach non-English speakers. Further, offering instruction "to improve" speech may send the mixed message of criticizing not only the language but also the person. Robbins (1989) described a unit of study designed to emphasize "Broadcast English" as a register to be used in certain situations (e.g., job interviews and reporting and presenting in class). Other suggestions include the use of journal writing, an effective tool for helping students to write on any topic they choose. Teachers, in turn, can read the journal entries and respond. The classroom teacher may also try using reading materials that deal with the culture of the student. It is highly likely that bicultural readers comprehend and remember materials that deal with their own culture more than those of another culture.

PROACTIVE STRATEGIES FOR MULTICULTURAL LEARNERS WITH COMMUNICATION DISORDERS

To work with multicultural learners with speech and language disorders or communication disorders, it is critical to form and maintain partnerships that effectively facilitate the community of learning that occurs in the home, school, and community environments. The types of parent-teacher-community partnerships that are formed and maintained are related to an understanding of both multicultural students with exceptionalities and their diverse cultural and linguistic backgrounds. The ASHA (2005) confirmed that

> in order to effectively meet the needs of an increasingly diverse multicultural clientele, it is very helpful for speech-language-hearing professionals to be aware of the historical, social and political factors that have contributed to the development of various speech communities throughout the United States.

Several critical factors concerning multicultural families and their involvement with schools are important to note:

- The participation of parents in an educational partnership with school staff may be affected by their comfort level when dealing with the schools. For some parents/family members of multicultural learners, like Bernice, Louis's mother, schools are not often seen as very user-friendly places. If parents/family members feel uncomfortable with the school's conceptualization of their involvement, they may choose to abstain from any of the roles made available to them by school personnel (Voltz, 1995).
- Many parents with limited verbal skills and little experience in negotiating the educational system may find it difficult to identify and to access appropriate educational resources for their children (Sileo, Sileo, & Prater, 1996). Dealing with any bureaucracies, including school systems, can be a frustrating and an overwhelming process. These parents may rarely have the capacity to participate in educational partnerships, especially when they sense that they are dealing with a system that does not recognize that they suffer from the double whammy of dealing with both race and disability (Haughton, 1993).
- Parents who have had negative experiences themselves with schools may not be willing to participate as partners in the educational process (Thorp, 1997). Some of these negative experiences may be more subtle; other experiences may be more overt. For example, when parents feel that there is little or no attempt to accurately represent the historical contributions of African Americans in the school curriculum, they may be reluctant or even unwilling to form partnerships with teachers and others involved in the education of their children. Parents, including those who have children with exceptionalities, usually understand that knowledge of one's racial identity and cultural heritage is critical in promoting positive self-esteem in children and in socializing them to effectively cope with racism (McAdoo, 1997).

Valuing Language Minority/English-Language Learners

Teachers and service providers are dream makers. Therefore, they need to know if students have communication disorders or language differences. It is believed approximately two thirds of youngsters from what are described as "language minority" households speak a non-English language at home (McLeod, 1996). Students from refugee and immigrant backgrounds frequently have little or no English-language skills when they come to school. Many are assigned to special ELL classes. However, their oral and written skills often remain underdeveloped. This is often referred to as the "Limited English Proficiency forever" syndrome. For some, the difficulty of trying to learn Standard English and develop speaking and writing proficiency is highly stressful and eventually leads them to drop out. Teachers and speech and language professionals should recognize that the time to develop proficiency in English varies and depends on many factors. As McLeod pointed out:

> Many students come to school with limited English proficiency (LEP); their speaking, listening, reading, or writing skills in English are not sufficient to allow them to fully participate in traditional all-English core curriculum classes. . . . Further, language minority, LEP, and immigrant youth are highly likely to be poor, to be members of ethnic or racial minority groups, and to attend segregated and poor schools. Their families and communities may suffer stress resulting from inadequate health, social, and cultural services; low employment rates; and illegal and dangerous activities in their neighborhoods. (p. 3)

Taking Advantage of Home and School Cultures

Regular classrooms have their own culture. All children arrive at school with ways of speaking and interacting with adults and peers and with ideas about the purpose of schools (Gersten, 1996). Often, however, the skills and strategies acquired to get along in a child's community may not be compatible with the demands of the school setting (Cole & Taylor, 1990; Craig & Washington, 1994, 2000; Craig, Washington, & Thompson-Porter, 1998). Hence, these children may be at risk for becoming doubly disadvantaged. It is critical to understand that

- their patterns of language use, behaviors, and values do not match those required in the school setting;
- teachers, administrators, or primary caregivers fail to take advantage of the strengths that these students possess;
- the greater the gap between the child's culture and the school's culture, the greater likelihood of failure or low pupil achievement; and the greater the overlap between the child's culture and the school's culture, the greater the likelihood of success or high pupil achievement.

Most multicultural learners interact with two cultures on a daily basis: the culture of the home and the white culture of schools and other social institutions. It is very important, then, that these learners be taught at an early age that their culture is different, not deficient, and that their culture should be acknowledged and valued. For instance, in some Vietnamese families, parents encourage their youngsters to master English communication, but may become concerned when, after entering school, their youngsters lose important vestiges of their native language.

Moreover, it is not uncommon for elderly members of the family to never fully master the English language.

It is important that general and special educators become sensitive to issues related to home and school cultures. They must understand that cultural conflicts can occur when both cultures are not fully recognized. For children to be successful in school, effective collaboration between home and school must occur at all levels. For some families, the school is not viewed as "user-friendly." In contrast, some teachers, as in Jennifer's case, may feel that multicultural parents may be apathetic about their children's educational and socioemotional development. This points out the need for sensitivity to cultural and linguistic differences by all. Morsink, Thomas, and Correa (1991) suggested that understanding the acculturation process of families from various multicultural groups is a necessary process for working effectively with children with special needs. Ovando (2003) observed that teachers of ELLs do not necessarily need to speak the first languages of their students; however, it is helpful to have a broad understanding of the history, traditions, folklore, attitudes, and values of cultural groups with which they work. Meyer, Bevan-Brown, Harry, and Sapon-Shevin (2003) noted that special education models are firmly rooted in Western European cultural values. For example, the special education structure that requires written communication and formal face-to-face conferences might provide a disconnect between the family and the school, especially if the family has had difficulty in relating to the school personnel in the past. An atmosphere of trust between multicultural parents and school personnel must be developed before advocacy for the child can take place.

A Culturally Responsive Educator

1. Understands the difference between language disorder and language difference.
2. Knows the complexity of speech and language impairments.
3. Values language as a part of culture.
4. Understands the impact of demographic changes on linguistic differences in classrooms and schools.
5. Teaches students with communication disorders in culturally responsive ways.
6. Assesses communication disorders in multidimensional ways.
7. Uses bilingual professionals in working with multicultural learners.
8. Works with parents, family members, and guardians when a child has a communication disorder.
9. Uses a developmental perspective rather than a deficit perspective when working with learners with communication disorders.
10. Differentiates between the various components of communication disorders.

Conclusion

Most would agree that the United States is a nation comprised of persons from different backgrounds, experiences, ethnic and cultural groups, and expectations. As a result, it is the responsibility of teachers and service providers to provide academic, social, and emotional supports that empower individual cultural and language differences. For many multicultural learners, problems of misidentification, labeling, and inappropriate schooling still remain. This chapter presented strategies that general and special educators can use to work with multicultural learners with communication disorders. Specifically, educators must value community and family involvement. In addition, they must understand when students have language disorders or language differences as they explore the different types of communication disorders. Finally, they must understand that collaboration with the child's parents can have a major impact on the child's communicative development and skills. This is true for all children, but especially for students like Louis whose first language is not the majority language.

Discussion Questions

1. Briefly explain the needs of learners with communication disorders.
2. Summarize why it is beneficial to distinguish between a language difference and a language disorder when working with multicultural learners.
3. Design an activity that you might use to create better awareness of the distinct features and qualities of other languages. For example, use game formats, create a collage, or write a children's story as you design your project.
4. Analyze the special concerns that you need to address in working with language minority/ELLs.
5. As a practitioner, describe changes you would make in your methodology when teaching a recently immigrated student who does not have command of the English language.

References

Adger, C. T., Wolfram, W., & Detwyler, J. (1993, Fall). Language differences: A new approach for special educators. *Teaching Exceptional Children, 26,* 44–48.

American Speech-Language-Hearing Association (1982). Definitions: Communication disorders and variations. *ASHA, 24,* 949–950.

American Speech-Language-Hearing Association (1983). Position paper: Social dialects. *ASHA, 25,* 23–24.

American Speech-Language-Hearing Association (2001, August). Communicating in a diverse society. Retrieved June 21, 2004, from www.asha.org/about/news/tipsheets/Diverse_society.htm

American Speech-Language-Hearing Association (2005). Multicultural history and demographic profile of the United States. Retrieved June 16, 2005, from www.asha.org/about/leadership-projects/multicultural/readings/reading_1.htm

Bernstein, R. (1984). Cues to post-vocalic voicing in mother-child speech. *Journal of Phonetics, 12,* 285–289.

Bountress, N. G. (1994). The classroom teacher and the language different student: Why, when, and how of intervention. *Preventing School Failure, 38,* 10–15.

Carmack, F., & Thomas, P. J. (1990). *Speech and language: Detecting and correcting special needs.* Boston: Allyn & Bacon.

Cole, P. A., & Taylor, O. L. (1990). Performance of working-class African American children on three tests of articulation. *Language, Speech, and Hearing Services in Schools, 21,* 171–176.

Craig, H., & Washington, J. (1994). The complex syntactic skills of poor, urban, African American preschoolers at school entry. *Language, Speech, and Hearing Services in Schools, 25,* 181–190.

Craig, H. K., & Washington, J. A. (2000, April). An assessment battery for identifying language impairments in African American children. *Journal of Speech, Language, and Hearing Research, 43,* 366–379.

Craig, H., Washington, J., & Thompson-Porter, C. (1998). Performances of young African American children on two comprehension tasks. *Journal of Speech, Language, and Hearing Research, 41,* 445–457.

Culatta, R., Tompkins, J., & Werts, M. (2003). *Fundamentals of special education: What every teacher needs to know.* Boston: Allyn & Bacon.

Delpit, L. (2002). Introduction. In L. Delpit & J. Dowdy (Eds.), *The skin that we speak: Thoughts on language and culture in the classroom* (p. xvii). New York: New Press.

Gersten, R. C. (1996). The double demands of teaching English language learners. *Educational Leadership, 53,* 18–22.

Gollnick, D., & Chinn, P. (2002). *Multicultural education in a pluralistic society* (6th ed.). Upper Saddle River, NJ: Merrill/Prentice Hall.

Haughton, C. D. (1993). Expanding the circle of inclusion for African Americans with disabilities. *The Black Collegian, 24,* 63–68.

Hedge, M. N. (1995). *Introduction to communication disorders.* Austin, TX: PRO-ED.

Heward, W. L. (2003). *Exceptional children* (7th ed.). Upper Saddle River, NJ: Merrill/Prentice Hall.

Hodgkinson, H. (2000/2001, December/January). Educational demographics: What teachers should know. *Educational Leadership, 58,* 6–11.

Hodgkinson, H. (2005, May 2). *Demographics for change.* Paper presented at the University of Central Florida Faculty Development Summer Conference, Orlando, FL.

Kuder, S. J. (2003). *Teaching students with language and communication disabilities.* Boston: Allyn & Bacon.

Lord, M. (2002, January 28/February 4). Teaching America. *U.S. News & World Report,* pp. 28–29.

Lue, M. (2001). The culturally and linguistically diverse exceptional learner. In M. Lue (Ed.), *A survey of communication disorders for the classroom teacher* (pp. 69–87). Boston: Allyn & Bacon.

Manning, M. L. (2000, Winter). Understanding diversity, accepting others: Realities and directions. *Educational Horizons,* pp. 77–79.

Martin, P., & Midgley, E. (1994). Immigration to the United States: Journey to an uncertain destination. *Population Bulletin, 49,* 2–47.

McAdoo, H. (1997). *Black families.* Thousand Oaks, CA: Sage.

McLaughlin, B., & McLeod, B. (1996, June). Educating all our students: Improving education for children from culturally and linguistically diverse backgrounds: Final Report of the National Center for Research on Cultural Diversity and Second Language Learning. Santa Cruz, CA: University of California. Retrieved June 21, 2004, from www.ncela.gwu.edu/pubs/ncrcdsll/edall.htm

McLeod, B. (1996). School reform and student diversity: Exemplary schooling for language minority students. *NCBE Resource Collection Series,* pp. 1–37.

Meyer, L., Bevan-Brown, J., Harry, B., & Sapon-Shevin, M. (2003). School inclusion and multicultural issues in education. In J. A. Banks & C. A. McGhee Banks (Eds.), *Multicultural education: Issues and perspectives* (pp. 327–352). New York: Wiley.

Morsink, C. V., Thomas, C. C., & Correa, V. I. (1991). *Interactive teaming: Consultation and collaboration in special programs.* Upper Saddle River, NJ: Merrill/Prentice Hall.

National Center on Educational Statistics (2005). Language minority school-age children: Participation in education: The condition of education. Retrieved June 15, 2005, from nces.ed.gov/programs/coe/2005/section1/indicator05.asp

Nieto, S. (2004). *Affirming diversity: The sociopolitical context of multicultural education* (4th ed.). Boston: Pearson Education.

Obiakor, F. E., & Ford, B. A. (2002). School accountability and reform. Implications for African Americans with disabilities. In F. E. Obiakor & B. A. Ford (Eds.), *Creating successful learning environments for African American learners with exceptionalities* (pp. 3–15). Thousand Oaks, CA: Corwin Press.

Orfield, G. (2001, Fall). Schools more separate. Consequences of a decade of resegregation. *Rethinking Schools Online, 16* (1). Retrieved June 20, 2004, from www.rethinkingschools. org/archive/16_01/16_01.shtml

Ovando, C. (2003). Language diversity and education. In J. A. Banks & C. A. McGhee Banks (Eds.), *Multicultural education: Issues and perspectives* (pp. 268–291). New York: Wiley.

Parker, R. (2005, April 7). Survey maps cultural diversity in the United States. *Black Issues in Higher Education, 22*(4), 18–23.

Payne, K. T., & Taylor, O. L. (1998). Communication differences and disorders. In G. H. Shames, E. H. Wiig, & W. A. Secord (Eds.), *Human communication disorders: An introduction* (5th ed., pp. 118–154). Boston: Allyn & Bacon.

Polloway, E., Patton, J., & Serna, L. (2001). *Strategies for teaching learners with special needs* (7th ed.). Upper Saddle River, NJ: Merrill/Prentice Hall.

Robbins, J. F. (1989, February). "Broadcast English" for nonstandard dialect speakers. *Education Digest, 54,* 52–53.

Rodriquez, D., Parmar, R., & Signer, B. (2001). Fourth-grade culturally and linguistically diverse exceptional students' concepts of number line. *Exceptional Children, 67,* 199–210.

Roseberry-McKibbin, C. (1995, Summer). Distinguishing language differences from language disorders in linguistically and culturally diverse students. *Multicultural Education,* 12–16.

Roseberry-McKibbin, C. (2000). Multicultural matters: The culture of poverty. *Communication Disorders Quarterly, 21,* 242–245.

Sileo, T. W., Sileo, A. P., & Prater, M. A. (1996). Parent and professional partnerships in special education: Multicultural considerations. *Intervention in School and Clinic, 31,* 145–153.

Thomas, C., Correa, V., & Morsink, C. (2001). *Interactive teaming: Enhancing programs for students with special needs* (3rd ed.). Upper Saddle River, NJ: Merrill/Prentice Hall.

Thorp, E. K. (1997). Increasing opportunities for partnership with culturally and linguistically diverse families. *Intervention in School and Clinic, 32,* 261–269.

Turnbull, R., Turnbull, A., Shank, M., Smith, S., & Leal, D. (2002). *Exceptional lives: Special education in today's schools* (3rd ed.). Upper Saddle River, NJ: Merrill/Prentice Hall.

U.S. Department of Census (2000). USA quick facts from the U.S. Census. Retrieved June 21, 2004, from quickfacts.census.gov/qfd/states/00000.html

Van Riper, C., & Erickson, R. (1996). *Speech correction: An introduction to speech pathology and audiology* (9th ed.). Boston: Allyn & Bacon.

Vaughn, S., Bos, C., & Schumm, J. (2000). *Teaching exceptional, diverse, and at-risk students in the general education classroom* (2nd ed.). Boston: Allyn & Bacon.

Voltz, D. L. (1995). Learning and cultural diversities in general and special education classes: Frameworks for success. *Multiple Voices, 1,* 1–11.

Chapter 5

Working with Multicultural Learners with Cognitive Disabilities

Festus E. Obiakor and Cheryl A. Utley

Chapter Outline

Thinking About Multicultural Special Education

Joseph, an African American child, was the only son of Mr. and Mrs. Williams. When he was a baby, he fell from the couch on his head. In first grade, he had many difficulties with language (i.e., receptive and expressive processes), prereading skills, spelling assignments, and math quizzes. During a psychological evaluation, Joseph was administered the traditional intelligence and achievement tests and adaptive behavior tests. His intelligence quotient (IQ) on the Wechsler Intelligence Scale-Revised (WISC-R) was 69, and he was diagnosed with a mild cognitive disability. His scores on the adaptive behavior scale showed that his social and emotional behaviors were functional and adequate for first grade. His special education teacher, Mrs. Thorne, noticed that he had considerable artistic talent, and she began to hope he would be a graphic designer. His parents, although interested in their son's education, were unclear about the teacher's perceptions of Joseph. During parent-teacher conferences, Mrs. Thorne was careful to explain the reports about Joseph's progress in language and reading. In addition, Mr. and Mrs. Williams were intimidated by the jargon used by professionals who made up the multidisciplinary team. But the teacher took time to explain those terms in simpler, easy-to-understand language. Collaboratively, Joseph's individualized education plan (IEP) was developed and included placement in a self-contained classroom.

Joseph's special education teacher was very structured and instruction was direct and consistent. She saw his potential for learning new skills and observed that he responded to reading stories in which he saw pictures of African American boys, girls, and adults like himself and his family. She used mnemonic strategies (i.e., cognitive procedures used to achieve the storage of information in long-term memory) to help Joseph improve his memory and to complete a variety of tasks. She taught problem-solving skills and used computer-based instruction. As time went on, his receptive and expressive language showed improvement when he was asked questions that let him connect his own cultural experiences to the themes of stories he read. The vocabulary from reading stories were his spelling words, and he was able to demonstrate that he could accurately remember and spell words when instruction involved his visual and auditory modalities. He was motivated to learn to read history books. Behavior problems were minimized because his teacher used culturally sensitive behavior management techniques. For example, when Joseph was acting out, his teacher did not reprimand him in an aversive manner; instead, she had peer role models to help him differentiate between appropriate and inappropriate behaviors. Because of Joseph's creative and artistic ability, he drew, colored, and painted pictures of people, objects, and events from stories that he read, and they were placed on the walls of the hallway throughout the school. Joseph won first place in an art contest in which he painted pictures of students participating in the Special Olympics and extracurricular activities at school.

Joseph's parents were contacted on a weekly basis to discuss his academic, creative, and behavioral strengths in school. Their involvement in school increased as their feelings of intimidation lessened, and they began to participate in parent-teacher association (PTA) and other fund-raising activities at school. Before long, Joseph was moved from a self-contained classroom to a resource room with the majority of his instruction in the regular education classroom. As he progressed through middle and high school, his IEP reflected a transition plan for him to begin working in the community in an art shop. His academic program concentrated on developing academic functional reading, writing, and mathematical skills. His prevocational program involved attending school for a half day followed by working in the art shop where he learned how to mount photographs in frames. Joseph became an independent young adult living in the community and working a full-time job at Hallmark Card Company. Because of his artistic skills, he was often asked to attend local community events where he painted pictures of the event. He was responsible for creating pictures to accompany poems for different occasions such as weddings, birthdays, and holidays. He continued to receive awards for his artistic talent, took care of his own personal needs, and began to serve as a role model for young adults with cognitive disabilities who were being transitioned from school to community.

- *How did Joseph's teacher get his parents to reduce their feelings of intimidation by educational professionals?*
- *What did Joseph's teacher do to maximize his potential as a student and her own potential as a teacher?*

Joseph's case reveals how general and special education professionals and service providers can maximize the potential of learners with cognitive disabilities, especially those who come from multicultural backgrounds. These individuals endure "double jeopardy" (i.e., problems associated with cultural/racial valuing and problems associated with disability valuing). As a consequence, there appears to be efforts to water down their curriculum and concentrate on the restrictive labels that they are given based on test instruments that are not good predictor variables of individual capabilities, learning styles, and cultural values (Bessent Byrd, 2002; Valencia & Suzuki, 2001). But great teachers like Joseph's teacher frequently make a difference in their students' education and survival. This chapter examines issues surrounding the definition, assessment, and educational practices for multicultural learners with cognitive disabilities. In addition, it explores Joseph's case from the perspectives of curricular and pedagogical modifications within a cultural framework.

IDENTIFICATION AND ASSESSMENT OF STUDENTS WITH COGNITIVE DISABILITIES

The educational and psychological identification and assessment of students with cognitive disabilities make up a systematic process of gathering relevant information to make legal and instructional decisions about the provision of services. The 1975 Education for All Handicapped Children Act (P.L. 94-142) and the subsequent 2004 Individuals with Disabilities Education Improvement Act (P.L. 108-446) indicated that the identification of all children eligible for special education services must adhere to the following explicit guidelines for the use of tests:

- IQ tests must never outweigh other test results in making diagnostic decisions.
- IQ tests must be viewed as only one piece of evidence in making diagnoses and assessments.
- IQ tests must be translated, modified, and administered in the child's native language without undue influence from linguistic differences.

Despite the legal provisions of these laws, educational and measurement trends have influenced the assessment process, some of which are centered on the debate that intelligence is (a) one entity that comprises a set of factors; and (b) a product of the interaction between people and their environment, and therefore, is subject to change. In addition, significant revisions in the American Association on Mental Retardation (AAMR) definition of mental retardation (also referred to as cognitive disabilities) has shaped the assessment process (Luckasson et al., 2002). About a decade ago, MacMillan and Reschly (1997) noted that "slight shifts in the upper limit have rather dramatic consequences in terms of the percentage of the population eligible. For example, a shift from IQ 70 and below to a criterion of IQ 75 and below results in *twice as many people being eligible.* Because of the acceleration of the curve in this portion of the normal curve, there are more cases falling in the interval of 69 to 75 (2.80%) than in the entire range scoring IQ 70 and below (2.68%)" (p. 57).

To obtain an IQ score, the mental age (MA) is divided by the chronological age (CA) and multiplied by 100:

$$\frac{MA}{CA} \times \frac{100}{1} = IQ$$

The MA reflects a person's mental or capability age and the CA reflects a person's chronological or actual age. The mean of all IQ tests (e.g., Wechsler Intelligence Scales for Children-Third Edition [WISC-III] and Stanford-Binet, Fourth Edition) is 100. The standard deviation (SD) for the WISC-III is 15 and that of the Stanford-Binet is 16. (Note: SD is a score that is positively deviated from the mean.) If an individual scores within the mild range, the IQ is about 2.0 to 3.0 SD below the mean. When an individual scores within the moderate or trainable range, the IQ is 3.0 SD below the mean. Finally, when an individual scores within the severe/profound range, the IQ is 4.0 below the mean (see Figure 5.1). Clearly, cognitive disabilities encompass the aforementioned components of mental disabilities. This is particularly relevant in this era of *inclusive education* when the focus is not on a person's cognitive label but on his or her unique educational needs.

More than two decades ago, Grossman (1983) stated that impairments in adaptive behavior demonstrate significant limitations in an individual's effectiveness

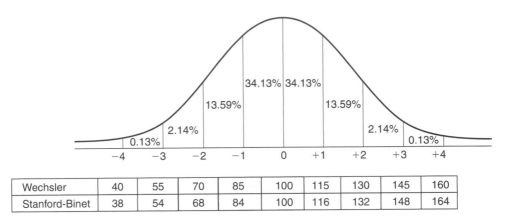

| Wechsler | 40 | 55 | 70 | 85 | 100 | 115 | 130 | 145 | 160 |
| Stanford-Binet | 38 | 54 | 68 | 84 | 100 | 116 | 132 | 148 | 164 |

FIGURE 5.1   Bell–Shaped Curve

in meeting the standards of maturation level and cultural group, as determined by clinical assessment and, usually, standardized scales. The debate concerning adaptive behavior has centered on its inclusion in the definition of cognitive disabilities and assessment. Some professionals have suggested that a score of 70 or less on an IQ test is the only criterion necessary for a diagnosis of cognitive disabilities, while other researchers have suggested age-appropriate learning, personal independence, and/or social responsibility must be considered in the diagnostic process. With regard to adaptive behavior assessment, school-based practices must include in-school behaviors (i.e., functional academic skills), conceptual skills, social skills, and daily living skills (Luckasson et al., 2002). In Joseph's case, the identification and assessment process relied heavily on the IQ test score as the primary measure for his placement in special education. A valid assessment of his abilities was not conducted. There was no consideration of (a) cultural factors that may influence the IQ and adaptive behavior test scores, and (b) documentation of limitations in adaptive skills that occur within the context of community environments typical of the individual's age peers. It appears unethical to use a white culture-bound test to assess prevalence of cognitive disabilities among people from multicultural backgrounds. Moreover, it appears unethical to use information obtained from this test to plan educational services for multicultural persons with cognitive disabilities to learn to function adequately in the majority white culture.

RESPONDING TO LEARNING CHARACTERISTICS OF MULTICULTURAL STUDENTS WITH COGNITIVE DISABILITIES

General and special educators must respond to the learning characteristics of multicultural students with cognitive disabilities to address their instructional needs. Following are discussions on these characteristics and their impact on and relationship with instructional provisions.

Receptive and Expressive Language

Receptive and expressive language impairments occur more frequently among students with cognitive disabilities as compared to "normal"-achieving peers (Conners, 2003; Langone, 1996). Language impairments may consist of an inability to articulate sounds or pronounce words. For these students, speech and language impairments may be diagnosed as a secondary disabling condition. Impairments may also be due to hearing problems that affect speech production. Additional factors that adversely affect receptive and language developments in students with cognitive disabilities include poor environmental conditions, cultural differences, language barriers, and a lack of exposure to positive role models. According to Warren and Yoder (1998), intervention goals should be based on a "continuum of optimally effective, developmentally appropriate communication and language intervention procedures" (p. 360). Appropriate interventions and instructional strategies should vary according to a child's developmental level and across multiple areas. As the child develops cognitively, responsive interaction approaches must be implemented to facilitate the acquisition of higher levels of receptive and expressive language skills (Brady & Warren, 2003).

Generalization of Skills

Generalization refers to the extent to which students with cognitive disabilities have extended what they have learned across settings and over time (Conners, 2003; Stokes & Osnes, 1989) and to a unique situation (Rosenthal-Malek & Bloom, 1998; Wehmeyer, 2002). Research has shown that these students have impairments in their ability to transfer or generalize information and skills learned in one setting or one way to new situations that involve different people, expectations, and skills (Langone, Clees, Oxford, Malone, & Ross, 1995; Meese, 2001). A skill is not learned until it has been generalized in multiple settings. To enhance generalization skills, Rosenthal-Malek and Bloom (1998) suggested a variety of behaviorally oriented learning principles such as varying settings, time of day, materials, and community-based instruction. In addition, they recommended the use of cognitive learning strategies (e.g., shadowing, verbatim notes, organization and elaboration, graphic organizers, and semantic mapping) to facilitate the spontaneous use of new skills in novel situations. Clearly, multicultural students with cognitive disabilities have difficulty distinguishing and paying attention to relevant cues in learning and social situations and attending to several different cues simultaneously (Zeaman & House, 1979). In addition, these students tend to exhibit a high level of distractibility when external stimuli are presented. To deal with these situations, instructional strategies must focus on teaching students to pay close attention to the relevant parts of any task by color coding the important components of school tasks.

Memory

Earlier research on the memory capabilities of students with cognitive disabilities showed that they differed in the rate at and efficiency with which they can acquire, remember, and use newly learned knowledge as compared to normal-achieving peers. From this line of research, memory characteristics of students with cognitive disabilities include problems associated with memory-related processes and short-term to long-term memory skills (Merrill & Taube, 1996; Scruggs & Laufenberg, 1986). In addition, research has shown that students with cognitive disabilities are less likely to use spontaneous rehearsal procedures and are unable to benefit from incidental learning cues in their environment as compared to their normal-achieving peers (Henley, Ramsey, & Algozzine, 1993). This is critical for multicultural learners who frequently survive based on cues and opportunities for growth from their communities. More recently, Bray et al. (in press) noted that memory studies with students with cognitive disabilities, as compared to normal-achieving peers, showed that they are equivalent in visual recognition, automatic processing, spread of activation, short-term retention rate, stimulus organization, organization of semantic memory, and long-term retention skills. It behooves general and special educators to facilitate memory processes by (a) using mnemonics as mediators to help learners with poor memory to complete a variety of tasks, (b) teaching appropriate problem-solving skills, and (c) using computer-based instruction. Multicultural learners will clearly benefit from these intervention approaches.

Motivation and Self-Direction

Motivation is an important aspect of learning. Because of their past history of negative experiences, multicultural students with cognitive disabilities may lack the necessary motivation needed to be successful learners. A frequently mentioned motivational characteristic of students with cognitive disabilities is their lower expectancy of success and higher expectancy of failure than their normal-achieving peers (Zigler & Balla, 1981). The cycle of academic failure frequently leads to feelings of learned helplessness in which these students are not motivated to achieve academically or exhibit symptoms of maladaptive motivational orientations on attentional tasks (Obiakor, 1999). An important characteristic of these students is self-direction. Self-direction is defined as one's ability to control the events that ultimately affect one's life. Studies on locus of control, an individual's belief concerning the relationship between efforts and achievements, have shown that students with cognitive disabilities have a history of not being self-directed. This is especially critical for multicultural learners because of the history of sociocultural problems (e.g., racism and prejudice) that they confront. Research suggests that these students demonstrate a tendency toward an external locus of control in which individuals contribute outcomes to forces outside of themselves (e.g., luck and fate; Levin, 1992). In studies examining locus of control in students with cognitive disabilities, Weisz (1990) found that these students have an external locus of control and that under conditions of failure feedback showed a significant decline in their use of effective strategies. It is important that general and special educators provide them with novel situations that are motivating and rewarding.

REACHING STUDENTS LIKE JOSEPH

Because Joseph is an African American with cognitive disability, he may show unique patterns of learning (referred to as *cognitive styles*) and multiple intelligences (Bessent Byrd, 1995). Although there is variability among African American children with and without cognitive disabilities, Bessent Byrd described learning patterns of African American children as the following:

- Responding to more kinesthetic/tactile learning with hands-on activities
- Responding to things in terms of the whole instead of isolated parts
- Preferring inferential reasoning
- Focusing on people rather than things
- Preferring learning by doing
- Being more proficient in nonverbal than verbal communication
- Preferring learning characteristics characterized by variation in activities
- Preferring group learning activities
- Approximating space and numbers rather than adhering to exactness or accuracy

Effective general and special educators who are culturally aware and sensitive to the academic, social, and behavioral needs of African American students with cognitive disabilities are culturally responsive. Culturally responsive teachers base their beliefs, methods, and strategies on what we have learned through the teacher effectiveness literature. For example, see the traits of culturally responsive teachers in Table 5.1.

Culturally Centric Curriculum and Pedagogy

Bessent Byrd (2002) developed a learning-centered cultural centrism model, which has the learner at the core of the curriculum in educational processes. She noted that this model

> serves five functions critical to the success of the African American learner [such as Joseph] with cognitive disabilities. Such a curriculum (a) affirms the child's identity, (b) ensures understanding of the child's own culture, (c) promotes understanding of other individual cultures, (d) serves as a foundation for valuing a common culture, and (e) provides cohesion that sustains a nation. The self-understanding, understanding of others, awareness for and appreciation of commonalities, with recognition of connection with others, are direly

TABLE 5.1 *Traits of Culturally Responsive Teachers/Service Providers*

Self-Understanding
- Sees self as part of each child's community.
- Models behaviors expected of the child.
- Evinces awareness of own values and belief systems.
- Manifests awareness and control of own prejudices.
- Exemplifies determination and commitment to teaching.
- Maintains a sense of humor.

Child Focus
- Likes children.
- Gives each child an identity base and enhances self-esteem.
- Helps each child to develop prerequisite skills and abilities.
- Promotes equitable teacher-student relationships.
- Encourages children to learn collaboratively.
- Makes expectations known to the child in a friendly, firm, calm, and confident manner.
- Reacts appropriately to child's display of hostility.
- Praises that which is praiseworthy.
- Values multiple simultaneous exchanges; neither expects nor requires silence often.

Content Mastery
- Knows the sequence of developmental stages.
- Understands cultural indices of the child and family.
- Understands and recognizes intellectual, emotional, social, and cultural strengths of the child.
- Knows subject matter and relates it to the child's experience and life.

Strategic Proficiency
- Draws upon cultural experiences of the child and family to include authentic cultural perspectives in the curriculum.
- Uses the child's culture to help create meaning and understanding of the world.
- Possesses a repertoire and varied teaching styles and adjusts them to accommodate varied learning styles among children.
- Maintains participatory, dynamic, and spontaneous classrooms.
- Displays flexibility in the context of a structured learning environment.
- Maintains a high rate of academically engaged time.
- Expands the child's capacity to appreciate and deal with differences in others and helps him or her to perceive self in an international or global perspective.

Source: Bessent Byrd, H. (1995). Curricular and pedagogical procedures for African American learners with academic and cognitive disabilities. In B. A. Ford, F. E. Obiakor, & J. M. Patton (Eds.), *Effective education of African American exceptional learners: New perspectives* (pp. 123–150). Austin, TX: PRO-ED.

needed to cement a patriotic bond of all citizens—black, white, red, yellow, and brown—of the United States (p. 58)

Consonant with the culturally centric curriculum is the multicultural multicognitive curriculum. Components of this curriculum consist of cognition, curriculum, culture, and pedagogy. *Cognition* refers to the teaching-learning experience, which is guided by the teacher's goals, decision, and planning. This component also includes cognitive style and multiple intelligences frameworks. *Curriculum* is the content that is taught to students with cognitive disabilities with a focus on functionality of skills. *Culture* is the third component and refers to the context of the educational environment. Lastly, *pedagogy* refers to the specific strategies used to impart knowledge.

Many definitions of culturally responsive pedagogy exist in the literature (Banks & Banks, 1997; Gay, 1994; Ladson-Billings, 1994; Villegas, 1991). Gay (2002) posited that culturally responsive pedagogy is "using the cultural knowledge, prior experiences, frames of reference, and performance styles of ethnically diverse students to make learning encounters more relevant to and effective for them. It teaches *to* and *through* the strengths of these students" (p. 29). Similarly, Bessent Byrd (2002) concluded that:

1. Culture can be a powerful variable that influences teaching and learning.
2. Effective teaching can be supportive of culturally responsive pedagogy.
3. Teacher knowledge and reflection can be important when designing and implementing a culturally responsive lesson.
4. Realistic expectations can be important components of cultural responsiveness.

On the whole, effective culturally responsive pedagogy entails (a) teachers and students producing together, (b) developing language and literacy across the curriculum, (c) making meaning through connecting with students' lives, (d) teaching complex thinking, and (e) teaching through conversation (Bessent Byrd, 2002; Gay, 1994). A logical extension is that culturally responsive pedagogy motivates general and special educators to have self-understanding, mastery of content, real pedagogical power, and a knowledge base regarding multiple intelligences and learning styles.

A Culturally Responsive Educator

1. Understands the traditional dilemmas of multicultural learners with regard to intelligence testing.
2. Knows that all learners have multiple intelligences and learning styles.
3. Values the "double jeopardy" situation in which multicultural learners with cognitive disabilities find themselves.

4. Understands that multicultural learners with cognitive disabilities can learn.
5. Knows that different professional thinking represents different paradigms or models.
6. Is flexible in responding to individual differences.
7. Does not mistake cultural differences for mental deficiency.
8. Works collaboratively with colleagues and parents.
9. Understands that effective teaching can have a positive influence on multicultural learners with cognitive disabilities.
10. Sees education as a continuous process of growth.

Conclusion

This chapter examined pertinent issues related to the education of multicultural learners with cognitive disabilities. Given the changing demographics of student populations and the controversial issues related to the classification of multicultural students, their learning characteristics must be taken into consideration. It is imperative that general and special education practitioners understand that multicultural learners with cognitive disabilities can learn when taught appropriately. They need to focus their efforts on classroom and school learning environments and move away from perspectives that divert their attention from quality instruction and behavior management issues. Additionally, these professionals must continue to examine their collaborative relationships within and across school districts and communities to achieve major changes in how multicultural learners with cognitive disabilities are provided services. They must also realize that IQ test scores do not determine a person's ability to succeed in school or in life, and that good teaching and learning are important for students' growth.

Discussion Questions

1. Briefly explain why Joseph did not maximize his potential in first grade.
2. Discuss why multicultural learners with cognitive disabilities find themselves in a "double jeopardy" situation.
3. Examine why it is not productive to categorize all students with cognitive disabilities from one perspective.

4. Develop four culturally responsive activities for a multicultural learner with cognitive disabilities.
5. All learners with cognitive disabilities are not brain-damaged. In two short paragraphs, give reasons why.

References

American Association on Mental Retardation (AAMR) (1992). *Mental retardation: Definitions, classification, and systems of support.* Washington, DC: Author.

Banks, J. A., & Banks, C. (1997). *Multicultural education: Issues and perspectives.* Needham Heights, MA: Allyn & Bacon.

Bessent Byrd, H. (1995). Curricular and pedagogical procedures for African American learners with academic and cognitive disabilities. In B. A. Ford, F. E. Obiakor, & J. M. Patton (Eds.), *Effective education of African American exceptional learners: New perspectives* (pp. 123–150). Austin, TX: PRO-ED.

Bessent Byrd, H. (2002). Instructional strategies for African American learners with cognitive disabilities. In F. E. Obiakor & B. A. Ford (Eds.), *Creating successful learning environments for African American learners with exceptionalities* (pp. 55–65). Austin, TX: PRO-ED.

Brady, N. C., & Warren, S. F. (2003). Language interventions for children with mental retardation. In L. Abbeduto (Ed.), *International review of research in mental retardation: Language and communication in mental retardation* (Vol. 27, pp. 231–250). San Diego, CA: Academic Press.

Bray, N. W., Reilly, K. D., Huffman, L. F., Grupe, L. A., Fletcher, K. L., Villa, M., et al. (in press). Mental retardation and cognitive competencies. In W. Bechtel & G. Graham (Eds.), *The Blackwell companion to cognitive science.* Oxford, England: Basil Blackwell.

Conners, F. A. (2003). Reading skills and cognitive abilities of individuals with mental retardation. In L. Abbeduto (Ed.), *International review of research in mental retardation: Language and communication in mental retardation* (Vol. 27, pp. 191–223). San Diego, CA: Academic Press.

Education for All Handicapped Children Act (1975), Pub. L. No. 94–142.

Gay, G. (1994). *At the essence of learning: Multicultural education.* West Lafayette, IN: Kappa Delta Pi.

Grossman, H. J. (1983). *Classification in mental retardation: 1983 revision.* Washington, DC.

Henley, M., Ramsey, R. S., & Algozzine, R. (1993). *Characteristics and strategies for teaching students with mild disabilities.* Boston: Allyn & Bacon.

Individuals with Disabilities Education Improvement Act (2004), Pub. L. No. 108-446.

Langone, J. (1996). Mild mental retardation. In P. J. McLaughlin & P. Wehman (Eds.), *Mental retardation and developmental disabilities* (2nd ed., pp. 113–130). Austin, TX: PRO-ED.

Langone, J., Clees, T. J., Oxford, J., Malone, M., & Ross, G. (1995). Acquisition and generalization of social skills by high school students with mild mental retardation. *Mental Retardation, 33,* 186–196.

Levin, V. (1992). *Locus of control: Its relationship to gender, ethnicity, and at-risk students.* (ERIC Document Reproduction Service No. ED360605)

Luckasson, R., Borthwick-Duffy, S., Buntinx, W. H., Coulter, D. L., Craig, E. M., Reeve, A., et al. (2002). *Mental retardation: Definition, classification, and systems of support* (10th ed.). Washington, DC: American Association on Mental Retardation.

MacMillan, D. L., & Reschly, D. (1997). Issues of definition and clarification. In W. E. Maclean, Jr. (Ed.), *Ellis' handbook of mental deficiency, psychological theory, and research* (3rd ed., pp. 47–74). Mahwah, NJ: Erlbaum.

Meese, R. L. (2001). *Teaching learners with mild disabilities: Integrating research and practice.* Belmont, CA: Wadsworth/Thomson Learning.

Merrill, E. C., & Taube, M. (1996). Negative priming and mental retardation: The processing of distractor information. *American Journal on Mental Retardation, 101,* 63–71.

Obiakor, F. E. (1999). Teacher expectations: Impact on "accuracy" of self-concepts of multicultural learners. In F. E. Obiakor, J. O. Schwenn, & A. R. Rotatori (Eds.), *Advances in special education: Multicultural education for learners with exceptionalities* (Vol. 12, pp. 205–216). Stamford, CT: JAI Press.

Obiakor, F. E. (2001). *It even happens in "good" schools: Responding to cultural diversity in today's classrooms.* Thousand Oaks, CA: Corwin Press.

Raymond, B. E. (2000). *Learners with mild disabilities: A characteristics approach.* Needham Heights, MA: Allyn & Bacon.

Reschly, D. J., & Ward, S. M. (1991). Uses of adaptive behavior measures and overrepresentation of black students in programs for students with mild mental retardation. *American Journal on Mental Retardation, 96,* 257–268.

Rosenthal-Malek, A., & Bloom, A. (1998). Beyond acquisition: Teaching generalization for students with developmental disabilities. In A. Hilton & R. Ringlaben (Eds.), *Best and promising practices in developmental disabilities* (pp. 139–155). Austin, TX: PRO-ED.

Rueda, R., & Simon, K. (2001). Cultural and linguistic diversity as a theoretical framework for understanding multicultural learners with mild disabilities. In C. A. Utley & F. E. Obiakor (Eds.), *Special education, multicultural education, and school reform: Components of quality education for learners with mild disabilities* (pp. 74–89). Springfield, IL: Charles C Thomas.

Scruggs, T. E., & Laufenberg, R. (1986). Transformational mnemonic strategies for retarded learners. *Education and Training of the Mentally Retarded, 21*(3), 165–173.

Stokes, T. F., & Osnes, P. G. (1989). An operant pursuit of generalization. *Journal of Learning Disabilities, 23,* 32–37.

Utley, C. A., & Obiakor, F. E. (2001). *Special education, multicultural education and school reform: Components for a quality education for learners with mild disabilities.* Springfield, IL: Charles C Thomas.

Valencia, R. R., & Suzuki, L. A. (2001). *Intelligence testing and minority students: Foundations, performance factors, and assessment issues.* Thousand Oaks, CA: Sage.

Warren, S., & Yoder, P. (1998). Facilitating the transition from preintentional to intentional communication. In A. Wetherby, S. Warren, & J. Reichle (Eds.), *Transitions in prelinguistic communication* (Vol. 7, pp. 365–385). Baltimore: Brookes.

Wehmeyer, M. L. (2002). *Providing access to the general curriculum: Teaching students with mental retardation.* Baltimore: Brookes.

Weisz, J. R. (1990). Cultural–familial mental retardation: A developmental perspective on cognitive perspective and "helpless" behavior. In R. M. Hodapp, J. A. Burack, &

E. Zigler (Eds.), *Issues in the developmental approach to mental retardation* (pp. 137–159). New York: Cambridge University Press.

Zeaman, D., & House, B. J. (1979). A review of attention theory. In N. R. Ellis (Ed.), *Handbook of mental deficiency: Psychological theory and research* (2nd ed., pp. 31–51). Hillsdale, NJ: Erlbaum.

Zigler, E., & Balla, D. (1981). Issues in the personality and motivation in mentally retarded persons. In M. Begab, H. C. Haywood, & H. L. Garber (Eds.), *Psychosocial influences in retarded performance* (pp. 197–218). Baltimore: University Park Press.

Chapter 6

Working with Multicultural Learners with Learning Disabilities

Patrick A. Grant and Sunday O. Obi

Chapter Outline

Thinking About Multicultural Special Education

Don was an American Indian student with problems related to poor academic perform- ance. More specifically, his poor reading ability appeared to be the root of his behavior problems. His parents first noticed Don's learning problems during his preschool and kindergarten years. While other children were learning their letter names and numbers, Don was struggling to remember even a few letter names. Yet he scored above average on intelligence tests. Some of his teachers asked how Don could have an average IQ, yet perform so poorly in school?

As Don advanced through first, second, and third grades, he continued to struggle in school. Mrs. Fernandez, his third grade teacher, had a conference with his parents, Peggy and Bill, to discuss Don's lack of progress. At this meeting, his teacher sug- gested that Don remain in third grade for another year. His parents were mortified upon hearing such news and immediately told his teacher that they would hire a tutor for him. After a few months of repeating third grade, Don still failed to make progress. A note requesting permission to have him tested to determine if he had a learning disability was sent home. His parents agreed to the evaluation, and within a few days they were asked to attend a meeting about the assessment results. During the meeting, the school psychologist reviewed the results of Don's performance on an intelligence test and an achievement test along with some other supporting observa- tions and test scores. As expected, Don qualified to receive special education services, and it was suggested that he attend a learning disabilities (LD) resource room for half a day each day.

Don's sixth-grade teacher, Mr. Swanz, decided to try some new modified teaching techniques with his class. About 5 months after the implementation of the strategies, Don was not only making above average grades, but he was also on the honor roll for the first time. As a result, he felt more confident about school. During high school, Don began to develop effective note taking and study routines. Many of these routines incor- porated techniques and strategies he learned from Mr. Swanz. Years later Mr. Swanz heard that Don was considering going to college to become a teacher. With help of spe- cial admission policies designed for people with learning disabilities, he received three acceptance letters. Don began college and continued to maximize his potential in his courses.

- *Why were Don's school problems perplexing to his teachers and parents?*
- *What inspired Don to major in education in college?*

The issue of whether a student has a learning disability or learning difference has continued to be controversial in general and special education. The learner, the learning environment, the subject matter to be learned, and the individual teaching the learner all have been known to affect learning. When any of these variables appears problematic, the potential for learning is not maximized. Then the learner might begin to question himself or herself, and the teacher might begin to question the learner. This phenomenal disconnect might lead to misidentification, misassessment, mislabeling, misplacement, and misinstruction of multicultural students with learning problems. Research has shown that differences in intelligence scores between multicultural learners (e.g., African Americans, American Indians) and whites are almost eliminated when educational and socioeconomic adjustments are made (Books-Gunn, Klebanov, & Duncan, 1996; Herrnstein & Murray, 1994; Kagan, 1971; Schaefer, 2006; Young, 2003).

To understand issues confronting learning and teaching of multicultural students with learning disabilities, it is important to look at historical contexts. This is especially relevant to the case of Don, an American Indian. As the original inhabitants of North America, the American Indians were the first to be subordinated by Europeans (see Schaefer, 2006). In the past, the American Indian who survived contact with some white people was usually removed, often from his or her ancestral home. The U.S. government tried to weaken tribal institutions through a succession of laws, beginning with the Allotment Act of 1887. Every effort to strengthen tribal autonomy, such as the 1934 Recognition Act, did so by encouraging American Indians to adopt the white society's way of life. Today, the Pan-Indian movement speaks for a diverse American Indian people with many needs: settlement of treaty violations, economic development, improved education, effective health care, religious and spiritual freedom, control over natural resources, and greater self-rule. As Schaefer pointed out, American Indian children are actively learning only 20 of the surviving 154 American Indian languages. While much of the country debates the need for a larger percentage of new immigrants to master English, the major concern of American Indians is maintaining the tie to their linguistic past and making it a viable part of the present.

It is important to note that American Indians are not monolithic. According to Ogunwole (2002), the different tribes include Cherokee, Navajo, Choctaw, Sioux, Chippewa, Apache, Black Feet, Iroquois, and Pueblo. These tribes speak different languages. Despite the diversity among American Indians, the conditions in which they generally find themselves make school or classroom problems inevitable. Studies of American Indian children using intelligence tests that do not require knowledge of English consistently show scores at or above the level of middle-class urban children. Yet, in the upper grades, a *crossover effect* occurs (when previously high-scoring American Indian students score below average because intelligence tests are given in English rather than their native language). When they drop behind their white peers, they are classified as underachievers (Bureau of Indian Affairs, 1988; Coleman et al., 1966; Fuch & Havighurst, 1972). For Don in the introductory case, having an exceptionality like a learning disability makes his problems perplexing and multidimensional. Consequently, Don's success in school and in life calls for well-prepared teachers and service providers. That need is the thrust of this chapter.

CONCEPTUAL FRAMEWORKS OF LEARNING DISABILITIES

Learning disability is a perplexing category of exceptionality. Hunt and Marshall (2002) reported that children with learning disabilities have always existed, but for many years, educators failed to recognize their unique problems and characteristics. Burkhardt, Obiakor, and Rotatori (2004) and Lloyd (1996) noted that the term *children with learning disabilities* means those children who have a disorder in one or more of the basic psychological processes involved in understanding or in using language, spoken or written, whose disorder may manifest itself in imperfect ability to listen, think, speak, read, write, spell, or do mathematical calculations. Such disorders include such conditions as perceptual disabilities, brain injury, minimal brain dysfunction, dyslexia, and developmental aphasia. Learning disability does not include children who have learning problems, which are primarily the result of visual, hearing, or motor disabilities; mental retardation; emotional disturbance; or of environmental, cultural, or economic disadvantage. Based on the 1990 Individuals with Disabilities Education Act (IDEA), a student has a learning disability if he or she (a) does not achieve at the proper age level and ability level in one or more or several specific areas when provided with appropriate learning experiences; and (b) has a severe discrepancy between achievement and intellectual ability in one or more of the following areas: oral expression, listening comprehension, written expression, basic reading skills, reading comprehension, mathematics calculation, and mathematics reasoning. The key element of the federal definition is the emphasis on the performance of students with learning disabilities, which is often tied to their ability to receive or express information (see Hunt & Marshall, 2002). These characteristics become loaded with misconceptions when multicultural learners exhibit them (Grant & Grant, 2002; Obiakor & Utley, 2004). Clearly, multicultural learners such as Don bring to school different behavioral and learning styles that could be easily misinterpreted as learning problems.

The category of learning disabilities was created long before 1963 when Dr. Samuel Kirk introduced it at a meeting of parents advocating special educational services for their children who were having difficulty in school (Kirk, 1975). In earlier decades, these children's difficulties had been variously categorized as mild exogenous mental retardation (mild mental retardation caused by brain injury), minimal brain dysfunction (behavior associated with brain injury, although brain damage that cannot be verified), perceptual impairment (persistent difficulty in making sense of sensory stimulation), hyperactivity (excessive and socially inappropriate behavior accompanied by problems in learning), and slow learning (a child whose achievement is not far enough below average to indicate mental retardation) (see Hallahan & Cruickshank, 1973; Hallahan & Kauffman, 1977; Mann, 1979; Wiedherhold, 1974). These difficulties create intensive problems for many multicultural learners whose mental and learning capabilities are viewed from very deficit perspectives (Obiakor, 1999; Obiakor, Grant, & Dooley, 2002). Don's case presents an excellent example of the plight of these learners in school programs.

The term *learning disability* has gained almost universal acceptance among regular educators, special educators, and the general public in the United States and in many foreign countries (Mazurek & Winzer, 1994; Winzer, 1993). Hallahan, Kauffman, and Lloyd (1996) reported that the history of learning disabilities could be summarized in relation to how the field has developed. For instance, learning disabilities (a) represent an interdisciplinary field that is international and multicultural in scope; (b) have a variety of possible causes; (c) are, in part, a social construct; (d) are heterogeneous in nature; (e) vary in severity and pervasiveness; (f) are characterized by intra-individual differences; (g) affect a diverse group of people; (h) may coexist with other disabilities or giftedness; (i) require training in systematic approaches to tasks; (j) require educators to minimize the contribution of poor teaching; and (k) are developmental disorders persisting over the life span. Additionally, it must be acknowledged that advances in the field of learning disabilities can occur only through careful, persistent research.

The field of learning disabilities is complicated by controversy in the areas of definition, prevalence, and demographics. Kirk (1962) defined *learning disability* as follows:

> A learning disability refers to retardation, disorder, or delayed development in one or more of the processes of speech, language, reading, writing, arithmetic, or other school subject resulting from a psychological handicap caused by a possible cerebral dysfunction and/or emotional or behavioral deprivation, or cultural and instructional factors. (p. 263)

Kirk's definition has five components, namely, (a) subaverage achievement (e.g., in reading, writing, arithmetic) or achievement-related behaviors (e.g., in speech or language); (b) intra-individual differences in achievement-related behaviors; (c) psychological "handicaps" (often referred to as psychological processes); (d) cerebral dysfunction; and (e) exclusion of other disabling conditions (e.g., mental retardation) and environmental conditions. A student of Kirk, Bateman (1965), offered the following definition:

> Children who have learning disorders are those who manifest an educationally significant discrepancy between their estimated intellectual potential and actual level of performance related to basic disorders in the learning process, which may or may not be accompanied by demonstrable central nervous system dysfunction, and which are not secondary to generalized mental retardation, educational or cultural deprivation, severe emotional disturbance, or sensory loss. (p. 220)

Bateman's definition differed from Kirk's in at least two ways. First, it did not include reference to emotional factors as a cause of learning disabilities. In fact, it mentioned severe emotional disturbance as one of the disabilities that does not cause learning disabilities. No major definitions since Bateman's have mentioned emotional disturbance as a possible causal factor. Second, and even more important, it included reference to a discrepancy between intellectual potential and actual performance.

The federal government defined learning disabilities in the 1975 Public Law 94-142, and later in the 1990 and 1997 amendments and reauthorization. Based on the 1975 law, learning disability is defined as follows:

> A disorder in one or more of the basic psychological processes involved in understanding or in using language, spoken or written, which may manifest itself in an imperfect ability to listen, think, speak, read, write, spell, or to do mathematical calculations. The term includes such conditions as perceptual handicaps, brain injury, minimal brain dysfunction, dyslexia, and developmental aphasia. The term does not include children who have problems that are primarily the result of visual, hearing, or motor disabilities, or mental retardation, emotional disturbance, or of environmental, cultural, or economic disadvantage. (see Hunt & Marshall, 2002, p. 140)

Although the federal definition governs the identification of and services to children with learning disabilities, there are variations between states and among school systems. In an attempt to clarify the identification, some states specify an intelligence range. Others add the concept of a discrepancy between potential and achievements, sometimes quantifying the discrepancy using test scores. *These slightly different parameters are indicative of a lack of clear consensus about exactly what learning disabilities are.* Despite the apparent logic of explaining learning disabilities as a discrepancy between intellectual potential and academic achievement, many people have criticized the concept. Researchers (e.g., Stanovich, 1989) have pointed to at least four problems inherent in the ability achievement discrepancy concepts:

1. Disputes continue regarding the definition and measurement of intelligence.
2. The intelligence of students with learning disabilities may be underestimated by IQ tests because the latter depend on the former to some extent.
3. It is difficult to distinguish between groups of poor readers whose achievement is discrepant from IQ.
4. Using discrepancy makes it difficult to identify young children because they are not yet old enough to have demonstrated a discrepancy.

More than a decade ago, the U.S. Department of Education (1994) noted that public schools identified approximately 2.3 million students 6 to 21 years of age as learning disabled, which represented 4.09% in this age range. However, this appeared to be a slight underestimation because the number of students in private schools identified with learning disabilities have tripled. *This rapid growth may be because learning disabilities is an ill-defined category, with confusing diagnostic criteria.* Hallahan (1992) speculated that there may be other reasons for some of the growth. The field of learning disabilities was quite new in 1976 when the government started keeping prevalence data, and it may have taken professionals several years to decide how to identify children. As he pointed out, a number of social and cultural changes that have occurred in the last 30 years have heightened children's vulnerability to develop learning disabilities. Earlier, Baumeister, Kupstas, and Klindworth (1990) suggested that an increase in poverty has placed more children at risk for biomedical problems, including central nervous system dysfunctions. Hallahan further speculated that stress on parents may result in them being less able to provide the social support necessary to help their children, who themselves are experiencing an increasing amount of stress. The result may be that children who in a previous time of less stressful lifestyle and more support would have gotten by in their schoolwork are now experiencing failure. Issues raised by Baumeister et al. and Hallahan are especially critical for multicultural parents and their children and youth.

THE IMPERATIVE NATURE OF MULTICULTURAL EDUCATION

Heward (2003) argued that multicultural learners come to school with rich and complex cultural backgrounds that may be influenced by the family, home, and local community. To reach these learners, general and special educators must accept and respect their unique characteristics and diverse backgrounds. Additionally, several authors (e.g., Gay, 1997; Gollnick & Chinn, 2002; Obiakor & Utley, 2004; Prater, 2002) suggested that culturally responsive instructional practices must be used to enhance students' opportunities to reach their potential. The need for a culturally responsive pedagogy is even more critical when referring to multicultural learners with disabilities. For instance, Prater acknowledged that current visibility of people from different social classes and ethnic groups must force schools to interact with families from different cultures as they redesign their programs. This fact must be recognized and respected when working with students and planning their educational experiences to provide parity of opportunity. Earlier, Gay acknowledged that despite legal mandates prohibiting discrimination, educational inequalities continue to prevail at crisis levels. More than two decades ago, the College Entrance Examination Board (1985) in its report, *Equality and Excellence*, concluded that "although many of the legal barriers to educational opportunity have been removed, education to a large extent remains separate and unequal in the United States" (p. vii). This inequality becomes clear when one analyzes pervasive problems experienced by African Americans, Latinos, and American Indians. The situation is not quite as serious for Asian Americans, at least on some standardized test measures of school achievement, school attendance, and graduation rates.

The controversial issue is whether educators and psychologists have used assessment procedures, too often designed and standardized with a middle-class orientation, to unfairly classify and label children from culturally and linguistically diverse backgrounds as individuals with mental retardation who require special education services (Baca & Cervantes, 1984). There is some controversy over whether most cases of mild mental retardation and placement in programs requiring special education services can be accounted for in terms of an assessment bias against intellectually intact, ethnically diverse, disadvantaged children. Clearly, society is enriched by the traditional values of people from different national origins, different language backgrounds, different areas of the country, and different genders. According to Robbins, Lindsey, Lindsey, and Terrell (2002), the learner who enters the classroom has not only his or her own learning styles but his or her own distinctive cultural background and experiences. As a person in charge of students' learning, the teacher or service provider also brings to the classroom some distinctive experiences and cultures. As a result, teachers must understand, appreciate, and respect the various cultures represented in their classrooms and try to proactively design instructional strategies that include *all* learners. Yet, diversity in schools comes with the dilemma of having been steeped in customs, knowledge, language, modes of thought, and styles of behavior that may not be well matched with school expectations, as in Don's case. The fact remains that no two learners or groups of learners process information in the same way; and no two learners read, speak, or think in the same way (Robbins et al., 2002).

It is common knowledge that the school curriculum is built on middle-income white expectations for the appropriate language to learn, the best knowledge to learn, and the behaviors that are most acceptable. Rather than celebrate the differences among different people, there is an underlying message that the white middle-class ways of behavior and thinking are more important than any other. Don would have failed completely if his teacher had not tried new and innovative strategies. Since whites represent almost 80% to 90% of all teachers in the educational system, there is a greater tendency to refer African American students based on personal stereotypes (Smith, 1994). Although Don's teacher is white, he wanted to maximize his potential by modifying his methods and engaging in good teaching. According to Smith, good teaching entails (a) the kinds of expectation teachers communicate to students, (b) the teacher's ability to deal with special needs in the classroom, (c) the teacher's knowledge of normal child development, and (d) the teacher's sensitivity to different learning strategies/behavioral styles that students bring to the school environment.

About three decades ago, Adelman (1971) noted that when teachers do not personalize instructions to accommodate individual differences, the number of children with learning problems increases. Later, Larsen (1978) contended that some students might be erroneously identified as learning disabled because they are not afforded appropriate learning opportunities. This misidentification leads to why many multicultural learners end up being misdiagnosed, misreferred, and most often misplaced. General and special educators must understand that many other factors may contribute to the misclassification of multicultural learners as behaviorally disordered instead of learning disabled (Turnbull, Turnbull, Shank, & Smith, 2004). Don's case showed that while he was able to pass tests, he was not able to be successful in his school work—he still needed help, which his teacher provided.

WORKING WITH MULTICULTURAL LEARNERS WITH LEARNING DISABILITIES

To work with multicultural learners with learning disabilities, general and special educators must focus on appropriate identification and assessment, along with developing new and proven strategies that meet the needs of individual learners.

Culturally sensitive teaches and service providers have good command of their subject matter and use a variety of techniques (Obiakor & Utley, 2004; Richards & Dooley, 2004). They see each learner as an individual and express to the learner, in myriad ways, their interest in the learner's success and ability to learn. Such professionals know their learners' learning styles and teach to those styles. They work with learners to experiment with, and to become comfortable with, alternative learning styles; and they recognize that each learner needs to know the information by preparing him or her to succeed in a variety of settings (see Obiakor & Utley, 2004; Richards & Dooley, 2004). Furthermore, they try to avoid cultural destructiveness as a practice or policy and collaborative efforts to match teaching with assessment.

About two decades ago, Ysseldyke et al. (1983) found no reliable psychometric differences between students labeled learning disabled and those who were perceived to be low achievers. In addition, identification as learning disabled depended on the criteria used, with different children being identified depending on the definition applied. If that child moved to a different school district, he or she might no longer be identified as being learning disabled (Shea & Bauer, 1994). More than a decade ago, Algozzine (1991) argued that the move toward excellence in education might increase the likelihood that low-performing students would be referred to as having learning disabilities. For multicultural learners, these referrals are most often based on behavioral and teacher expectations rather than pedagogical imperatives needed to enhance school success. In order to diagnose a child with a suspected learning disability, the following procedures and criteria should be considered (see Obiakor & Utley, 2004; Richards & Dooley, 2004).

Doing Clinical Interviews

A clinical interview involves a series of interviews with the child to assess where the ultimate problem may lie. When interviewing the multicultural student with suspected learning disabilities, it is important to look and listen for confusion over questions, poor use of vocabulary, problems expressing ideas and thoughts, awkward gait, poor memory, short attention span, lack of focus, poor fine-motor skills, and a history of academic difficulties (Burkhardt et al., 2004; Pierangelo & Giuliani, 2002).

Making Assessments Ecological

Ecological assessment involves observing multicultural students in a variety of settings such as classrooms, playgrounds, and other structured and nonstructured settings to determine where they manifest their greatest difficulties. For appropriate assessments, general and special educators may observe social withdrawal, alienation from peers, inability to focus in unstructured settings, and "class clown" type of behavior as a means of being removed from an academically stressful setting (Obiakor & Utley, 2004; Pierangelo & Giuliani, 2002; Richards & Dooley, 2004).

Interviewing Parents

Parental interviews require personal meetings with parents to determine the essential background history that may be needed for appropriate diagnosis. For a multicultural student with a suspected learning disability, general and special educators must try listening during interviews for statements such as (a) has difficulty dressing himself or herself; (b) avoids homework; (c) is disorganized; (d) has a short attention span; (e) forgets easily; (f) forgets to bring books home; (g) gets stomachaches in the morning before school; (h) gets frequent headaches; (i) has few friends; (j) is unwilling to try new things; and (k) gives up easily (Obiakor & Utley, 2004; Pierangelo & Giuliani, 2002; Prater, 2002; Richards & Dooley, 2004).

Doing Teacher Interviews

Teacher interviews may require several meetings with the classroom teacher to ascertain the child's basic intellectual, social, and academic performance. For multicultural learners with potential learning disabilities, the interviewer must be aware of certain LD symptoms that may appear in the classroom. Some examples may include poor memory, gross-motor coordination difficulties, lack of focus, short attention span, procrastination, failure to hand in written work or homework, lack of confidence, self-derogatory statements such as "I'm so stupid," consistently low academic performance in certain subjects over time, social difficulties, lack of motivation for schoolwork, poor handwriting, and poor fine-motor skills (Burkhardt et al., 2004; Pierangelo & Giuliani, 2002; Richards & Dooley, 2004).

Interpreting Intelligence Tests Multidimensionally

For many multicultural learners with learning disabilities, the psychologist administers an individual intelligence test to look for an average to above average potential intellectual level. This does not mean that the student's IQ must be in the average range. Many multicultural learners are commonly misdiagnosed as having a learning disability when, in actuality, they may be (a) prone to learning differently, (b) slow learners, (c) those with emotional issues, or (d) underachievers not performing for reasons other than a learning disability. Moreover, a major criticism of IQ tests is that they regulate access to educational opportunities and relegate students from multicultural backgrounds to special education programs (Obiakor & Utley, 2004; Richards & Dooley, 2004; Smith-Beirne, Patton, & Ittenbach, 1994). To reach multicultural learners, IQ tests must be interpreted multidimensionally.

Understanding Achievement Testing

Children with learning disabilities usually exhibit a severe discrepancy between potential ability (as measured on an individual IQ test) and academic achievement. This is a debatable criterion because it is possible that a multicultural learner functioning on grade level, according to standardized achievement tests, may actually have a severe discrepancy if one takes into account ability levels (Pierangelo & Giuliani, 2002; Turnbull, Turnbull, Shank, Smith, & Leal, 2002). As Turnbull et al. (2002) reported, in diagnosing learning disabilities, it is necessary to use a nondiscriminatory approach to ensure compliance with the mandates of IDEA. An important aspect of nondiscriminatory evaluation for multicultural learners with learning disabilities is establishing a discrepancy between ability as measured by an IQ test, and achievement as measured by a standardized test.

Although many general and special education professionals understand the biases inherent in standardized tests as they relate to the multicultural learner, it is sometimes satisfying to put a label on a disability or at least to identify a condition that can be treated. With proper assessment comes proper instruction/intervention for *all* learners. One of the best ways for teachers to address the needs of multicultural learners with learning disabilities is to adapt instruction and materials. Many textbooks include teacher's manuals to assist in the presentation of instruction. Too often, however, the lessons in the manual are brief and potentially confusing. General and special education teachers must modify these lessons before presenting them to the class (see Hunt & Marshall, 2002). Multicultural learners with learning disabilities have different learning styles and cultural values, as in the case of Don. As a result, parents and extended family members must be involved in the educational process (Obiakor & Utley, 2004; Prater, 2002; Richards & Dooley, 2004).

Reviewing Cumulative Reports and Records

For many multicultural learners with learning disabilities, a review of cumulative records by general and special educators may reveal a consistently low group of achievement scores in certain subjects over a period of years, past teachers' comments showing a pattern to the child's present teacher reports, a historical pattern of academic difficulties, frequent absences (which may occur when the child feels frustrated and overwhelmed by the work), and a discrepancy between ability and class performance as indicated by report card patterns. Educators must review and consistently analyze and remodel (Burkhardt et al., 2004; Pierangelo & Giuliani, 2002; Richards & Dooley, 2004).

Hurley and Tinajero (2001) stated that although progress has been made in many areas of teaching students with cultural and linguistic differences, the one area that is still in need of development is assessment. Additionally, Fradd and Lee (2001) contended that the issue of assessment is particularly controversial with respect to high-stakes standardized tests. Such tests may be culturally incompatible for some students and may be linguistically impossible for students who have not reached a level of English language development consistent with the examination (see Hurley & Tinajero, 2001).

Incorporating Innovative Teaching Techniques

Teachers and service providers are essential links between children with learning disabilities and the interventions and services that can help them (Burkhardt et al., 2004; Richards & Dooley, 2004). There is no student with a learning disability who cannot learn, if a teacher has received appropriate preparation and is willing to spend the time, using his or her expertise to reach and teach that child. To most effectively help multicultural children with learning disabilities, teachers should do the following:

Know the "Warning Signs."   All students exhibit difficulties at one time or another with spoken or written language, memory, attention, concentration, organizational skills, physical coordination, and social behavior. However, if a student consistently displays difficulty with a group of these behaviors, it is a good indication of a possible learning disability (Richards & Dooley, 2004).

Participate in Ongoing Workshops and Staff Development Programs. Good teachers are constantly learning, updating their teaching skills, and sharing successes (and challenges) with fellow educators. The support and advice of these colleagues help to better address the needs of multicultural students with learning disabilities and to improve classroom skills. General and special educators should seek the help of colleagues and professional learning disability organizations. In addition, they should draw on their expertise and demonstrate willingness to acknowledge what they do not know (Burkhardt et al., 2004; Obiakor & Utley, 2004; Richards & Dooley, 2004).

Design a Learning Profile of Each Student.   General and special educators should monitor each multicultural student's ability and involvement in the classroom. By being aware of the learning styles, work level, reasoning ability, classroom participation, comprehension, and progress of a student, they can effectively build on the existing strengths and weaknesses of multicultural learners with learning disabilities (Burkhardt et al., 2004; Obiakor & Utley, 2004; Richards & Dooley, 2004).

Develop Effective Teaching Techniques.   When students have learning disabilities, their brains sometimes work differently from those of other children. That does not mean that they are a "little dumb" ("LD"); it just means that they "learn differently" ("LD"). In other words, simply slowing the pace while using traditional teaching methods will not work. General and special educators should use innovative techniques to maintain student interest and improve opportunities to learn. In addition, they should develop and modify curricula and testing to ensure that multicultural students obtain the information and skills to be evaluated accordingly (Richards & Dooley, 2004). Some examples include:
- Always gaining a student's attention before giving directions or initiating class instruction.

- Calling the student by name to alert him or her to focus attention on the classroom activity.
- Using visual aids to capitalize on a student's visual processing and providing the auditory/visual association needed to learn new concepts and language.
- Writing assignments on the board so the student can copy them in a notebook.
- Providing the student with the list of assignments as needed.

General and special educators should make sure that multicultural students with learning disabilities have enough time to answer test questions. They should change testing procedures if the testing mechanism itself interferes with a student's ability to demonstrate knowledge. It is critical to note that not all of these recommendations apply to *all* students. Individual strategies should be developed to address the needs of individual students with learning disabilities. Implementing changes such as these in the classroom can minimize the impact of learning disabilities upon academic achievement (Obiakor & Utley, 2004; Richards & Dooley, 2004).

Provide Individualized Instruction.   Frequently, students with learning disabilities have more difficulty than others in grasping concepts and communicating information in class. To be effective, teachers should modify their instruction to meet the various learning styles and abilities of multicultural students with learning disabilities (Obiakor & Utley, 2004; Richards & Dooley, 2004).

Provide a Structure for Learning.   Many students with learning disabilities have difficulty organizing information, developing work habits, and coping with change. They must be taught to monitor their own progress and regulate the time and effort they spend on each assignment. Teachers should maintain consistent teaching routines and methods for *all* learners, including those from multicultural backgrounds (Richards & Dooley, 2004).

Build Students' Self-Concepts.   Educators should build confidence among multicultural students by delivering information in a gradually more progressive manner, allowing them time to master a topic at one level before moving on to more difficult material. In addition, they should recognize and help them appreciate the value of their creativity (Obiakor, 1999; Richards & Dooley, 2004).

Meet with Parents to Discuss Their Child's Problems at School.   Parents and guardians are often unaware of their child's problems at school. Teachers should meet with them and discuss the situation in an open and supportive manner. In addition, they should ask parents' permission to administer an educational evaluation of the multicultural student when such an evaluation seems warranted. It is important that they work with parents and guardians to provide the multicultural student with a comprehensive approach to coping with his or her learning disability.

Consistencies must be maintained in the student's instruction and self-discipline by sharing strategies with parents and guardians that can be used during weekends or vacations (Obiakor & Utley, 2004; Prater, 2002).

Understand the Laws and Procedures That Regulate Special Education Programs.   Educators should become familiar with laws protecting the rights of multicultural students with learning disabilities and advise parents about proper legal and school procedures. Additionally, they should help ensure that their school meets legal standards and requirements when conducting educational evaluations, parental advisory meetings, program development, and placement of multicultural students with learning disabilities (Obiakor & Utley, 2004; Richards & Dooley, 2004).

Advocate on Behalf of Students.   It is imperative for the emotional well-being of multicultural students with learning disabilities to be protected. These students must be seen as equal members of the school community. Teachers can work to ensure that school authorities offer these students equal opportunity, and they can oppose any discriminatory or exclusionary act that would further stigmatize these students with learning disabilities (Burkhardt et al., 2004; Obiakor & Utley, 2004).

A Culturally Responsive Educator

1. Insists that family support is a must in facilitating successful educational experiences for multicultural learners with learning disabilities.
2. Knows that caring and "good" teachers are essential in the success of *all* learners.
3. Utilizes nondiscriminatory assessments to adequately identify, assess, categorize, place, and instruct multicultural learners with learning disabilities.
4. Understands that school support systems are necessary for the success of *all* learners.
5. Understands that how a child learns is a major component in constructing a pedagogical framework for multicultural learners, especially those with learning problems.
6. Knows that it is important to adapt the classroom environment to meet the needs of at-risk learners.
7. Provide adaptable materials to meet the needs of students with different learning styles.
8. Utilizes multicultural peer tutors to increase opportunities for learning.
9. Avoids unwarranted assumptions about multicultural learners with learning problems.
10. Allows multicultural learners to maximize their learning potential.

Conclusion

This chapter has explored ways to work with multicultural learners with learning disabilities. In addition, it has focused on the problems faced by students such as Don, especially because they are "double disabled," not only because of an identified disabling condition but also because of their racial origin. In order to get along in predominantly white schools, they have to play stereotypical roles to be accepted, and they often find themselves being accused of "acting white" when they are in their home setting. For the multicultural learner with a learning disability, the pressure to do well, fit in, and satisfy others, may lead to dropping out, suicide, continuous fighting, or constant outbursts that are totally unacceptable to general and special education teachers and administrators. It appears that the survival of multicultural students with learning problems must come from being exposed to caring teachers who are willing to try new techniques, involve the family in the child's education, and demonstrate a definite understanding of the child's needs. Multicultural learners deserve opportunities to utilize their fullest potential. Surely, notwithstanding the legal protections under IDEA, there needs to be a more humane safeguard that supersedes the letter of the law in working with *all* learners, especially those from multicultural backgrounds.

Discussion Questions

1. Briefly explain traditional problems facing multicultural learners with learning disabilities.
2. Describe visible signs of learning disabilities and explain how cultural variables are attached to these signs.
3. Identify and explain learning characteristics of multicultural learners with specific learning disabilities.
4. Evaluate strategies to empower multicultural families whose children have learning disabilities.
5. Summarize how the potential of multicultural learners like Don can be maximized in inclusive settings.

References

Adelman, H. S. (1971). The not so specific learning disability population. *Exceptional Children, 37,* 528–533.

Algozzine, B. (1991). Decision–making and curriculum-based assessment. In B. Y. L. Wong (Ed.), *Learning about learning disabilities* (pp. 40–55). San Diego, CA: Academic Press.

Baca, L. M., & Cervantes, H. T. (1984). *The bilingual special education interface.* St. Louis, MO: Times/Mirror Mosby.

Bateman, B. (1965). An educational view of a diagnostic approach to learning disorders. In J. Hellmuth (Ed.), *Learning disorders* (Vol. 1, pp. 219–239). Seattle, WA: Special Child.

Baumeister, A. A., Kupstas, F., & Klindworth, L. M. (1990). New morbidity: Implications for prevention of children's disabilities. *Exceptionality, 1*(1), 1–6.

Beirne-Smith, M., Patton, J., & Ittenbach, R. (1994). *Mental retardation* (4th ed.). Upper Saddle River, NJ: Merrill/Prentice Hall.

Books-Gunn, J., Klebanov, P. K., & Duncan, G. J. (1996). Ethnic difference in children's intelligence test scores: Role of economic deprivation, home environment and maternal characteristics. *Child Development, 4*(67), 396–408.

Bureau of Indian Affairs. (1988). *Report of BIA education: Excellence in Indian education through the effective school process.* Washington, DC: U.S. Government Printing Office.

Burkhardt, S., Obiakor, F. E., & Rotatori, A. F. (2004). *Current perspectives on learning disabilities: Advances in special education* (Vol. 16). Oxford, England: Elsevier/JAI Press.

Coleman, J. S., Campbell, E. Q., Hobson, C. J., McPartland, J., Mood, A. M.., Weinfold, F. D., et al. (1966). *Inequality of educational opportunity.* Washington, DC: U.S. Office of Education.

College Entrance Examination Board (1985). *Equality and excellence: The educational status of Black Americans.* New York: Author.

Fradd, S. H., & Lee, O. (2001). Needed: A framework for integrating standardized and informal assessment for students developing academic language proficiency in English. In S. R. Hurley & J. V. Tinajero (Eds.), *Literacy assessment of second language learners* (pp. 130–148). Boston: Allyn & Bacon.

Fuch, E., & Havighurst, R. J. (1972). *To live on this earth: American Indian education.* Garden City, NY: Doubleday.

Gay, G. (1997). Educational equality for students of color. In J. A. Banks & C. A. McGee-Banks (Eds.), *Multicultural education: Issues and perspectives* (3rd ed., pp. 195–228). Boston: Allyn & Bacon.

Gollnick, D. M., & Chinn, P. G. (2002). *Multicultural education in a pluralistic society* (6th ed.). Upper Saddle River, NJ: Merrill/Prentice Hall.

Grant, P. A., & Grant P. B. (2002). Working with African American students with specific learning disabilities. In F. E. Obiakor & B. A. Ford (Eds.), *Creating successful learning environments for African American learners with exceptionalities* (pp. 67–77). Thousand Oaks, CA: Corwin Press.

Hallahan, D. P. (1992). Some thoughts on why the prevalence of learning disabilities has increased. *Journal of Learning Disabilities, 25,* 523–528.

Hallahan, D. P., & Cruickshank, W. M. (1973). *Psycho-educational foundations of learning disabilities.* Upper Saddle River, NJ: Prentice Hall.

Hallahan, D. P., & Kauffman, J. M. (1977). Labels, categories, behaviors: ED, LD, and EMR reconsidered. *Journal of Special Education, 11,* 139–149.

Hallahan, D. P., Kauffman, J. M., & Lloyd, J. W. (1996). *Introduction to learning disabilities.* Needham Heights, MA: Allyn & Bacon.

Herrnstein, R. J., & Murray, C. (1994). *The bell curve: Intelligence and class structure in American life.* New York: Free Press.

Heward, W. L. (2003). *Exceptional children: An introduction to special education* (7th ed.). Upper Saddle River, NJ: Merrill/Prentice Hall.

Hunt, N., & Marshall, K. (2002). *Exceptional children and youth: An introduction to special education* (3rd ed.). Boston: Houghton Mifflin.

Hurley, S. R., & Tinajero, J. V. (Eds.). (2001). *Literacy assessment of second language learners.* Boston: Allyn & Bacon.

Kagan, J. (1971, December 4). The magical aura of the IQ. *Saturday Review of Literature, 4,* 92–93.

Kirk, S. A. (1962). *Educating exceptional children.* Boston: Houghton-Mifflin.

Kirk, S. A. (1975). Behavioral diagnosis and remediation of learning disabilities. In S. A. Kirk & J. J. McCarthy (Eds.), *Learning disabilities: Selected papers* (pp. 7–10). Boston: Houghton-Mifflin.

Larsen, S. C. (1978). Learning disabilities and the professional educator. *Learning Disability Quarterly, 1,* 5–12.

Lloyd, J. (1996, December 28). What is learning disability? [1 paragraph]. *The Curry School of Education at the University of Virginia, Office of Special Education: A Web resource for Special Education.* [Online] Available from curry.edschool.virginia.edu/go/cise/ose/home.html

Mann, L. (1979). *On the trail of process.* New York: Grune & Stratton.

Mazurek, K., & Winzer, M. A. (1994). *Comparative studies in special education.* Washington, DC: Gallaudet University Press.

Obiakor, F. E. (1999). Teacher expectations of minority exceptional learners: Impact on "accuracy" of self-concepts. *Exceptional Children, 66,* 39–53.

Obiakor, F. E., Grant, P. A., & Dooley, E. A. (2002). *Educating all learners: Refocusing the comprehensive support model.* Springfield, IL: Charles C Thomas.

Obiakor, F. E., & Utley, C. A. (2004). Multicultural learners with learning disabilities: Beyond Eurocentric perspectives. In S. Burkhardt, F. E. Obiakor, & A. F. Rotatori (Eds.), *Current perspectives on learning disabilities: Advances in special education* (Vol. 16, pp. 35–64). Oxford, England: Elsevier/JAI Press.

Ogunwole, S. V. (2002). *The American Indian and Alaskan Native Population: Census 2000 brief.* Washington, DC: U.S. Government Printing Office.

Pierangelo, R., & Giuliani, G. A. (2002). *Assessment in special education: A practical approach.* Boston: Allyn & Bacon.

Prater, L. (2002). Family and schooling. In F. E. Obiakor, P. A. Grant, & E. A. Dooley (Eds.), *Educating all learners: Refocusing the comprehensive support model* (pp. 32–48). Springfield, IL: Charles C Thomas.

Richards, A., & Dooley, E. (2004). Curriculum modifications for students with learning disabilities. In S. Burkhardt, F. E. Obiakor, & A. F. Rotatori (Eds.), *Current perspectives on learning disabilities: Advances in special education* (Vol. 16, pp. 95–111). Oxford, England: Elsevier/JAI Press.

Robbins, K. N., Lindsey, R. B., Lindsey, D. B., & Terrell, R. D. (2002). *Culturally proficient instruction: A guide for people who teach.* Thousand Oaks, CA: Corwin Press.

Schaefer, R. T. (2006). *Racial and ethnic groups* (10th ed.). Upper Saddle River, NJ: Pearson/Prentice Hall.

Shea, T. M., & Bauer, A. M. (1994). *Learners with disabilities: A social systems perspective of special education.* Dubuque, IA: Brown & Benchmark.

Smith, C. R. (1994). *Learning disabilities: The interaction of learner, task, and setting* (3rd ed.). Boston: Allyn & Bacon.

Stanovich, K. E. (1989). Has the learning disabled field lost its intelligence? *Journal of Learning Disabilities, 22*(8), 487–492.

Turnbull, R., Turnbull, A., Shank M., & Smith S. J. (2004). *Exceptional lives: Special education in today's schools* (4th ed.). Upper Saddle River, NJ: Merrill/Prentice Hall.

Turnbull, R., Turnbull, A., Shank, M., Smith, S., & Leal, D. (2002). *Exceptional lives: Special education in today's schools* (3rd ed.). Upper Saddle River, NJ: Merrill/Prentice Hall.

U.S. Department of Education. (1994). *Sixteenth annual report to Congress on the implementation of the Individuals with Disabilities Education Act.* Washington, DC: Author.

Wiedherhold, J. L. (1974). Historical perspectives on the education of the learning disabled. In L. Mann & D. Sabatino (Eds.), *The second review of special education* (pp. 103–152). Philadelphia, PA: Journal of Special Education Press.

Winzer, M. A. (1993). *The history of special education: From isolation to integration.* Washington, DC: Gallaudet University Press.

Young, J. (2003, October 10). Researchers change racial bias on the SAT. *Chronicle of Higher Education,* A34–A35.

Ysseldyke, J. E., Thurlow, M. L., Graden, J. L., Wesson, C., Algozzine, B., & Deno, S. L. (1983). Generalizations from five years of research on assessment and decision-making: The University of Minnesota Institute. *Exceptional Education Quarterly, 4*(1), 75–93.

Chapter 7

Working with Multicultural Learners with Behavioral Problems

Cheryl A. Utley and Spencer J. Salend

Chapter Outline

Thinking About Multicultural Special Education

Roberto's father, an African American, was an electrical engineer and his mother, a Latina, was a registered nurse. The family moved from Puerto Rico to an affluent suburban neighborhood. Roberto, age 5, spoke and understood both Spanish and English. He attended kindergarten in a private school and his teacher, Ms. Jones, observed that his classroom behavior interfered with his mastery of schoolwork and positive interactions with his peers. An initial interview with Ms. Jones revealed that she found him to be disruptive and disrespectful in the classroom. She reported that his behavior included "calling out frequently," "talking back," and "not understanding what 'No' means." Ms. Jones added that Roberto was not failing but that his academic performance was below his ability level. He appeared to understand and complete his pre-reading and math assignments when motivated to do so, but his attention was often sporadic and insufficient. Ms. Jones noted that Roberto had a habit of elaborately rearranging his work area, asking for directions to be repeated, and checking with his classmates whenever he was given a class assignment. He paid closer attention when an assignment interested him or the method of teaching was relatively new or involved working with his classmates.

Observations of Roberto in school showed he often called out answers to questions and left his seat without permission to talk with his peers. When called on by the teacher, he often answered questions with an irrelevant comment. These behaviors frequently interfered with his ability to complete his work and elicited laughter from his peers, who described him as the "class clown." When asked about school, Roberto said he did not like it because his teacher was always yelling at him because he did not follow class rules. The thing he liked about school was being with his friends. He noted that he learned best when he was interested and when he worked in small groups with other children. Roberto's family was frustrated by his school behavior and felt that he was smart and capable of doing better work. His family also discussed how they could work more closely with him to help him complete homework assignments. Ms. Jones tried several things to improve Roberto's behavior. She used a classroom discipline system that consisted of students changing their name cards from green to yellow to orange to red for each infraction of the rules. A red card meant a call to the child's parents. In one month, Roberto had 10 red cards and 5 orange cards. As a result, Ms. Jones spoke with his family on a regular basis about his inappropriate behavior in class. On some occasions, his behaviors were severe enough that he was sent to the principal's office for supervision. In fact, traditional behavior interventions did not lead to an improvement in his behavior. After trying some intervention strategies, Ms. Jones recommended that Roberto be evaluated for special education. Before long, a team of professionals met regarding his behaviors. Interestingly, the team did not believe he deserved to be placed in a special education program, and to a larger measure, felt that more multidimensional variables must be considered before arriving at this conclusion.

- *Why was it important to understand Roberto's home and cultural backgrounds?*
- *Why did the team of professionals not recommend Roberto for special education placement even though he exhibited different behavioral patterns in school?*

The Individuals with Disabilities Education Amendments (IDEA) of 1997 noted that "greater efforts are needed to prevent the intensification of problems connected with mislabeling . . . among minority children with disabilities" (Section 601 [c] [8] [A]). The Individuals with Disabilities Education Improvement Act (IDEIA) of 2004 reiterated this proposition. Multicultural learners with behavior problems are significantly more likely to be removed from general education programs and educated in more restrictive, less inclusive, and substantially separate educational settings (Osher, Woodruff, & Sims, 2001). Scholars and educators who study discipline in the context of race and ethnicity have found that African American males and females, followed by Latinos, Filipinos, and whites were disciplined more frequently and strictly (Coutinho, Oswald, & Best, 2002; Lo & Cartledge, 2001; National Research Council, 2002). Specifically, African American children have been identified one and a half to four times the rate of white children in the disability category of behavior disorders (Oswald & Coutinho, 2001).

To minimize the risk of poor classroom experiences, general and special education professionals have been urged to rethink issues of assessment and intervention as they discover how to maximize the potential of multicultural learners with presumed behavior problems (Obiakor et al., 2004). As Obiakor et al. noted, it is essential that educators understand that (a) poor identification may lead to poor assessment, (b) poor assessment may lead to poor labels and categories, (c) poor labels and categories may lead to poor placement, (d) poor placement may lead to poor instruction/intervention, and (e) poor instruction/intervention may lead to more problem behaviors. Ms. Jones, Roberto's teacher in the introductory case, was not quick to label him. She attempted some intervention techniques. Even the team of professionals felt that Roberto did not deserve to be placed in a special education program. In this chapter, we discuss Roberto's case along the dimensions of identification, assessment, categorization, and instruction. In addition, we suggest alternative ways to handle Roberto's behavior problems.

THE IDENTIFICATION OF ROBERTO

The legal context and foundation for the identification of students with behavioral problems are described in IDEA '97. Ideally, the goals of this process are to determine whether a student is eligible for special education services and to plan his or her educational program. Initially, the identification process involves a multiple process of applying general measures to large groups of students—screening—and moving through a series of more elaborate and focused steps, converging on a classification and determination that a given student is eligible for special education services (Kauffman, 2005; Obiakor & Utley, 2004; Utley & Obiakor, 2001). For instance, Kauffman and Utley and Obiakor concluded that screening and identifying antisocial behavior embody the following principles:

- The procedure should be proactive rather than reactive.
- Whenever possible, a variety of people (e.g., the teacher, parent, trained observer) should be employed and students' behavior should be evaluated in a variety of settings (e.g., classroom, playground, lunchroom, home).
- Screening should take place as early as possible in students' school careers, ideally at preschool and kindergarten levels (i.e., prior to the child developing a history of maladaptive behavior and school failure).
- Teacher nominations and rankings or ratings are appropriate in the beginning of the screening process, but should be supplemented, if possible, by direct observation, examination of school records, peer or parent ratings, and other sources of information that might be available in order to minimize chances of misidentification.

In the majority of schools, the identification process begins when the general education teacher makes a request for help because a student's behavior is so disturbing that it can no longer be tolerated. The teacher decides that the child's academic achievement level is not acceptable or classroom behaviors are unacceptable. In other words, the teacher finds himself or herself no longer optimistic about the capacity to deal effectively with certain students in the context of the general education classroom, and perceives that these students are difficult to teach and unresponsive to classroom interventions. These personal feelings on the part of the teacher could lead to intentional or unintentional misidentification of students, especially those who exhibit different cultural and behavioral styles. Although Roberto's teacher was not quick to label him, the identification process of his inappropriate behaviors appeared unidimensional—it did not include a variety of assessment measures (e.g., classroom and playground observations, authentic assessments, and portfolio) linked to interventions across settings (e.g., school and home) and people in Roberto's life.

Prereferral Process

A comprehensive team of professionals and family members come together to make important decisions concerning the education of students. The special education identification process that the comprehensive team follows for students who are experiencing difficulties in school usually starts with the prereferral process. *Prereferral is a preventive problem-solving process* assisting educators like Ms. Jones before considering a referral for a special education placement. The team collaborates with teachers to gather information about students and to develop and use methods to successfully educate students like Roberto within inclusive classrooms. Prereferral interventions are determined based on individual students' strengths and challenges; educational, social, and medical history; language and cultural backgrounds; as well as the teacher's concerns and the nature of the learning environment (Salend, 2005). The implementation and effectiveness of these interventions are then assessed over a period of time prior to evaluating a student for special education.

Prereferral strategies are especially important for multicultural learners who are experiencing difficulties in school (Knotek, 2001). In addition to identifying the source of students' difficulties in school, effective prereferral interventions with students from diverse backgrounds include *using a multicultural curriculum, understanding how cultural and linguistic backgrounds affect learning and behavior*, and *involving families in all school and classroom activities* (Ortiz, 2001). However, in the case of Roberto, although Ms. Jones attempted to address his behavior problems via her classroom management system, no formal prereferral process was employed. Unfortunately, this is a common occurrence for multicultural learners, who are more likely than their white peers to attend schools that offer limited access to prereferral and ancillary services (Ochoa, Robles-Pina, Garcia, & Breunig, 1999).

THE ASSESSMENT OF ROBERTO

When prereferral strategies are not effective (or not employed, as in the case of Roberto), the planning team, with the consent of the student's family, determines if a student is eligible for special education. To determine eligibility for special education services, standardized assessment procedures as well as interviews and observations are used to determine if the student has a disability that adversely affects educational performance. One major problem linked to the shortcomings of existing standardized assessment procedures is bias, which means that a disproportionate number of multicultural learners like Roberto are misclassified as having disabilities (Council for Children with Behavioral Disorders, 1989; Obiakor et al., 2004; Salend, 2005). In their research, Obiakor et al. reiterated that standardized norm-referenced tests:

1. Foster undemocratic attitudes because they are used to form homogeneous classroom groups that rigidly limit educational, vocational, economic, and other social opportunities.
2. Strictly shape school curricula and restrict educational change.
3. Are not in any way useful for instructional purposes.
4. Are occasionally conducted incompetently by professionals with no perception and recognition of the meaning of culture and language of diverse student groups and are therefore unable to elicit a level of performance that accurately reflects students' underlying competence.
5. Are biased and unfair to individuals from culturally and socioeconomically different backgrounds. On a regular basis, they reflect white middle-class values and attitudes rather than experiential, linguistic, cognitive, and cultural values of all students.
6. Foster expectations that may be damaging by contributing to both the low self-esteem and [the] self-fulfilling prophecy that results in low-level achievement for individuals who score low.

7. Encourage a view of human beings as having only innate, fixed abilities and characteristics.
8. Represent in some fashion an invasion of privacy.
9. Reflect the appraisal of only a part of the changes in students' school performance. (pp. 16–17)

The Council for Children with Behavioral Disorders (CCBD) (1989) identified factors that contribute to the misdiagnosis of multicultural learners with behavioral problems. The CCBD concluded that "direct observations of the teaching/learning interactions should provide enough information to determine the adequacy of existing instructional formats and durations" (p. 270). It also recommended a functional approach to assessment that "examines the student's performance within the context of existing instructional practice" (p. 270). Therefore, to limit the bias associated with standardized tests, the IDEA '97 requirements mandated that assessments must be multidimensional and broad enough to include interviews, samples, observations, portfolios, criterion-referenced, and other classroom-based activities (Obiakor, 2004; Salend, 2005). Apparently, in Roberto's case, there was little culturally relevant assessment information provided by Ms. Jones, the teacher. She provided a brief description of his academic performance, noting that he was not performing according to his ability. There was no specific test information regarding his reading and math abilities; and there was no information regarding instructional conditions and the contexts under which instruction was taught. With regard to Roberto's inappropriate behavior, Ms. Jones provided informal classroom observational data gathered throughout the school day. However, without a systematic system of classroom observation procedures, data collection procedures are sporadic and not consistently used as a means to develop a culturally responsive behavior management program. In reality, the assessment process for students whose behaviors impede their learning or the learning of others must include a team's willingness to conduct a functional behavior assessment (FBA), that is, a process of gathering information to examine the causes and functions of student behaviors and to identify factors that appear to lead to and maintain the behavior (Orza & Zirpoli, 2004; Salend, Duhaney, & Montgomery, 2002; Sugai, Horner, & Sprague, 1999).

Obiakor et al. (2004) noted that multicultural learners with behavioral problems have "different behavioral patterns that frequently result in inappropriate interpretations, classifications, and labels and dysfunctional educational programs" (p. 16). Therefore, in the case of multicultural learners such as Roberto, it is important to identify and assess behavioral patterns that may be attributed to cultural factors by performing a culturally sensitive FBA (see Salend & Taylor, 2002). According to Salend and Taylor, conducting a culturally sensitive FBA involves general and special educators' willingness to:

• **Create a Diverse Multidisciplinary Team.** This means expanding the composition of the team to include family and community members and culturally sensitive professionals who help to gather information regarding the student's cultural perspective and experiential and linguistic backgrounds. Logically, this assists the team in identifying whether the student's behavior has a cultural explanation.

- **Consider Whether the Behavior Is Related to the Student's Cultural and Linguistic Background.**   This means examining the relationship between the behavior and the student's cultural and language backgrounds. It also means determining if behavioral and communication problems between students and teachers are related to their different cultural perspectives.

- **Define the Problem Behavior(s).**   This means defining the behavior and outlining its observable features using culturally sensitive and comprehensible language.

- **Gather Additional Information About the Student and the Behavior.** This means using multiple sources and methods to obtain information regarding the student's skills, strengths, and challenges. It also means using cultural, linguistic and experiential backgrounds, interests, preferences, self-concepts, attitudes, and health issues as well as contexts in which behaviors occur.

- **Record Behavior and List and Analyze the Antecedents and Consequences.** This means observing the student during typical classroom activities and analyzing the potential antecedents and consequences related to his or her behavior. It also means trying to identify the perceived function of the student's behavior, including how it relates to his or her cultural, experiential, and language backgrounds.

- **Formulate and Validate Hypothesis Statements.**   This means considering sociocultural factors and assessing the impact of the student's cultural perspective and language background on behavior to develop specific hypotheses related to why the behavior occurs and the context of the behavior, including the possible antecedents and consequences. It also means considering global hypotheses concerning how variables in the student's life in school, at home, and in the community affect the behavior and employing direct observations to validate their accuracy.

- **Develop Behavior Intervention Plans.**   This means creating and implementing behavior intervention plans (BIP) to delineate how the classroom environment will change to address the behavior and the student's unique educational, social, behavioral, cultural, and linguistic characteristics and needs. It also means including goals for culturally appropriate replacement behaviors and culturally appropriate instructional strategies and behavioral supports. For example, a BIP for Roberto should include such culturally responsive instructional and classroom management strategies as they relate to curriculum, home, and community life. Logically, these strategies should use culturally appropriate reinforcers, cooperative learning groups, peer mediation, and group-oriented behavior management techniques.

THE CATEGORIZATION OF ROBERTO

After the assessment data are collected, the multidisciplinary team meets to review the data and determine if students are eligible for special education. For multicultural learners, the analysis should focus on cultural, linguistic, and experiential factors that affect student learning, behavior, and language development (Obiakor & Utley, 2004; Salend, 2005). Before students are categorized, some critical questions must be answered. More than a decade ago, Damico (1991) offered questions that can guide educators and service providers in examining the data to assess the extent to which students' diverse life experiences and cultural and linguistic backgrounds serve as explanations for the difficulties they may be experiencing in schools. These questions include:

- What factors and conditions may explain the student's learning, behavioral, and/or language difficulties (e.g., stressful life events, lack of opportunity to learn, racism, acculturation, experiential backgrounds)?
- To what extent does the student demonstrate the same learning, behavioral, and/or language difficulties in community settings as in school?
- To what extent are the student's learning, behavioral, and/or language difficulties due to normal second language acquisition, dialectical differences, or cultural factors?
- Did bias occur prior to, during, and after assessment, such as in the reliability, validity, and standardization of the test as well as with the skills and learning styles assessed?
- To what extent were the student's cultural, linguistic, dialectic, and experiential backgrounds considered in collecting and analyzing the assessment data (e.g., selection, administration, and interpretation of test results, prereferral strategies, learning styles, and family involvement)?

In the case of Roberto, the team debated his eligibility for special education. Surely, Roberto exhibited behaviors that deviated from the norms in the classroom. These behaviors prevented him from academically performing to his maximum levels in school. But there is a big difference between the inability to perform school tasks and the unwillingness or refusal to perform school tasks. In the end, the team of professionals was right in deciding that Roberto's behaviors did not qualify him for a special education categorization or placement. The team probably felt that some initial steps deserved to be taken before arriving at that conclusion. A logical extension is that this team understood the power of words, that is, that words can uplift and denigrate people (Obiakor & Smith, 2005). Clearly, the team proved that one cannot generalize that all professionals are out to label multicultural learners. Some professionals are willing to think about the ramifications of categories on students' self-empowerment (Obiakor & Beachum, 2005).

CULTURALLY RESPONSIVE INTERVENTIONS FOR ROBERTO

As previously noted, boys more often than girls tend to use hostility and coercion in social situations and become disruptive when solving problems (Cartledge & Milburn, 1995). In Roberto's case, he often called out answers to questions and left his seat without permission to joke around with his classmates. On the playground, Roberto's interpersonal relationships with his classmates were somewhat distant, and his playground behavior consisted of coercing peers, dominating playground activities, making up his own rules for games, and ridiculing others. What was the school's role in promoting academic and behavioral success, mental and emotional wellness, and a caring classroom environment for him? Although his teacher was not quick to label him, she had a poorly defined discipline system that lacked cultural responsiveness in managing inappropriate behaviors (Algozzine & Kay, 2002; Obiakor et al., 2004; Utley, Kozleski, Smith, & Draper, 2002).

IDEA (1997) and IDEIA (2004) mandated schools to develop behavioral intervention plans and supports for *all* students who exhibit problematic behaviors that interfere with their learning and that of their peers. To this end, Utley et al. (2002) suggested that general and special educators initiate positive behavioral support (PBS). PBS is based on an empirical database rooted in applied behavior analysis and, more recently, methods for solving school-related behavioral issues. There is evidence suggesting that classroom discipline and culturally responsive teaching procedures must be developed to reduce inappropriate behaviors and teach prosocial skills. Sugai, Sprague, Horner, and Walker (2000) noted that:

> The use of culturally appropriate interventions also is emphasized in the PBS approach. *Culturally appropriate* describes interventions that consider the unique and individualized learning histories (social, community, historical, familial, racial, gender, etc.) of all individuals (children with problem behaviors, families, teachers, community agents, etc.) who participate in the PBS process and approach. Data-based problem solving and individualized planning processes can help to establish culturally appropriate interventions; however, individual learning histories ultimately can affect how data are summarized, analyzed, and used. (p. 134)

As indicated, culturally responsive programs are effective if they promote positive relationships among peers and adults (e.g., positive behavior support, cooperative learning, and social skills as key ingredients in managing classroom behaviors). In Roberto's case, the discipline system of using color-coded cards was ineffective in preventing or minimizing his disruptive behaviors. Merely telling him the rules was insufficient. Classroom rules must be taught and expectations of acceptable behavior in and outside of school must be clearly defined. Apparently, rules must be designed to maximize on-task behaviors and minimize off-task behaviors to provide students with a safe learning environment and prevent students from disturbing other students.

Grossman (2004) and Kamps (2002) suggested some teaching rules for students with behavioral problems. They agreed that general and special educators must help students to accomplish the following:

- **Describe and demonstrate the desired behavior.** This means that students should describe specifically what they should do to behave themselves and demonstrate and model desired behaviors.
- **Practice the desired behaviors.** This means that students should go through activities in which the rules come into play or role-play interpersonal situations in which they apply.
- **Use feedback to correct mistakes.** This means that students should take advantage of feedback on how they are doing and correct their mistakes.
- **Know the rules before compliance.** This means that students should make rules and comply with them before consequences are enforced.

Since multicultural learners come to school with their own particular learning, behavioral, and motivational styles, which are influenced by their cultural backgrounds, general and special educators must be well prepared to teach them. Day-Vines and Patton (2003) emphasized that general and special educators must

- consider their personal attitudes, biases, and assumptions,
- value children and their languages,
- recognize that the culture of the school and the culture of the child's family may not be well synchronized,
- recognize that children bring cultural values to school,
- incorporate children's need for multidimensional pedagogical styles,
- affirm students' cultural identity with power-enhancing confidence builders to enable their successful development,
- provide culturally relevant instructional materials,
- provide family involvement and community partnerships,
- maintain realistic expectations for *all* children,
- avoid filtering all behaviors through the singular lens of race, ethnicity, culture, or class,
- seek new information from cultural informants or knowledgeable community members.

Clearly, the educational program for multicultural learners like Roberto can be enhanced by teachers like Ms. Jones using a multicultural curriculum that acknowledges the voices, histories, experiences, and contributions of *all* learners (Banks & Banks, 2004). Incorporating content and instructional materials that acknowledge the experiences and histories of multicultural learners allows them to find meaningful connections between themselves and the curriculum, which can decrease the difficulties they encounter in school. Therefore, educators can minimize the extent to which these learners are referred for special education services by focusing curriculum and instruction on higher-level critical thinking skills and authentic activities that relate to their lives. For example, through use of interdisciplinary units addressing multicultural curricula and instructional resources (e.g., literature, multimedia, community members, personal interviews), students like Roberto can explore various topics and relate them to their cultural, linguistic, and experiential backgrounds. In Roberto's case, rather than structuring learning so that he works individually or competitively, general and special education teachers can organize instruction so that he can work collaboratively with his classmates (Salend, 2005; Utley & Obiakor, 2001). In cooperative learning arrangements, students work with their peers to achieve a shared academic goal. Teachers must structure the learning environment so that each class member contributes to the group's goal. Cooperative learning is especially worthwhile for heterogeneous student populations because it helps them to actively participate and stay engaged in the learning process (Jenkins, Antil, Wayne, & Vadasy, 2003). In addition, it promotes friendships and encourages mutual respect, self-esteem, and learning among students of various academic abilities and different language, racial, and ethnic backgrounds.

A Culturally Responsive Educator

1. Believes there is no perfect human being.
2. Does not misjudge human behaviors.
3. Understands that behavior is learned.
4. Assesses human behaviors from a holistic perspective.
5. Knows that misidentification leads to miscategorization of cultural and behavioral styles.
6. Considers cultural and linguistic differences before judging human differences.
7. Engages in functional behavioral assessment to understand multicultural learners.
8. Designs behavior intervention plans for his or her multicultural learners.
9. Is proactive in managing inappropriate behaviors of multicultural learners.
10. Believes inappropriate or appropriate behaviors do not occur in isolation.

Conclusion

As schools become more inclusive and diverse, general and special educators must develop an in-depth understanding of cultural aspects of behavior as they relate to emotional or behavioral problems of learners. Behavioral standards, expectations, biases, and judgments on deviance are culture-bound; therefore, value judgments about behaviors are not culture-free. In the introductory case, Roberto's behaviors were different and sometimes difficult, yet the team of professionals did not support his placement in a special education program. The team believed more intervention techniques needed to be initiated before making some conclusive judgments. We agree that behavior is learned within the framework of a particular ethnic group or culture, standards, and school-based expectations. Put another way, we agree that what is considered to be acceptable and "normal" in a child's culture may be viewed as unacceptable and incompatible in the public school context (i.e., students' behaviors in the school context may mirror a child's particular cultural heritage, home environment, and different school standards and codes of conduct).

For multicultural learners with behavioral problems, there appears to be problems of how they are identified, assessed, categorized, placed, and instructed. These intriguing tasks conjure some cultural overtones in spite of how "good" or "bad" a teacher or service provider is. This was true in Roberto's case, where the teacher's reactions manifested themselves even though she was not quick to label him. We believe that without considering children's social and cultural backgrounds in addition to holistic and multidisciplinary approaches to studying behaviors, misassessment, miscategorization, misplacement, and misintervention may be inevitable. We conclude that general and special educators must design programs that enhance learning opportunities for multicultural learners with behavior problems. These learning roadways must include a culturally enriched curriculum designed to help develop students' understanding of their learning and promote social skills development and a caring learning community in their education.

Discussion Questions

1. Explain how the identification process of Roberto could have become more culturally sensitive and appropriate to meet his academic and behavioral needs.
2. Identify two questions that must be asked during the prereferral process to identify cultural and language differences that are inherent in a student's behavioral and learning situations.
3. Analyze how an assessment process can relate to the development of culturally responsive interventions.
4. What is considered acceptable in a child's culture may be viewed as unacceptable and incompatible in the public school context. Do you agree? Explain the reasons for your answer.
5. Behavior is learned. In one paragraph, evaluate this statement.

References

Algozzine, R., & Kay, P. (2002). *Preventing problem behaviors: A handbook of successful prevention strategies*. Thousand Oaks, CA: Corwin Press.

Banks, J. A., & Banks, C. A. (2004). *Handbook of research on multicultural education* (2nd ed.). San Francisco: Wiley.

Cartledge, G., & Milburn, J. F. (1995). *Teaching social skills to children and youth: Innovative approaches*. Boston: Allyn & Bacon.

Council for Children with Behavior Disorders (1989). Best assessment practices for students with behavioral disorders: Accommodation to cultural diversity and individual differences. *Behavioral Disorders, 14*(4), 263–278.

Coutinho, M. J., Oswald, D. P., & Best, A. A. (2002). Gender and sociodemographic factors and the disproportionate identification of minority students as emotionally disturbed. *Behavior Disorders, 27,* 109–125.

Damico, J. S. (1991). Descriptive assessment of communicative ability in Limited English proficient students. In E. Hamayan & J. S. Damico (Eds.), *Limiting bias in the assessment of bilingual students* (pp. 157–218). Austin, TX: PRO-ED.

Day-Vines, N. L., & Patton, J. M. (2003, February–March). The perils, pitfalls, and promises of the No Child Left Behind Act of 2001: Implications for the education of African American and other minority learners. *T/TAL Link Lines*, pp. 1–5.

Grossman, H. (2004). *Classroom management for diverse and inclusive schools*. Oxford, England: Rowman & Littlefield.

Individuals with Disabilities Education Amendments Act, 20 U.S.C. §§ 1400 *et seq.* (1997).

Individuals with Disabilities Education Improvement Act of 2004. Pub. L. No. 108-446.

Jenkins, J. R., Antil, L. R., Wayne, S. K., & Vadasy, P. F. (2003). How cooperative learning works for special education and remedial students. *Exceptional Children, 69,* 279, 292.

Kamps, D. M. (2002). Preventing problems by improving behavior. In B. Algozzine & P. Kay (Eds.), *Preventing problem behaviors: A handbook of successful prevention strategies* (pp. 11–36). Thousand Oaks, CA: Corwin Press.

Kauffman, J. M. (2005). *Characteristics of emotional and behavioral disorders of children and youth* (8th ed.). Upper Saddle River, NJ: Merrill/Prentice Hall.

Knotek, S. (2001). Bias in problem solving and the social process of student study team: A qualitative investigation of two SST's. *The Journal of Special Education, 37,* 2–14.

Lo, Y. Y., & Cartledge, G. (2001). They are more than just reports: Using office discipline referrals to increase school disciplinary effectiveness. *Principal Magazine, 20*(2), 1–3.

National Research Council (2002). *Minority students in special and gifted education*. Washington, DC: National Academy Press.

Obiakor, F. E. (2004, October). *Impact of changing demographics on public education for culturally diverse learners with behavior problems: Implications for teacher preparation*. Keynote Address at the Eagle Summit, University of North Texas Institute for Behavioral and Learning Differences, Dallas, TX.

Obiakor, F. E., & Beachum, F. D. (2005, Winter). Developing self-empowerment in African American students using the comprehensive support model. *The Journal of Negro Education, 74,* 18–29.

Obiakor, F. E., Enwefa, S., Utley, C. A., Obi, S. O., Gwalla-Ogisi, N., & Enwefa, R. (2004). *Serving culturally and linguistically diverse students with emotional and behavioral disorders*. Arlington, VA: The Council for Children with Behavioral Disorders.

Obiakor, F. E., & Smith, D. J. (2005). Understanding the power of words in multicultural education and interaction. In R. Hoosain & F. Salili (Eds.), *Language in multicultural education* (pp. 77–92). Greenwich, CT: Information Age.

Obiakor, F. E., & Utley, C. A. (2004). Educating culturally diverse learners with exceptionalities: A critical analysis of the *Brown* case. *Peabody Journal of Education, 79,* 141–156.

Ochoa, S. H., Robles-Pina, R., Garcia, S. B., & Breunig, N. (1999). School psychologists' perspectives on referrals of language minority students. *Multiple Voices, 3*(1), 1–13.

Ortiz, A. A. (2001, December). *English language learners with special needs: Effective instructional strategies.* Washington, DC: ERIC Clearinghouse on Languages and Linguistics.

Orza, J. L., & Zirpoli, T. J. (2004). Cultural influences on behavior. In T. J. Zirpoli, *Behavior management: Applications for teachers* (4th ed., pp. 470–518). Upper Saddle River, NJ: Merrill/Prentice Hall.

Osher, D., Woodruff, D., & Sims, A. (2001). Schools make a difference: The overrepresentation of African American youth in special education and the juvenile justice system. In D. Losen & G. Orfield (Eds.), *Racial inequality in special education* (pp. 93–116). Cambridge, MA: Harvard Education Press.

Oswald, D. P., & Coutinho, M. J. (2001). Trends in disproportionate representation in special education: Implications for multicultural education policies. In C. A. Utley & F. E. Obiakor (Eds.), *Special education, multicultural education, and school reform: Components of a quality education for students with mild disabilities* (pp. 53–73). Springfield, IL: Charles C Thomas.

Salend, S. J. (2005). *Creating inclusive classrooms: Effective and reflective practices for all students* (5th ed.). Upper Saddle River, NJ: Merrill/Prentice Hall.

Salend, S. J., Duhaney, L. M., & Montgomery, W. (2002). A comprehensive approach to identifying and addressing issues of disproportionate representation. *Remedial and Special Education, 23*(5), 289–299.

Salend, S. J., & Taylor, L. (2002). Cultural perspectives: Missing pieces in the functional assessment process. *Intervention in School and Clinic, 38*(2), 104–112.

Sugai, G., Horner, R. H., & Sprague, J. R. (1999). Functional assessment based behavior support planning: Research to practice to research. *Behavioral Disorders, 24*, 253–257.

Sugai, G., Sprague, J. R., Horner, R., & Walker, H. M. (2000). Preventing school violence: The use of office discipline referrals to assess and monitor school-wide discipline interventions. *Journal of Emotional and Behavioral Disorders, 8*(2), 94–102.

Utley, C. A., Kozleski, E., Smith, A., & Draper, I. L. (2002). Positive behavior support: A proactive strategy for minimizing behavior problems in urban multicultural youth. *Journal of Positive Behavior Interventions, 4*(4), 196–207.

Utley, C. A., & Obiakor, F. E. (2001). *Special education, multicultural education, and school reform: Components of a quality education for students with mild disabilities.* Springfield, IL: Charles C Thomas.

Chapter 8

Working with Multicultural Learners with Gifts and Talents

Vera I. Daniels

Chapter Outline

Thinking About Multicultural Special Education

Jabari, a 10-year-old African American male, was a fifth grader who attended an elementary school in an economically disadvantaged school district. There were 25 other students in Jabari's class, and all were African American. His teacher, Mrs. Jones, a 27-year-old white teacher, said that Jabari was quite different from the other students in her class. Jabari did his class work quickly; acquired, retained, and learned new information easily; and demonstrated remarkable critical thinking skills. Even when Jabari appeared not to be attentive to instruction, he surprisingly demonstrated good understanding of the skills and answered inquiry-type questions correctly 99% of the time. Mrs. Jones also noted that when Jabari finished his class work, rather than sitting quietly to wait for his classmates to complete theirs, he continually interrupted the class by asking questions that were beyond the scope of the class activity. Because of these behaviors, Mrs. Jones described Jabari as a child with unusual skills and abilities.

After objectively thinking about Jabari's exceptional abilities, Mrs. Jones decided to list all of Jabari's strengths and shortcomings. In addition to those already noted, Mrs. Jones added the following: Jabari was very inquisitive, had knowledge of information on a variety of topics, and had good reading and comprehension skills. Jabari had an unusually large vocabulary, and his responses to inquiry-based questions had more breadth and depth than typical responses of youngsters his age. Also, Jabari demonstrated a remarkable ability to think logically and reason using intellectual standards. He performed well on class activities, always completed his in-class assignments before his peers, and obtained a 95 to 100% accuracy rate on these tasks. Jabari liked to be alone and enjoyed intellectually stimulating challenges. Even though he worked cooperatively in small group settings, he frequently asked Mrs. Jones why he had to be part of a group. Despite his dislike for group activities, his peers looked up to him.

Mrs. Jones came from an upper-class background. She had no firsthand experiences with students from multicultural backgrounds, and she had limited experiences interacting with individuals of diverse ethnic and racial groups. However, she had taken a course in multicultural education and one in learning theories. Mrs. Jones was puzzled as to why Jabari was in her class. Being new to the school, she decided to speak with several of Jabari's former teachers, all of whom were African American. His former teachers said that Jabari was a very smart student who created havoc in their classrooms by asking off-the-wall questions or questions that had nothing to do with the class activity; and he always wanted to do things different from the rest of the class. In general, they all described Jabari as a child who loved to "show off." When asked if they had ever thought about referring Jabari for gifted education, all of them said "no."

When asked why not, none of them could give a plausible reason, other than that they viewed Jabari as being a nuisance, a show-off, and a child who just wanted attention.

Mrs. Jones was perplexed by what she heard. She was even more convinced that something was uniquely different about Jabari and was determined to find out what it was. First, Mrs. Jones adjusted her instruction to be more responsive to Jabari's needs and learning style. For 5 consecutive weeks following the implementation of curricular modifications, Mrs. Jones noticed an even more remarkable increase in Jabari's learning and performance. Next, she contacted Jabari's mother, shared her observations of Jabari's unique skills and abilities, and recommended that Jabari undergo a formal evaluation for giftedness. Approximately 3 weeks after her meeting with Jabari's mother, Jabari underwent testing for giftedness, and later he was placed in a class for gifted learners. This class was comprised of 10 white and 4 Latino youngsters. Two months later, Mrs. Broadstreet, Jabari's gifted education teacher, told Mrs. Jones that Jabari had adjusted well in her class, and that he had excelled tremendously since being there. Mrs. Jones was elated to hear the good news and was pleased that she had been able to recognize Jabari's extraordinary skills and abilities. Jabari hugged and thanked Mrs. Jones and asked if he could come back to her class as a volunteer peer tutor to satisfy his school service requirement.

- *Why do you think that Jabari's former teachers were unable to recognize that the behaviors exhibited by Jabari were signs or indicators of giftedness?*
- *What do you think were the key factors that caused Mrs. Jones to recommend a functional assessment to determine if her suspicions about Jabari's learning potential were plausible?*

Jabari's situation is not unique. There are many youngsters with gifts and talents from multicultural backgrounds and disadvantaged environments. Students with gifts and talents can be found among all racial, cultural, ethnic, socioeconomic, and linguistic backgrounds (Daniels, 2003). Yet gifted multicultural students who are economically disadvantaged and those whose first language is not English are not visible in gifted programs (Frasier, García, & Passow, 1995). The disparity in multicultural student representation in gifted programs may be attributed to historical, philosophical, psychological, theoretical, procedural, and sociopolitical factors (see Frasier et al.), as well as test bias and the lack of available assessment approaches that are grounded by the worldviews, ethos, and cultures of multicultural groups. Despite the shortcomings of traditional assessment procedures and the reliance on such measures for assessment and identification purposes, these procedures have substantially affected the disproportionate representation of multicultural students in gifted education programs. Concerns about the disproportionate representation of these students (especially African American, Latino, and American Indian, as well as students from other underrepresented populations) in gifted programs evolved as a result of gaps in the knowledge base (e.g., articles, reports, research studies, and other publications) in the field of gifted education focusing on gifted multicultural students, and from the difficulty of educators, policymakers, and other stakeholders in finding solutions to reverse this persistent and pervasive problem (Ford, 1998; Ford, Baytops, & Harmon, 1997). Although the causes of multicultural underrepresentation are not fully understood, it is evident that forces such as poverty, discrimination, prejudice, low socioeconomic status, school bias, teacher bias, inequitable school experience, ineffective prereferral strategy, low teacher referral, and teacher quality are among the contributing factors.

Looking back at Jabari's case, we can hypothesize a number of mitigating factors as to why he was not referred for gifted education prior to fifth grade. The issue of teacher quality in conjunction with teacher bias and the forces of poverty seem to be among the major contributing factors. Other factors contributing to the underidentification of multicultural learners in gifted and talented programs include varying conceptions of intelligence, definitions of giftedness, and the inability of teachers to recognize the potential of these students. Teacher deficiency in the use of culturally responsive or culturally sensitive pedagogy, their refusal to use alternative instructional practices to empower student learning, and school district policies and procedures that underscore and guide gifted programs are also included among these factors. Assessment and identification systems, particularly those that look at the construct of giftedness from a unidimensional rather than a multidimensional or multifaceted (multimodal) assessment approach, and the lack of standardized assessments appropriate for use with students who are English-language learners (Daniels, 2003; Ford, 1998; Obiakor, 1999) also contribute to disproportionate representation in gifted programs.

Support for multidimensional approaches to assessment stem from the contention that these approaches draw heavily on qualitative and quantitative information to portray a more accurate and equitable identification. In addition, they stem from the notion that such approaches ensure that identification practices are inclusive, rather than exclusive; they also ensure practices that identify potentially gifted students, underachievers, multicultural students, and other students from historically underrepresented groups (Ford, 1996). Clearly, sources of information for multidimensional assessment approaches vary widely. They may include indices of students' cognitive abilities from group and individual intelligence tests, performance scores on achievement and informal tests, biographical inventories, artifacts or samples of student work from the student portfolio, checklists, teacher nominations, parent nominations, and peer or self-nominations (Clark, 2002; Coleman, 2003; Daniels, 2003; Ford, 1996; Piirto & Heward, 2003). They may also include direct observations, information about students across multiple class and time periods, and extracurricular or leisure activities (see Clark, 1997; Coleman, 2003; Piirto & Heward, 2003). In Jabari's case, Mrs. Jones took a multidimensional approach. She objectively outlined Jabari's learning and behavioral assets as well as his limitations. Impressively, she queried his former teachers about their observations of him.

CHARACTERISTICS OF MULTICULTURAL LEARNERS WITH GIFTS AND TALENTS

Children with gifts and talents possess an array of abilities and skills. Some demonstrate outstanding cognitive and intellectual abilities, aptitude, and leadership. Others demonstrate extraordinary talents, creative abilities, psychomotor skills, and extraordinary abilities in the visual and performing arts (Daniels, 2003). In addition, these children are described as those who obtain IQ (intelligent quotient) scores that are three or more standard deviations above the mean on intelligence tests. Using Gardner's (1983) concept of multiple intelligences, many indicators of giftedness can be found among children of all racial, ethnic, linguistic, and socioeconomic backgrounds. These indicators, based on Gardner's theory, can be subsumed under the auspices of seven distinct intelligences—linguistic intelligence, logical and mathematical intelligence, visual and spatial intelligence, musical intelligence, bodily kinesthetic intelligence, interpersonal intelligence, and intrapersonal intelligence—each of which corresponds to a particular type of giftedness. Given this premise, teachers who are cognizant of these indicators of giftedness (i.e., have knowledge and awareness of behaviors that denote special skills, abilities, and talents) are more likely to recognize multicultural students with gifts and talents. Further, teachers cognizant of these constructs are better able to identify curricula, instructional modifications, and strategies that unmask the gifts of high-ability children of multicultural groups. For instance, in Jabari's case, the indicators of giftedness were obvious. Mrs. Jones was able to recognize these indicators almost immediately (e.g., he was a critical thinker and a quick learner with the ability to acquire, retain, and learn information). What was of concern was that his former teachers did not recognize or identify these behaviors as indicators of giftedness.

Academic and Learning Capabilities

Students with gifts and talents share many characteristics that are similar to those of other students. What is different about these students, in comparison to their age-mates, is the degree and extent of these characteristics (Roberts, 2003). In general, they have unusual cognitive and information-processing abilities. They can acquire, retain, and learn new information easily and rapidly. They can easily comprehend abstract and complex concepts and relationships; conceptualize, generalize, and synthesize information; and easily manipulate large amounts of information. In addition, they are intellectually curious and highly verbal. They show a propensity for learning, have an excellent memory, and have a sustained level of attention and concentration. These children can also perceive and recognize relationships among seemingly unrelated facts, ideas, and thoughts. They are usually early readers, often ahead of their age-mates as reflected by their performance on academic tasks. These learners are achievement-oriented and easily bored if they are not given work that they consider challenging (Hallahan & Kauffman, 2003). Sometimes, they daydream and exhibit high levels of energy that may get them in trouble (Roberts, 2003).

Students with gifts and talents have a large vocabulary, a good memory for things heard or read (Van Tassel-Baska, 1998), and the ability to think logically or reason by analogy (Schwartz, 1997). They ask probing questions, are widely informed about many topics, and are independent workers. Additionally, these youngsters have lots of initiative and can effortlessly produce original and/or unusual products and ideas. Although many intellectually gifted children display highly exceptional abilities in the cognitive arena, it is important to remember that not all gifted children will display all of these characteristics. It is equally important to note that some gifted and talented youngsters may exhibit inter- or intraindividual differences (Piirto & Heward, 2003); and "when teachers fail to respond to the intraindividual and interindividual differences of students . . . instruction becomes loaded with inappropriate assumptions, prejudicial expectations, negative stereotypes, and illusory conclusions" (Obiakor, 1999, p. 41). In Jabari's case, it was obvious that he exhibited a substantial amount of extraordinary abilities that warranted assessment for giftedness. Unfortunately, he was not given the opportunity to demonstrate his true abilities. His former teachers regarded his inquisitiveness and astuteness as annoying, show-off, and attention-seeking behaviors. Mrs. Jones, on the other hand, had a different perspective of Jabari's behaviors. She viewed his behaviors as characteristic of giftedness and actively sought to address them.

Social and Emotional Abilities

One of the most common misconceptions about students with gifts is that they are socially inept and emotionally unstable (Hallahan & Kauffman, 2000). Although some of them may feel different, misunderstood, and socially isolated (Hunt & Marshall, 2002), most are healthy, self-sufficient, emotionally well adjusted, independent, stable, sensitive (Hallahan & Kauffman, 2003), and insightful (Silverman, 1993; Van Tassel-Baska, 1998). Even though they are generally well liked by their peers (Hallahan & Kauffman, 2003), some hide or camouflage their giftedness to be more socially acceptable to their peers (Davis & Rimm, 2004). Additionally, they tend to show an advanced level of moral behavior and a keen sense of justice (Silverman, 1993; Van Tassel-Baska, 1998). They are quick to question authority; respond to perceived injustices to themselves and others when they perceive those in authority are illogical, irrational, erroneous, or unjust (Silverman, 1993); point out incongruencies in situations; and have a strong sense of pride, self-worth, and strong leadership ability (Schwartz, 1997). Sometimes, they tend to be hypersensitive, highly emotional, empathetic, and impulsive (Clark, 1997; Silverman, 1993; Van Tassel-Baska, 1998); and they get upset and display maladaptive behaviors when they feel they are discriminated against and prevented from realizing their full potential (Hallahan & Kauffman, 2003).

Students with gifts and talents have an excellent sense of humor, a vivid imagination, and a capacity for reflection (Silverman, 1993; Van Tassel-Baska, 1998). Many display characteristics of perfectionism (Silverman, 1993) and are frustrated when they are unable to meet the expectations that they have of themselves and the expectations that others (e.g., parents and teachers) have of them (Hardman, Drew, & Egan, 2005). Others feel pressured to achieve at high academic levels and to select particular professions (see Hardman et al.). Although they have many extraordinary and remarkable skills, abilities, and talents, they are confronted with a number of social-emotional challenges. As Van Tassel-Baska noted, these students

1. understand the ways in which they are different from other children and the ways in which they are the same,
2. appreciate and treasure their own individuality and individual differences of others,
3. understand and develop social skills that allow them to cope adequately within relationships,
4. develop an appreciation for their high-level sensitivity that manifests itself in humor, artistic endeavors, and intensified emotional experiences,
5. gain realistic assessment of their abilities and talents and how they can be nurtured,
6. develop an understanding of the distinction between "pursuit of excellence" and "pursuit of perfection,"
7. learn the art and science of compromise.

In Jabari's case, he was a relatively well-adjusted youngster, considering his current school placement. Although he enjoyed being alone and was very adamant in his feelings about not wanting to participate in small group activities (e.g., continually questioning why he had to be a part of a group), he was a cooperative team player. Also, as a result of being placed in a gifted education program, he seemed to freely interact with his peers. In fact, Jabari asked Mrs. Jones if he could volunteer as a peer tutor in her class to satisfy his school service requirement.

EDUCATIONAL CONSIDERATIONS FOR MULTICULTURAL LEARNERS WITH GIFTS AND TALENTS

The characteristics and needs of children with gifts and talents play an important role in defining appropriate instruction for them. To identify learning needs and facilitate the learning of these students, teachers need to have knowledge of the cultural particularities as well as the cognitive, academic, and affective (social-emotional) characteristics of these youngsters. They need to have an understanding of their learning style preferences and how to capitalize on them. Additionally, they must have knowledge of and skills in using culturally responsive pedagogy.

Learning Style Preferences

Learning styles describe how a person thinks, perceives, remembers, understands, internalizes, learns, reacts, and responds to various information, circumstances, situations, and events within his or her instructional setting (Saracho, 1988). As a group, multicultural learners, including those with gifts and talents, tend to show preferences for certain cognitive orientations and learning style preferences (Clark, 2002). Yet the teaching methods used in schools are in stark contrast to the learning styles of most of these learners (Daniels, 2003). Implications of the interaction effects of learning styles, teaching effectiveness, and student performance (across the spectrum of class or race) have been discussed extensively in the literature (e.g., Clark, 2002; Ford, 1996, 1998; Franklin, 1992; Patton & Townsend, 1997).

The choices that teachers make when providing instruction to multicultural students with gifts and talents depend, to a large degree, on their understanding of the cultures and learning styles of these youngsters and their individualistic teaching styles. Many multicultural learners (e.g., African American, Latino, and Asian American/Pacific Islanders) are field-dependent/field-sensitive learners (Daniels, 2003; Ford, 1996; Franklin, 1992; Shade, 1994). Field-dependent learners (especially African Americans) tend to be holistic, relational, global, concrete, visual, kinesthetic, and tactile learners (Ford, 1996; Ford & Webb, 1994). They approach learning intuitively rather than logically or analytically (Ford, 1996, 1998; Shade, 1994); find their success in cooperative rather than competitive learning situations; prefer group work rather than individual learning experiences (Ford & Webb, 1994); and prefer tactile and kinesthetic learning and teaching experiences (Ford, 1996). Field-dependent students also depend on authority and are strongly interested in helping people (Grossman, 1990).

Latino students share many learning style preferences similar to those of African American students. Although there is limited research on the learning style preferences of Latino students (Griggs & Dunn, 1995), they exhibit some learning style preferences that are culturally specific. Large numbers of Latino students have preferences for a cool environment, formal design, conformity, peer-oriented learning, kinesthetic instructional resources, a high degree of structure, and variety in instruction (see Griggs & Dunn). They often seek close relationships with teachers and are more comfortable learning broad concepts rather than component facts and specifics (Guild, 1994). Asian American/Pacific Islander students prefer to learn by observation, memorization, patterned practice, and rote rather than discovery learning (Sileo & Prater, 1998; Timm & Chiang, 1997). They seek teacher approval, make personal and academic decisions based on what the teacher thinks (Manning & Baruth, 2004), and seldom express their opinions, ideals, or abilities voluntarily. On the other hand, field-independent students tend to be more independent and analytical learners (Ford, 1996, 1998) rather than global/concrete learners. They prefer to work by themselves or to receive impersonal, direct types of instruction. These students are intrinsically motivated and thrive on competitive learning situations (Ford, 1996). Field-independent students are also task-oriented learners. They exhibit greater competence in using their cognitive abilities in instructional environments to learn and comprehend new and difficult information, and they favor instruction that is direct and impersonal (Saracho, 1993). Further, these students are less interactive with their classmates, and they have a general tendency to prefer working independently on academic tasks.

American Indian students are largely field-independent and reflective thinkers (Guild, 1994; Kaulback, 1997); and they are generally soft spoken, cooperative, and patient. These students have acute skills in visual discrimination and in the use of imagery (Guild, 1994). In addition, American Indian students tend to process information globally rather than analytically and prefer to learn using visual/perceptual/spatial information and the use of mental images to enhance their memorization, recall, and understanding of words and concepts (Manning & Baruth, 2004; Utley, 1983). Although schools sanction field-independent, abstract, and analytical styles of teaching and learning (Ford, 1996), the instructional methods that perpetuate these practices are incongruent with the learning styles (field-dependent) of many multicultural students. Teaching these students in ways that complement their learning styles can improve academic performance; accentuate gifts and talents that may otherwise be unrecognized; and reduce underachievement, low academic performance, and school dropout (Daniels, 2001). Interestingly, Jabari had a clearly defined learning preference, which did not fit the typical profile of youngsters of his cultural group. Jabari was a field-independent learner, whereas most African Americans are field-dependent/field-sensitive learners. Having knowledge of learning style preferences and knowing their effect on teaching effectiveness, Mrs. Jones modified her instruction to accommodate Jabari's learning style. Interestingly, Jabari then demonstrated an even more remarkable increase in his learning performance.

Educational Programming

Efforts to provide multicultural learners with gifts and talents with equitable educational opportunities have been inundated with problems, despite the range of educational programming and service delivery options (e.g., enrichment, accelerated, and combination programs; cluster programs, pull-out programs, special classes, and ability grouping). For some reason, many of the existing programs do not infuse critical elements that provide for the individual needs of gifted and talented multicultural learners. In addition, there appears to be an absence of federal policy mandating the development and implementation of an individualized education plan such as that prescribed for students with disabilities (Daniels, 2003). As it stands, the literature focusing on instructional, curricular, or programming options for gifted multicultural learners is limited. It is known, however, that these learners perform at higher levels when they receive instruction that is culturally responsive. Gay (2002) defined culturally responsive teaching as

> using the cultural characteristics, experiences, and perspectives of ethnically diverse students as conduits for teaching them more effectively. It is based on the assumption that when academic knowledge and skills are situated within the lived experiences and frames of reference of students, they are more personally meaningful, have higher interest appeal, and are learned more easily and thoroughly. (p. 106)

Teachers and service providers who lack a repertoire of practical ideas, strategies, and techniques within a culturally laden paradigm are culturally inept in their interpretation of the affective, social, emotional, psychological, and motivational needs of students with gifts and talents. In addition, they have inappropriate attitudes and instruct learners in ways that are incongruent with evidence-based effective teaching practices that optimize the ability of gifted multicultural students to develop their potential and achieve success. It is clear that Mrs. Jones was an avid user of field-dependent instructional practices because her students were African American. Thus, she did not consider alternative approaches to instruction. However, upon conducting a functional assessment of Jabari's academic and social behaviors, Mrs. Jones refocused her instruction to match Jabari's learning preferences to further validate her suspicions of his special abilities before referring him for gifted education.

Culturally Responsive Teaching

A number of factors can enhance giftedness. Some of these factors include recognizing indicators of giftedness and accomplishments of students from cultural perspectives; creating stimulating and nurturing learning environments; matching teaching-learning styles; involving students in class projects that have purpose, direction, meaning, and specific outcomes; using innovative teaching techniques; infusing technology in teaching; and using meaningful, challenging, and conceptually rich culturally embedded differentiated curricula. Also, a number of factors can inhibit giftedness. Among these factors are boredom; poor teaching; limited opportunities to learn; inappropriate curricula; family disorganization; abuse, neglect, and drugs; teachers' attitudes; and school climates (Daniels, 2001, 2003). Experiential deprivation during childhood, a lack of cognitive stimulation, limited language development, learning style differences, lack of positive role models, low teacher and parent expectations, peer pressure, a lack of parental involvement, strained or difficult relationships with parents or guardians, cultural differences, racial biases, and lack of opportunities are also potential contributors to inhibition. Successful teaching of multicultural students, including those with gifts and talents, requires instruction by teachers who not only have a knowledge base of diverse cultures and the particularities of specific ethnic groups, but who also use culturally responsive pedagogy (Gay, 2002). Many scholars and educators (e.g., Clark, 2002; Ford, 1996; Ford & Trotman, 2001; Franklin, 1992; Gay, 2002; Obiakor, 1999; Van Tassel-Baska, 1998) agree that culturally responsive teaching styles positively influence the way multicultural students learn.

Ford (1996) identified some critical characteristics of culturally competent and responsible teachers. As she described, such teachers possess:

1. **Self-Awareness and Self-Understanding**—These teachers are aware of themselves as cultural beings and knowledgeable about their own cultural heritage and how it affects them. In addition, they are aware of their biases, attitudes, and values and how they influence the educational process. In other words, they are comfortable with students of different racial, ethnic, and cultural backgrounds; and they seek educational training, experiences, and consultation to enhance their effectiveness in teaching and working with multicultural learners.

2. **Cultural Awareness and Understanding**—These teachers are aware of their negative reactions toward students of different cultures and strive to be nonjudgmental. They are aware of how cultural differences influence and conflict with their teaching as well as with their students' learning; and they are aware of culturally sensitive identification and assessment practices. In other words, they seek to address educational inequities and advocate for multicultural learners who are confronted with injustices. They are actively involved in family and community events with these learners outside the school setting, and they work with their students' families to enhance the educational process.

3. **Social Responsiveness and Responsibility**—These teachers seek to increase both their awareness and their students' awareness and understanding of students of different cultures. In addition, they try to increase unity and harmony among students of different cultures within their classroom and seek ways to address issues of social injustices. In other words, they are able to address inequities that may arise in the classroom; seek to encourage and empower students to be proactive; and are aware of and respectful of cultural differences.

4. **Use of Appropriate Techniques and Strategies**—These teachers have an understanding of social and institutional barriers that prevent multicultural learners from having an equitable education. They are knowledgeable of teaching practices and how they may conflict with multicultural values. In other words, they are willing to adapt teaching styles to their students' learning styles. In addition, they modify curriculum and instruction to be culturally sensitive and are willing to engage students in a variety of ways to help them learn.

Ford's ideas were reiterated by Villegas and Lucas (2002) when they noted that a culturally responsive teacher and practitioner

> (a) is socioculturally conscious, that is, recognizes that there are multiple ways of perceiving reality and that these ways are influenced by one's location in the social order; (b) has affirming views of students from diverse backgrounds, seeing resources for learning in all students rather than viewing differences as problems to be overcome; (c) sees himself or herself as both responsible for and capable of bringing about educational change that will make schools more responsive to all students; (d) understands how learners construct knowledge and is capable of promoting learners' knowledge construction; (e) knows about the lives of his or her students; and (f) uses his or her knowledge about students' lives to design instruction that builds on what they already know while stretching them beyond the familiar. (p. 21)

Successful teaching of multicultural learners with gifts and talents also requires the establishment of culturally responsive classroom environments. Ford and Trotman (2001) identified several characteristics of culturally responsive classrooms. In their view, culturally responsive classrooms have culturally relevant pedagogy, equity pedagogy, a holistic teaching philosophy, a communal philosophy, a respect for students' primary language, culturally congruent instructional practices, culturally sensitive assessment, student-family-teacher relationships, and teacher diversity. Thus, culturally responsive teachers place students at the center of teaching and learning. They feel obligated and responsible for their students' cognitive, academic, and affective well-being (see Ford & Trotman); and they employ teaching methods tailored toward improving the intellectual, social, emotional, political, and cultural growth of their students (Ladson-Billings, 1995). In the case of Jabari, Mrs. Jones demonstrated characteristics of a culturally responsive teacher. She conducted a functional assessment of Jabari's behavior and response style and recognized indicators of giftedness Jabari exhibited. Then she placed him at the center of teaching and learning; and she felt obligated and responsible for ensuring that he received cognitive, academic, and affective nurturing so he would flourish. Mrs. Jones matched her teaching style to Jabari's learning style and made a decision to refer him for gifted education so that he could be taught in an appropriate learning environment. In addition, she was self-aware and understanding of her biases. She was culturally aware and able to redefine her frame of reference to address the inequities within her thinking about multicultural students.

A Culturally Responsive Educator

1. Understands that students with gifts and talents can be found among people of all racial, cultural, ethnic, socioeconomic, and linguistic backgrounds.
2. Knows that all students with gifts and talents cannot learn in the same way and that optimal learning occurs when teachers know their students' learning styles and consider these styles when creating environments for learning.
3. Understands that students who exhibit giftedness or show exceptional abilities often are not detected or recognized because of lack of knowledge of indicators of potential giftedness.
4. Has a substantive knowledge base of cultural characteristics, experiences, and perspectives of multicultural learners.
5. Knows indicators and characteristics of giftedness and uses culturally responsive pedagogical strategies to teach.
6. Creates culturally responsive classroom environments for multicultural learners with gifts and talents.
7. Understands that multicultural learners with gifts and talents need highly qualified service providers and professionals who are sensitive to their needs.
8. Knows that multicultural learners with gifts and talents are confronted with a number of socioemotional challenges.

9. Uses multidimensional methods to assess multiple intelligences of multicultural learners.
10. Values emotional intelligence and creativity as important instructional ingredients for students with gifts and talents.

Conclusion

Although students with gifts and talents can be found across the spectrum of racial, ethnic, cultural, and linguistically diverse backgrounds, they are still underrepresented in gifted programs. It is not clear as to how this pervasive problem can be reversed, but it is clear that meeting the needs of multicultural learners with gifts and talents will require teaching behaviors and strategies that are culturally responsive and aligned to their learning styles. Jabari's case presents a very interesting perspective and raises a number of questions about teacher quality, teacher accountability, and student learning. When Jabari's former teachers observed that he was different from other students, they did not nurture or cultivate his academic growth. They viewed his behaviors as those of a child who wanted to show off and be at the center of attention. Mrs. Jones, on the other hand, used her knowledge of multicultural education and learning theories and her professional dispositions to facilitate and transform Jabari's learning and educational experiences. She was able to "think outside the box" to accomplish her goal of ensuring that Jabari's abilities were not stifled by a failure of the educational system to recognize his unique abilities.

The misguided perceptions of teachers of multicultural learners and the stereotypical assumptions they sometimes have about the capabilities of these learners are central to disproportionate placements in gifted programs. Jabari's case underscores the fact that even those teachers who meet the standard(s) of highly qualified do not necessarily have the skills to recognize and respond to the needs of multicultural learners with gifts and talents. Mrs. Jones, in this situation, respected cultural differences; and she believed Jabari, though from a nondominate group, was a highly capable learner. She based her perceptions of Jabari's abilities on his academic performance in her class; his ways of thinking, talking, and behaving; and his former teachers' perspectives of his behavior. By exposing Jabari to an intellectually enriching curriculum with high performance standards, Mrs. Jones was able to validate her suspicions of Jabari's unique abilities, which ultimately led to Jabari being provided appropriate educational services. One can argue that the academic lag of multicultural students and their lack of high visibility in gifted programs can be attributable to low teacher expectations, thus making the source of the problem one of educational inequity, rather than one of cultural or genetic underpinnings. One might also argue that there is a clearly defined relationship between student learning and teacher quality. Regardless, Jabari's case explicitly underscores the fact that for optimal learning to occur, students from culturally diverse backgrounds need culturally responsive teachers. In addition, it draws attention to the fact that not all teachers who have met the criteria of highly qualified have the knowledge, skills, and dispositions to address academic and social learning needs of multicultural learners with gifts and talents.

Discussion Questions

1. Briefly analyze why Jabari's former teachers did not recognize that he had special skills and/or abilities until Mrs. Jones became his teacher.
2. As a future teacher, explain why is it important for teachers to be knowledgeable about the indicators of giftedness that are culturally sensitive to multicultural learners. Analyze two behavioral indicators that showed that Jabari exhibited special skills and abilities.
3. Discuss how schools can better inform teachers of the characteristics of multicultural learners with gifts and talents.
4. Summarize the primary source(s) of information that Mrs. Jones used to identify Jabari's special gifts and abilities.
5. Explain why a course in multicultural education, such as that taken by Mrs. Jones, can facilitate one's understanding of the unique skills and abilities of multicultural learners.

References

Clark, B. (1997). *Growing up gifted: Developing the potential of children at home and at school* (5th ed.). Upper Saddle River, NJ: Merrill/Prentice Hall.

Clark, B. (2002). *Growing up gifted: Developing the potential of children at home and at school* (6th ed.). Upper Saddle River, NJ: Merrill/Prentice Hall.

Coleman, M. R. (2003). *The identification of students who are gifted* (ERIC Digest No. E644). Arlington, VA: The Council for Exceptional Children.

Daniels, V. I. (2001). Responding to the learning needs of multicultural learners with gifts and talents. In C. A. Utley & F. E. Obiakor (Eds.), *Special education, multicultural education, and school reform: Components of a quality education for learners with mild disabilities* (pp. 140–154). Springfield, IL: Charles C Thomas.

Daniels, V. I. (2003). Students with gifts and talents. In F. E. Obiakor, C. A. Utley, & A. F. Rotatori (Eds.), *Effective education for learners with exceptionalities: Advances in special education* (pp. 325–348). Oxford, England: Elsevier Science/JAI Press.

Davis, G. A., & Rimm, S. B. (2004). *Education of the gifted and talented* (5th ed.). Boston: Allyn & Bacon.

Ford, D. Y. (1996). *Reversing underachievement among gifted black students: Promising practices and programs.* New York: Teachers College Press.

Ford, D. Y. (1998). The underrepresentation of minority students in gifted education: Problems and promises in recruitment and retention. *Journal of Special Education, 32*(1), 4–14.

Ford, D. Y., Baytops, J. L., & Harmon, D. A. (1997). Helping gifted minority students reach their potential: Recommendations for change. *Peabody Journal of Education, 72,* 201–216.

Ford, D. Y., & Trotman, M. F. (2001). Teachers of gifted students: Suggested multicultural characteristics and competencies. *Roeper Review, 23,* 235–239.

Ford, D. Y., & Webb, K. S. (1994). Desegregation of gifted educational programs: The impact of *Brown* on underachieving children of color. *Journal of Negro Education, 63,* 358–375.

Franklin, M. E. (1992). Culturally sensitive instructional practices for African-American learners with disabilities. *Exceptional Children, 59,* 115–122.

Frasier, M. M., García, J. H., & Passow, A. H. (1995). *A review of assessment issues in gifted education and their implications for identifying gifted minority students.* Storrs, CT: The National Research Center on the Gifted and Talented, University of Connecticut.

Gardner, H. (1983). *Frames of the mind: The theories of multiple intelligences.* New York: Basic Books.

Gay, G. (2002). Preparing for culturally responsive teaching. *Journal of Teacher Education, 53,* 106–116.

Griggs, S., & Dunn, R. (1995). Hispanic-American students and learning styles. *Emergency Librarian, 23,* 11–16.

Grossman, H. (1990). *Trouble-free teaching: Solutions to behavior problems in the classroom.* Mountain View, CA: Mayfield.

Guild, P. (1994). The culture/learning style connection. *Educational Leadership, 51,* 16–21.

Hallahan, D. P., & Kauffman, J. M. (2000). *Exceptional learners: Introduction to special education* (8th ed.). Needham Heights, MA: Allyn & Bacon.

Hallahan, D. P., & Kauffman, J. M. (2003). *Exceptional learners: Introduction to special education* (9th ed.). Boston: Allyn & Bacon.

Hardman, M. L., Drew, C. J., & Egan, M. W. (2005). *Human exceptionality: School, community, and family* (8th ed.). Boston: Allyn & Bacon.

Hunt, N., & Marshall, K. (2002). *Exceptional children and youth: An introduction to special education* (3rd ed.). Boston: Houghton Mifflin.

Kaulback, B. (1997). Styles of learning among Native American children: A review of research. In B. J. Shade (Ed.), *Culture, style, and the educative process: Making schools work for racially diverse students* (2nd ed., pp. 92–104). Springfield, IL: Charles C Thomas.

Ladson-Billings, G. (1995). Toward a theory of culturally relevant pedagogy. *American Educational Research Journal, 32,* 465-491.

Manning, M. L., & Baruth, L. G. (2004). *Multicultural education of children and adolescents* (4th ed.). Boston: Allyn & Bacon.

Obiakor, F. E. (1999). Teacher expectations of minority exceptional learners: Impact on "accuracy" of self-concepts. *Exceptional Children, 66,* 39–53.

Patton, J. M., & Townsend, B. L. (1997). Creating inclusive environments for African American children and youth with gifts and talents. *Roeper Review, 20,* 13–17.

Piirto, J., & Heward, W. L. (2003). Giftedness and talent. In W. L. Heward, *Exceptional children: An introduction to special education* (7th ed., pp. 526–565). Upper Saddle River, NJ: Merrill/Prentice Hall.

Roberts, J. L. (2003). Persons who are gifted and talented. In R. M. Gargiulo (Ed.), *Special education in contemporary society: A introduction to exceptionality* (pp. 315–361). Belmont, CA: Wadsworth/Thomson Learning.

Saracho, O. N. (1988). Cognitive styles: Implications for the preparation of early childhood teachers. *Early Child Development and Care, 38,* 1–11.

Saracho, O. N. (1993). Sociocultural perspectives in the cognitive styles of young students and teachers. *Early Child Development and Care, 84,* 1–17.

Schwartz, W. (1997). *Strategies for identifying the talents of diverse students.* (ERIC Reproduction Service No. ED410323)

Shade, B. J. (1994). Understanding the African American learner. In E. R. Hollins, J. E. King, & W. C. Hayman (Eds.), *Teaching diverse populations: Formulating a knowledge base* (pp. 175–189). New York: State University of New York Press.

Sileo, T. W., & Prater, M. A. (1998). Creating classroom environments that assess the linguistic and cultural backgrounds of students with disabilities: An Asian Pacific American perspective. *Remedial and Special Education, 19,* 323–337.

Silverman, L. K. (Ed.). (1993). *Counseling the gifted and talented.* Denver, CO: Love.

Timm, J., & Chiang, B. (1997). Among culture and cognitive style. In B. J. Shade (Ed.), *Culture, style, and the educative process: Making schools work for racially diverse students* (2nd ed., pp. 105–117). Springfield, IL: Charles C Thomas.

Utley, C. A. (1983). *A cross-cultural investigation of field-independence/field-dependence as a psychological variable in Menominee Native American Euro American grade school students.* Unpublished doctoral dissertation, University of Wisconsin–Madison, Madison.

Van Tassel-Baska, J. (1998). *Excellence in educating gifted & talented learners* (3rd ed.). Denver, CO: Love.

Villegas, A. M., & Lucas, T. (2002). Preparing culturally responsive teachers: Rethinking the curriculum. *Journal of Teacher Education, 53*(1), 20–32.

Chapter 9

Working with Multicultural Learners with Autism

Tina Taylor Dyches, Lynn K. Wilder, Bob Algozzine, and Festus E. Obiakor

Chapter Outline

Thinking About Multicultural Special Education

A special educator worked with the mother of Chul Woo, a 10-year-old boy with autism, assisting her in designing and implementing a behavior management program to address her son's problematic behavior at home. Chul Woo was Korean by ethnicity, although his parents were long-time residents of the United States. Chul Woo's father, Hyun Jin, worked for many years for a technology company, and his mother, Mee Sook, had been in the United States since she was 14. Both were university graduates, and Mee Sook spoke proficient English. Both parents had high expectations for their four other children; all but their son with autism were involved in gifted/talented programs, music lessons, art lessons, karate, and Korean school.

When Mee Sook and Hyun Jin learned that Chul Woo had autism, they immediately sought programs available to help their son. Chul Woo attended preschool, and Mee Sook learned several signs in American Sign Language so she could communicate with him. Although he later learned to speak in order to make basic requests, at age 10 he initiated meaningful speech less than 50% of the time. Most of his speech consisted of repeating what others had said; he was unable to explain or describe his feelings or to participate in a reciprocal conversation. He made repeated requests (mostly to his mother), which could be very tiresome. Rarely did he talk to his brothers; he only spoke when he felt his rights were being violated by his younger brother (e.g., when he felt interrupted while playing his video or computer games). Chul Woo typically did not choose to engage with others even during family activities; however, he enjoyed being tickled by his family. In designing an appropriate behavioral program, Mee Sook told the special educator that she wanted to see her son gain basic social, behavioral, and communication skills so he could play and interact with others.

Chul Woo received his elementary education at various public school programs for children with autism. Although his mother was satisfied with most of his special education teachers, Chul Woo continued to have behavioral challenges. One behavior the family found particularly troublesome was that he pounded his fists against the wall for intervals of up to 20 minutes. His mother found consultants and therapists who agreed to supervise an applied behavioral analysis program for him, but this proved to be too costly for the family. When Mee Sook found a doctor who specialized in autism and in special diets for children with autism, she began taking Chul Woo to see this doctor, whose office was in a large city one hour away from the family's home. Although she felt that she had seen an improvement in his health and ability to focus, Mee Sook was frustrated with her son's school situation. Many of his fellow students moved on to a class for children with less severe developmental problems, but Chul Woo "stayed back" in the class for students with more severe problems, despite her work with diet and other interventions. Apparently, Chul Woo had excellent parental support and good professional collaboration, but there were a few disappointments on the school front.

- *What role can Chul Woo's culture play as the family works with educational and medical systems to meet his needs?*
- *What are the prospects and problems of collaboration and consultation between Chul Woo's parents and educational professionals?*

The social, behavioral, and communication repertoires that Chul Woo exhibited are not atypical for a 10-year-old boy with autism. However, in addition to understanding his unique autistic characteristics and determining effective interventions for him, his teacher needs to examine the cultural factors implicit in his family. Home visits and frequent communication with the family are highly recommended for this purpose (see Campbell-Whatley & Gardner, 2002). One cultural factor teachers must consider is the importance of family roles and responsibilities. As a matter of fact, Chul Woo's father held traditional Korean views regarding the male's role in the family. He participated infrequently in housework and childrearing, noting that it was his responsibility to watch over family finances. His cultural framework, including the traditional male favoritism that exists in many Asian cultures (Smith, 2004), had implications for his son's education. First, the teacher communicated largely with the mother regarding Chul Woo's skills, and in collaboration with the parents, chose some classroom interventions and instruction based on what his mother could realistically reinforce at home, as well as what behavior his father preferred to see in his son. His mother appeared well informed about autism and was motivated to participate in meaningful interventions. However, his father did not participate directly in interventions.

Other cultural characteristics of Chul Woo's family were an emphasis on harmony, avoidance of conflict, and suppression of anger. His pounding behavior was of great concern because it disturbed the expected peaceful and harmonious atmosphere of his home. The parents chose this as the most problematic behavior that they desired the behavior specialist to help them replace. In addition, the culture of this family emphasized education and the arts; therefore if Chul Woo could have learned to listen, view with interest, or create his own works, his family would have been pleased. It is critical that professionals understand the cultural variables of different groups, since children with autism can be found in every nation, geographic area, and ethnic group. The Autism Society of America (2004b) Web site notes that autism "knows no racial, ethnic, or social boundaries. Family income, lifestyle, and educational levels do not affect the chance of autism's occurrence." This suggests that some environmental and cultural factors must be exonerated concerning the etiology of the disorder. Interestingly, the data from the Annual Report to Congress on the Individuals with Disabilities Education Act (IDEA) revealed significant differences in the occurrence of autism across ethnic groups in the United States for school-aged children (see Dyches, Wilder, & Obiakor, 2001; Dyches, Wilder, Sudweeks, Obiakor, & Algozzine, 2004).

Although past approaches to special education might be criticized for focusing solely on individualization according to student disability and not considering culture, the need for responding to cultural differences is gaining favor. Recent attention has been given to the importance of multicultural factors on learners with autism and their families (Dyches et al., 2001, 2004; Zionts & Zionts, 2003). Clearly, the family culture of a learner with autism has a great impact on several educational factors: whether the child is assessed and labeled as autistic, if and where the child receives services, how the parents should be approached in this collaborative relationship, and how the child should be instructed. This chapter defines autism, delineates characteristics of children with autism, discusses the assessment and classification of autism across cultures, and suggests educational strategies for multicultural learners with autism.

DEFINING AUTISM

Autism is a developmental disorder with neurological origins, present from birth or early in development. Considered to be a lifelong disorder, autism affects one's social skills, communication skills, and repertoire of behavior. Autism is manifested along a broad spectrum, meaning the skills and deficits vary greatly from one individual to another. For example, some children with autism may have normal or high IQs, while approximately 44 to 75% have intellectual disabilities (American Psychiatric Association, 1994; California Department of Developmental Services, 2003). Social skills may vary from social quirkiness to severe self-absorption. Some children with autism are highly verbal, while approximately half do not have functional speech (Prizant, 1996). Also, some have mildly odd patterns of behavior or interests, while many have persistent destructive and disruptive behavioral challenges.

Autism is categorized by the American Psychiatric Association (1994) as a Pervasive Developmental Disorder (PDD). Five main disorders are considered under this broad umbrella term: autistic disorder, Rett's disorder, childhood disintegrative disorder, Asperger's disorder, and pervasive developmental disorder not otherwise specified (PDD-NOS) (see Figure 9.1). It is generally accepted that all of the PDDs, except Rett's disorder (which has a distinct causation and characteristics that differ from those of the other PDDs), are similar enough to be called Autistic Spectrum Disorders (National Research Council, 2001). However, according to the Individuals with Disabilities Education Act of 1997 (IDEA '97), only autism is currently accepted as a distinct educational classification. In this chapter when we refer to autism, we are considering this spectrum of similar disorders, unless otherwise noted.

In 1981, the Secretary of Education moved autism from the federal category of severe emotional disturbance to that of other health impairments. The decision to change categorizations, made in consultation with the National Society for Autistic Children and the National Institute for Neurological and Communicative Disorders and Stroke, was based on evidence that autism is biologically rather than

FIGURE 9.1 Pervasive Developmental Disorder (PDD)

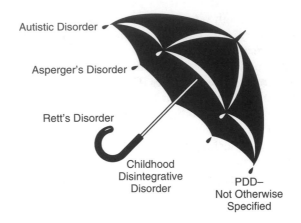

Autistic Disorder

Asperger's Disorder

Rett's Disorder

Childhood Disintegrative Disorder

PDD–Not Otherwise Specified

psychologically caused. Since 1990 autism has been a separate category in the federal classification system, and the 1991–92 school year was the first in which data were collected on the number of children and youth identified with autism. About 5,400 students with autism were identified at that time (U.S. Department of Education, 1993); recent figures include more than 78,000 students with autism. This increase of 1300% suggests that educational programs for children with autism are more common than ever before in history (U.S. Department of Education, 2002). The shift in categories reflects the recurrent debate among professionals about autism. Since Leo Kanner, a psychiatrist at Johns Hopkins University, first brought the disorder to public attention in 1943, professionals have debated the extent to which autism is a biological condition or is the result of family, environmental, or psychosocial factors. There is agreement that autism is a complex, brain-based developmental disorder in which multiple areas of functioning are affected.

CHARACTERISTICS OF AUTISM

Three main characteristics of autism are (a) impairment in reciprocal social interaction, (b) impairment in verbal and nonverbal communication, and (c) restrictive, repetitive, and stereotyped patterns of behavior, interests, and activities (American Psychiatric Association, 1994). These three characteristics have implications for cultural interpretations. Although these cultural interpretations should not be applied *carte blanche* to all multicultural families, or even to all families in the same cultural group, they should be viewed as a set of frameworks that families might employ when interacting with others (Park, 1996). The challenges that students like Chul Woo typically experience are highlighted in the following subsections.

Social Skills

Autism is primarily a social disorder. Deficits in social skills of learners with autism greatly affect their ability to communicate and behave appropriately with others. These social skills are most often unusual and delayed, resulting in challenges in relating to others. Many students have difficulty using nonverbal behaviors such as eye contact, facial expression, body postures, and gestures. Eye contact may not be valued by some families' cultures, particularly those in which looking an authority figure in the eye may be considered disrespectful, rude, argumentative, or even hateful (Lian, 1996). Teachers who neglect to learn the family's culturally based stance on nonverbal behaviors and continue to systematically teach children with autism to make eye contact may be violating the family's cultural values.

Deficits in social skills might be difficult for some families to accept, particularly those in cultures that value proper behavior in relationships as one of the highest virtues to be developed. For example, Chul Woo's family adhered to the philosophical teachings of Confucianism and expected their children to follow, with propriety, a "system of well-defined social relationships with one another" (Park, 1996, p. 196). Teachers should be aware of learners with autism who live in families with these social expectations, so they can understand compatible priorities in teaching skills that lead to such proper relationships (e.g., obedience to authority figures, respect for elders, and use of teachers' titles rather than their first names). In addition, students with autism experience extreme difficulty exhibiting developmentally appropriate peer relationships. This deficit may be of particular concern to Chul Woo's family, which considers social skills more important than academic goals (Park, 1996). Teachers must ascertain family priorities while developing the student's IEP so that the emphasis is placed on goals the family values.

Communication Skills

Communication impairments are some of the greatest challenges of learners with autism because these impairments affect children's ability to relate socially with others. Many of these learners are nonverbal and are unable to compensate via alternative modes of communication such as gesture, mime, pointing, or other natural techniques. Often learners with autism are taught to use augmentative communication devices such as picture boards, communication books, and computer software and hardware. However, teachers must be especially careful in suggesting such devices for multicultural learners, because the use of augmentative communication devices or systems is viewed as not natural and even more stigmatizing than unaided systems in some cultures (Harry et al., 1995).

Learners with autism who are able to speak are challenged in their ability to initiate, sustain, and terminate a conversation. These are skills Chul Woo had not yet developed. His teacher used a technique called *scripted communication*, which provides common conversational scripts to be memorized and used in daily interactions. Scripted communication may be an appropriate strategy for multicultural learners whose families interrelate better with oral involvement, such as chanting and storytelling (Benson, 1996). Many individuals with autism, like Chul Woo, display unusual abilities with verbal skills such as echoing (i.e., repeating back what has just been said) and perseverating (e.g., repeating the same words or phrases, or talking about the same subject for extended periods of time). This style of communication was demonstrated by Raymond Babbitt, the autistic man in the popular movie *Rainman,* who constantly counted the time left until he could watch his favorite show—"Four minutes 'til Wapner." These communicative behaviors were problematic for Chul Woo's parents, because they valued children who spoke only when spoken to and did not question authority. Sometimes, highly verbal learners with autism appear to be challenging others with their relentless questioning, yet they may only be trying to make sense of an environment they do not yet understand.

Behavioral Repertoire

Restrictive, repetitive, and stereotyped patterns of behavior, interests, and activities of many learners with autism often prevent them from learning effectively. These behaviors become problematic when their duration and intensity are excessive and interfere with productive academic and social activities. In some cases, learners with autism are over- or underresponsive to sensory stimulation (e.g., light, noise, and touch). These behaviors may be interpreted differently based upon one's cultural orientation. For example, Chul Woo's family, followers of Confucianism, valued the principles of good conduct (Park, 1996), and their children were expected to behave in school by being quiet rather than participating actively. These children were expected to follow adult directions with exactness rather than to be creative in their learning, and to trust the teacher instead of learning through inquiry and debate (Lian, 1996). Many learners with autism are naturally reluctant to actively engage in social learning. As a result of their cultural views, Chul Woo's parents were not concerned about his reticent behavior, which his teachers interpreted as being nonparticipatory and aloof.

On the other hand, some learners with autism, including many who are African American, may demonstrate higher verve in the classroom and be labeled hyperactive by their teachers (Benson, 1996). They may be exposed to "simultaneous variable stimulation" (Benson, 1996, p. 259) at home, where energy levels are high, people move about frequently, and visual/auditory entertainment is ongoing. Such learners may be bored in school environments where stimulation is low, and they may need frequent movement, touching, and playing to facilitate their learning. Some students with autism exhibit repetitive body movements such as rocking, pacing, spinning, and hand flapping. These self-stimulatory behaviors range from mildly odd to extremely self-encompassing. Families who do not want to draw attention to behavior that society considers deviant may shelter their children from the community to prevent embarrassing situations. Chul Woo's father did not like public attention, so he rarely took his son out of the house.

Although there are many characteristics which, when viewed as a whole, constitute a condition called *autism,* some argue that autism has its own culture (Dyches et al., 2001, 2004). Generally speaking, the symptoms of autism are innate within the individual, not necessarily learned through observation or imitation. Because many learners with autism have poor imitation skills and are not totally aware of social norms, their autistic characteristics are likely innate rather than learned. However, these behaviors may be misinterpreted when viewed prejudicially through different cultural lenses.

ASSESSMENT AND CLASSIFICATION OF MULTICULTURAL LEARNERS WITH AUTISM

The American Psychiatric Association (1994) indicated that autism occurs in 2 to 5 individuals per 10,000; however, more recent data indicate this figure could be as high as 1 in 323 births (California Department of Developmental Services, 2003). It is assumed that autism occurs across racial, ethnic, religious, and socioeconomic groups, yet there are reported differences in the prevalence of autism across racial categories. While investigating data from the United States Department of Education, Dyches and her colleagues (2001) found that students with autism of Asian/Pacific Islander or African American culture were served at approximately twice the rate of students with autism who were Latino or American Indian/Alaskan.

The discrepancies shown above have yet to be explained. Families from some nonwhite cultures may be reluctant to have their children identified as having autism, or identified as having a disability at all. Also, families of some socioeconomic groups may advocate for a diagnosis of autism to avoid the social stigma associated with mental retardation, a condition that often accompanies autism. It may be that some characteristics of autism are not considered problematic by people of some cultures (e.g., avoiding eye contact or displaying hyperactive or aggressive behaviors), which would result in the child not being referred. It is critical that scholars and educators continue to investigate questions regarding differences in prevalence across races.

INSTRUCTION OF MULTICULTURAL LEARNERS WITH AUTISM

The student is central in teaching-learning situations. For instructions to be culturally relevant, families must be involved as integral parts of the teaching and learning of all students, with or without disabilities (Obiakor & Wilder, 2004). As commonly recognized, when professionals become familiar with and show respect for the culture of a child's family, there is the likelihood of the family feeling appreciated and subsequently working collaboratively with the professionals to improve their child's social/behavioral and academic learning. As a result, professionals must examine their personal worldviews, family structure beliefs, interaction styles, disability perspectives, and other social behaviors to facilitate cross-cultural collaborations (Flexer, Baer, Luft, & Simmons, 2001; Obiakor, 2003). When a student has a significant disability such as autism, education professionals typically concern themselves mainly with the disability, often ignoring the learner's cultural and linguistic factors (Harry et al., 1995). But professionals who attend to these factors are able to better individualize services for students with disabilities. For example, it is critical that education teams assess multicultural students with autism in their native language. Communication skills are deficits for all students with autism, and non-native language assessment may magnify the extent of students' autism. Further, multicultural students with autism should have access to bilingual or English-language learner (ELL) services. Unfortunately, students who receive such services are often considered to be lucky rather than entitled (Harry et al., 1995).

The National Research Council (2001) recommended four main elements for effectively serving students with autism: (a) early intervention, (b) active and intense educational programming, up to five hours per day for five days per week for a full year, (c) planned teaching opportunities, and (d) adult attention in one-to-one or small group settings to facilitate mastery of educational goals. Essential components of effective programs for children and adolescents with autism include emphasis on functional activities and skills needed to be successful in the real world, chronological age–appropriateness of activities, data-based instructional decisions, instruction in school and nonschool environments, and social integration to the maximum extent possible. Clearly, people with autism are entitled to the highest quality of life possible, and they should be treated at all times with the same dignity and respect accorded to everyone else.

Evidence-based effective educational strategies for many learners with autism include a language experience approach, milieu teaching, behavior chain interruption, sign language, natural language teaching, language shaping technique, semantic/pragmatic language instruction, direct instruction, picture exchange communication system, visual strategies, choice making, peer-mediated instruction, pivotal response training, applied behavior analysis, and social stories (Bakken & Bock, 2001). For multicultural learners with autism, there are many effective teaching strategies that include high levels of communication, integrated and thematic curriculum, interactive cross-age tutoring, collaborative learning, and language and literacy instruction in the student's native language (Garcia, 1997, 2002); explicit instruction model and strategy instruction model (Miller, 2002); individual help, peer interaction, games, flashcards, songs, hands-on activities, writing assignments, and rewards for learning (Schultz, 2002); mastery learning, experiential learning, learning activity packets and learning centers, independent study, and peer tutoring (Bennett, 1999); multiple intelligences recognition, reciprocal interaction teaching, and integration of multimedia (Delgado & Rogers-Adkinson, 1999); and use of a teaching style similar to that commonly experienced in the culture (Franklin, 1992). There are some strategies that appear to work for both autistic and multicultural groups. They include individual help (i.e., one adult/paraeducator helps one student); peer and cross-age tutoring (i.e., same-age and older students helping students); direct or explicit instruction and mastery learning (i.e., systematic, sequential learning where the student must master the material before moving on); and experiential learning (i.e., using real-life experiences to promote learning, such as new vocabulary). No doubt, information regarding strategies that are effective specifically with multicultural students with autism is emerging.

As indicated, resources for multicultural families who are raising children with autism and for those who serve these families are also beginning to develop. These resources include Web sites, books/pamphlets, and augmentative communication resources. The Autism Society of America hosts a comprehensive and informative Web site that presents information in Spanish (see www.autismsociety.org). Further, some federal agencies include extensive information about autism on their Web sites (see the Centers for Disease Control and Prevention, www.cdc.gov/ncbddd/Spanish/spautism.htm and the National Institutes of Health, health.nih.gov/result.asp/62). Autism Online (www.autismonline.org) is dedicated to linking families of children with autism with support, education, resources, and products in their own language and includes information in at least 20 languages, from Arabic to Urdu. Some books originally written in English are now available in other languages, including popular books such as *Visual Strategies for Improving Communication* (Spanish and Arabic), *The Picture Exchange Communication System (PECS) Training Manual* (French and Spanish), *Children with Autism: A Parents' Guide* (Spanish), and *Siblings of Children with Autism: A Guide for Families* (Spanish). Other less widely known books/pamphlets are available in languages other than English, including *Facts About Autism* (Spanish), *Helping People with Autism Manage Their Behavior* (Spanish), and *Learning Together* (Spanish and Korean), all published by the Indiana Resource Center for Autism. Further, *Autism—Hope Through Behavioral Therapy* is available in Turkish. Presently, augmentative communication resources are available in languages other than English. For example, *Boardmaker,* a program that uses pictures to help people communicate, is available with picture labels in 21 languages, from Catalan to Turkish. *Picture This—Pro,* another picture-based program, is available in five languages. The *Picture Communication Symbols* book and guide are also available in several languages other than English. A sophisticated software communication program, *Speaking Dynamically Pro,* is in development for 12 languages from Danish to Swedish, with the capability of using recorded voice in any language. Many other communication devices have the capability of using recorded voice. Finally, the International Society for Augmentative and Alternative Communication (www.isaac-online.org) is an organization that promotes the best possible communication for individuals with complex communication needs. This international society has chapters in 15 countries.

MULTIDIMENSIONAL VISION FOR THE 21ST CENTURY

As previously discussed, students with autism exhibit impairments in reciprocal social interaction. Even students with mild autism frequently require instruction in social skills, perhaps one-on-one with an adult. To improve a student's social interaction, general and special education teachers must first consider the student's culture, including what may be expected and appropriate in his or her family, and then work with IEP (individualized education plan) team members to choose culturally appropriate social skills. Next, teachers or service providers must task analyze the specific social skill by breaking the skill down into small parts (e.g., the skill of following directions can be broken down first, to follow basic one-part directions, then multipart directions). Then, teachers or service providers must teach the skill step by step in an orderly sequence, allowing mastery learning before progressing to the next step (Snell & Brown, 2000).

To teach multicultural learners like Chul Woo to follow directions, general and special education professionals must begin with testing them to determine which parts of the task they can and cannot perform. Teachers or service providers must then target one area of difficulty, such as learning to give items when requested. This response should be one that Chul Woo would need to master in his school or home context (experiential learning) and should be important to his family (Durán, 1988). Teachers or service providers must then present the request either verbally or visually with pictures and/or written words. Verbal requests should be short in the beginning stages of instruction (e.g., "Give me the toy" rather than "Would you stop banging that toy on your desk and just give it to me"). A visual representation of the request may be helpful, because learners with autism tend to have relative strengths in reading visual cues. If Chul Woo is still unable to follow the direction at this point, his teacher or service provider must gently prompt him to comply with the request. This professional would then gradually fade or remove the prompts as Chul Woo followed directions without help. Chul Woo must be encouraged and rewarded after each step to help him to understand expectations and know if they were met (Young, West, Marchant, Morgan, & Mitchem, 1997). Once it was understood that Chul Woo could demonstrate sufficient understanding of this direction, he could be presented with more complex directions by removing visual cues, using more difficult and varied language, and practicing the skill in various environments.

It is known that learners with autism display restrictive, repetitive, and stereotyped patterns of behavior, interests, and activities. Successful strategies for dealing with such behaviors include conducting a functional behavioral assessment to determine the function of the unusual behavior, then developing a behavioral intervention plan or positive behavioral support plan based on the functional assessment (Gresham, Watson, & Skinner, 2001). This process provides a framework for behavioral problem solving. Of course, the bottom line is that teachers and service providers must always consider whether the behavior that is considered unusual at school is acceptable or even expected within the culture of the home.

A Culturally Responsive Educator

1. Understands that autism is a spectrum disorder that manifests itself differently in each child in spite of cultural or racial differences.
2. Knows that deficits in social skills of multicultural learners with autism greatly affect their ability to communicate and behave appropriately with others.
3. Does not reject his or her students with autism because they have different cultural, learning, communication, and social styles.

4. Understands that restrictive and repetitive behaviors, interests, and activities of multicultural learners with autism may impede effective education.
5. Knows that autism may be viewed differently according to the culture of the family.
6. Individualizes instruction for students according to culture as well as exceptionality.
7. Becomes familiar with the family culture of the learner with autism.
8. Knows that prevalence of autism differs across cultures.
9. Engages in culturally sensitive assessment and instruction for multicultural learners with autism.
10. Agrees that all students should be treated with dignity despite their abilities or inabilities.

Conclusion

This chapter focused on ways to work with multicultural learners with autism. In addition, it highlighted difficulties inherent in assessing, classifying, and serving this population. However, opportunities available to people with other disabilities (e.g., group living homes) and increasing transition services (e.g., supported employment opportunities) are helping to make successful independent living more common for *all* learners with autism. The keys to successful life experiences for multicultural learners with autism are the same as they are for other people with disabilities: fostering independence; providing supportive learning environments; and increasing communication, socialization, and employment skills. The Autism Society of American (2004a) concluded:

> Individuals with autism, like everyone, are individuals first and foremost. They have unique strengths and weaknesses. . . . [and] goals need to be tailored to [an] individual's . . . ability and functioning level. Some children may need help in understanding social situations and developing appropriate responses. Others may . . . need assistance managing their behaviors. No one program will meet the needs of all individuals with [autism] . . . [and] treatment approaches and educational programs should be tailored to your child's individual needs, should be flexible and should be re-evaluated on a regular basis.

Discussion Questions

1. Briefly explain how the characteristics of learners with autism can be interpreted culturally.
2. Describe how educational professionals can serve multicultural students with autism.

3. Summarize how being familiar with the culture of the family of a student with autism may assist the professional in better serving that student.
4. Choose a teaching strategy and describe how this strategy can facilitate the learning of a multicultural student with autism.
5. In your own words, define autism using a cultural perspective.

References

American Psychiatric Association. (1994). *Diagnostic and statistical manual of mental disorders* (4th ed.). Washington, DC: Author.

Autism Society of America. (2004a). *Treatment and education.* Retrieved July 7, 2004, from www.autism-society.org/site/PageServer?pagename=TreatmentEducationOverview

Autism Society of America. (2004b). *What is autism?* Retrieved July 7, 2004, from www.autism-society.org/site/PageServer?pagename=whatisautism

Bakken, J. P., & Bock, S. J. (2001). Developing appropriate curriculum for students with autistic spectrum disorders. In T. Wahlberg, F. E. Obiakor, S. Burkhardt, & A. F. Rotatori (Eds.), *Advances in special education. Autistic spectrum disorders: Educational and clinical interventions* (pp. 109–132). Oxford, England: Elsevier Science/JAI Press.

Bennett, C. I. (1999). *Comprehensive multicultural education: Theory and practice* (4th ed.). Boston: Allyn & Bacon.

Benson, G. T. (1996). Issues in the education of African American students with disabilities. In E. Durán (Ed.), *Teaching students with moderate/severe disabilities, including autism: Strategies for second language learners in inclusive settings* (2nd ed., pp. 194–214). Springfield, IL: Charles C Thomas.

California Department of Developmental Services. (2003). *Autistic spectrum disorders changes in the California caseload: An update: 1999 through 2002.* Sacramento, CA: California Department of Developmental Services. Retrieved January 23, 2004, from www.dds.ca.gov/Autism/pdf/AutismReport2003.pdf

Campbell-Whatley, G. D., & Gardner, R. (2002). *Strategies and procedures for designing proactive interventions with a culturally diverse population of students with emotional or behavioral disorders and their families/caregivers.* Arlington, VA: Council for Children with Behavioral Disorders, Council for Exceptional Children.

Delgado, B. M., & Rogers-Adkinson, D. (1999). Educating the Hispanic-American exceptional learner. In F. E. Obiakor, J. O. Schwenn, & A. F. Rotatori (Eds.), *Advances in special education: Multicultural education for learners with exceptionalities* (pp. 53–71). Stamford, CT: JAI Press.

Durán, E. (1988). *Teaching the moderately and severely handicapped student and autistic adolescent: With particular attention to bilingual special education.* Springfield, IL: Charles C Thomas.

Dyches, T. T., Wilder, L. K., & Obiakor, F. E. (2001). Autism: Multicultural perspectives. In T. Wahlberg, F. E. Obiakor, S. Burkhardt, & A. F. Rotatori (Eds.), *Advances in special education: Autistic spectrum disorders: Educational and clinical interventions* (pp. 151–180). Oxford, England: Elsevier Science/JAI Press.

Dyches, T. T., Wilder, L. K., Sudweeks, R., Obiakor, F. E., & Algozzine, B. (2004). Multicultural perspectives on autism. *Journal of Autism and Developmental Disorders, 43*(2), 211–222.

Flexer, R. W., Baer, R., Luft, P., & Simmons, T. J. (2001). *Transition planning for secondary students with disabilities.* Upper Saddle River, NJ: Merrill/Prentice Hall.

Franklin, M. E. (1992). Culturally sensitive instructional practices for African-American learners with disabilities. *Exceptional Children, 59*(2), 115–122.

Garcia, E. (1997). The education of Hispanics in early childhood: Of roots and wings. *Young Children, 52*(3), 5–14.

Garcia, E. (2002). *Student cultural diversity: Understanding and meeting the challenge* (3rd ed.). Boston: Houghton Mifflin.

Gresham, F. M., Watson, T. S., & Skinner, C. H. (2001). Functional behavioral assessment: Principles, procedures, and future directions. *School Psychology Review, 30*(2), 156–172.

Harry, B., Grenot-Scheyer, M., Smith-Lewis, M., Park, H., Xin, F., & Schwartz, I. (1995). Developing culturally inclusive services for individuals with severe disabilities. *Journal for the Association of Persons with Severe Disabilities, 20,* 99–109.

Lian, M. G. (1996). Teaching Asian American children. In E. Durán (Ed.), *Teaching students with moderate/severe disabilities, including autism* (2nd ed., pp. 239–253). Springfield, IL: Charles C Thomas.

Miller, S. (2002). *Validated practices for teaching students with diverse needs and abilities.* Boston: Allyn & Bacon.

National Research Council. (2001). *Educating children with autism.* Washington, DC: National Academy Press.

Obiakor, F. E. (2003). *The eight step approach to multicultural learning and teaching* (2nd ed.). Dubuque, IA: Kendall/Hunt.

Obiakor, F. E., & Wilder, L. K. (2004). Issues, practices, and solutions in transitioning ethnically diverse learners with emotional/behavioral disability. In D. Cheney (Ed.), *Transition of students with emotional or behavioral disability from school to community: Current approaches for positive outcomes* (pp. 15–39). Arlington, VA: Council for Children with Behavioral Disorders, Council for Exceptional Children.

Park, H. (1996). Korean-American families of children with disabilities: Perspectives and implications for practitioners. In E. Durán (Ed.), *Teaching students with moderate/severe disabilities, including autism: Strategies for second language learners in inclusive settings* (2nd ed., pp. 194–214). Springfield, IL: Charles C Thomas.

Prizant, B. (1996). Brief report: Communication, language, social, & emotional development. *Journal of Autism and Developmental Disorders, 26,* 173–178.

Schultz, F. (2002). *Multicultural education* (8th ed.). Guilford, CT: McGraw-Hill/Dushkin.

Smith, T. B. (2004). *Practicing multiculturalism: Affirming diversity in counseling and psychology.* New York: Pearson/Allyn & Bacon.

Snell, M. E., & Brown, F. (2000). *Instruction of students with severe disabilities* (5th ed.). Upper Saddle River, NJ: Merrill/Prentice Hall.

U.S. Department of Education. (1993). *Fifteenth annual report to Congress on the implementation of the Individuals with Disabilities Education Act.* Washington, DC: Author.

U.S. Department of Education. (2002). *Twenty-fourth annual report to Congress on the implementation of the Individuals with Disabilities Education Act.* Washington, DC: Author.

Young, K. R., West, R. P., Marchant, M., Morgan, J. C., & Mitchem, K. (1997). *Prevention plus: A comprehensive program for the prevention of antisocial behavior.* Logan, UT: Utah State University Institute for the Study of Children, Youth, and Families at Risk.

Zionts, P., & Zionts, L. (Eds.) (2003). Multicultural aspects in the education of children and youth with autism and other developmental disabilities [Special issue]. *Focus on Autism and Other Developmental Disabilities, 18*(1), 2–3.

Chapter 10

Working with Multicultural Learners with Traumatic Brain Injury

Sandra Burkhardt and Anthony Rotatori

Chapter Outline

Thinking About Multicultural Special Education

At 4 years of age, Darius sustained a fractured skull when he was struck by a hit-and-run driver while playing on the curb by his family's apartment; his mother was killed. He was treated at the county hospital and received rehabilitation services at a prominent facility. Upon discharge, Child Services placed Darius with his maternal grandmother who kept him enrolled in aftercare services at the rehabilitation center for 3 years. Twice weekly, they took two buses and walked several blocks to keep appointments that monitored the progress of his speech and language, fine and gross motor skills, and aptitude for preschool tasks, including learning colors, letters, and counting. Darius's grandmother worked with him daily and showered him with love, praise, discipline, and challenges.

Darius was enrolled in the neighborhood public school that was ranked in the bottom 1% of schools in the school system. He qualified for special education eligibility under traumatic brain injury (TBI), but his grandmother was told that he actually acted better and learned more quickly than many of the other children in the general education classroom. The grandmother and a sympathetic kindergarten teacher persisted in arranging for Darius to receive speech and language services and learning disability remediation for mathematics; however, the school district had only one part-time special educator who could provide limited minutes of services. Classroom teachers worked with the grandmother to maintain good home-school communication and to support Darius when he encountered difficulties. The grandmother arranged to have Darius sing in the church choir and learn to play an instrument in the school band.

Darius's family is African American, low income, with considerable support in the community through the grandmother's church and extended family. During transition planning to high school, Darius was found eligible for inclusion in a magnet public high school program that recognized his musical talents and leadership abilities. His special education services for high school included school social work services, career planning, and learning disabilities resource assistance. At age 15, Darius, a C student in his freshman year, is taking college prep courses as part of his plans for the future. Darius's grandmother continues to encourage and support his progress, although she still worries about "spoiling" him.

- *How can Darius's teacher learn how to support Darius as he optimizes his potential during his recovery from TBI?*
- *What can school personnel do to assist Darius in his return to school?*

In 1990, the Education of All Handicapped Children Act (EHA Part B, P.L. 94-142) was revised and renamed the Individuals with Disabilities Education Act

(IDEA, P.L. 101-476), and TBI was added as an eligibility category. Thus, the academic needs of learners with TBI became assigned to the home school with general and special education teachers required to address the educational characteristics of these learners. The IDEA defined TBI as

> an acquired injury to the brain caused by an external physical force, resulting in total or partial functional disability or psychosocial impairment, or both, that adversely affects a child's educational performance. The term applies to open or closed head injuries resulting in impairments in one or more areas, such as cognition; language; memory; attention; reasoning; abstract thinking; judgment; problemsolving; sensory, perceptual and motor abilities; psycho-social behavior; physical functions; information processing; and speech. The term does not apply to brain injuries that are congenital or degenerative, or to brain injuries induced by birth trauma. (cited in NICHCY, 2004, p. 1)

Types of TBI include open, penetrating wounds, such as gunshots, and closed head, or nonpenetrating, injury, as in shaken baby syndrome (Committee on Child Abuse and Neglect, 2001). TBI may be categorized on a continuum from mild to severe. Mild TBI is most common and usually does not require hospitalization, although it can lead to long-term disability (Youse, Le, Cannizzaro, & Coelho, 2002). Causes of TBI include blunt trauma, penetrating wounds, or acceleration-deceleration forces to the head. For children under 14 years of age, violence and accidents as well as sports-related brain injury result in about 3,000 deaths per year and 29,000 hospitalizations (Centers for Disease Control and Prevention [CDC], 2003a). Common causes of TBI include car accidents, sports accidents, falls, and physical abuse (Council for Exceptional Children [CEC], 2001). Physical assault has become an increasing cause of injury, with domestic and urban violence as well as child abuse affecting infants (CDC, 2002a, b).

In the aftermath of TBI, an individual may display loss of function in the following realms: sensory, perceptual and motor abilities; speech and language; attention; memory; cognition; abstract thinking; speed and accuracy of information processing; reasoning and judgment; problem solving; motivation; and emotional expression, including mood regulation. Mental fatigue, poor stamina, sleep disturbance, headache, depression, and seizures are associated with TBI (CEC, 2001). The neuropsychological consequences of TBI in children and adolescents ranging in age from 6 to 18 years include poor performance on speeded tasks, memory impairment, decreased recall, and difficulties in processing novel or complex visual-spatial stimuli (Lord-Maes & Obrzut, 1996). Poor long-term and short-term memory following TBI may affect reading, writing, planning, comprehending, and sequencing (NICHCY, 2004). In some cases, students with mild TBI display learning characteristics associated with learning disabilities, attention deficits, mild mental retardation, and behavior disorders (CEC, 2001). In fact, young children with TBI are at particular risk for negative effects of injury in the development of cognition, language, social-emotional regulation, motor coordination, and adaptive living skills. The case of Darius illustrates how early intervention minimizes negative effects of TBI for young children, if intervention is intensive and long-term (e.g., Lowenthal, 1998).

MULTICULTURAL ISSUES AND TBI

Multicultural issues affect our understanding of TBI in at least two ways: risk factors and recovery indicators. In the case of Darius, his placement in the supportive care of his grandmother after injury had a favorable impact on his recovery. The close ties of his grandmother to resources within the African American community provided support for both Darius and her. Multicultural factors, including racial identity, family values, religious affiliation, and place of residence, contributed to positive outcomes for Darius. Diverse services available within a large urban school system provided school programming that evolved from initially limited resources to comprehensive programming that built on Darius's strengths, minimized his deficits, and preserved his cultural identity. To maximize the potential of diverse students, D'Andrea and Daniels (2001) proposed the RESPECTFUL model, which includes recognizing *gender, age, and stage of development, race and ethnicity, economic status, family influence, place of residence,* and *language fluency.* Males are twice as likely as females to sustain TBI (CDC, 2003b), although assault due to being struck has been known to be the leading cause of all nonfatal violence-related injuries (not only brain injury) for girls. There are about 1,500 assaults on boys under the age of 1 year; 10,882 assaults on boys aged 1–4 years; 29,831 assaults on boys aged 5–9 years; and 78,970 assaults on boys aged 10–14 years (CDC, 2002b). Incidence of assault on girls included over 1,500 assaults on girls under the age of 1 year; 6,189 assaults on girls aged 1–4 years; 14,600 assaults on girls aged 5–9 years; and 35,898 assaults on girls aged 10–14 years (CDC, 2002a).

Risks of TBI related to age, developmental stage, and dependency include child abuse, with 25% of shaken babies dying from TBI and survivors displaying permanent damage to sensory and cognitive capabilities (Journal of the American Medical Association [JAMA], 2003). Attention to multicultural issues in regard to educating students with TBI may be particularly important. TBI is a disability that is acquired during the course of *environmental events.* Thus, social factors associated with *how* TBI is acquired and *who* acquires TBI may predict different outcomes for the individual with TBI. For example, Max et al. (1998) determined that symptoms of oppositional defiant disorder (ODD) in children and adolescents in the first two years after TBI were predicted by the following: preinjury family functioning, family social class, and presence of preinjury ODD symptoms. Changes in preinjury ODD symptoms at 6 months, 1 year, and 2 years postinjury were associated with socioeconomic status, with severity of injury becoming a predictor of ODD at 2 years postinjury. Max et al. concluded that the contribution of psychosocial factors *is greater* than severity of TBI in accounting for ODD symptoms during the first, although not the second year postinjury. In other words, factors such as socioeconomic class and discrimination, which affect many multicultural learners, may be particularly important in determining the recovery of a learner with TBI.

Trauma as a Multicultural Issue

The "T" in TBI stands for *trauma*. Levi, Drotar, Yeates, and Taylor (1999) discovered a higher rate of post-traumatic stress (PTS) symptoms in children following severe TBI in comparison to PTS symptoms in children who had sustained orthopedic injuries, even when ethnicity, social disadvantage, and age at time of injury were accounted for. Ivey, D'Andrea, Ivey, and Simek-Morgan (2002) noted that the experience of trauma is a potential diversity factor that may profoundly affect one's worldview. The experience of trauma may, in and of itself, change the ways in which individuals develop and view themselves, others, the future, and the past. TBI involves both physical and emotional suffering for victims and their families. An individual child's future potential may be compromised by TBI. Pain, hospitalizations, surgeries, disfigurement, and scarring may result in continuing adjustment difficulties in recovery from TBI. Some children who sustain TBI are old enough to remember the physical trauma of injury and treatment, to register the emotional pain of functional loss, and to reflect on the social circumstances that contributed to the injury. It is likely that increased psychological and social support for adjustment may be needed for these children compared to children who were injured without awareness of the nature of the injurious event.

Darius's case highlights some general diversity issues related to the risk of TBI. Burnett, Silver, Kolakowsky-Hayner, and Cifu (2000) reported that, among ethnic minorities, African Americans and Latinos appear to have the greatest incidence of TBI. In a comparison of 852 individuals of ethnic minority status and 1,518 individuals of nonminority status served by 17 model programs for the treatment of TBI, individuals of ethnic minority status with TBI were young, male, single, unemployed, and had limited years of education. The most frequent cause of TBI for minorities and nonminorities combined was motor vehicle crashes, including pedestrian accidents. In general, minorities experienced less severe brain injury, spent less time in rehabilitation, and received less frequent and less intense therapies than nonminorities. Ability after rehabilitation was rated as the same for both minorities and nonminorities (Burnett et al., 2003). In terms of recovery rates, there is a paucity of research regarding ethnicity and TBI, with most studies finding similarities rather than differences between minority and nonminority populations with TBI (Burnett et al., 2003). Accurate estimates of the impact of TBI on racial and ethnic minorities may be hampered by follow-up studies in which minorities are systematically omitted. Corrigan et al. (2003) determined that "selective attrition" of follow-up on patients was associated with race and ethnicity, socioeconomic disadvantage, cause of injury, and hospital payer source.

Transportation-related TBI accounted for a greater proportion of TBI among African American children than among white children (CDC, 1997). African American children aged 1 to 4 years have approximately twice as high a risk of death from TBI compared to same-age white or other race children (Thurman, Alverson, Dunn, Guerrero, & Sniezek, 1999). Violence is the leading cause of TBI among ethnic minorities who sustain TBI (Burnett et al., 2000). African Americans have the highest death rate from TBI (Thurman et al., 1999). Assault and firearms are responsible for a greater proportion of TBI among African Americans than whites (CDC, 2003c).

DEVELOPMENTAL ATTRIBUTES OF TBI

Increased vulnerability to injury may be common during childhood, with typical developmental stages contributing to the incidence of head injury. For young children, acquisition of capabilities, such as walking or riding a bicycle, without adequate accompanying judgment, such as monitoring traffic, create risk periods in which children's capacities to *sustain* injury exceed their ability to *prevent* injury (Burkhardt, 1995). The socialization patterns of some older children put them and those around them at risk for head injury. Beyond typical childhood risks, such as car accidents, falls, and sports injuries, social problems like gang violence, access to weapons, substance abuse, and involvement in crime bring additional risks of head injury to children at increasingly younger ages (CDC, 2003c; JAMA, 2003). For children from the ages of birth through 14 years of age, pedestrian and bicycle accidents and improper safety devices used when riding as passengers in a motor vehicle result in increased incidence of injury (CDC, 2003c).

Following TBI, a child's development is affected in at least two ways. First, TBI may, in some cases, permanently derail normal development (Burkhardt, 1995); and second, plasticity of the central nervous system may afford young victims of TBI increased opportunity for neurological compensation. When adults sustain brain injury, they have a vast fund of consolidated knowledge and abilities upon which to draw during rehabilitation. Children have short histories of previous learning. However, education presents many formal and informal opportunities for new learning. Thus, for children with TBI, the promise of ongoing development, particularly in the presence of intervention to support recovery, brings with it the possibility that maturation and experience will mitigate the effects of TBI in the years following the injury. In the case of Darius, he returned to school and benefited greatly from his educational experiences. His grandmother ensured optimal development for him by securing educational and rehabilitation services throughout the course of his development.

Family Influences

Both the risks of TBI and the potential for recovery from TBI begin in the family (Youse et al., 2002). Poverty, poor educational opportunities, teen pregnancies, and substance abuse may contribute to chaotic and poorly run households in which children are at increased risk of accidents, physical abuse, or neglect. For most multicultural children with TBI, reunion after injury involves eager and devoted family members who assist with their return to the home and school. In the case of Darius, recovery depended on placing him with a strong, positive family member. However, Yeates et al. (2002) identified race as a moderating factor in parent as well as family outcomes following TBI of a child family member, with the negative effects of TBI becoming greater over time for African American parents compared to white parents, independent of socioeconomic status. When the family is not a resource for the child with TBI, hospital, social service, court, and school staff direct the school reentry process. Thus, foster children, abused children, and children with TBI from poor families may face great obstacles with postinjury adjustment (JAMA, 2003). Other family members may also be affected by the impact of TBI. Swift et al. (2003) determined that brother-sister relationships for children with TBI were of poorer quality than brother-sister dyads of children with orthopedic injuries, with behavior problems in the child with TBI predicting sibling behavior problems.

Economic Issues

Two aspects of economic resources affect access to rehabilitation services following TBI: limited access to care based on the type of insurance coverage available (Burnett et al., 2003), and the relatively low amount of funding available to treat TBI compared to the excessive costs associated with treatment (CDC, 2004). For many multicultural, low-income families, school services may constitute the primary rehabilitative services that a learner with TBI receives. In the absence of private health care insurance and/or financial resources to hire clinical service providers, poor families must rely on public schools to meet their children's needs following head injury. Poverty has been associated with a higher incidence of postinjury behavioral problems (Schwartz et al., 2003).

Place of Residence

Place of residence may increase risk of TBI in terms of motor vehicle, bicycle, and pedestrian accidents as well as urban violence for teens. Congested urban areas may expose even young children to motor vehicle accidents as pedestrians. Urban violence, including gunshots, increase risk of TBI for innocent bystanders as well as violent youth. Neighborhood is also related to recovery. Urban areas are more likely to have access to advanced treatment centers than rural areas (NICHCY, 2004). For Darius, his place of residence near a major rehabilitation center had a significant impact on continuing support for recovery. Additionally, the variety of educational placements available in a large, urban school system afforded his grandmother the opportunity to seek an appropriate, publicly funded school setting for high school. Limited special education resources may make it difficult for small school districts to accommodate the needs of multicultural learners with TBI.

Language Fluency

As a multicultural issue, *language* traditionally refers to native tongue and second languages. However, it is worth highlighting that one of the major residual effects of TBI includes speech and language impairment. Special education and clinical speech services target restoration of premorbid levels of linguistic capability for students with TBI. Youse et al. (2002) emphasized the importance of cultural competence in speech and language interventions with multicultural learners. They recommend the following guidelines for intervention:

- Evaluate the cultural and linguistic context.
- Use assessments and interventions for TBI that are culturally appropriate.
- Heed how the cultural and linguistic background of individuals with TBI influences their feelings about health and health care.
- Examine clinician biases and beliefs.

Because TBI often disrupts both expressive and receptive language, sometimes on a permanent basis, some multicultural learners with TBI may find themselves in the subculture of persons whose speech production lacks intelligibility (Cahill, Murdoch, & Theodoros, 2000, 2002; Netsell, 2001). Care must be exercised to distinguish linguistic characteristics based on multicultural differences from true language deficits due to injury.

EDUCATING MULTICULTURAL LEARNERS WITH TBI

The treatment of TBI begins with medical intervention; however, return to home and school is a milestone of recovery. The major developmental tasks of school-age years (i.e., academic progress and making friends) may be compromised by the effects of TBI. For teens with TBI, cognitive and behavioral impairments may result in alterations in vocational and career planning. For some multicultural learners who suffered from poor social adjustment prior to head injury, there is a risk for even poorer social functioning following TBI. The National Dissemination Center for Children with Disabilities (2004) suggested guidelines for teachers of children with TBI (see Table 10.1).

On the whole, effective intervention for persons with TBI from multicultural groups should result in restoration of age-appropriate cultural competence (ASHA, 2002). Guidelines for working with students with TBI who are members of these multicultural groups include the following:

- Identification of culturally normative values and beliefs that may affect the learner's attitudes toward family involvement, injury, and health management responsibilities
- Culturally relevant and meaningful assessment and intervention measures
- Use of interpreters and translators for training and remediation
- Culturally sensitive referrals for resources within the learner's community

Effective behavior management is an essential component for optimizing recovery from TBI. As in Darius's case, his grandmother worried that he might be spoiled because she no longer used corporal punishment for his disruptive behaviors following TBI. In general, he was at risk for the use of inadequate behavior management practices at school and home. It is important that general and special educators address problem classroom behaviors, particularly in the case of learners from multicultural backgrounds, with constructive management approaches.

TABLE 10.1   *Guidelines for Teachers of Children with TBI*

- Find out about TBI and the child's present needs.
- Provide the learner with more time for schoolwork and tests.
- Give step-by-step directions and provide written directions or pictures as needed.
- Teach new tasks by modeling and demonstration and provide examples of new concepts.
- Establish routine and give advance notice of changes to routine.
- Provide time to practice new skills.
- Use daily planners and organizers.
- Modify work to allow for fatigue.
- Reduce distractions in the learning environment.
- Maximize the learner's chances for success by teacher flexibility.

Ewing (1995) emphasized that behavioral management strategies that ignore multicultural values, customs, and beliefs are used by many educators without understanding how practices and expectations of education can contribute to ineffective learning and destructive school behavior (p. 106). Teachers and service providers must be aware that students with TBI may exhibit more behavior problems than their peers without disabilities (see Asarnow, Satz, Light, Lewis, & Neuman, 1991; Greenspan & MacKenzie, 1994; Parker, 1994). There is often the belief and hope that full recovery will make special education unnecessary. Similarly, there may be the expectation that mild brain damage or closed head injury will have few, if any, effects on learning. Because of overlapping symptoms, TBI may be identified with educational and emotional difficulties, such as learning disability, mental retardation, or behavioral disorder (NICHCY, 2004).

Behavior management has been identified as an effective intervention for students with behavioral difficulties associated with TBI, particularly antecedent management strategies that assist in avoiding inappropriate behaviors (Feeney & Ylvisaker, 1995, 1997; Kehle, Clark, & Jenson, 1996; Ylvisaker, Feeney, & Szekers, 1998). Additionally, Tyler and Savage (2003) stressed that, for students with TBI, contingency management associated with traditional behavioral management may not be appropriate. A meta-analysis of behavioral outcome studies for all persons (not specifically children) with acquired brain injury failed to identify the "best practice" that would provide consistent behavioral regulation and durable results (Ager & O'May, 2001). Furthermore, Egnor (2003) stressed that such concerns led Congress to attach an amendment to IDEA 1997 that endorsed *positive behavioral interventions and supports (PBIS)* for students with challenging behaviors. As Egnor noted, the amendment requires that, in the case of a child with a disability whose behavior impedes his or her learning or that of others, the IEP team shall "consider, when appropriate, strategies, including positive behavioral interventions, and supports to address that behavior [Section 614 (d) (3) (B) (i)]" (p. 177).

It appears that Darius's recovery exemplifies the positive happenings that can be the result of the home and the school working together. Such collaborative efforts can be good news for many multicultural learners with TBI. It is estimated that 70% of students with TBI eligibility receive high school diplomas, the second highest graduation rate among learners with disabilities (CEC, 2002). Successful return to school following TBI may require an individualized education program and a flexible plan to address identified needs (NICHCY, 2004). Assessment of the child's intact abilities, short-term deficits, and capacity for restoration of functioning should guide intervention. Remedial services should promote maximal recovery of functions. Compensatory strategies must be provided when it is established that normal functioning will not be restored. Some learning that happens automatically for other children may require repetition, practice, reinforcement, and explanation for children with TBI. Additionally, behavioral problems that may develop as a residual of TBI include overactivity, aggression, temper tantrums, low frustration tolerance, helplessness, a lack of self-direction, impulse control difficulties, irritability, apathy, poor anger control, social disinhibition, and poor planning, organizing, and problem solving (Smith, Polloway, Patton, & Dowdy, 2001; Tyler & Savage, 2003).

PBIS is an "application of a behaviorally based systems approach to enhancing the capacity of schools, families, and communities to design effective environments that improve the fit or link between research-validated practices and the environments in which teaching and learning occur" (Office of Special Educational Programs, 2000, p. III-8). This approach to managing disruptive behaviors such as temper tantrums, aggression, or significant agitation involves a *functional behavioral assessment (FBA)* of the specific problem behavior (see Sugai & Horner, 1999). The FBA helps to identify events that set off and maintain the problem behavior (see Halvorsen & Neary, 2001). According to Smith (2004), such an assessment enables the teacher to "understand the relationship between what happens in the student's environment and how the student behaves . . . and why inappropriate behaviors occur and continue" (p. 465). This understanding leads to a positive intervention that stresses the development of appropriate behaviors. Following the FBA is the behavior intervention plan (BIP), which consists of positive reinforcement (e.g., a teacher's verbal praise for a student's calm reaction to a stressful transition) and environmental supports (e.g., a gentle reminder to the student 10 minutes prior to an upcoming transition). Also, the student with TBI may be taught self-control strategies such as self-monitoring, self-description, self-evaluation in terms of valued goals, goal-oriented self-instruction, and self-reinforcement (see Baldwin & Baldwin, 2001). Such strategies provide an angry or agitated student with TBI proactive behaviors to reduce inappropriate behaviors, while increasing appropriate behaviors that will lead to successful learning and mastery.

Another effective tool for behavior management of students with TBI who exhibit inappropriate problem behaviors is self-concept development. According to Webb-Johnson, Obiakor, and Algozzine (1995), "The self-perceptions of youth demonstrating behaviors that often differ from established school norms may be enhanced as a result of embracing self-concept as a construct with three dimensions of self-knowledge, self-esteem, and self-ideal" (p. 161). Embedded in these dimensions is the MECCA program, developed to allow learners to increase more effective self-perceptions that will empower them to "accept life's challenges through intrapersonal and interpersonal growth" (Webb-Johnson et al., 1995, p. 161). To a large measure, the MECCA program is a culturally sensitive behavior management approach that may prevent teachers from routinely devaluing a multicultural student's cultural backgrounds and experiences (see Webb-Johnson et al.).

A Culturally Responsive Educator

1. Understands that all learners, including those from different cultures, can acquire TBI.
2. Knows that diversity factors are associated with increased risk of TBI.
3. Understands that all students with TBI, in spite of their cultural differences, often exhibit more inappropriate behaviors compared to their same-age peers.
4. Acknowledges that the "T" in TBI stands for trauma. As a result, an individual with TBI may be psychologically affected by the experience.
5. Knows that TBI is a medical condition that should include culturally sensitive, professional medical and educational interventions.
6. Seeks more school district in-service workshops on how to work with multicultural learners with TBI.
7. Respects behavioral management strategies that are positive, proactive, and culturally appropriate.
8. Values culturally sensitive transitional programming for students with TBI.
9. Learns the facts about TBI before making prejudicial judgments about multicultural learners and their families.
10. Understands that multicultural factors affect both risk factors for TBI and resources for recovery.

Conclusion

This chapter examined the risks of TBI for multicultural learners and offered some guidelines for successful reintegration of multicultural learners with TBI into the classroom. Regarding the TBI, impacts of diversity factors including race and ethnicity, socioeconomic status, family resources, and place of residence are presented. The case of Darius demonstrates that although risk factors may contribute to the occurrence of TBI, key postinjury interventions, including culturally sensitive home-school collaboration, responsive special education services, and positive behavior management strategies, provide multicultural learners who have TBI with optimal opportunities for recovery.

Discussion Questions

1. Using the case of Darius, explain the benefits of teacher-parent collaboration.
2. Discuss how gender and race affect risk of TBI for preschool and school-age children.
3. Explain why a professional must understand the characteristics of TBI.
4. Discuss the advantages of culturally sensitive behavior management for students with TBI.
5. Briefly evaluate how socioeconomic factors and place of residence affect services for students with TBI.

References

Ager, A., & O'May, F. (2001). Issues in the definition and implementation of "best practice" for staff delivery of interventions for challenging behavior. *Journal of Intellectual & Developmental Disability, 26,* 243–256.

American Speech-Language-Hearing Association. (2002). *Working with culturally and linguistically diverse groups.* Retrieved February 17, 2004 from www.asha.org/about/publication/leader-online/archives/2002/q2/020625a3.htm

Asarnow, R. F., Satz, P., Light, R., Lewis, R., & Neuman, E. (1991). Behavior problems and adaptive functioning in children with mild and severe closed head injury. *Journal of Pediatric Psychology, 16,* 543–555.

Baldwin, J. D., & Baldwin, J. I. (2001). *Behavior principles in everyday life.* Upper Saddle River, NJ: Prentice Hall.

Burkhardt, S. (1995). Counseling issues for children with traumatic brain injury. In A. Rotatori, J. Schwenn, & F. Litton (Eds.), *Counseling special populations: Research and practice perspectives* (Vol. 9, pp. 207–240). Greenwich, CT: JAI Press.

Burnett, D. M., Kolakowsky-Hayner, S. A., Slater, D., Stringer, A., Bushnik, T., Zafonte, R., et al. (2003). Ethnographic analysis of traumatic brain injury patients in the national model systems database. *Archives of Physical Medicine and Rehabilitation, 84,* 263–267.

Burnett, D. M., Silver, T. M., Kolakowsky-Hayner, S. A., & Cifu, D. X. (2000). Functional outcomes for African Americans and Hispanics treated at a traumatic brain injury model systems center. *Brain Injury, 14,* 713–718.

Cahill, L. M., Murdoch, B. E., & Theodoros, D. G. (2000). Variability in speech outcome following severe childhood traumatic brain injury: A report of three cases. *Journal of Medical Speech-Language Pathology, 8,* 347–352.

Cahill, L. M., Murdoch, B. E., & Theodoros, D. G. (2002). Perceptual analysis of speech following traumatic brain injury in childhood. *Brain Injury, 16,* 415–446.

Centers for Disease Control and Prevention. (1997). *Appendix B: Traumatic brain injury in children and youth as a public health problem.* Retrieved February 17, 2004 from www .cdc.gov/doc.do?id-900f3ed800109c8

Centers for Disease Control and Prevention. (2002a). *10 leading causes of nonfatal violence-related injury: United States, 2002, all races, females.* Retrieved February 17, 2004 from www.cdc.gov/ncipc/wisqars/nonfatal/quickpicks/quickpicks_2002/violfem.htm

Centers for Disease Control and Prevention. (2002b). *10 leading causes of nonfatal violence-related injury: United States, 2002, all races, males.* Retrieved February 17, 2004 from www.cdc.gov/ncipc/wisqars/nonfatal/quickpicks/quickpicks_2002/violmal.htm

Centers for Disease Control and Prevention. (2003a). *Traumatic brain injury facts.* Retrieved February 17, 2004 from www.cdc.gov/doc.do?id=0900f3ec800081d7

Centers for Disease Control and Prevention. (2003b). TBI topic home. Retrieved March 3, 2004 from www.cdc.gov/node.do?id=0900f3ec8000dbdc&askpectId=C60308

Centers for Disease Control and Prevention. (2003c). *Traumatic brain injury facts: The problem.* Retrieved February 17, 2004 from www.cdc.gov/doc.do?id=0900f3ec80001d7

Centers for Disease Control and Prevention. (2004). *Traumatic brain injury in the United States: Assessing outcomes in children—Other TBI issues.* Retrieved February 17, 2004 from www.cdc.gov/doc.do?id=0900f3ec8000f8aa

Committee on Child Abuse and Neglect. (2001). Shaken-baby syndrome: Rotational cranial injuries—technical report. *Pediatrics, 108,* 206–210.

Corrigan, J. D., Harrison-Felix, C., Bogner, J., Dijkers, M., Terrill, M. S., & Whiteneck, G. (2003). Systematic bias in traumatic brain injury outcome studies because of loss to follow-up. *Archives of Physical Medicine and Rehabilitation, 84*(2). Abstract retrieved March 2, 2004 from www2.archives-pmr.org/scripts/om.dll/serve?action=search DB&searchDBfor=ar

Council for Exceptional Children. (2001, March). Traumatic brain injury: The silent epidemic. *Today, 7.* Retrieved February 17, 2004 from www.cec.sped.org/bk/cectoday/archives/march_2001/cectoday_03_2001_01.h

Council for Exceptional Children. (2002, May 10). *Public policy and legislative information: CEC policy update.* Retrieved February 17, 2004 from www.cec.sped.org/pp.legupd 051002.html

D'Andrea, M., & Daniels, J. (2001). RESPECTFUL counseling: An integrative model for counselors. In D. Pope-Davis & H. Coleman (Eds.), *The interface of class, culture and gender in counseling* (pp. 417–466). Thousand Oaks, CA: Sage.

Egnor, D. (2003). *IDEA reauthorization and the student discipline controversy.* Denver, CO: Love.

Ewing, N. (1995). A neglected factor in behavior management. In F. E. Obiakor & B. Algozzine (Eds.), *Managing problem behaviors: Perspectives for general and special educators* (pp. 96–114). Dubuque, IA: Kendall/Hunt.

Feeney, T. J., & Ylvisaker, M. (1995). Choice and routine: Antecedent behavioral interventions for adolescents with severe traumatic brain injury. *Journal of Head Trauma Rehabilitation, 10,* 67–86.

Feeney, T. J., & Ylvisaker, M. (1997). A positive, communication-based approach to challenging behavior after ABI. In A. Glang, G. H. S. Singer, & B. Todis (Eds.), *Children with acquired brain injury: The school's response* (pp. 229–254). Baltimore: Brookes.

Greenspan, A. L., & MacKenzie, E. J. (1994). Functional outcome after pediatric head injury. *Pediatrics, 94,* 425–432.

Halvorsen, A. T., & Neary, T. (2001). *Building inclusive schools: Tools and strategies for success.* Boston: Allyn & Bacon.

Ivey, A. E., D'Andrea, M., Ivey, M. B., & Simek-Morgan, L. (2002). *Theories of counseling and psychotherapy: A multicultural perspective* (5th ed.). Boston: Allyn & Bacon.

JAMA & Archives Journals. (2003). *JAMA patient page: Inflicted brain injury in children.* Retrieved February 17, 2004 from www.medem.com/medlb/article_detaillb.cfm?article_ID-ZZZ4SS4 FOJD&sub_ca

Kehle, T. J., Clark, E., & Jenson, W. R. (1996). Interventions for students with traumatic brain injury: Managing behavioral disturbances. *Journal of Learning Disabilities, 29,* 632–642.

Levi, R., Drotar, D., Yeates, K., & Taylor, H. (1999). Posttraumatic stress symptoms in children following orthopedic or traumatic brain injury. *Journal of Clinical Child Psychology, 28,* 232–243.

Lord-Maes, J., & Obrzut, J. (1996). Neuropsychological consequences of traumatic brain injury in children and adolescents. *Journal of Learning Disabilities, 29,* 609–617.

Lowenthal, B. (1998). Traumatic brain injury in early childhood: Developmental effects and interventions. *Infant-Toddler Intervention, 8,* 377–388.

Max, J., Castillo, C., Bokura, H., Robin, D., Lindgren, S., Smith, W., et al. (1998). Oppositional defiant disorder symptomatology after traumatic brain injury: A prospective study. *Journal of Nervous & Mental Disease, 186,* 325–332.

National Dissemination Center for Children with Disabilities. (2004). *Traumatic brain injury: Fact sheet.* Retrieved February 17, 2004 from www.nichcy.org/pubs/fatshe/fs18txt.htm

Netsell, R. (2001). Speech aeromechanics and the dysarthrias: Implications for children with traumatic brain injury. *Journal of Head Trauma Rehabilitation, 16,* 415–425.

Office of Special Education Programs. (2000). Applying positive behavioral support in schools. *Twenty-second annual report to Congress on the implementing of the Individuals with Disabilities Education Act* (pp. III–7 through III–31). Washington, DC: U.S. Department of Education.

Parker, R. S. (1994). Neurobehavioral content of children's mild traumatic brain injury. *Seminars in Neurology, 14,* 67–73.

Schwartz, L., Taylor, H., Drotar, D., Yeates, K., Wade, S., & Stancin, T. (2003). Long-term behavior problems following pediatric traumatic brain injury: Prevalence, predictors, and correlates. *Journal of Pediatric Psychology, 28,* 251–263.

Smith, D. D. (2004). *Introduction to special education: Teaching in an age of opportunity* (5th ed.). Boston: Allyn & Bacon.

Smith, T. E. C., Polloway, E. A., Patton, J. R., & Dowdy, C. A. (2001). *Teaching students with special needs in inclusive settings* (3rd ed.). Boston: Allyn & Bacon.

Sugai, G., & Horner, R. H. (1999). Discipline and behavior support: Preferred procedures and practices. *Effective School Practices, 17,* 10–22.

Swift, E., Taylor, H., Kaugars, A., Drotar, D., Yeates, K., Wade, S., et al. (2003). Sibling relationship and behavior after pediatric traumatic brain injury. *Journal of Developmental & Behavioral Pediatrics, 24,* 24–31.

Thurman, D., Alverson, C., Dunn, K., Guerrero, J., & Sniezek, J. (1999). Traumatic brain injury in the United States: A public health perspective. *Journal of Head Trauma and Rehabilitation, 14,* 602–615.

Tyler, J. S., & Savage, R. C. (2003). Students with traumatic brain injury. In F. E. Obiakor, C. A. Utley, & A. Rotatori (Eds.), *Effective education for learners with exceptionalities* (pp. 299–350). Boston: JAI/Elsevier Sciences.

Webb-Johnson, G., Obiakor, F. E., & Algozzine, B. (1995). Self-concept development: An effective tool for behavior management. In F. E. Obiakor & B. Algozzine (Eds.), *Managing problem behaviors* (pp. 161–177). Dubuque, IA: Kendall/Hunt.

Yeates, K., Taylor, G., Woodrome, S., Wade, S., Stancin, T., & Drotar, D. (2002). Race as a moderator of parent and family outcomes following pediatric traumatic brain injury. *Journal of Pediatric Psychology, 27,* 393–403.

Ylvisaker, M., Feeney, T. J., & Szekers, S. F. (1998). Social-environmental approach to communication and behavior. In M. Ylvisaker (Ed.), *Traumatic brain injury rehabilitation: Children and adolescents* (2nd ed., pp. 271–298). Boston: Butterworth-Heinemann.

Youse, K. M., Le, K. N., Cannizzaro, M. S., & Coelho, C. A. (2002). *Traumatic brain injury: A primer for professionals.* Retrieved February, 17, 2004 from www.asha.org/about/publications/leader-online/archive/2002/12/020625a.htm

Chapter 11

Working with Multicultural Learners with Physical and Health Impairments

Joan Fleitas and Festus E. Obiakor

Chapter Outline

Thinking About Multicultural Special Education

Cara sat slumped in her seat, a scarf covering her bald head and two canes crisscrossed on the floor beside her. Her eyes were downcast as her classmates worked in groups of three on a history project. When approached by the teacher, she swallowed hard in an unsuccessful attempt to maintain her composure. Her eyes filled with tears as she admitted that she did not understand the assignment. She had been absent twice in one week, and her parents worried that their 10-year-old daughter might not continue in school following her diagnosis and initial treatment of Ewing's sarcoma, a type of bone cancer that commonly spreads to other areas of the body. The teacher was caring and continued to motivate Cara to work harder to keep up with her classmates.

The malignant tumor was in Cara's thigh bone (femur), and surgery involved removal of the bone and insertion of a titanium rod to maintain the form and function of her right leg. But that was just a part of it! She also endured chemotherapy, a potent group of drugs designed to catch and destroy any cancer cells that might have spread from her leg to other areas of her body. Because the chemotherapy attacks all rapidly developing tissue (characteristic of cancer cells), it certainly took its toll on Cara, affecting those normal cells in her body that also tended to divide rapidly, primarily her hair cells and the mucous membranes that lined her mouth and stomach. As a result, she lost her hair, had painful sores in her mouth, and experienced nausea, vomiting, and a great deal of fatigue.

Cara lived with her mother, father, grandmother, and two younger brothers in a three-bedroom apartment in Manhattan, New York. She shared a bedroom with her grandmother. Although her mother and grandmother were Filipino, her father, a Black Caribbean, was born on the island of St. Thomas, grew up in New York, and worked in the Philippines for 10 years prior to relocating to the United States.

Cara had a rough year in school, beginning with pain and swelling in her leg that was initially thought to be associated with a preadolescent growth spurt. She recalled, "When the doctor told us that I had cancer I was scared and confused; scared because my grandfather died of cancer in his lungs and now I had it in my leg. I wondered what I did to get this awful disease, and how much longer I'd have to live." It is important to note that though some Filipino parents view illness as a gift from God (i.e., good fortune to families), Cara's parents seemed devastated and had a difficult time coping with her illness.

When Cara returned to school, it was just awful. Even though the nurse from the hospital came to her classroom to explain about Ewing's sarcoma, and even though everybody said they would help her with her work, she felt so alone. She limped noticeably and used two canes to get around, and she could see everybody staring at her.

Some children were very nice to her at first, wanting to do absolutely everything for her, but they stopped being so friendly after they learned that she had cancer. Besides the physical sequela of ongoing cancer treatment, she felt angry and confused about being sick, and sometimes blamed herself for her predicament. Although her teachers and service providers were always there for her, Cara felt shy and deferential around other children. Coupled with this, she continued to experience fatigue, pain and fear . . . it all seemed too much for her.

Cara's classroom teacher had taken some courses on multicultural education and knew that Cara's lack of eye contact had some cultural attachment. Although some teachers erroneously classified Cara as an African American, her teacher recognized the richness of her mixed ethnic and cultural heritage. She consistently believed in Cara and tried to be culturally responsive in working with her.

- *How did Cara's teachers and service providers help her to maximize her potential in school?*
- *Why did Cara's teacher in Manhattan not erroneously label her?*

There are many learners with physical and health impairments, who, like Cara, come to school dressed not only in clothes, but in a complex tapestry woven of development, culture, and health. It is imperative that all of the threads of this fabric be recognized and treated with care if these learners are to flourish and achieve in educational settings. Surely, these settings must be least restrictive and demonstrate valuing of the humanity that students bring to school despite their disabilities, health problems, and cultural backgrounds. This is the main thrust of this chapter. We believe developmental factors are influenced by physical and health impairments, and developmental expectations in one culture differ from those in other cultural milieus. Under these circumstances, the task of the teacher is rendered more complex.

Students like Cara, with significant mobility and health issues, and with multicultural backgrounds, often have difficulty mastering typical age-appropriate developmental crises as defined by educators who use the stages of human development defined by Erikson (1950) as the norm. His theory arose from a Western tradition, so when students from multicultural groups are measured against its standards, there are problems with its universal application. Until recently, child development textbooks attended to culture as a separate entity rather than as a vertical thread that weaves its influence through each developmental stage. Eriksonian crises such as autonomy versus shame and doubt, and identity versus role confusion, are Western constructs, steeped in individualistic norms and goals. The age-appropriate crisis for Cara, industry versus inferiority, assumes that "I am what I can accomplish." However, there are significant challenges for her because she may be judged against that standard with regard to mobility impairment, decreased endurance, and frequent absences. Her Filipino/Caribbean ancestry provided her with a developmental construct that, like Erikson's industry, stressed the importance of achievement, but unlike that psychosocial challenge, stressed its importance only in the context of her role in the social group. She was brought up to value verbal hesitancy and ambiguity in her communication with others in order to avoid giving offense (Futrell, Gomez, & Bedden, 2003). Unfortunately, this pattern of communication might be misconstrued as inferiority, the negative corollary to industry. In Cara's case, the pressure to do well in school collided with the pressure of her illness, making it difficult to cope. However, most of her teachers and service providers believed in helping her to maximize her fullest potential even though she internalized some circles of failure because of her illness.

Learners like Cara, who enter school with physical and health impairments, and who give meaning to life through the lens of their culture, suffer from being held to a rigid developmental standard of performance. As a result, many do in fact feel inferior. The wide array of conditions they bring to the classroom include cerebral palsy, muscular dystrophy, diabetes, cancer, asthma, and many more disabilities and medical diagnoses (Kauffman & Hallahan, 2005). People with these physical or health impairments can be served under the umbrella of the 1975 Education for All Handicapped Children Act (P.L. 94-142) and its amendments and reauthorizations (e.g., the 1997 Individuals with Disabilities Education Act [IDEA] and the 2004 Individuals with Disabilities Education Improvement Act [IDEIA]). These laws, in concert with Section 504 of the Vocational Rehabilitation Act of 1973 (P.L. 93-112) and Title II of the Americans with Disabilities Act (P.L. 101-336), form the nondiscrimination frameworks for students with physical and health impairments in public education. In fact, most educators point to these laws as the motivation for bringing this population into the general education classroom and rarely ask the questions, "What does the inclusion of students with physical and health impairments yield for society?" and "What have we learned as a society about the exclusion of students with disabilities in schools?"

Clearly, there are psychosocial and functional aspects of chronic illness and disability (Falvo, 1991). The self, family members, teachers, and community members are all affected. As a matter of necessity, a comprehensive support model is needed to take advantage of all affected variables (Obiakor, Grant, & Dooley, 2002). Laws are promulgated to reduce poor treatment of persons with physical and health impairments; however, humans practicalize these laws by valuing the sacred existence of fellow humans. All aspects of human existence require understanding, valuing, caring, and practicality. Without these basic ingredients, the simplest form of human illness or disease could be emotionally devastating (American Academy of Family Physicians, 2004; American Diabetes Association, 1997; Cicero & Pierre, 2001; Falvo, 1991; Fleitas, 2000, 2002, 2003; Kemper & Stilwell, 1995; Shangold & Gross, 1981; Wood & Associates, 1998). For instance, Falvo wrote:

> Chronic illness and disability have a major impact on the psychological, familial, social, and vocational aspects of the lives of the individuals who are experiencing them. Although several factors influence the extent of the impact, every chronic illness or disability requires some alteration and adjustment in daily life. The type of impact is dependent on the nature of the condition, the individual's pre-illness/disability personality, the meaning of the illness or disability to the individual, the current life circumstances of the individual, and the degree of family and social support within the individual's environment. (p. 1)

Based on Falvo's statement, general and special educators are obligated to understand a medical condition in the context of its effects on the individual's ability to function within his or her community. In the introductory case, Cara's illness affected how she viewed herself, how her parents reacted to her adjustment in school, and how the teachers responded to her needs.

DEFINITIONS AND TERMS IN PHYSICAL AND HEALTH IMPAIRMENTS

More than a decade ago, Blackhurst and Berdine (1993) explained that a child with physical and health impairment is "one whose physical or health problems result in an impairment of normal interaction with society to the extent that specialized services and programs are required" (p. 352). They argued that those with physical and health impairments are typically grouped in categories, yet this categorical grouping isolates them from other children. They acknowledged that "most of the terms used to describe physical disabilities are based on medical usage, which is derived from Greek and Latin. Areas of the body are frequently designated with prefixes, whereas suffixes are used to designate conditions of the body" (p. 352). For instance, *hemi* refers to one side of the body, and *plegia* refers to paralysis or the inability to move. *Monoplegia* involves one limb; *hemiplegia* involves both limbs on the same side of the body; *paraplegia* involves the lower limbs; *diplegia* involves all four limbs, but the lower limbs more seriously than the upper; *triplegia* involves three limbs; *quadriplegia* involves all four limbs; and *double hemiplegia* involves upper limbs more seriously affected than the lower. Other important terms include *anterior*, meaning front; *posterior*, meaning back; *medial*, pertaining to the middle; *lateral*, farther from the midline; *superior*, meaning upper; and *inferior*, meaning lower (see Blackhurst & Berdine, 1993).

Physical and health impairments involve people who are grouped by their abilities to function in a particular way and those who are grouped according to medical diagnoses. According to Blackhurst and Berdine (1993), the familiar categories of physical and health impairments are "ambulation, which refers to a child's ability to move from place to place, and vitality, which refers to the health and ability to sustain life" (p. 352). Disabilities that affect *ambulation* include:

- **Cerebral palsy.** This is caused by a brain dysfunction. It is a nonprogressive disorder (i.e., it does not become progressively more debilitating) that affects gross and fine motor coordination. Literally, *cerebral* refers to the brain and *palsy* refers to paralysis. If this were to be consistently true, no person with cerebral palsy would succeed in school and life. In reality, many of them do succeed.
- **Muscular dystrophy.** This is a disease in which the voluntary muscles progressively weaken and degenerate until they can no longer function.
- **Spinal muscular atrophy.** This affects the spinal cord and may result in progressive degeneration of nerve cells.
- **Polio.** Also called poliomyelitis or infantile paralysis, this is a viral infection that affects or destroys the anterior horn cells in the spinal cord. When

these cells are destroyed, the muscles that they serve eventually die or become paralyzed.

- **Spinal cord injuries.** These can be caused by auto accidents, sports accidents, and accidents at work. As Blackhurst and Berdine (1993) pointed out, "an injury may result in quadriplegia or paraplegia. Depending on the damage that occurs, the injured portion may recover completely or not at all" (p. 360).
- **Spina bifida.** This is a congenital defect that results when the bones of a part of the spine fail to grow together.
- **Osteogenesis imperfecta.** This is known as brittle bone disease. It is an inherited disorder that does not have a cure. The bones of children with this disorder break easily, and the fractures cause the limbs to be small and bowed.
- **Multiple sclerosis.** This is a progressive disorder in which portions of the myelin sheath (tissues surrounding the spinal cord) are damaged and replaced by scar tissue, resulting in short circuiting of nerve impulses to muscles.
- **Juvenile rheumatoid arthritis.** This is a chronic condition. The first signs of the disease are general fatigue, stiffness, and aching of the joints as they swell and become tender.

Disabilities that affect *vitality* include:

- **Congenital heart defects.** The second most common type of birth defect, they are generally recognized at birth or in early childhood. They are mechanical in nature. Persons with these defects have shortness of breath, cyanosis (blue appearance of the skin), and low tolerance for exercise.
- **Cystic fibrosis.** This is a chronic genetic disorder that typically affects the nature of secretions produced by glands in the body, particularly the lungs and pancreas. According to Blackhurst and Berdine (1993), "when the lungs are affected, the mucus normally found in the lungs does not drain properly and when it builds up, blocks the passage of air to and from the affected area" (p. 367).
- **Diabetes.** This is an inherited metabolic disorder that affects the metabolism of sugar. Insufficient insulin is produced to process the sugar in the bloodstream. Type I diabetes requires injections of insulin to compensate for the lack of its production in the pancreas, and Type II diabetes requires a well-balanced diet with a restriction of simple sugars.
- **Asthma.** This is a chronic condition characterized by inflammation in the air passages, resulting in secretions and obstruction that produces wheezing or labored breathing. Blackhurst and Berdine (1993) noted that asthma tends to run in families. "The severity and duration of asthma attacks vary considerably" (p. 369). Asthma may be due to allergic reactions to foods (ingestants) or to particles in the air (inhalants).
- **Acquired immunodeficiency syndrome (AIDS).** This is acquired from the human immunodeficiency virus (HIV), which is spread through the exchange of body fluids.
- **Cancer.** This can take many different forms, including leukemia, lymphoma, and tumors that affect various organs, bone tumors, and brain tumors.

There are other disabilities that are related to physical and health impairments. Convulsive disorders include epilepsy and seizures. Epilepsy "is caused by brain dysfunctions that impair the brain's ability to control its normal electrical activity" (Blackhurst & Berdine, 1993, p. 370). As Blackhurst and Berdine noted, "when control is lost, electrical energy stimulates many different parts of the brain at the same time, and the individual may have a seizure" (p. 371). This can occur in anyone at any age. It can be *petit mal* (lasts for a short time) or *grand mal* (lasts for a long time).

FUNCTIONAL EDUCATIONAL NEEDS OF MULTICULTURAL LEARNERS WITH PHYSICAL AND HEALTH IMPAIRMENTS

With 12 million children with physical and health impairments in the United States (one in every five households), and with federal laws mandating educational inclusion in the least restrictive environment for these youngsters (IDEA, 1997; IDEIA, 2004), school systems are challenged to offer appropriate supports. The prevalence of children with special health care needs varies by age, with the numbers increasing as a child moves from preschool (7.8%) to elementary/middle (14.6%) to high school (15.8%). The numbers vary by race and ethnicity as well, with American Indian and mixed race children claiming the highest prevalence at almost 32% (Blumberg, Halfon, & Olson, 2003). As a consequence, it behooves general and special educators to plan functional educational programming for these children to increase their functional capacity (Falvo, 1991; Spector, 2000; Utley & Obiakor, 2001; Utsey, Ponterotto, Reynolds, & Cancelli, 2000). For example, Falvo asserted that:

> Functional capacity goes beyond specific tasks and activities. It also includes significant events and relationships in the individual's life, such as relationships with family, friends, employers, and casual acquaintances. No relationship exists in isolation. Just as the individual's reaction to the illness or disability influences the reaction of others, the reaction of others affects the individual's self-concept and perception of his or her own strengths and abilities. (p. 1)

Blanchett and Wolfe (2000) agreed that "when planning for instruction of students with health impairments, many general and special educators are faced with the dilemma of what to teach students during their brief but important time within the classroom" (p. 348). They added that since "students with health impairments often have a variety of needs, educators, along with parents and other individuals, must determine what skills and activities should be targeted for instruction" (p. 348). Clearly, these learners must acclimate to the culture of the health care system as well as to that of the classroom. Western medicine values a reliance on accurate diagnosis, prescription of treatment and supportive care based on that diagnosis, and determination of a prognosis and trajectory of the medical condition. Learners from multicultural backgrounds often value a more holistic approach to the understanding and treatment of illness and disability. It has only been fairly recently that cultural variations in the presentation of illness have even been noted (Harris, 2000;

Helman, 2000; Huang, 1993). For instance, Helman emphasized that health interventions cannot be meaningful prior to the development of an insight into a person's culture. He referred to the cultural "lens" of a society (i.e., a perception of the world or a lens through which people view life as an issue that must be tackled in educational programs). For Cara in the introductory case, developmental issues and culture combined to influence her perceptions of her health care experience. As two separate "lenses," they colored the ways in which she understood the hospital and the medical treatment prescribed for the resolution of bone cancer. Without attending to both, educators and health care providers frequently fail to provide empathetic and effective care. Although people of different cultures share basic concepts, they view these cultures from different angles and perspectives, leading them to behave in manners that may be considered deviant by educators and health providers (Lewis, 1999; Luckmann, 1999; Rodd, 1996). Although there are educators and health providers like Cara's teacher who treat multicultural students with physical and health impairments with care, there are some in educational and medical communities who are myopic, only focusing on diagnosing the deviance from the norm (see Fleitas, 2000). This behavior of teachers and service providers makes participation in family, social, and work activities difficult.

Many learners with physical and health impairments have pragmatic as well as psychosocial concerns. Despite the mandate included in the ADA (1990) for building accessibility, not all facilities are in compliance. When a student with a physical disability is educated in an inclusive setting, accessibility and accommodation issues must be addressed (Blanchett & Wolfe, 2000; Kauffman & Hallahan, 2005). General and special education teachers for the most part have been educated to educate, not to attend to health problems of their students, problems that had been the purview of nurses in school settings. Yet the growing number of students with physical and health impairments in classrooms has necessitated a change. Like Cara's teacher, these teachers must be aware of the educational ramifications of a number of childhood diseases and disabilities. They must also be responsive to the needs that these health conditions activate. Children no longer remain in hospitals for weeks and months. Instead, often after a few days, they return to school with medical needs that create tension in the classroom. Such tension is visible in teachers as well, who are often poorly informed of the nature of the health problems and of their roles should problems occur. In addition, a fine line must be drawn between paying too little attention to students with physical and health impairment and patronizing them, thus increasing both physical risks and frustrations (Weist, Finney, Barnard, Davis, & Ollendick, 1993). Given the trauma in Cara's life and in the life of her family, efforts to ensure strong ties in the classroom setting are critical antecedents to fostering her resilience. Fortunately, her teacher understands that! In fact, collaborative and consultative efforts must be made to respond to her health needs in a sensitive and culturally competent manner.

On the whole, general and special education teachers are powerful people in the lives of *all* students, and as such, they have tremendous influence over the nature of educational and social climates in the classroom. Lightfoot, Wright, and Sloper (1999), in their study of learners with physical and health impairments, reported that even within the same school, teachers reacted very differently to medical needs of learners with physical and health impairments. This proves that teachers are not exempt from cultural myths and stereotypes—they are universal. Cara revealed herself as a student who did not want to disappoint her parents but felt overburdened by illness. In addition, the parents seemed frustrated because of their daughter's illness and her inability to maximize her educational potential (Cho, Singer, & Brenner, 2000; Garcia, Mendez-Perez, & Ortiz, 2000; Wohls, 1993). This is why cultural respect and valuing must be at the center of what educators, service providers, and health professionals do (Saina & Cauble, 2004). In Cara's situation, the teacher's knowledge base prevented her from engaging in misinterpretations. She did not mislabel Cara—she recognized medical symptomatology as a factor contributing to Cara's "inattention" in the classroom. In spite of all the frustrations surrounding her job, the teacher was focused on trying to do the right thing. She understood the importance for *all* learners with physical and health impairments to be integrated into the life of the classroom in a safe and socially appropriate manner (Blanchett & Wolfe, 2000; Carroll, 2004; Delpit, 1996; Fleitas, 2003; Kauffman & Hallahan, 2005). In addition, she focused on collaborating and consulting with parents and colleagues to provide functional educational needs for *all* her students, including Cara.

A Culturally Responsive Educator

1. Participates in a multidisciplinary planning process to ensure success in school reentry after hospitalization or extended absences, focusing on both medical and cultural issues.
2. Monitors needs that flow from medical and cultural diversity and addresses them with multidimensional strategies.
3. Creates a classroom milieu that values diversity, reflects respect and caring, and promotes academic achievement.
4. Includes students with impairments in as many activities as possible, providing assistance as necessary.
5. Facilitates positive peer interactions by formal or informal information sharing about impairments with *all* students.
6. Offers opportunities for *all* students to express individual and cultural differences.
7. Gains an understanding of student physical and health impairments and keeps an updated care plan for each student for effective management.
8. Has the skills and resources to evacuate nonambulatory students in emergencies and handle health crises.
9. Involves parents in decision making and lets them know that they are the experts in relation to their children.
10. Understands both cultural preferences and appropriate responses to medical needs.

Conclusion

This chapter focused on ways to maximize the fullest potential of multicultural learners with physical and health impairments. Many students like Cara struggle alone with classroom activities that seem overwhelming. Having such an intensive illness and coming from a multicultural background, Cara can profit from careful planning to ensure that her fundamental needs for safety, acceptance, achievement, and inclusion are met. A multidisciplinary, concerted effort must be made to truly educate her in the least restrictive environment while maintaining high standards of performance and offering flexible strategies to achieve success.

There is no doubt that Cara's illness has put a burden on her parents. It is critical that general and special educators ensure that teachers and service providers hear their voices and show understanding of their plight. If the central goal is *to leave no child behind,* proactive efforts must be made to educate multicultural learners with physical and health impairments in collaborative and consultative fashions.

Discussion Questions

1. Discuss how the hospital, home, and school can collaborate and consult to minimize stressors that affect students like Cara.
2. Explain the nature of stigma and recommend strategies to combat it in the classroom.
3. Explore ways of enhancing communication with parents and health professionals.
4. Analyze the constraints related to effective management of physical and health impairment in the context of cultural diversity.
5. Describe strategies of inclusion that would better serve Cara as she copes with both medical and educational stressors.

References

American Academy of Family Physicians (2004). *Family doctor: Your essential guide to health and well being.* Leawood, KS: Author.

American Diabetes Association (1997). *Diabetes A to Z: What you need to know about diabetes—simply put* (3rd ed.). Alexandria, VA: Author.

Americans with Disabilities Act of 1990, Pub. L. No. 101-336.

Blackhurst, A. E., & Berdine, W. H. (1993). *An introduction to special education* (3rd ed.). New York: HarperCollins.

Blanchett, W. J., & Wolfe, P. S. (2000). Working with persons with physical and health impairments. In F. E. Obiakor, S. A. Burkhardt, A. F. Rotatori, & T. Wahlberg (Eds.), *Intervention techniques for individuals with exceptionalities in inclusive settings: Advances in special education* (pp. 239–259). Stamford, CT: JAI Press.

Blumberg, S. J., Halfon, N., & Olson, L. M. (2003, June). The national survey of early child-hood health. *Pediatrics, 113,* 1899–1906.

Carroll, D. W. (2004). Multiracial children: Practical suggestions for parents and teachers. *Communiqué, 32*(7). Retrieved September 27, 2004 from www.nasponline.org/publications/cq327multiracial.html

Cho, S., Singer, G., & Brenner, M. (2000). Adaptation and accommodation for young chil-dren with disabilities: A comparison of Korean and Korean American parents. *Topics in Early Childhood Special Education, 20,* 236–250.

Cicero, K., & Pierre, C. (2001). *Kitchen counter cures.* Wixon, MI: Baker.

Davidhizer, R. (1999, July/August). Assessing culturally diverse pediatric clients. *Pediatric Nursing, 25,* 371–377.

Delpit, L. D. (1996). *Other people's children: Cultural conflict in the classroom.* New York: New Press.

Education for All Handicapped Children Act of 1975, Pub. L. No. 94-142.

Erikson, E. H. (1950). *Childhood and society.* New York: Norton.

Falvo, D. R. (1991). *Medical and psychological aspects of chronic illness and disability.* Gaithersburg, MD: Aspen.

Fleitas, J. (2000). *Band-aides and blackboards.* Retrieved May 15, 2004 from www.faculty.fairfield.edu/fleitas/seeme.html

Fleitas, J. (2002). *Band-aides and blackboards.* Retrieved March 15, 2004 from www.faculty.fairfield.edu/fleitas/teachtips.html

Fleitas, J. (2003). Educating children and youth with serious medical conditions: Perils and potential. In F. E. Obiakor, S. A. Burkhardt, A. F. Rotatori, & T. Wahlberg (Eds.), *Effective education for learners with exceptionalities: Advances in special education* (pp. 283–298). Oxford, England: Elsevier Science/JAI Press.

Futrell, M., Gomez, J., & Bedden, D. (2003). Teaching the children of a new America. *Phi Delta Kappan, 84,* 381–385.

Garcia, S., Mendez-Perez, A., & Ortiz, A. (2000). Mexican-American mother's beliefs about disabilities: Implications for early childhood intervention. *Remedial and Special Education, 21,* 90–100, 120.

Harris, C. H. (2000). Educating toward multiculturalism. *OT Practice,* pp. 7–8.

Helman, C. (2000). *Culture, health and illness.* Oxford, England: Butterworth and Heinemann.

Huang, G. (1993). *Beyond culture: Communicating with Asian American children and their fami-lies.* ERIC/CUE Digest #94. Retrieved April 20, 2004 from www.ericfacility.net/data-bases/ERICDigests/ed366673.html

Individuals with Disabilities Education Act of 1997, Pub. L. No. 105-117.

Individuals with Disabilities Education Improvement Act of 2004, Pub. L. No. 108-446.

Kauffman, J. M., & Hallahan, D. P. (2005). *Special education: What it is and why we need it.* Boston: Allyn & Bacon.

Kemper, D. W., & Stilwell, D. (1995). *Healthwise handbook: A self-care manual for you* (12th ed.). Boise, ID: Healthwise.

Lewis, R. D. (1999). *When cultures collide.* London, England: Brealey.

Lightfoot, J., Wright, S., & Sloper, P. (1999). Supporting pupils in mainstream school with an illness or disability: Young people's views. *Child: Care, Health and Development, 25*(4), 267–283.

Luckmann, J. (1999). *Transcultural communication in nursing.* Albany, NY: Delmar.

Obiakor, F. E., Grant, P., & Dooley, E. (2002). *Educating all learners: Refocusing the comprehen-sive support model.* Springfield, IL: Charles C Thomas.

Rodd, J. (1996). Children, culture and education, the importance of culture in children's education. *Childhood Education: International Focus Issue, 72,* 325–329.

Saina, D., & Cauble, B. (2004). *Applying cultural knowledge to child welfare practice.* Retrieved August 8, 2004 from www.socwel.ku.edu/cws/modules/acktocwp.pdf

Shangold, M. M., & Gross, E. C. (1981). *Women's medical problems.* New York: Hearst Books.

Spector, R. E. (2000). *Cultural diversity in health & illness* (5th ed.). Upper Saddle River, NJ: Prentice Hall.

Utley, C. A., & Obiakor, F. E. (2001). Multicultural education and special education: Infusion for better schooling. In C. A. Utley & F. E. Obiakor (Eds.), *Special education, multicultural education, and school reform: Components of quality education for learners with mild disabilities* (pp. 3–29). Springfield, IL: Charles C Thomas.

Utsey, S. O., Ponterotto, J. G., Reynolds, A. L., & Cancelli, A. A. (2000). Racial discrimination, coping, life satisfaction, and self-esteem among African-Americans. *Journal of Counseling and Development, 78,* 72–80.

Vocational Rehabilitation Act of 1973, Pub. L. No. 93-112.

Weist, M. D., Finney, J. W., Barnard, M. U., Davis, C. D., & Ollendick, T. H. (1993). Empirical selection of psychosocial treatment targets for children and adolescents with diabetes. *Journal of Pediatric Psychology, 18,* 11–28.

Wohls, J. (1993). On belonging: A place to stand, a gift to give. In A. P. Turnbull, J. A. Patterson, S. K. Behr, D. L. Murphy, J. G. Marquis, & M. J. Blue-Banning (Eds.), *Cognitive coping, families, and disability* (pp. 151–163). Baltimore: Brookes.

Wood, F. W., & Associates. (1998). *Nature's prescriptions: Foods, vitamins, and supplements that prevent disease.* Peachtree City, GA: FC&A.

Chapter 12

Working with Multicultural Learners with Hearing Loss

Kathleen M. Chinn, C. Jonah Eleweke, and Eric J. López

Chapter Outline

Thinking About Multicultural Special Education

Christina was a 14-year-old Latina student who was deaf. She had lived in the United States for about 6 years. Prior to coming to the United States, Christina lived with her family in Mexico. Her mother was a Mexican Indian and her father was Mexican. Christina's mother spoke both Mixtec and Spanish; her father spoke and wrote Spanish. Neither of Christina's parents read or wrote English. Christina and her family lived in a rural border state about 50 miles from the border of Mexico. Her father was a farm laborer and her mother worked in the family home.

Christina was enrolled in the local public school system 5 years ago. During the enrollment process her mother was interviewed. When she was asked about Christina, she replied that Christina could wash clothes, make beds, clean house (including sweeping and mopping), cook, and wash dishes. In her estimate, Christina was a bright child. Upon formal in-school testing (using a combination of two IQ tests, the UNIT and the TONI-2), it was determined that Christina had an IQ of about 70 (UNIT: IQ of 68, TONI-2: IQ of 72).

Based on a profound hearing loss and low IQ scores, Christina was placed in a self-contained special education classroom all day, labeled "hearing impaired," and considered to have possible mild mental retardation. Luckily, for half of her day she was with a special education certified teacher who happened to be a child of deaf adults (CODA). Thus, for half of the day, Christina was exposed to American Sign Language (ASL). Within 6 months, she had reached the third-grade level in math skills, was writing simple sentences in English, and was gaining Spanish written vocabulary. Five years later, Christina was educated for half a day in a self-contained classroom for the deaf and was mainstreamed with an interpreter for the rest of the day. Although Christina made leaps and bounds in her education, her mother still expected that as an adult, Christina would clean and take care of people's houses, a goal different from her teacher's expectations. Before long, her mother decided that she wanted to learn American Sign Language. Christina's teacher began to develop a tape of ASL vocabulary translated into Spanish so that Christina's mother could begin to communicate with her. In the end, Christina's teacher and mother continued the collaboration that helped Christina to grow and bloom. They developed mutual respect for each other and everyone gained.

- *What steps did Christina's teacher take to help Christina to maximize her potential in class?*
- *What is Christina's prognosis for successful adulthood, given the amount of progress she made in the past 5 years?*

This chapter focuses on working with multicultural learners with hearing loss like Christina. Children who are deaf and are of other cultures face many of the same problems in accessing education and other services in the United States. Increasing numbers of children and young people from multicultural groups require educators with multicultural experience who possess cross-cultural sensitivity. Evidence indicates that in 1990, 20% of the U.S. population were foreign-born ethnic minorities. This number is expected to increase because at least one million immigrants, the majority of them ethnic minorities, enter the United States annually (Gargiulo, 2003). Bynoe (1998) noted that the majority of people living in 23 of the 25 major cities in the United States were diverse minority ethnic people with diverse linguistic and cultural backgrounds. Further, it has been observed that multicultural students constitute the majority of students in states like Texas, California, and New York as well as in cities such as Detroit, Atlanta, Miami, Baltimore, and Chicago (Gargiulo, 2003; Heward, 2000). Data from the U.S. Department of Education (2003) indicated that 38.8% of students in public schools were ethnic minorities, which is a significant increase from 29.6% in 1986. As the data revealed, the number of students who spoke a language other than English at home increased by more than 50% from 6.3 million in 1979 to 13.7 million in 1999 (see U.S. Department of Education, 2003).

During the 1990s several research projects were conducted regarding immigrant and migrant deaf children of Latino heritage (Gerner de Garcia, 1993, 1995a, 1995b; Rodriguez & Santiviago, 1991). However, in the last 5 years, research on multiculturalism in deaf studies has begun to lessen. Yet evidence reveals that the number of multicultural learners with hearing loss in most multiethnic societies, for example, the United States, Canada, and the United Kingdom, has continued to increase (Gargiulo, 2003; Rodda & Eleweke, 2003). Evidence indicates that these learners constitute approximately 41 to 43% of the deaf school-age population in the United States (Andrews & Martin, 1998; Mitchell, 2004). Their representation in schools, according to data from the IDEA Child Count (Mitchell, 2004), are as follows: white (59%), African American (16%), and Latino (19%), for the three major ethnic groups. However, according to the data from the Gallaudet Research Institute (2004), the percentages of ethnicity for the three dominant groups are: white (51.5%), African American (15.4%), and Latino (24.2%). Further, current information from the Gallaudet Research Institute indicates that in the southern and western United States, the percentages of Latino students increased to 25.7% and 24.2%, respectively. In general, the representation of white children is decreasing and the representation of multicultural children is increasing. Specifically, the Center for Assessment and Demographics (1995) reported 59% white students and 41% minority students for the 1994–95 school year, in contrast with 67% white and 33% minorities in the 1983–84 school year.

The increasing numbers of multicultural learners with hearing loss in schools notwithstanding, Doe (1994) noted that these learners are in a "multiple minority" category and are faced with formidable barriers to the development of their potential because of prejudice and ignorance. Earlier, Reagan (1990) remarked that a child who is both deaf and a member of a multicultural group is indeed faced with a social and educational "double whammy." Similarly, Schirmer (2000) observed that double minority membership places deaf individuals in double jeopardy and further argued that these learners are forced to deal with the issues of stereotyping, prejudice, and discrimination in their attempt to access relevant services in the community. Put another way, an understanding of and sensitivity to these learners is essential in the provision of services that are appropriate, respectful, and helpful. In the absence of such an understanding and sensitivity, service providers can misinterpret their communication and behavior.

Multicultural learners with hearing loss like Christina, who have no English and American Sign Language skills, have consistent problems in accessing meaningful education and related services in the community. Reagan (1990) argued that regardless of how well intentioned, current educational and other social services are not adequate in addressing the needs of these learners. Indeed, Schirmer (2000) observed that although deaf individuals have the same diverse racial, ethnic, and linguistic backgrounds as other ethnic minorities, educators and service providers seem less likely to acknowledge the differential educational experiences that they bring to the table. As Reagan pointed out, "We will be faced with a growing challenge to develop innovative and effective techniques for meeting the social, cultural, and linguistic needs of children who are caught not in a bilingual and bicultural matrix, but rather in a multilingual and multicultural one" (p. 79). Clearly, these learners have difficulties in accessing existing services because their home culture may, to varying degrees, differ from that of the dominant hearing culture as well as from the mainstream deaf culture. To respond to the educational needs of students like Christina, the foci must be on the important areas of (a) language and communication, (b) assessment and placement, and (c) cultural issues and role models (e.g., parents and professionals).

LANGUAGE AND COMMUNICATION

The foremost issue affecting the access of education and related services by multicultural learners with hearing loss centers on language and communication (Eleweke & Rodda, 2000; Odgen, 1997; Turnbull, Turnbull, Shanke, & Smith, 2004). Recall in the introductory case, Christina took two nonverbal IQ tests. No oral language was used for either test. Instead, eye gaze, gesture, and pointing were used to conduct the test. Any test presented in English or ASL would have been improper because Christina came to the educational setting with no verbal language (English or ASL). In the case of Christina, who came to the United States with no experience of the dominant culture or language, it is not surprising that she received IQ scores much lower than her potential. The reason for this is that performance on standardized assessment instruments are affected by both culture and language. Therefore, with bilingual children, improper assessment instruments can lead to improper educational decisions that affect adversely their optimum development. Many of these learners have parents who are nonsigning monolinguals, for example, Spanish speakers. Thus, these learners are not exposed to English at home but are expected to learn to read and write English in the academic setting. In addition, they may be taught sign language in school. However, depending on the school's policy, the sign language may be ASL or a Manually Coded English (MCE) form of signing. ASL is a complete language in its own right that has rules for use and communication (Paperkamp & Mehler, 1999; Stokoe, 1963). In contrast, MCE systems attempt to use ASL signs to represent English language words, inserting markers for morphemes. Although it sounds good, the essence of meaning of the communicative gesture is lost. Further, it distorts the flow of the visual language.

Cummins (1992) noted that children who do not acquire a first language completely may not be able to fully acquire a second language. This is a major concern given that MCEs are not complete languages. In addition, ASL develops in a natural way, and it is taught from child to child or many times from older child to younger child. In addition, it is the language of the Deaf culture (Bat-Chava, 2000; Lane, Hoffmeister, & Bahan, 1996). Moreover, most multicultural learners frequently join the Deaf culture in adulthood. The major characteristic of deaf members of the Deaf community is the use of ASL. Therefore, most experts in the field of deaf education prescribe ASL. In the case of multicultural learners with hearing loss like Christina who have no English and ASL skills, there are some critical questions. Are there interpreters who can ensure that the test instructions are appropriately conveyed in their native language? Do learners hear well enough to make use of the oral instruction in, say, Spanish? If the answers to these questions are not in the affirmative, then there is real danger that multicultural learners like Christina are wrongly tested and placed in educational programs.

ASSESSMENT AND PLACEMENT

Assessment and referral processes for children who are deaf are different from those of many children referred for special education. Some children are deaf congenitally, that is, they are deaf at or become deaf shortly after birth; others lose their hearing prelingually, that is, prior to language development (i.e., before age 2); and some children are deaf adventitiously, that is, they lose their hearing after language has developed (i.e., after age 2). According to Billings and Kenna (1999); Cherian, Singh, Chacko, and Abraham (2002); Morzaria, Westerberg, and Kozak (2004); and Walch, Anderhuber, Kole, and Berghold (2000), causative factors of hearing loss include prenatal factors (e.g., heredity factors), perinatal factors (e.g., lack of oxygen), or postnatal factors (e.g., illnesses). Early hearing screening is mandated at birth for all newborn infants in the United States and thus performed prior to leaving the hospital (Hayes, 1999, 2001). Otoacoustic emission (OE) and auditory brainstem response (ABR) are two of some of the tests used to identify hearing loss in infants (Furst, Bresloff, Levine, Merlob, & Attias, 2004; Jakubkova, Kabatova, & Zavodna, 2003). Generally, upon failing OE, an ABR is performed. Some children who have hearing loss are missed because of false positive screening results. In some children, hearing loss occurs later in life from high fever, meningitis, and other factors that are identified by audiological assessments (Baroch, 2003). Factoring in children who are prelingually deaf, the age of identification for children with hearing loss in the United States is between 13 to 20 months (Harrison & Roush, 1996; Kittrell & Arjmand, 1997; Pendergast, Lartz, & Fiedler, 2002). After identification, parents are referred by a physician to a parent infant training program or to a public school program if the child loses his or her hearing after the preschool years. At entry into parent infant training, preschool, or regular school, other diagnostics are performed to determine developmental skills, language, IQ, and later academic achievement levels, as mandated by IDEA (Moores, 2001).

For many multicultural learners with hearing loss, there appears to be little or no information about the onset or diagnosis of hearing loss. Christina was enrolled in a school that recognized her hearing loss. Although the audiologist spoke Spanish and English, Christina had no knowledge of Spanish, English, or sign language. Further, she had never been to school. Was it surprising, therefore, that she performed poorly on all tests? Legislative amendments in the United States, for example, the 1990 Americans with Disabilities Act (ADA) and the 1990 Individuals with Disabilities Education Act (IDEA), require that assessments be performed in a nondiscriminatory manner (Bysshe, 1995). Mason (2005) suggested that when assessing children who are deaf or hard of hearing, culture and language as well as a disability must be taken into account. This was certainly not the case for Christina. However, she was able to make academic progress, including a 3 academic year improvement in mathematic skills. Notwithstanding the use of ASL, Christina's IQ test scores remained at 70. Clearly, it was more than expressive and receptive language that affected her ability to perform on the IQ test. Lane et al. (1996) agreed that learners like Christina may face double prejudice in education and other social services. As they explained,

> Deaf children from non-English-speaking homes are three to four times more likely to be labeled learning disabled, mentally retarded, or emotionally disturbed. . . . Deaf students are seriously disadvantaged in psychological and achievement testing because of the English language and cultural biases of the tests. . . . Black and Hispanic deaf children score well below white peers on achievement tests. They are more likely to drop out of high school or to be tracked into vocational rather than academic programs. . . . These educational "handicaps" of minorities within the deaf world take their toll on life fulfillment, . . . economic success and minority leadership in subsequent years. (p. 164)

CULTURAL ISSUES AND ROLE MODELS

Children who are deaf and multicultural may belong to any or to all of the following: the Deaf culture; their native country's culture; a shared culture, as in Christina's case, the Latino culture; and the American culture. Rodda and Eleweke (2003) explained that failure of educators and service providers to be culturally sensitive to multicultural learners could affect their interaction in the classroom. In the classroom, multicultural learners may exhibit behaviors that appear to the teacher as inappropriate, when instead it may be a cultural attribute. A common gesture of respect in Latino children, for example, is to drop eye gaze when the teacher is addressing them. However, in the white American culture, this may be misunderstood as a sign of guilt or lying. When educating children of different cultures, teachers and service providers should be aware of cultural influences and not assume that the children know or will display the characteristics that are representative of the dominant school culture. Further, these professionals should investigate students' home culture and allow them to share their culture with other class members. This also applies when professionals interact with parents of children from diverse cultures.

It is important to note that parents and professionals can be role models. Parents of multicultural children may not speak English. It is therefore imperative for an interpreter to be present at all conferences, individualized education plan (IEP) meetings, and any other time a teacher needs to contact or talk with them. Few parents learn to sign adequately with their children (Joseph & Alant, 2000; Lederberg & Everhart, 1998). Thus, it is difficult to ensure that instructions and directions to parents are relayed exactly to the child. The lack of multicultural adults who can serve as role models is another problem. Lane et al. (1996) observed that multicultural learners comprise more than one-third of all deaf school children in the United States, but only 7% of their teachers are multicultural. As a result, there is a near absence of role models for many of the children, who find little in their curriculum that relates clearly to their lives and personal idiosyncrasies.

Since parents are good role models, it is important that they are involved in the education of their children. When the needs of multicultural family members are included in the service delivery plan, parents are able to work toward the success of the plan for the benefit of their child with hearing loss. Family members can have input in formal planning and implementation of the program of care, and they also can be excellent advocates for their children and programs (Luterman, 1991; Turnbull & Turnbull, 2001). The provision of services that accommodate the needs of family members as well as those of the child with hearing loss is vital, particularly during children's preschool years when they spend most of their time with their families. Services provided at this stage have a significant impact on children's social, emotional, linguistic, and intellectual development (Pendergast et al., 2002). Therefore, information about services should be provided to parents to help them understand that their children's development can be advanced.

EFFECTIVE PROGRAMMING FOR MULTICULTURAL LEARNERS WITH HEARING LOSS

The starting point of any serious concern for the provision of accessible and appropriate education for multicultural learners like Christina must be awareness and recognition of their needs by educational institutions and service providers. It is imperative that educational institutions and service providers are aware of the need of these learners to acquire English and ASL skills to enhance effective communication and access relevant services and education. For students like Christina, enrollment into English-language learner (ELL) and ASL programs should be considered the top priority. These students must be given the appropriate assistance to facilitate the acquisition of English and ASL skills if they are to receive meaningful education. As a result, a partnership between the ELL programs, colleges/universities, local school boards, and local Association for the Deaf must be established to ensure improved coordination and utilization of available resources for multicultural learners with hearing loss. Working together, these agencies must plan the best means for their learners to acquire English and ASL skills prior to testing and placement in schools. It should be noted that other children of multicultural backgrounds who have special needs may also benefit from bilingual programs.

To enhance effective programming for multicultural learners with hearing loss, funding is an absolute necessity. Financial support by the various governments (i.e., federal, state, and provincial) is crucial to the provision of accessible and appropriate services for all learners. Considering the background of multicultural learners, it is almost impossible for parents to enroll their children in ELL and ASL programs. Consequently, there is a need for funding support that would enable multicultural learners like Christina to enroll in ELL and ASL classes, and that would ensure that important support services in terms of personnel and material resources are available. Further, governments should provide financial support for the establishment of Deaf Literacy Projects (DLP) in schools. Such projects could be the most effective means of imparting English literacy and ASL skills to multicultural learners, ensuring their academic success. For instance, through such projects, Christina can be assisted to acquire necessary skills.

The provision of effective education for multicultural learners with hearing loss like Christina makes it imperative for school boards in the United States to employ itinerant specialists in deafness, ethnicity, deaf culture, and communication, at least on a part-time basis. Such professionals would be of immense assistance in several areas to facilitate the provision of accessible and appropriate education for multicultural learners with hearing loss. The specialists, for instance, would be responsible for coordinating information on available resources. In addition, the specialists would work with different service providers and institutions to identify difficulties multicultural learners might encounter in accessing education and other services. Employing qualified deaf people who are themselves minorities would also have the advantage of providing multicultural learners with good role models. The provision of effective education underlines the need for increased partnership between agencies specializing in deafness, schools, and service providers to ensure that services are appropriate and accessible. By effective collaboration, new programs and services could be developed. If relevant agencies work together, they can provide various services to enhance different choices for multicultural learners. Further, if these agencies work together, learners like Christina would be able to access services and obtain education that would lead to secure employment. Collaboration by these agencies would ensure that appropriate services and supports would be available. If the agencies work together, they can provide multicultural learners and their families with better advice concerning educational opportunities, resources, and options available. In addition, collaboration and consultation would facilitate the establishment of appropriate support services to address the individual needs of learners like Christina.

Finally, effective bilingual-bicultural (BiBi) programs are imperative in the provision of true and meaningful multicultural education to all learners, including those with hearing loss like Christina. There is no doubt that English-language literacy is important for deaf people for effective functioning in the schools and the larger hearing society because so much information is in the print form of the spoken English language. How is such literacy to be developed? Since people with deafness do not match the assumptions of the medical-deficit model, Ladd (1994) and Reagan (1990) suggested that they have to be members of two cultures, the Deaf culture and one of the hearing cultures. But if the BiBi perspective is to be fully developed, it is important to be clear about the nature of Deaf culture, particularly the importance of "natural" sign languages for deaf people. According to Jacobs (1996), approximately 10% of deaf children are born to deaf parents and naturally acquire sign language as their native language. The other 90% are born to hearing parents. Jacobs noted that not recognizing that these deaf children have a culture different from their hearing parents' and not recognizing the rights of the children to become encultured into something that their parents cannot give them (i.e., Deaf culture) could be attributed to their later developmental difficulties with English literacy, and indeed, other facets of their development. Although Paul (1998) observed that no widely accepted definition for bilingualism in deafness exists, the term may refer to proficiency in two languages (i.e., ASL and print English). As a result of hearing loss, which may preclude deaf individuals from acquiring English as a first language, some professionals have argued for the development and use of sign language/English bilingual programs (see Paul, 1998; Paul & Quigley, 1994; Schirmer, 1994, 2000). Essentially, the bilingual approach could (a) enhance the knowledge and use of sign and written/spoken language (i.e., important features of Deaf and hearing cultures); (b) enrich deaf individuals socially, emotionally, and academically; and (c) promote interaction in different social settings.

EDUCATIONAL SUPPORT SERVICES

In addition to the deaf education curriculum, children who are deaf or hard of hearing may require ancillary support. Primarily, these support programs are made of speech language therapy, occupational therapy, and sometimes physical therapy. It is not always appropriate for deaf children to receive speech language therapy. It is only appropriate if the student has sufficient hearing to benefit from such therapy. Better speech language therapy techniques focus on the development of language skills.

Since some causes of hearing loss affect the vestibular system as well as causing secondary disabilities, it is not uncommon for occupational and sometimes physical therapy to be prescribed. Occupational therapy works at increasing fine motor skills and balance and protective reflexes, whereas physical therapy works to increase gross motor skills, ambulation, strength, and flexibility. All these services are necessary to help multicultural learners with hearing loss to maximize their potential.

A Culturally Responsive Educator

1. Understands that multicultural learners with hearing loss have a "double-whammy" problem.
2. Knows that instructional modification is an absolute necessity for multicultural learners with hearing loss.
3. Is aware that language is an integral part of culture.
4. Understands that demographic shifts are occurring in many cities of the United States.
5. Knows the laws that protect his or her students.
6. Understands that culture and language must be taken into account in performing assessments.
7. Creates classroom enrichments that are culturally sensitive.
8. Collaborates and consults with parents of children with hearing loss.
9. Avoids negative assumptions about multicultural learners.
10. Sees himself or herself as a role model to his or her multicultural learners.

Conclusion

This chapter focused on how to maximize the educational potential of multicultural learners with hearing loss. Clearly, a classroom that celebrates diversity proves welcoming to *all* learners, irrespective of their physical, emotional, social, and ethnic differences. To ensure the provision of effective education for multicultural learners with hearing loss like Christina, it is important to respond to the "double-whammy" issue (i.e., the interplay of culture and disability valuing). For many students with hearing loss, language acquisition is an important part of survival. Learners with hearing loss have problems with receptive language, but do not want to disappoint the teacher. To overcome this problem, teachers and service providers must never assume that students understand their questions or the subject matters to which they are exposed. Instead of asking close-ended questions, these students should be asked open-ended questions that require more than one- or two-word answers. Efforts must be made to minimize criticism and environments must be least restrictive.

It is important that general and special educators become familiar with a family's culture prior to advising the family about what to do to help the child with a hearing loss. They must take time to get to know the families and try to encourage them to talk with social workers if they have financial or other needs. They must encourage them to join organizations that can help them with issues related to children with disabilities. In addition, they must encourage them to learn languages that would benefit them with regard to the provision of materials, phone numbers, and contacts related to services and organizations. The appropriate use of sign language interpreters or bilingual specialists is essential to make sure that educational transitions from stage to stage are less traumatic.

Discussion Questions

1. Briefly explain how Christina's lack of English and ASL skills affected the results of the IQ tests given to her.
2. Describe how Christina's ethnic background affected her educational placement.
3. Evaluate why language is an integral part of culture.
4. Explain why multicultural learners with hearing loss have the "double-whammy" problem.
5. As an educator, discuss how you would become more culturally sensitive and responsive to the needs of multicultural learners like Christina.

References

Andrews, J. F., & Martin, G. (1998). *Hopwood*, affirmative action, and deaf children. *American Annals of the Deaf, 143*(4), 305–313.

Baroch, K. A. (2003). Universal newborn hearing screening: Fine-tuning the process. *Current Opinions on Otolaryngology, Head, and Neck Surgery, 11*(6), 424–427.

Bat-Chava, Y. (2000). Diversity and deaf identity. *American Annals of the Deaf, 145*(5), 420–428.

Billings, K. R., & Kenna, M. A. (1999). Causes of pediatric sensorineural hearing loss: Yesterday and today. *Archives of Otorhinolaryngology, Head, and Neck Surgery, 125*(11), 1284.

Bynoe, F. P. (1998). Rethinking and retooling teacher preparation to prevent perpetual failure in our children. *Journal of Special Education, 23*(1), 37–40.

Bysshe, J. (1995). Deafness in childhood: Are deaf children getting the education they need? *Professional Care of Mother and Child, 5*(1), 11–13.

Center for Assessment and Demographics, Gallaudet University. (1995). *1994–95 Annual survey of deaf and hard of hearing children and youth.* Washington, DC: Author.

Cherian, B., Singh, T., Chacko, B., & Abraham, A. (2002). Sensorineural hearing loss following bacterial meningitis in non-neonates. *Indian Journal of Pediatrics, 69*(11), 951–955.

Cummins, J. (1992). The role of primary language development in promoting educational success for language minority students. In D. P. Dolmon (Ed.), *Schooling and language minority students: A theoretical framework* (pp. 3–50). Los Angeles: California State University.

Doe, T. (1994). Multiple minorities: Communities within the deaf community. In C. J. Erting, R. C. Johnson, D. L. Smith, & B. O. Snider (Eds.), *The deaf way: Perspectives from the international conference on deaf culture* (pp. 464–469). Washington, DC: Gallaudet University Press.

Eleweke, C. J., & Rodda, M. (2000). Factors contributing to parents' selection of a communication mode to use with their deaf children. *American Annals of the Deaf, 145*(4), 375–381.

Furst, M., Bresloff, I., Levine, R. A., Merlob, P. L., & Attias, J. J. (2004). Interaural time coincidence detectors are present at birth: Evidence from bineural interaction. *Hearing Research, 187*(1), 63–72.

Gallaudet Research Institute (2004). *2003–2004 Regional and national summary.* Retrieved May 25, 2005, from gri.gallaudet.edu/Demographics/2004_National_Summary.pdf

Gargiulo, M. R. (2003). *Special education in contemporary society: An introduction to exceptionality.* Belmont, CA: Wadsworth/Thompson.

Gerner de Garcia, B. A. (1993). Addressing the needs of Hispanic deaf children. In K. M. Christensen & G. L. Delgado (Eds.), *Multicultural issues in deafness* (pp. 69–90). White Plains, NY: Longman.

Gerner de Garcia, B. A. (1995a). ESL applications for Hispanic children. *Bilingual Research Journal, 19*(384) 452–467.

Gerner de Garcia, B. A. (1995b). Communication and language in Spanish-speaking families with deaf children. In C. Lucas (Ed.), *Sociolinguistics in deaf communities (Vol. 1).* Washington, DC: Gallaudet University Press.

Harrison, M., & Roush, J. (1996). The age of suspicion, identification and intervention for infants and young children with hearing loss: A national survey. *Ear & Hearing, 17*(1), 55–62.

Hayes, D. (1999). State programs for universal newborn hearing screening. *Pediatric Clinicians of North America, 46*(1), 89–94.

Hayes, D. (2001). Newborn hearing screening: Selected experience in the United States. *Scandinavian Audiology, 53*, 29–32.

Heward, L. W. (2000). *Exceptional children: An introduction to special education.* Upper Saddle River, NJ: Merrill/Prentice Hall.

Jacobs, R. (1996). Just how hard is it to learn ASL: The case for ASL as a truly foreign language. In C. Lucas (Ed.), *Multicultural aspects of sociolinguistics in the deaf communities* (pp. 183–226). Washington, DC: Gallaudet University Press.

Jakubkova, J., Kabatova, Z., & Zavodna, M. (2003). Identification of hearing loss in newborns by transient otoacoustic emissions. *International Journal of Pediatric Otorhinolaryngology, 67*(1), 15–18.

Joseph, L., & Alant, E. (2000). Strangers in the house: Communication between mothers and their hearing impaired children who sign. *South African Journal of Communication Disorders, 47*, 15–24.

Kittrell, A. P., & Arjmand, E. M. (1997). The age of diagnosis of sensorineural hearing impairment in children. *International Journal of Pediatric Otorhinolaryngology, 4*(2), 97–106.

Ladd, P. (1994). Deaf culture: Finding it and nurturing it. In C. J. Erting, R. C. Johnson, & D. L. Smith (Eds.), *The deaf way: Perspectives from the international conference on deaf culture* (pp. 5–15). Washington, DC: Gallaudet University Press.

Lane, H., Hoffmeister, R., & Bahan, B. (1996). *A journey into the deaf-world.* San Diego, CA: DawnSign Press.

Lederberg, A. R., & Everhart, V. S. (1998). Communication between deaf children and their hearing mothers: The role of language, gesture, and vocalizations. *Journal of Speech, Language and Hearing Research, 41*(4), 887–899.

Luterman, D. M. (1991). *Counseling the communicatively disordered and their families.* Austin, TX: PRO-ED.

Mason, T. C. (2005). Cross cultural instrument translation: Assessment, translation and statistical applications. *American Annals of the Deaf, 150*(1), 67–72.

Mitchell, R. E. (2004). National profile of deaf and hard of hearing students in special education from weighted survey results. *American Annals of the Deaf, 149*(4), 336–349.

Moores, D. F. (2001). *Educating the deaf: Psychology, principles, and practices* (5th ed.). Boston: Houghton Mifflin.

Morzaria, S., Westerberg, B. D., & Kozak, F. K. (2004). Systematic review of the etiology of bilateral sensorineural hearing loss in children. *International Journal of Pediatric Otorhinolaryngology, 68*(9), 1193–1198.

Odgen, P. W. (1997). *The silent garden: Raising your deaf child.* Washington DC: Gallaudet University Press.

Paperkamp, S., & Mehler, J. (1999). Signed and spoken language: A unique underlying system? *Journal of Language and Speech, 42,* 333–346.

Paul, P. V. (1998). *Literacy and deafness: The development of reading, writing and literate thought.* Needham Heights, MA: Allyn & Bacon.

Paul, P., & Quigley, S. (1994). ASL/English bilingual education. In P. L. McAnally, S. Rose, & S. P. Quigley (Eds.), *Language learning practices with deaf children* (pp. 219–253). Austin, TX: PRO-ED.

Pendergast, S. G., Lartz, M. N., & Fiedler, B. C. (2002). Ages of diagnosis, amplification and early intervention of infants and young children with hearing loss: Findings from parent interviews. *American Annals of the Deaf, 147*(1), 24–29.

Reagan, T. (1990). Cultural considerations in the education of deaf children. In D. F. Moores & K. P. Meadows-Orlans (Eds.), *Education and developmental aspects of deafness* (pp. 73–84). Washington, DC: Gallaudet University Press.

Rodda, M., & Eleweke, C. J. (2003). Providing accessible services to minority ethnic deaf people: Insights from a study in Alberta, Canada. *American Annals of the Deaf, 147*(5), 45–55.

Rodriguez, O., & Santiviago, M. (1991). Hispanic deaf adolescence: A multicultural minority. *Volta Review, 93*(5), 89–97.

Schirmer, B. R. (1994). *Language and literacy development in children who are deaf.* New York: Macmillan.

Schirmer, B. R. (2000). *Psychological, social and educational dimensions of deafness.* Needham Heights, MA: Allyn & Bacon.

Stokoe, W. (1963). *Sign language structure: An outline of the visual communication structures of the American deaf* (Studies in Linguistics Occasional Papers No. 8). Washington, DC: Gallaudet University Press.

Turnbull, A., & Turnbull, H. R. (2001). *Families, professionals, and exceptionality: Collaborating for empowerment* (4th ed.). Upper Saddle River, NJ: Merrill/Prentice Hall.

Turnbull, R., Turnbull, A., Shank, M., & Smith, S. J. (2004). *Exceptional lives: Special education in today's schools*. Upper Saddle River, NJ: Merrill/Prentice Hall.

U.S. Department of Education. (2003). *The condition of education*. Washington, DC: Author.

Walch, C., Anderhuber, W., Kole, W., & Berghold, A. (2000). Bilateral sensorineural hearing disorders in children: Etiology of deafness and evaluation of hearing loss. *International Journal of Pediatric Otorhinolaryngology, 53*(1), 31–38.

Chapter 13

Working with Multicultural Learners with Visual Impairments

Wendy Sapp

Chapter Outline

Thinking About Multicultural Special Education

Gloria was born in Mexico City and diagnosed with optic nerve hypoplasia when she was 6 months old. The doctors told her family that she would never see well and that they should "take her home and love her." Her family moved to the United States when she was 2 years old, because her father was looking for work. Her parents spent 18 months as migrant farm workers, moving seasonally. Despite their frequent moves, Gloria's father learned to speak English fairly well and found a job at a factory that would keep the family from moving so often. When Gloria developed an ear infection, her mother took her to the free clinic in town where a social worker noticed Gloria's visual impairment. The social worker explained, through an interpreter, that Gloria could receive special services because of her visual impairment even though she was not old enough to start school. That night Gloria's parents discussed what the social worker told them. They knew they could take care of their daughter, but they also wanted to provide everything they could for her.

After a long and confusing assessment process, Gloria began receiving services from a teacher of students with visual impairments. Gloria was accepted into a Head Start program where the staff spoke English and Spanish. Over time, the teacher of students with visual impairments, the Head Start teacher, and Gloria's parents developed a positive working relationship and learned from each other. The teacher of students with visual impairments explained how the visual impairment affected Gloria's learning. The Head Start teacher described the typical development of children and how Gloria interacted with other children. Gloria's parents talked about what Gloria did at home and what they would like her to learn to do. Working as a team, the professionals and family were able to provide a positive learning environment for Gloria.

- *How did the professionals involved in Gloria's referral and education show respect for Gloria and her parents?*
- *Despite their reservations, why do you think Gloria's parents enrolled her in special education?*

Visual impairments, like the one Gloria experienced, refer to any limitation in visual functioning that affects a person's ability to engage in daily tasks. Most people who are visually impaired have some useable vision and are referred to as having *low vision*. When people have little or no useable vision, they are said to be *blind*. Visual impairments include low vision and blindness. Visual impairments occur in people of all ages, ethnicities, races, genders, and religions. The influences of ethnicity, race, gender, and religion are well documented, as are the influences of having a visual impairment. Only rarely, however, has anyone considered the interaction between the effects of culture and visual impairment (Milian & Erin, 2001). This chapter provides an understanding of the interaction of visual impairments and culture, including demographic information, and an overview of how the education of students with visual impairments may be influenced by a person's cultural and ethnic beliefs.

In the United States, visual impairments affect between 1 and 4 infants, children, and teenagers per 1,000 (Chaing, Bassie, & Javitt, 1992; Ferrell, 1998; Nelson & Dimitrova, 1993). Advances in medical care in the United States mean that many visual conditions can now be prevented or controlled so that the visual impairment is less severe. At the same time, advances in medicine have resulted in the survival of children born extremely prematurely and children with neurological damage. These children are at high risk for developing visual impairments as well as cognitive and motor impairments. Children who move to the United States from other countries may not have received the same medical care that is provided in the United States and may experience visual impairments not frequently seen in children born in the United States.

HISTORICAL PERSPECTIVES

Historically, cultures around the world have moved through five stages of social perspective on visual impairments: separation, protection, self-emancipation, education, and assimilation (Tuttle & Tuttle, 1996). These stages are not as linear as they may seem from this list. No society has progressed smoothly and effortlessly through these stages. Cultures experience great variability, with several different stages existing simultaneously or quickly changing because of world events.

Limited records of preliterate societies reveal that many cultures completely separated people with visual impairments from society, resulting in their deaths. For example, in Sparta, babies who were blind were left to die in the mountains (Koestler, 1976). The protection stage developed largely as an outgrowth of Western religions—religious communities and individuals took an interest in providing charity to people with a variety of disabilities, including blindness. Self-emancipation began first in Eastern and Middle Eastern countries, with countries such as China establishing guilds of workers who were blind and establishing standards and skills training (Vaughn, 1998). In Europe, individuals who were blind occasionally achieved success through their own initiatives rather than through societal support (Hatlen, 2000). Formal education began in Europe with the establishment of the Institute for the Blind in Paris by Valentin Haüy in 1784, and the concept of a residential school for children who were blind quickly spread throughout the Western world. Later, assimilation became popular. The assimilation view is that individuals with visual impairments are integral members of their communities who should contribute to and participate in their society throughout all stages of their lives.

ETIOLOGIES OF VISUAL IMPAIRMENTS IN CULTURAL GROUPS

Around the world, rates and etiologies of visual impairments vary from nation to nation. Within the United States, the prevalence of visual impairments and the frequency of certain etiologies vary based on ethnic group. Because etiologies can influence the degree and severity of visual impairment, it is important to consider the different types of visual impairments. There are three main reasons for the difference in overall prevalence and etiologies: access to health care, environmental factors, and genetic predisposition. Many ethnic groups in the United States have limited access to adequate health care, health education, and nutrition (Cabil & Gold, 2001). Many visual impairments are preventable with proper health care and nutrition, and the severity of a visual impairment may be reduced with early identification and treatment. Environmental factors also can contribute to increased risks for visual impairments when cultural and work environments place people at high risk for acquiring a visual impairment. Genetic predisposition can result in higher rates of certain hereditary visual impairments within a population.

Overall, the three most common causes of visual impairment in children in the United States are cortical visual impairment, retinopathy of prematurity, and optic nerve hypoplasia (Ferrell, 1998; Hatton et al., 2001; Steinkuller et al., 1999). These are the most common causes of visual impairments in children of European descent and Asian descent. Other ethnic groups may experience slightly different rates of certain types of visual impairments. Another relatively common form of visual impairments is albinism, a recessive hereditary condition resulting in a lack of pigment in the skin, hair, and eyes. Albinism occurs in all ethnic groups and accounts for 6 to 8% of all visual impairments in children (Ferrell, 1998; Hatton et al., 2001). Children with albinism are often teased and treated differently because of their appearance. The impact is greatest on children of non-European descent, because they tend to look "more different" from the other members of their family and community (Gold, 2002).

Genetic and cultural factors can influence the prevalence of visual impairments in ethnic groups. Visual impairments are twice as likely to occur in African Americans compared to white Americans of the same social status (Cabil & Gold, 2001). African Americans are at higher risk for certain medical conditions such as sickle cell anemia, diabetes, and hypertension, which can lead to visual impairments such as retinopathy, glaucoma, and cataracts. Lack of appropriate medical care and compliance can increase the risk that a medical condition will result in a visual impairment or the worsening of a visual impairment (see Cabil & Gold). Latinos are a diverse group of people from Mexico, Central and South America, Puerto Rico, Cuba, and other smaller countries (U.S. Bureau of Census, 1999), and Latinos live in every state in the United States. Although the Latino population is very diverse, a higher percentage of Latino children live in poverty than the national average, meaning that these children often lack adequate health care to prevent and treat visual impairments. In a national study of children with visual impairments, Ferrell (1998) found the rate of visual impairments among Latinos to be comparable to that of other ethnic groups. American Indians, who live both on and off reservations, are at risk for visual impairment due to the prevalence of poverty and genetic factors. Trauma has been identified as the single largest cause of visual impairments among American Indians, with fighting and accidents the primary causes for the trauma (Rearwin, Jubilee, Tang, & Hughes, 1997). As Rearwin et al. indicated, the lack of running water in many homes on reservations also results in an inability to wear contacts or an increased risk of infection from wearing contacts.

BELIEFS ABOUT VISUAL IMPAIRMENTS

Culture, religion, and ethnicity influence people's beliefs about visual impairments. Visual impairment may be attributed to a variety of causes outside those identified by modern Western medicine. The treatment and management of visual impairments are approached differently depending on cultural and religious factors. The importance of education for people with visual impairments varies based on cultural beliefs.

Beliefs About Causes of Visual Impairments

In mainstream U.S. culture, most people attribute visual impairments to medical causes and pursue medical treatment options, if any exist. In addition, many alternative or supplementary explanations are accepted for the cause of visual impairments. These alternative beliefs are usually the result of a religious or world view that attributes events to factors not measurable by Western science. Often people accept a medical diagnosis to explain *how* a visual impairment occurs, but they turn to other belief systems to understand *why* the visual impairment happened. Sometimes, practitioners of a religion may interpret causes of visual impairments very differently. For example, many Christians believe a child with a visual impairment is a gift from God to the parents, but others believe the visual impairment is punishment for sin (Erin, Rudin, & Njoroge, 1991; Ruconich & Schneider, 2001; Skinner, Bailey, Correa, & Rodriquez, 1999).

There are also cultural beliefs regarding visual impairments. For instance, many, but not all, Asian Americans believe in fate, or Karma, and in strong connections between the spirit and the body (Love, 2001). As a result, many Asian Americans interpret visual impairments as fate, the result of a misdeed (Chung, 1996). Others believe disharmony between the body and nature result in visual impairments (Spector, 1996). The belief in the influence of fate and in spirit-body connections may not be a major factor in the belief system of all Asian Americans, and it is important not to assume that all Asian Americans will attribute visual impairments to these factors. It is equally true that these beliefs exist in varying degrees in other cultures as well, so practitioners should not be surprised to see similar beliefs in people of other backgrounds. In the same dimension, American

Indians have a variety of belief systems but many include multiple causalities for disabilities and illness (Joe & Malach, 1998). Supernatural causes may include witchcraft, spirit loss, and spells. Some American Indians may also believe visual impairments are the result of disturbances to the natural balance such as breaking a cultural taboo, acculturation into the mainstream, or accidents. Traditional American Indian culture views disabilities differently from mainstream white culture, and no American Indian language has a word for "disability" (Topor, 2001). Many American Indian cultures view each person's abilities individually rather than assuming that someone with a "disability" cannot accomplish tasks. In fact, many with "disabilities" have been highly respected by their communities (e.g., Sequoyah, who was "physically disabled," created the first written form of an American Indian language).

General and special education teachers working with children with visual impairments must consider cultural and ethnic factors that influence the family's perspectives about the visual impairment. A child's visual impairment will be an integral part of the child's developing self-concept and self-esteem (Tuttle, 1987), thus the family's beliefs about the visual impairment may affect the child's self-concept (Obiakor, 1999; Obiakor & Stile, 1989, 1990). Teachers also need to evaluate their own beliefs concerning causes of visual impairments and how their beliefs may differ from the beliefs of their students. Teachers must respect beliefs of children and families about the cause of the visual impairment even when they disagree. If the child or family asks the teacher's opinion, the teacher may share beliefs in a nonthreatening way. The only time a teacher should intervene in response to a family's belief is if a child's health or life is in jeopardy.

Beliefs About Treatment of Visual Impairments

When a child is diagnosed with a visual impairment, the ophthalmologist, a medical doctor who specializes in treating the eyes, will recommend appropriate medical treatment options, if any exist. Especially when there are no options or only limited options, parents frequently pursue a second and even a third opinion. As children and their parents struggle with accepting the visual impairment, they may choose to pursue Western medical treatment only, alternative treatments only, a combination of Western and alternative treatments, or no treatment at all (Ruconich & Schneider, 2001; Topor, 2001). For instance, American Indians who consult a shaman or Christians who visit a faith healer are samples of alternative treatments that are pursued by members of some cultural groups. Often, people will continue to follow the treatment recommended by the ophthalmologist while concurrently pursuing other options.

Unfortunately, many cultural and ethnic groups do not have access to high-quality medical care because of poverty or geographical location. People with limited access to medical care tend to pursue only emergency care rather than regular examinations or follow-up visits (Cabil & Gold, 2001). Without regular examinations, many treatable visual impairments may not be identified, resulting in permanent or more severe visual impairments. For example, if a child has glaucoma, regular exams are necessary to monitor treatment and adjust medications even though the child may not be experiencing any pain or noticeable changes in vision. If glaucoma is not treated properly, it can result in total blindness. In addition to treating the medical condition, emotional support is critical for children and their families. Some cultural groups frequently prefer to find emotional support through extended families and religious organizations (Alston, McCowan, & Turner, 1994; Cabil & Gold, 2001; Erin et al., 1991). Other times, families may prefer to meet with families of the same or different cultures who are experiencing similar disabilities. Teachers and professionals working with students with visual impairments should assist families in locating the types of support they desire.

Although medical treatment is not typically a part of education, teachers and service providers are placed in an unusual position regarding treatment for children with visual impairments. Students frequently tell their teachers about their families' searches for alternative treatments. Teachers and service providers may be asked to enforce certain treatments such as wearing glasses, patching, or administering eye drops. As a result, they should listen when children talk about treatment, both traditional and nontraditional. They should not judge the treatments the family chooses to pursue unless the treatment poses a threat to the health or life of the child. In addition, they should follow parents' instructions regarding treatments at school and not assume that they know more than parents about treatment. For example, many teachers assume that glasses will improve the vision of a child with low vision and should be worn at all times. In reality, glasses may improve vision, they may provide protection, they may be designed only for specific tasks (e.g., reading), or they may not be prescribed at all. Teachers' primary role in the treatment of visual impairments is to implement doctors' and parents' instructions without consciously or unconsciously judging treatment options. For example, a child who is blind may tell a teacher that her family took her to a faith healer. The child may say, "He said God must want me to be blind or else I'd be able to see." The teacher should respond, "How does that make you feel?" This leads to a conversation guided by the child's needs rather than the teacher's opinion about faith healers or God's role in disabilities.

Beliefs About Education

Families and schools often have differing opinions about long-term goals for the student, parent roles in education, and access to special education services. The purpose of special education is to provide the appropriate education and services to prepare a child to be a contributing member of society. When schools and families differ on what constitutes a "contributing member of society," conflicts can arise. Federal law requires that parents be involved in the educational process of their children in special education, but traditional parent-professional partnerships contradict values from several cultures. Often, families new to the United States do not know that their child can receive educational services.

Some cultures believe children with visual impairments do not need to gain independent skills, because they will be taken care of by their family or community

(Milian & Conroy, 2001; Topor, 2001). Often, these cultures do not encourage any child to help with daily tasks like cooking and cleaning. Tasks required for daily life are largely the responsibility of adults, and children do not begin practicing these skills until adolescence. Children with typical sight spend a lifetime observing adults engaging in daily living tasks, and they draw on those visual experiences when they begin practicing these tasks. Children with visual impairments have limited understanding of the tasks that were going on around them unless they were actively participating in them. As these children develop daily living skills, they may make messes (e.g., spill the juice when pouring it), and they may get occasional bumps and bruises. Parents from cultures that place a strong emphasis on caring for children or on maintaining a neat appearance may find it especially difficult to allow children to have the experiences necessary to learn. Teachers need to provide opportunities for children with visual impairments to begin developing skills of daily living at home, at school, and in the community. For example, it is not uncommon for children with visual impairments to have difficulty learning to tie their shoes. When a child's shoes become untied, a teacher can allow him or her as much time as necessary to tie the laces without pressure to tie them quickly and without making the child feel that the teacher or other students are watching.

Some cultures believe certain jobs or careers are appropriate for people with visual impairments. For example, historically in Japan and Korea, people who were blind became masseuses, and in Thailand they sold lottery tickets (Love, 2001). Even within mainstream U.S. culture, there are many misconceptions about the jobs that are available to people with visual impairments. Family and community perceptions about potential independence and employability will influence a family's participation in their child's education. By providing adult role models with visual impairments, from the same ethnic or cultural background when possible, parents and children can learn about the limitless potential for people with visual impairments who receive the appropriate education. The American Foundation for the Blind has an electronic database of working adults with visual impairments who are willing to serve as role models. Teachers, service providers, and families can access the database, Career Connect, at *www.afb.org*.

Many cultures do not understand the concept of parent-professional partnerships in developing educational plans. Some cultures, such as Asian Americans, have respect for teachers as professionals and would consider it rude to offer suggestions (Love, 2001). Certain cultures also do not reinforce the same skills that schools often encourage. For example, many children with visual impairments need to learn to be assertive in requesting needed assistance and in declining unneeded assistance. Many cultures encourage children to remain quiet and would consider assertive behaviors disrespectful. By developing a relationship with the family, teachers and service providers can better develop culturally appropriate ways of addressing the student's needs (see Table 13.1 for the roles of general and special educators). In many countries around the world, children with visual impairments are not provided with a public education. In some countries, no educational services are available for

TABLE 13.1   *The Roles of General and Special Educators*

When the family believes the visual impairment will be cured through non-Western interventions, general and special educators must

- listen respectfully to the child and parents as they discuss alternative treatments,
- suggest that the family continues receiving educational services to address the visual impairment for the present time,
- recommend that parents continue with medical treatment if any has been recommended.

When the family believes the child will go into a specific career, because that is what "blind people do," general and special educators must

- listen respectfully to parents' views,
- connect parents with adults with visual impairments to provide role models on the potential for people with visual impairments,
- contact possible sources of role models including the teacher of students with visual impairments, Career Connect, at *www.afb.org.*

When the family believes the family will take care of the child, because he or she cannot take care of himself or herself, general and special educators must

- praise the family for taking such good care of their child,
- provide role models for children and adults with visual impairments from similar cultural backgrounds,
- discuss the benefits of independence within a family structure (e.g., positive feelings of being able to contribute to the family),
- discuss times the child may need to be independent (e.g., in an emergency situation).

When the family believes the child cannot learn, because he or she has a visual impairment, general and special educators must

- give examples of children in the same situation who learned age-appropriate skills or concepts,
- brainstorm ways that the child can learn from them,
- connect parents with other parents of children with visual impairments through an organization such as NAPVI, at *www.napvi.org.*

children with visual impairments; in others, education for children with visual impairments is available only for families who can pay for it. Additionally, in some countries, the only educational option for children with visual impairments is to attend a residential school. Parents who recently immigrated may not realize their child with a visual impairment has an opportunity for an education that does not require tuition or attending a distant residential school. These parents need to be taught about education laws, especially those that stipulate that, regardless of residency status, children with disabilities are guaranteed a free and appropriate education from birth until the child graduates from high school. Sometimes, these services are provided in the child's home school. By developing community outreach and partnerships, schools can help educate parents so they know about services available to their children.

WORKING WITH MULTICULTURAL STUDENTS WHO ARE ENGLISH-LANGUAGE LEARNERS

Many families from multicultural backgrounds are fluent English speakers, but others speak little or no English. Under federal civil rights laws, public schools are required to provide assistance to students who are English-language learners (ELLs). To determine the English-language skills of children who speak a language other than English at home, schools evaluate the children's English skills through language proficiency tests. Most proficiency tests have many visual components such as pointing to the correct picture, identifying a picture, and creating a story about pictures. These items are inaccessible to children who are blind, and the items may be unclear or impossible to see for children with low vision. A test must be modified by a professional, usually a teacher of students with visual impairments. The professional who modifies the test must be familiar with the language proficiency test, the child's cultural background, the child's visual functioning, and guidelines for adapting tests for children with visual impairments. Unfortunately, once modified, the standardization of the test is no longer valid.

Authentic assessments are an alternative proposed for children who are ELL and may prove especially important for children with visual impairments who are unable to participate in commercially available standardized tests (Milian & Conroy, 2001). Authentic assessments use multiple measures of factors related to language acquisition, including learning, motivation, and attitudes tied to classroom learning. They include performance assessments, portfolio assessments, and student self-assessments (O'Malley & Valdez Pierce, 1996). Used in conjunction with modified standardized tests, authentic assessments may provide the best understanding of a student's language proficiency and progress. Just as children who are ELL are tested using visual methods, English instruction is often very visual (Milian & Conroy, 2001). Using pictures as a teaching tool is encouraged because it does not penalize children who have little or no literacy in their first language, and because it is thought to encourage "thinking in English" rather than translating word for word. Unfortunately, visual teaching materials are not appropriate for many children with visual impairments because they are inaccessible. Modifications can be made to many activities through simple techniques such as providing real objects for each picture; giving the child an individual copy of the picture to be held as close as necessary; and using large, clear, uncluttered pictures. Because of the tremendous variability in visual functioning among children with visual impairments, classroom modifications for each child must be determined individually. For students with visual impairments, the teacher of students with visual impairments can help other teachers know what modifications are appropriate for each child.

MULTICULTURAL LEARNERS WITH VISUAL IMPAIRMENTS AND ADDITIONAL DISABILITIES

Approximately 40 to 60% of children with visual impairments have additional disabilities, many of which are severe (Ferrell, 1998). Additional disabilities can include deafness or hearing impairment, physical impairments, cognitive impairments, learning disabilities, and health issues. For these children, the families' cultural and ethnic backgrounds influence how the visual impairment and the additional disabilities are perceived. Some cultures and families are more accepting of certain types of disabilities. For example, accepting that a child is visually impaired is often easier for parents than accepting a significant cognitive impairment. Some cultures, however, consider blindness to be a "worse" disability than others; as a consequence, parents may pretend a child with low vision has typical sight while accepting a physical or cognitive impairment.

The cultural interpretation of different disabilities frequently affects how a family views educational opportunities. Families who recently came to the United States may be unaware that their child with severe disabilities is guaranteed a free and appropriate education in public schools. Other families may not realize the possibilities for adults with multiple impairments, thus they may fail to understand the purpose of education for their child. School systems should work with health care providers and social service agencies to ensure that all families know of educational services available to their children regardless of disability.

RESOURCES FOR EDUCATORS

Professionals interested in learning more about the interaction of visual impairment and cultures should consult Milian and Erin's (2001) work, *Diversity and Visual Impairments: The Influence of Race, Gender, Religions, and Ethnicity on the Individual,* for some useful information. Consumer organizations for people with visual impairments and their families, such as the National Organization for Albinism and Hypopigmentation (NOAH), provide resources specific to the needs of individuals of diverse backgrounds. Many organizations have informational materials about blindness and braille materials available in a variety of languages. The following are examples of Web sites:

- American Foundation for the Blind, *www.afb.org*
- American Printing House for the Blind, *www.aph.org*
- National Association of Parents of Children with Visual Impairments, *www.napvi.org*
- National Braille Press, *www.nbp.org*
- National Organization for Albinism and Hypopigmentation, *www.albinism.org*

- Lighthouse International, *www.lighthouse.org*
- Seedlings, *www.seedlings.org*

A Culturally Responsive Educator

1. Understands that children with visual impairments are found in all cultural, ethnic, and religious cultures.

2. Knows that cultural interpretations about the causes of visual impairments influence a family's perception about the child and his or her educational opportunities.

3. Believes every child with a visual impairment is unique and will require individualized and specific modifications in educational planning.

4. Understands that the teacher of students with visual impairments is a good resource for information about visual impairments.

5. Accepts families' rights to pursue non-Western treatments for their children's visual impairments.

6. Discovers what skills are important to the family and tries to find common ground for the student's education.

7. Assists multicultural students with visual impairments by appropriately modifying materials and instruction with the assistance of a teacher of students with visual impairments.

8. Values cultural differences in designing multicultural educational programming.

9. Modifies assessment strategies to reach all learners, including those with visual impairments.

10. Explains the powerful influence of race, gender, religion, and ethnicity on people with visual impairments.

Conclusion

Children with visual impairments are members of all cultural, ethnic, religious, and language groups. As Gloria's case indicated, when working with children and families, general and special education professionals must view the entire picture, including the visual impairment, the cultural factors, and the interaction between the visual impairment and culture. Teachers and service providers of students with visual impairments are good resources for information about a student's visual impairment and its impact on learning. Developing positive, accepting relationships with students and their families will help teachers and related professionals to understand their students' cultures and learn ways to modify instruction to better meet their needs.

Discussion Questions

1. Briefly explain steps you can take to improve the classroom situation of your student with a visual impairment.
2. Looking back at Gloria's case in the introduction, examine why teamwork is an asset in educational programming.
3. Discuss reasons why tests must be modified for students with visual impairments.
4. Explain cultural and religious situations that affect the education of students with visual impairments.
5. As a professional, explain why you must continue to learn about visual impairments and cultural variables that affect education.

References

Alston, R. J., McCowan, C. J., & Turner, W. L. (1994). Family functioning as a correlate of disability adjustment for African Americans. *Rehabilitation Counseling Bulletin, 37,* 277–289.

Cabil, L., & Gold, M. E. (2001). African Americans with visual impairments. In M. Milian & J. N. Erin (Eds.), *Diversity and visual impairments: The influence of race, gender, religions, and ethnicity on the individual* (pp. 57–77). New York: AFB Press.

Chaing, Y., Bassie, L. J., & Javitt, J. C. (1992). Federal budgetary costs of blindness. *Milbank Quarterly, 70,* 319–340.

Chung, E. L. (1996). Asian Americans. In M. C. Julia (Ed.), *Multicultural awareness in the health care professions* (pp. 77–110). Boston: Allyn & Bacon.

Erin, J. N., Rudin, D., & Njoroge, M. (1991). Religious beliefs of parents of children with visual impairments. *Journal of Visual Impairment and Blindness, 85,* 157–162.

Ferrell, K. A. (1998). *Project PRISM: A longitudinal study of developmental patterns of children who are visually impaired (Final report).* Greeley, CO: University of Northern Colorado, Division of Special Education.

Gold, M. (2002). The effects of the physical features associated with albinism on the self-esteem of African American youth. *Journal of Visual Impairment and Blindness, 93,* 133–142.

Hatlen, P. (2000). Historical perspectives. In M. C. Holbrook & A. J. Koenig (Eds.), *Foundations of education (Vol. 1): History and theory of teaching children and youths with visual impairments* (2nd ed., pp. 1–54). New York: AFB Press.

Hatton, D. D., & Model Registry of Early Childhood Visual Impairment Collaborative Group. (2001). Model registry of early childhood visual impairment: First-year results. *Journal of Visual Impairment and Blindness, 95,* 418–433.

Joe, J., & Malach, R. S. (1998). Families with roots. In E. Lynch & M. J. Hanson (Eds.), *Developing cross-cultural competence* (pp. 89–119). Baltimore: Brookes.

Koestler, F. (1976). *The unseen minority: A social history of blindness in the United States.* New York: American Foundation for the Blind.

Love, C. Y. (2001). Asian Americans and Pacific Islanders with visual impairments. In M. Milian & J. N. Erin (Eds.), *Diversity and visual impairments: The influence of race, gender, religions, and ethnicity on the individual* (pp. 79–107). New York: AFB Press.

Milian, M., & Conroy, P. (2001). Individuals who speak English as a second language. In M. Milian & J. N. Erin (Eds.), *Diversity and visual impairments: The influence of race, gender, religions, and ethnicity on the individual* (pp. 343–381). New York: AFB Press.

Milian, M., & Erin, J. N. (Eds.) (2001). *Diversity and visual impairments: The influence of race, gender, religions, and ethnicity on the individual.* New York: AFB Press.

Nelson, K. A., & Dimitrova, G. (1993). Severe visual impairment in the United States and in each state, 1990. *Journal of Visual Impairment and Blindness, 87,* 80–85.

Obiakor, F. E. (1999). Teacher expectations of minority exceptional learners: Impact on "accuracy" of self-concept. *Exceptional Children, 66,* 39–53.

Obiakor, F. E., & Stile, S. W. (1989). Enhancing self-concept in students with visual handicaps. *Journal of Visual Impairment and Blindness, 83,* 255–257.

Obiakor, F. E., & Stile, S. W. (1990). The self concept of visually impaired and normally sighted middle school children. *Journal of Psychology, 124,* 199–206.

O'Malley, J. M., & Valdez Pierce, L. (1996). *Authentic assessment for English language learners: Practical approaches for teachers.* Reading, MA: Addison-Wesley.

Rearwin, D. T., Jubilee, H. E., Tang, O. D., & Hughes, J. W. (1997). Causes of blindness among Navajo Indians: An update. *Journal of the American Optometric Association, 68,* 511–517.

Ruconich, S., & Schneider, K. (2001). Religions and their views of blindness and visual impairments. In M. Milian & J. N. Erin (Eds.), *Diversity and visual impairments: The influence of race, gender, religions, and ethnicity on the individual* (pp. 193–222). New York: AFB Press.

Skinner, D., Bailey, D., Correa, V., & Rodriquez, P. (1999). Narrating self and disability: Latino mothers' construction of identities vis-á-vis their child with special needs. *Exceptional Children, 65,* 54–63.

Spector, R. E. (1996). *Cultural diversity in health and illness* (4th ed.). Stamford, CT: Appleton & Lange.

Steinkuller, P. G., Du, L., Gilbert, C., Foster, A., Collins, M. L., & Coats, D. K. (1999). Childhood blindness. *Journal of the American Association for Pediatric Ophthalmology and Strabismus, 3,* 2–32.

Tuttle, D. W. (1987). The role of the special education teacher-counselor in meeting students' self-esteem needs. *Journal of Visual Impairment and Blindness, 81,* 156–161.

Tuttle, D. W., & Tuttle, N. R. (1996). *Self-esteem and adjusting with blindness: The process of responding to life's demands.* Springfield, IL: Charles C Thomas.

U.S. Bureau of the Census. (1999, March). *Hispanic population in the United States* [Online]. Available at www.census.gov/population/www/socdemo/hispanic/ho99.html

Vaughn, C. E. (1998). *Social and cultural perspectives on blindness.* Springfield, IL: Charles C Thomas.

Part III

Lifespan Issues and Multicultural Special Education

Chapter 14

Early Childhood Multicultural Special Education

Arletha J. McSwain and James M. Patton

Chapter Outline

Thinking About Multicultural Special Education

For the past 15 years, Michael's father had been either incarcerated or in a drug reha-bilitation program. Michael never had a positive relationship with his father. Because of drug abuse, his father missed countless and meaningful occasions in his life. He remembered all the times his father came home and stole everything out of Michael's pockets. He would wake up the next morning expecting to have the money he had worked for, but it would be gone. Sometimes, he would sleep with a knife under his pil-low because he was tired of things being taken away from him. He remembered his first experience entering a "drug house" and confronting his father about Christmas presents stolen from under the tree.

Throughout Michael's early grade school years, he was a student in basic learning classes and was identified as being at risk. He had no paternal support as a young child. As a consequence, high school was a challenge for him. He continued to be placed in basic classes and always scored below average on standardized tests. He remembered being advised by his guidance counselor that college would not be the place for him. She said that he needed to think about joining the military or taking up a trade. The re-sults from the career placement inventory suggested that he should become a bus driver or a custodian. But Michael's resiliency as a young child was supported by some of his teachers. As a result, he became determined to succeed as an adolescent and adult.

In 2000, Michael graduated from Bethune Cookman College's Project MODEL (Males of Diversity Exhibiting Leadership), a federally funded project from the U.S. Department of Education's Office of Special Education. This program celebrated and honored his worth as an African American male as well as believed in his potential to become a licensed teacher in early childhood special education. In 2003, he graduated with a master of arts in education from the University of South Florida.

- *What happens to a young child like Michael in early education, especially when he is labeled at risk?*
- *How can general and special educators be prepared to work with students such as Michael in ways that are culturally responsive?*

Early childhood special education illustrates an enriching theoretical frame-work that undergirds early experiences for infants, toddlers, and preschoolers (Bowe, 2000). Theoretically, the benefits of early experiences are irrefutable (Erickson, 1963; Freud, 1965; Piaget, 1962; Vygotsky, 1978). The impact of the early developmental years in providing a foundation for lifelong learning is well estab-lished. During these years, preschoolers profit from a broad range of essential skills in the developmental areas, especially if these experiences are culturally mediated

(Allen & Schwartz, 2001; Gay, 2000). There is an abundance of evidence from psychological research supporting the substantial impact of early experiences on the development of preschoolers (Haddad & Garralda, 1992; Lizardi, Klein, Ouimette, & Riso, 1995). In addition to the psychological research, medical research has contributed further evidence of the effects of early experiences on development (Hooper & Umansky, 2004).

The federal government's first commitment to early childhood special education was the Handicapped Children's Early Education Assistance Act of 1968. The objective of this act was to support national model programs that demonstrated and disseminated exemplary practices in early education. As a result of this act, the Handicapped Children's Early Education Program (HCEEP) was created to direct and offer technical support. In 1974, the Economic Opportunity and Community Partnership Act recognized the need for early intervention by requiring Head Start programs to serve a minimum of 10% of children with disabilities. In 1975 came the Education for All Handicapped Children Act (P.L. 94-142), a landmark piece of legislation that guaranteed the right of children with disabilities to a free and appropriate education. With this act came the implementation of child find, which requires states to identify, assess, and provide special services to young children (Bowe, 2000). A major step taken by Congress, which specifically relates to infants, toddlers, and preschoolers, as well as their families, was the passing of the Education for All Handicapped Children Act Amendment of 1986 (P.L. 99-457). This act continued mandating services to preschool children with disabilities from age 3, as well as providing state incentives to implement intervention services to children from birth. With this act came the individualized family service plan (IFSP), which is comparable to the IEP, but recognizes the necessity of including the needs of the entire family relative to the child (Hooper & Umansky, 2004). Recently, the No Child Left Behind Act was signed into federal law. This act is designed to ensure that all children receive a high-quality education regardless of their background or race (Henniger, 2005).

Young children need advocates. Numerous organizations have emerged as advocates of early childhood special education. Prominent among them are three nationally recognized organizations that have long been committed to ensuring that young children and their families receive culturally and linguistically relevant services. These organizations are: (a) the National Association for the Education of Young Children (NAEYC), (b) the National Black Child Development Institute (NBCDI), and (c) the Division for Early Childhood (DEC) of the Council for Exceptional Children (CEC). As the NAEYC noted, "early childhood programs must have the ability to respond to the diverse developmental, cultural, linguistic and education interests and needs of all children" (p. 1).

CULTURAL COMPETENCY IN EARLY CHILDHOOD SPECIAL EDUCATION

Development and learning ensue from within and without and are predisposed to be culturally contextualized. Given the increasingly diverse cultural climate of today's classrooms, teachers working with young children with exceptionalities must be equipped to provide culturally responsive services to children and their families. To do such, early childhood special educators must become culturally competent and responsive in their curriculum, pedagogy, and other practices. Cultural competent responses, both theoretical and practical, go beyond cultural diversity or awareness. Specifically, cultural competency refers to a set of congruent attitudes, practices, policies, and structures that are brought together in educational systems to enable educators to work collaboratively and effectively with members of culturally distinct groups in a manner that values and respects the culture and world view of those groups (Hanley, 1999; Patton & Day-Vines, 2004). For instance, Patton and Day-Vines developed a cultural competency curriculum that provides constructs and practical suggestions useful to early childhood special educators. This curriculum is based on a cultural competence model developed by Pederson (1994), a model that delineates three distinct developmental stages of cultural *awareness*, *knowledge*, and *skills*. According to Pederson, it is important for early childhood special educators to acknowledge their own biases and explicitly and intrinsically held attitudes, stereotypes, and assumptions about themselves and their "other." This development requires that these educators engage in a form of *cultural therapy* that allows them to explore cultural "boulders" in their own "eyes" before they search for "motes" in the "eyes" of culturally diverse individuals.

The model proposed by Pederson (1994) suggests that early childhood special educators understand the deep structured cultural knowledge, axiologies, epistemologies, and world views of their own cultural/racial group and those of culturally distinct groups. This therapeutic movement, by definition, would also include the need to obtain cultural knowledge of the historical experiences with oppression endured by these groups, as well as issues related to cultural/racial nomenclature, culturally mediated instructional and behavioral strategies, social and education experiences, and mechanisms of support available within their indigenous communities. The third stage of the cultural competency model would require that early childhood special educators translate this newfound cultural awareness and knowledge into culturally responsive and competent skills that enable them to work more effectively with these culturally distinct groups. Apparently, culturally competent responses require the synchronization and integration of these three cultural stages into the curriculum, pedagogy, and instruction by early childhood special educators.

EARLY CHILDHOOD SPECIAL EDUCATION AND FAMILY INVOLVEMENT

Historically, early childhood special education programs have long valued family involvement. This includes respect for the family, acknowledging the family as the constant in a preschooler's life, and understanding that the preschooler's needs can only be fully met through family involvement and understanding of the sociocultural contexts in which families exist. Professionally, organizations such as the DEC, NBCDI, and NAEYC have stressed the significance of understanding and respecting the individuality of all families and the sociocultural constructs in which they exist (Bowe, 2000). Mounting numbers of multicultural families are prevalent in today's society (Garcia, 2001). Early childhood special educators provide services to children and families whose language and culture vary slightly or significantly from their own. This trend is bound to continue, given changes in cultural and class demographics. The early childhood special educator's customary and safe ways of relating and interacting with families are no longer adequate in responding competently to multicultural preschoolers and their families (Barrera, Corso, & Macpherson, 2003). For example, a skill necessary for being culturally competent is referred to as *mirroring.* "One of the core needs of all children is to have their behaviors and beliefs mirrored by the adults around them" (see Barrera et al., 2003, p. 18). This process maximizes the cognitive and healthy emotional development of a child's sense of identity. The absence of culturally and linguistically responsive mirroring and validation can cause bewilderment and disgrace, which may result in concomitant delays or interference in learning and development (Donovan & McIntyre, 1990). On the other hand, the presence and modeling of mirroring by early childhood special educators in the preschooler's learning environments, including the home, can considerably cultivate culturally responsive mirroring and validation for both children and their families. This is especially true with children and family members who are not from the dominant culture and whose language, values, beliefs, and behaviors typically have already been invalidated or mirrored from a deficit approach (see Barrera et al., 2003, p. 18).

Collecting culturally informed data about a family's perspectives and functioning relative to child-rearing practices guarantees individualized and culturally responsive communications, thus alleviating feelings of alienation often experienced by these families (Chen, Downing, & Peckham-Hardin, 2002). For example, many African American parents practice potty training of their child before the age of two. An early childhood special educator who believes waiting later is more developmentally appropriate for the preschooler may have difficulty supporting these parents' views, thus hampering respectful culturally mediated communications and interventions. It is imperative that early childhood special educators understand families' cultural and linguistic backgrounds (Allen & Majidi-Ahi, 1989; Correa, 1987; Lowenthal, 1996). Apparently, cultural and linguistic differences in interpretation of nonverbal communication can cause misinterpretation between families and early childhood special educators (Chen et al., 2002). As an example, during an IFSP conference, the early childhood special educator might become frustrated with a parent's lack of eye contact. Unbeknownst to her, in certain cultures, eye contact with professionals is a sign of disrespect (Axtell, 1991; Chan, 1998; Dresser, 1996; Sileo & Prater, 1998). Additionally, some Hispanic families see professionals as the experts and presume a passive role when interacting with them (Harry, 1992; Harry & Kalyanpur, 1994). Cognitive anchoring can be helpful in this regard. According to Barrera et al. (2003), "cognitive anchoring is the belief that other's behaviors make as much sense as one's own" (p. 53). Three strategies for this type of anchoring are *respect, reciprocity,* and *responsiveness.* The early childhood special educator needs to embrace these skills and anchor them in culturally responsive ways. By so doing, a mutually satisfying relationship between the early childhood special educator and families can be ensured.

ASSESSING YOUNG CHILDREN WITH SPECIAL NEEDS

Early childhood and general special educators need to know that almost any assessment instrument used with young children may be "culturally biased in favor of white, middle-class, suburban children and against African American or Latino, poor, rural or inner city children" (Bowe, 2000, p. 165). Disturbingly, traditional procedures and assessment choices for children are consistently predisposed to cultural and linguistic prejudice. "Most traditional assessments have been based on descriptions of middle-class, monoculture and monolingual children and their families" (Losardo & Notari-Syverson, 2001, p. 185). Further, components of standardized assessment items mirror too often the constructs, meanings, and formal language used in the dominant culture. Too often, children are penalized for differences in how they respond culturally to questions. In most norm-referenced assessments, children do better on language and cognitive tasks when materials are culturally and linguistically appropriate (Losardo & Notari-Syverson, 2001). As it stands, the reliability and validity of data on standardized instruments are questionable when it comes to assessing the array of achievement levels and mastery of skills of children from multicultural backgrounds (Bergen & Mosley-Howard, 1994). Responding to individual needs of young children who are developmentally, culturally, and linguistically diverse requires the early childhood special educator to look beyond the child's performance on traditional assessments and behaviors in traditional classrooms and take into consideration the frameworks of family or community (Losardo & Notari-Syverson, 2001).

Cultural and linguistic differences that exist in values, beliefs, and attitudes often contradict what standardized tests measure. For example, some of the more commonly used achievement tests emphasize written language and do not consider the rich oral language traditions of multicultural learners (Bergen & Mosley-Howard, 1994). A more appropriate approach is the use of alternative assessment models that are designed to counter biases associated with traditional assessments by considering the cultural and contextual influences as they relate to performance. In addition, these models take into account the child's motivation by placing a more concentrated focus on qualitative descriptions of intricate behaviors, which are not present in established quantitative assessment instruments. As an example, instead of assuming a child who is an ELL has a language deficit, the culturally competent early childhood special educator will assess a variety of factors such as levels of acculturation demonstrated by family members, including the extended family, the child's level of exposure to English, and the child's developmental capabilities (Losardo & Notari-Syverson, 2001). On the whole, when families' cultural and linguistic backgrounds differ from those of the early childhood educator, assessment and evaluation present significant challenges that must be tackled (McLean, 2001; Moore & Beatty, 1995; Santos de Barona & Barona, 1991).

Curriculum-based assessment approaches represent an alternative to norm-referenced quantitative assessment approaches used traditionally for young children. They counter problems of misidentification and misassessment. "Because of the direct congruence among testing, teaching and progress evaluation, curriculum-based assessment provides a direct link between the child's entry or baseline level of mastery and the child's level of ability after instruction is provided" (Losardo & Notari-Syverson, 2001, p. 162). The use of curriculum-based assessments that are culturally and linguistically responsive can provide meaningful instructional information that typically is not identified by the use of norm-referenced instruments. Curriculum-based assessment centers on tasks that are a significant part of the daily curriculum and make it easier for the early childhood special educator to collect information on a constant basis by observing and monitoring young children's learning. By doing so, the early childhood special educator can modify the curriculum and teaching strategies to meet the educational and social needs of the individual child (see Losardo & Notari-Syverson, 2001). This modification is especially important when providing intervention to multicultural preschoolers.

MULTICULTURAL INTERVENTION FOR YOUNG CHILDREN WITH EXCEPTIONALITIES

Early childhood general and special educators are usually prepared to work with the whole child. They are specifically prepared to identify, assess, and evaluate how the unique areas of growth and development amalgamate and affect one another (Klein, Cook, & Richardson-Gibbs, 2001). These educators have a divergent array of instructional and intervention strategies for teaching multicultural learners. It is important, therefore, that they value what these learners bring to schools. Although several early childhood curricula address the need to implement approaches that are multicultural in nature, preschool settings that thoroughly and consistently operate from a culturally responsive continuum that meets the needs of all preschoolers are few and far between. Early childhood special educators who speak the same languages as the preschoolers they are serving are in many instances practically nonexistent. In addition, these educators may not be aware of the intervention needs of multicultural children and their families (Guralnick, 2001). "On an individual level, the goal is to develop an extensive cultural repertoire. An individual who acquires understanding and competency in different linguistic and cultural systems is said to have an extensive repertoire" (Perez & Torres-Guzman, 2002, p. 18).

It is important to note that many early childhood special educators, however, are inclined to put into practice interventions and instructional strategies based on the theoretical constructs to which they were exposed during their formal education and training. Unfortunately, many of those constructs seldom consider and value culturally and linguistically responsive child-rearing practices. As a result, early childhood special educators must develop intervention and instructional practices as well as activities that reflect the social and cultural preferences of all groups (Bhagwanji, Santos, & Fowler, 2000). In addition, they must carefully discern the intervention or instructional content that best reflects the educational and social needs of multicultural children and families (Barrera et al., 2003). When this is done, only then will early childhood special educators be culturally responsive.

A Culturally Responsive Educator

1. Values the whole child.
2. Respects the different families that children come from.
3. Understands that labels can be detrimental to children's growth.
4. Is aware of strengths and weaknesses of young children with special needs.
5. Believes that assessment of multicultural learners must be culturally responsive.
6. Avoids misidentification of multicultural children.
7. Values culturally responsive instruction of young learners.
8. Continues to learn about innovative intervention techniques.
9. Does not separate the child from the family.
10. Uses resource persons to work with young children from multicultural backgrounds.

Conclusion

This chapter discussed the importance of early childhood special education as it relates to culturally and linguistically relevant services. Clearly, today's early childhood general and special educators must acquire the necessary cultural awareness, knowledge, and skills needed to provide culturally competent and responsive intervention and services. Further, Michael's case confirmed that it is imperative that early childhood special educators learn to build on the strengths and cultural capital that a child brings to the classroom. These educators need to engage in a form of "cultural competency" that allows them to examine and explore their assumptions, stereotypes, predilections, and images they hold toward one's cultural self and other "selves." Stated in another way, the first step on the road to cultural competency is to explore fully one's invisible "cultural and class knapsack" that one carries around to use as a "lens" for understanding one's own culture and that of someone else.

Responding in culturally appropriate ways to the needs and strengths of families continues to challenge early childhood general and special educators. Organizations like the NAEYC, NBCDI, and DEC offer important guidelines in this regard. Early childhood general and special education cannot be deemed culturally responsive when young multicultural children are assessed and evaluated in biased and culturally inappropriate ways. Assessment instruments and processes along with curricula, pedagogy, and intervention must mirror the cultural needs, attributes, and strengths of all young learners and their families. It is critical that early childhood special educators use interventions and practices that are culturally responsive in all aspects of their curriculum and instruction.

Discussion Questions

1. Michael was labeled at risk in the introductory case. Briefly explain why the label did not reflect his capabilities.
2. Discuss why teachers and service providers must avoid assumptions about parents in early childhood special education.
3. Explain why it is important for early childhood special educators to be culturally competent.
4. Evaluate why some well-intentioned professionals sometimes support early labeling of multicultural learners.
5. Appropriate assessment can lead to appropriate intervention for young children. Do you agree? Give reasons for your answer.

References

Allen, L., & Majidi-Ahi, S. (1989). Black American children. In J. Taylor & L. Haung-Nahame (Eds.), *Children of color: Psychological intervention with minority youth* (pp. 148–178). San Francisco: Jossey-Bass.

Allen, K., & Schwartz, I. (2001). *The exceptional child: Inclusion in early education.* Albany, NY: Delmar.

Axtell, R. E. (1991). *The do's and taboos of body language around the world.* New York: Wiley.

Barrera, I., Corso, R., & Macpherson, D. (2003). *Skilled dialogue: Strategies for responding to cultural diversity in early childhood education.* Baltimore: Brookes.

Bergen, D., & Mosley-Howard, S. (1994). Assessment perspectives for culturally diverse young children. In D. Bergen (Ed.), *Assessment methods for infants and toddlers: Transdisciplinary team approaches* (pp. 190–206). New York: Teachers College Press.

Bhagwanji, Y., Santos, R. M., & Fowler, S. A. (2000). *Culturally and linguistically sensitive practices in motor skills interventions for young children* (Culturally and Linguistically Appropriate Services [CLAS] Technical Report #1). Champaign, IL: University of Illinois at Urbana-Champaign, Early Childhood Research Institute on Culturally and Linguistically Appropriate Services.

Bowe, F. (2000). *Birth to five early childhood special education.* Albany, NY: Delmar.

Chan, S. (1998). Families with Asian roots. In E. W. Lynch & M. J. Hanson (Eds.), *Developing cross-cultural competence: A guide for working with children and their families* (2nd ed., pp. 251–354). Baltimore: Brookes.

Chen, D., Downing, J., & Peckham-Hardin, K. (2002). *Families & positive behavior support.* Baltimore: Brookes.

Correa, V. I. (1987). Working with Hispanic parents of visually impaired children: Cultural implications. *Journal of Visual Impairment and Blindness, 81,* 260–264.

Donovan, D. M., & McIntyre, D. (1990). *Healing the hurt child.* New York: Norton.

Dresser, N. (1996). *Multicultural manners. New rules of etiquette for a changing society.* New York: Wiley.

Erickson, E. (1963). *Childhood and society.* New York: Norton.

Freud, A. (1965). *Normality and pathology in childhood: Assessments of development.* New York: International Universities Press.

Garcia, E. (2001). *Hispanic education in the United States: Raíces y alas.* Lanham, MD: Rowman & Littlefield.

Gay, G. (2000). *Culturally responsive teaching: Theory, research, and practice.* New York: Teachers College Press.

Guralnick, M. (2001). *Early childhood inclusion: Focus on change.* Baltimore: Brookes.

Haddad, P. M., & Garralda, M. E. (1992). Hyperkinetic syndrome and disruptive early experiences. *British Journal of Psychiatry, 191,* 700–703.

Hanley, J. (1999). Beyond the tip of the iceberg: Five stages toward culturally competency. *Today's Youth: The Community Circle Journal, 3*(2), 9–12.

Harry, B. (1992). *Cultural diversity, families and the special education system: Communication and empowerment.* New York: Teachers College Press.

Harry, B., & Kalyanpur, M. (1994). Cultural underpinnings of special education: Implications for professional interactions with culturally diverse families. *Disability & Society, 9,* 145–165.

Henniger, M. (2005). *An introduction: Teaching young children.* Upper Saddle River, NJ: Merrill/Prentice Hall.

Hooper, S., & Umansky, W. (2004). *Young children with special needs.* Upper Saddle River, NJ: Merrill/Prentice Hall.

Klein, D., Cook, R., & Richardson-Gibbs, A. (2001). *Strategies for including children with special needs in early childhood settings.* Albany, NY: Delmar.

Lizardi, H., Klein, D. N., Ouimette, P. C., & Riso, L. P. (1995). Reports of the childhood home environment in early onset dysthymia and episodic major depression. *Journal of Abnormal Psychology, 104,* 132–129.

Losardo A., & Notari-Syverson, A. (2001). *Alternative approaches to assessing young children.* Baltimore: Brookes.

Lowenthal, B. (1996). Training early interventionists to work with culturally diverse families. *Infant-Toddler Intervention: The Transdisciplinary Journal, 6,* 145–152.

McLean, M. (2001). *Conducting child assessment* (CLAS Technical Report #2). Champaign, IL: University of Illinois at Urbana-Champaign, Early Childhood Research Institute on Culturally and Linguistically Appropriate Services.

Moore, S. M., & Beatty, J. (1995). *Developing cultural competence in early childhood assessment.* Boulder, CO: University of Colorado at Boulder.

National Association for the Education of Young Children. (n.d.). About NAEYC. Retrieved July 12, 2004, from naeyc.org/about/default.asp

Patton, J. M., & Day-Vines, N. L. (2004). *A curriculum and pedagogy for cultural competencies: Strategies to guide the training of special and general education teachers.* Richmond, VA: Department of Education.

Pederson, P. (1994). *A handbook for developing multicultural awareness* (2nd ed.). Alexandria, VA: American Counseling Association.

Perez, B., & Torres-Guzman, M. E. (2002). *Learning in two worlds: An integrated Spanish/English biliteracy approach.* Boston: Allyn & Bacon.

Piaget, J. (1962). *Play, dreams and imitation in childhood.* New York: Norton.

Santos de Barona, M., & Barona, A. (1991). The assessment of culturally and linguistically different preschoolers. *Early Childhood Research Quarterly, 6,* 363–376.

Sileo, T., & Prater, M. A. (1998). Parents and professional partnerships in special education: Multicultural considerations. *Intervention in School and Clinic, 3,* 145–153.

Vygotsky, L. S. (1978). *Mind in society: The development of higher psychological processes.* Cambridge, MA: Harvard University Press.

Chapter 15

Multicultural Special Education Transition Programming

Bertina H. Combes and Beth A. Durodoye

Chapter Outline

Thinking About Multicultural Special Education

Macy and her family lived in a suburban town near a larger metropolitan city. Her parents had three children, of which she was the youngest. They always held high expectations for their children's performance, especially in education. For instance, Macy's older sister Ann graduated from high school with honors and attended a private college for African American women. Macy's learning disabilities in reading and written language were diagnosed when she was in third grade. A shy child, she had a few close friends, and found making new friends and conversations with those outside of her friendship and family circle challenging. In school, her assignments were often modified, and she was given additional time to complete exams and in-class assignments.

As Macy approached ninth grade, her parents requested a meeting to discuss the upcoming school year. They wanted her to continue in the general education classroom taking courses that would prepare her for college. She was present at the meeting but had very little to say, though she was encouraged to participate by her parents and teachers. Macy's teachers were concerned about her social skills, academic readiness for some college prep courses, and her transition to independence. They suggested that these areas be further examined in upcoming individualized education plan (IEP) and individual transition plan (ITP) meetings. During these meetings, Macy and her family were listened to in collaborative and consultative fashions, and they were given tools to guide their thinking about Macy's long-term goals and life after high school. Even though Macy's teachers and service providers were mostly white, they were culturally sensitive and professionally respectful. It became an excellent experience for Macy.

- *What early preparations were made by Macy's teachers to transition her through school?*
- *How did the collaboration and consultation between Macy's teachers and parents help her in her transitions to independence?*

Transition can be defined as the process of moving from one life's stage or season to the next, ranging from infancy to senior adulthood. Over the years, special education has focused on these transition phases, beginning with the early childhood phase and moving from early intervention programs to preschool or educational programs (Wischnowski, Fowler, & McCollum, 2000). The term *transition* has also been used to describe the process of moving from facilities to communities for youth who have been incarcerated (Bullis, Yovanoff, Mueller, & Havel, 2002). However, considerable attention, especially in the last 20 years, has been directed toward the transition of adolescents and young adults to life after secondary schooling (deFur, 1999; Field & Hoffman, 1994; Mullins & Irving, 2000; Wehmeyer & Schwartz, 1995). Attending to the transitions between all life stages is important and worthy of study and discussion; however, the focus of this chapter is the transition from school to adult life.

Legislative requirement for transition services and planning was first authorized by 1990 amendments to the Individuals with Disabilities Education Act (IDEA) (P.L. 101-476). The act defined transition services as a coordinated set of activities for a student with disabilities designed within an outcome-oriented process. The process was to promote movement from school to postschool activities and encompass postsecondary education, vocational training, integrated employment (including supported employment), continuing and adult education, adult services, independent living, or community participation. Based on individual students' needs and taking into account the student's preferences and interests, transition planning includes "instruction-related services, community experiences, the development of employment and other post-school adult living objectives, and, when appropriate, acquisition of daily living skills and functional vocational evaluation" (IDEA, 1990, §602(a)(19)). Transition services and planning were considered so crucial to the life success of students like Macy that the amendments required the IEP to include a statement of the needed transition services for students beginning no later than age 16 and each year thereafter. If it is determined appropriate, planning could begin as early as age 14 or younger. In addition, when appropriate, a statement of interagency responsibilities or linkages (or both) before the student leaves the school setting is also to be included. New amendments expanded the concept of transition with the reauthorization of IDEA in 1997 (P. L. 105-17). Wehman (2002) noted that though modest in scope, these changes included the definition, age requirement for the initiation of transition services, inclusion of students with disabilities in statewide testing, discipline evaluation and service requirements, inclusion of general educators in the IEP and ITP teams, and the transfer of rights to students on attaining the age of majority. With regards to students from multicultural backgrounds, the amendments acknowledged their overrepresentation in special education, their high dropout rate, and their lack of transition into postsecondary options as compared to their white counterparts.

The major purpose of IDEA (1997), according to the new amendments, was to "ensure that all children with disabilities have available to them a free appropriate public education that emphasizes special education and related services designed to meet their unique needs and prepare them for employment and independent living" (§1400(d)1(A)). For the first time, emphasis was placed on preparation for employment and independent living. For deFur (1999), this implied that transition planning was to be the forethought of all special education services. According to Stodden (1998), other pieces of legislation began to reflect the values of the transition initiative as policy and legislation evolved throughout the early 1990s. In addition, education, employment, and human services began to complement and encourage common issues and values essential for cooperation between government agencies to effectively serve individuals with disabilities. Legislation that supports this position includes the Carl Perkins Vocational and Applied Technology

Act of 1990 (P.L. 98-524), the Americans with Disabilities Act of 1990 (ADA) (P.L. 101-336), the Vocational Rehabilitation Act Amendments of 1992 (P.L. 102-569), and the School-to-Work Opportunities Act of 1994 (P.L. 103-239). All were governmental efforts to support transition programming in general and special education.

FOUNDATIONS OF TRANSITION PLANNING FOR MULTICULTURAL LEARNERS

The goal of transition planning for Macy and other students is to facilitate a smooth transition into life after secondary schooling. Plans must address all areas of her life (e.g., career, vocation, recreation, leisure, and independent living). The process ought to begin as early as appropriate and include a variety of individuals and agencies who either know Macy, or who are familiar with services that might assist her in transitioning. Clark, Patton, and Moulton (2000) identified three key elements that need to be in place to ensure a seamless transition from school to postsecondary settings. First, there must be comprehensive planning. The planning must include assessment of needs and the development of an IEP. The second key element involves carrying out the plan. Finally, there must be ongoing coordination between the schools and agencies, service providers, and settings involved in the transition process.

Using Nondiscriminatory Assessment

Assessment may be considered the foundation of all transition planning. Sitlington, Nuebert, and Leconte (1997) described assessment as an ongoing process of collecting data on a student's strengths, needs, preferences, and interests as related to the demands of current and future working, educational, living, and personal-social environments. Assessment is the common thread in the process, forming the basis for defining goals and services included in the IEP. Data can be collected through informal or formal instruments. Informal assessment tools include a student's school records, work samples, portfolios, curriculum-based measures, criterion-referenced assessments, situational assessments, interviews, surveys, and behavioral assessments. Tools similar to the survey in Table 15.1 can guide the discussions among Macy, her family, and the IEP team as they design Macy's IEP and school program over her remaining school years. The nature of informal tools should allow multicultural students and their families to provide more detailed information about their long-term goals. Formal tools are also used for assessing transition goals and skills. Formal measures include standardized intelligence and achievement tests, adaptive behavior scales, personality inventories, and vocational and career aptitude scales. These measures may assist the team in considering a student's performance relative to similar students. Appropriate attention needs to be paid to selecting instruments that are technically sound. When interpreting and using results of any instruments, school personnel should consider both the cultural and economic backgrounds of the student.

TABLE 15.1   *Transition Needs and Preferences Survey*

This survey is designed to help the school determine what type of experiences and education you will need to prepare for life after graduation from high school. It will be used to develop a long-range plan (or transition plan) which will be discussed at the next IEP meeting.

Please answer the following questions based on what you know about yourself (or the student, if answered by a parent/guardian).

STUDENT NAME:	PARENT/GUARDIAN:
STUDENT AGE:	TODAY'S DATE:

1. What kind of work or education do you hope to see yourself in after graduation from high school?

Full-Time	Part-Time	
☐	☐	University or College–academically oriented four-year program
☐	☐	Community/Technical Colleges–technical/paraprofessional training
☐	☐	Adult Vocational Education–advanced job training (e.g., secretary)
☐	☐	Military Service–Army, Navy, Air Force, Coast Guard, Marines, etc.
☐	☐	Competitive Employment–a job trained by employer (or job coach)
☐	☐	Support Employment–a job with training then support from job coach
☐	☐	Sheltered Employment–low-pay work activities and training
☐	☐	Other: _____

2. What age do you want to exit school?   18   19   20   21   22

3. Is there a particular kind of work or education that you are currently interested in or other comments? If so, specify:

_____

_____

_____

4. Where do you hope to ultimately live as an adult?

☐ Independently in a home or apartment–generally requires more than minimum wage

☐ Independently in subsidized housing–usually requires minimum wage or higher income

☐ Wheelchair-accessible housing–ability to live on own or with personal care attendant

☐ Supported living–staff assists a few hours per day with cooking, shopping, budgeting, etc.

☐ Group home/foster care–staff provides 24-hour care and help in self-care, health, etc.

☐ With parents or relatives–sometimes with help of support staff or Medicaid services

☐ Other _____

5. Is there a neighborhood, city, or locality you hope to live in?

_____

6. What kinds of community participation do you hope will be available to you as an adult? (*Check all that apply*)

☐ Clubs or groups that meet to talk about a common interest (e.g., computers, astronomy). Specify, if possible.

_____

☐ Community recreational activities (e.g., YMCA, community centers, out with friends). Specify, if possible.
_____

☐ Religious and cultural activities (e.g., church, synagogue, temple, study groups). Specify, if possible.
_____

☐ Transportation for work and leisure activities (e.g., car, bus, friends, parents, bicycle). Specify type(s) and for what purpose. _____

☐ Continuing education (e.g., computers, cooking, sewing, home repair). Specify, if possible.
_____
_____

☐ Political participation (e.g., voting, involvement in political groups). Specify type of participation if possible.
_____

Other/Comments: _____
_____

7. Check any of the following services that you feel would be helpful to you in achieving your goals:

☐ Interest Inventories (e.g., OASYS) ☐ Entrance Exam Training (e.g., SAT)
☐ In-School Job Placement ☐ Job Shadowing (i.e., observing a job)
☐ Work Adjustment Training ☐ Guidance Counseling
☐ Community Work Experience ☐ Vocational Education
☐ Summer Jobs ☐ College Experience
Other/Comments: _____
_____

☐ Transportation and Driver Education ☐ Training in Handling Emergencies
☐ Consumer Sciences/Home Economics ☐ Training in Cooking and Nutrition
☐ Money Management Training ☐ Home Repair and Maintenance Training
☐ Sewing and Clothing Care Training ☐ First Aid Training
Other/Comments: _____
_____

☐ Language and Hearing Services ☐ Occupational or Physical Therapy
☐ Accommodations and Technology ☐ Self-Advocacy Training
☐ Relationships and Marriage ☐ Vocational Rehabilitation
☐ Psychology, Social Work, Psychiatry ☐ Community Awareness Activities
Other/Comments: _____
_____

☐ Evaluation(s) (Specify type needed): _____
☐ Referrals (Specify to whom): _____

Source: From Baer, R., McMahan, R., & Flexer, R. (1999). *Transition planning: A guide for parents and professionals.* Kent, OH: Kent State University. Reprinted with permission.

A variety of transition assessment models have been proposed (Clark, Patton, & Moulton, 2000; Sitlington, Clark, & Kolstoe, 2000). Often, these models reflect transition planning areas that later become the focus of the transition plan and curriculum. For instance, Clark et al. described common transition planning as community participation, daily living, employment, financial/income management, health, independent living, leisure/recreation, postsecondary education, relationships/social skills, transportation/mobility, and vocational training. Students and their families can provide critical information during the assessment process to develop effective transition plans.

Involving Multicultural Students and Their Family

Who better represents a student's interest than the student and his or her family? Student choice or participation was a key feature of the 1997 amendments of IDEA. The student's preferences, choices, and interests are to be incorporated into the IEP along with his or her cultures and values. The amendments provided for the student to be invited to the IEP meeting if the purpose of the meeting is the consideration of transition needs. When it is not possible for students to attend their meeting, schools should adopt measures to ensure that preferences and interests are considered. Although it might be suggested that the presence of a disability would make participation difficult, individuals with varying levels and types of disabilities have participated successfully in their own transition planning (Sitlington et al., 2000). Earlier, Wehmeyer (1998) highlighted the benefits of involving students in educational planning and decision making, which includes enhanced motivation to learn, improved educational outcomes, and opportunities to learn and practice self-advocacy skills.

Federal legislation has consistently outlined the necessity for significant individual and family involvement in the transition planning process. Specifically, the 1997 amendments required not only that parents be notified, but that the purpose of the meeting and those who would be in attendance be shared. Additionally, parents are to be notified that their son or daughter would be in attendance. The National Center on Secondary Education and Transition (NCSET, 2002) suggested that knowing their child has been invited provides parents the opportunity to discuss transition goals and activities, and to request that the school utilize transition strategies to increase the likelihood of their child's participation. A logical extension is that with prior notice, Macy's parents can concretely consider their own hopes and dreams for her future. Knowing that agencies will be invited may encourage parents to discuss agencies and support services that the school may not have considered.

Although federal legislation provides for family participation, research suggests that families, particularly those from multicultural backgrounds, are not always fully involved in the transition process (Hanley-Maxwell, Pogoloff, & Whitney-Thomas, 1998; Harry, Allen, & McLaughlin, 1995). The lack of or limited participation may be viewed as disinterest, but multicultural families might not participate in transition planning because of (a) issues related to time and resources to attend meetings or conferences; (b) belief that school personnel do not understand or respect their culture; (c) relative importance of transition planning to other more pressing and immediate family issues; and (d) apprehensions about the value of family contributions to the school-based transition process. Greenen, Powers, and Lopez-Vasquez (2001) reported that the lack of participation by multicultural families may be perceptional. In a survey of 308 African American, American Indian, Latino, and white parents, multicultural parents noted that they are active in the transition planning of their children. In some instances, their level of reported participation surpassed that of white parents. Professionals working with these parents reported multicultural parents as less involved than their white counterparts in the majority of transition activities. One explanation for the discrepancy centers on how professionals form their perceptions of parental involvement. Multicultural families may view the transition of a young person into adulthood from family and community perspectives rather than from experiences provided by educational or other institutions. Families may believe school-initiated transition planning is important, but that it is not the only setting where transition support should be sought (Harry, Allen, & McLaughlin, 1995).

Putting Together the Transition Planning Team

In addition to the student and his or her family, a variety of individuals must join together to assist with the development of a transition plan. The group includes those who developed the IEP—the student with a disability, parents and guardians, the special education teacher, a representative of the local education agency who is knowledgeable about the general education curriculum, an individual who can interpret evaluations, and a general education teacher if the student is involved in general or vocational education classes. These individuals are considered core participants. However, transition planning broadens the input by incorporating the expertise of other individuals, agencies, or services including those within the school setting (e.g., counselors, transition specialists, occupational therapists, job coaches, and mobility specialists). It might also include outside individuals, agencies, or services (e.g., community and spiritual leaders, vocational rehabilitation counselors and agencies, mental health and mental retardation agencies, Social Security Administration and other social services, community recreation services, postsecondary education and training institutions, disability advocacy groups, and group home or independent living center representatives). Table 15.2 highlights possible roles of transition team members.

Participation in the planning process requires that educators and professional service providers be cognizant of numerous issues that affect the student and his or her family. This is especially important for students who come from multicultural backgrounds. Educators and professional service providers cannot shy away from the realities that may be evidenced in their transition planning for multicultural students. Some of the planning experiences will be similar for both multicultural students and their peers, especially along socioeconomic lines. At the same time, educators and service providers must be aware of the potential for bias

TABLE 15.2 *Responsibilities of Transition Team Members*

Team Members	Responsibilities
Student*	• Identifies needs, strengths, preferences, and interests • Takes a leadership role in planning with supports • Participates in all planning activities • Identifies friends, family, and community members who can be part of the transition team • Assumes IDEA rights at age of majority

Parent/Guardian*
Also:
   Siblings
   Friends
   Advocates
	• Provides information regarding student needs, strengths, preferences, and interests
	• Participates in referrals to transition programs and adult services
	• Assists in procuring Social Security identification cards and transportation passes
	• Plans for long-term financial support, Social Security, trust funds, or other supports
	• Asks for assistance in obtaining community and residential services as needed
	• Provides opportunities for the student to try out adult roles and responsibilities
	• Identifies the person who will coordinate the transition plan
	• Identifies friends and community members who can be part of the transition team

Special Education*
Teacher
Collaborating with:
   Vocational education
   Work study
   Related services
   Guidance counselor
	• Helps student identify postsecondary goals and obtain needed transition services
	• Identifies school or community agency personnel to be included in transition planning
	• Prepares the student and the family for leadership roles in IEP/transition planning
	• Writes the statement of needed transition services in the IEP/transition plan
	• Coordinates transition services and activities in the IEP/transition plan
	• Provides information and assists families in developing referrals for adult services
	• Links the IEP to the student's course of study and required testing
	• Collects and monitors information about student progress
	• Provides or obtains accommodations and supports for all education services

Regular Education* **Teacher***	• Connects the IEP to the general education curriculum • Helps student to identify postsecondary goals and needed transition services • Provides classroom instruction to support the student's transition to adult environments

	• Collects and monitors information about student progress
	• Adapts curriculum and provides or obtains accommodations for regular education
	• Obtains or provides accommodations for state and regional proficiency tests
An Individual Who Can Interpret Evaluations*	• Provides assessment information regarding student needs, interests, and preferences
	• Provides assessment information regarding student strengths and aptitudes
	• Interprets assessments and evaluations for the student and the family
	• Identifies limitations of assessments and additional assessment needs
	• Works with the student and the family to identify assessment options
Representative of the Local Education Agency Familiar with the Curriculum*	• Provides information about programs offered throughout the school
	• Identifies how the student with a disability can be included in general education programs
	• Assists in obtaining technology, accommodations, and supports for inclusion and transition
	• Helps to identify how to address general education curriculum and competencies
	• Assists the transition team in obtaining accommodations and supports for student graduation and for participation in state and regional proficiency tests
Adult Service Providers, including VR services MR/DD. services Mental health Bureau of Employment Social Security Independent living center Employers Postsecondary educators Human services	• May provide job training and placement before and after graduation
	• May provide case management and service coordination services
	• Determine eligibility for SSI and Medicaid (generally VR and Social Security)
	• May provide independent living services
	• May provide functional vocational assessments and job counseling
	• May provide health services and supports
	• May provide technology and accommodations
	• May help fund postsecondary education or vocational training
	• May provide recreational and leisure opportunities
	• May provide counseling and behavioral supports
	• May assist in developing peer and coworker supports
	• May provide opportunities to try out postsecondary environments
	• May provide child support

*Core member

Source: From Baer, R., McMahan, R., & Flexer, R. (1999). *Transition planning: A guide for parents and professionals.* Kent, OH: Kent State University. Reprinted with permission.

and specific cultural dynamics that affect multicultural students and their families. For instance, Hoberman (1992) addressed service delivery in terms of vocational outcomes that are disproportionately poorer for multicultural versus white youth. Mental health center utilization data for multicultural youth indicate that their utilization of services is limited. In addition, they have higher rates of out-of-home placements, their parents receive fewer social services, and they are consistently routed through the juvenile justice system.

Transition plans may be effective or ineffective. By employing a culture-centered transition planning approach, team members can promote positive planning experiences for students for whom they are responsible. The transition team needs to understand how the intersection of race, disability, and other identities such as gender or age affect students and their family members. It cannot be assumed that because Macy has a learning disability, she identifies primarily with persons with disabilities. This may or may not be the case. Sue and Sue (2003) reminded educators and professional service providers that the client's disability may not be the primary focus of attention. This idea may be further explored through the RESPECTFUL counseling framework proposed by Lewis, Lewis, Daniels, and D'Andrea (2003). The RESPECTFUL model highlights factors that affect an individual psychologically and personally. Educators and professional service providers must consider each of these cultural factors in order to develop a more holistic view of the individual with whom they are working. Lewis et al. noted that these factors include (a) religious/spiritual identity, (b) economic class background, (c) sexual identity, (d) psychological maturity, (e) ethnic/racial identity, (f) threats to one's sense of well-being, (g) family background and history, (h) unique physical characteristics, and (i) location of residence and language differences. It is in Macy's best interest to be empowered to define her personal identities for herself. The student's identification of personal cultural alignments can guide the team to an assessment of appropriate needs.

Before the transition team can effectively work with multicultural families, they must be aware of their own ethnic and cultural backgrounds. This involves "self-knowledge and maturity," an area that may be considered one of several characteristics of a helper who is wise (Egan, 2002, p. 19). As Sue and Sue (2003) noted, five points of awareness are necessary to be a culturally competent provider. These are (a) moving from unawareness to awareness of one's own cultural background; (b) understanding how one's values affect multicultural clientele; (c) acknowledging racial and other identities that exist between the helper and client; (d) being aware of one's limitations; and (e) being prepared to deal with one's own negative thoughts, feelings, and actions regarding the "isms" (e.g., racism or ethnocentrism). Cultural awareness is a dynamic process that requires the full efforts of a team each time they interact with a student, his or her family, and the broader community. Clearly, keeping Macy's culture, family, and community in mind is a component of person-centered or lifestyle planning. These terms describe a process of planning that begins with a focus on the wants and needs of individuals. This process reflects new ways of thinking about disability and federal policy that focuses on personal choice and empowerment (Menchetti & Piland, 1998). Person-centered planning is most often used with individuals who have moderate to severe disabilities, or those who may have difficulty sharing their wishes and preferences.

Individualizing Transition Plans

Individual transition plans are written documents that detail the student's transition plans and services. Macy's parents tried to form an alliance with the transition team to generate specific duties and responsibilities for all involved. In some cases, transition is discussed during the annual IEP meeting along with any other goals the team has deemed appropriate. However, there are other times when the team comes together to discuss transition specifically. Amended regulations for implementing IDEA require that for students, including multicultural students, beginning no later than 14 years old (or earlier if deemed appropriate), one of the purposes of the annual IEP meeting will be a discussion of transition services needs. Beginning at least by age 16, the discussion will focus on planning for needed transition services. In both cases, the final regulations require that students be invited to attend their IEP meeting.

An important addition to the IEP/ITP is the provision that allows for the transfer of parental rights to students at the age of majority—the age when an individual acquires all the rights and responsibilities of being an adult. In most states, the age is 18. According to NCSET (2002), there is further recognition of the importance of the school's responsibility in assisting students to move from school to the adult world. In a state where age of majority transfer rights begin at least one year before a student reaches the age of majority, the student's IEP must include a statement that the student has been notified of his or her rights and that these rights will transfer to him or her on reaching the age of majority. Additionally, when the student reaches the age of majority, if rights transfer, the school must provide notice to the student and parents.

Developing Self-Determination

Self-determination is an integral component of transition planning and success. Emphasis on self-determination in transition planning has become increasingly important as general and special educators have come to acknowledge the rights of individuals with disabilities to participate in decisions made about them. Field, Martin, Miller, Ward, and Wehmeyer (1998) described self-determination as "a combination of skills, knowledge, and beliefs that enable a person to engage in goal-directed, self-regulated, autonomous behavior" (p. 2). It is a personal quality that compels individuals to be in control of themselves and their life. Those who possess self-determination are cognizant of their strengths and challenges, likes and dislikes, their history and what role their history has played in making them who they are. Self-determination has been divided into several components, types, or characteristics that lend themselves to teaching and evaluation. According to Test, Browder, Karvonen, Wood, and Algozzine (2002), those most commonly identified include choice/decision making, goal setting/attainment, problem solving, self-evaluation/management, self-advocacy, person-centered planning for IEPs, relationships with others, and self-awareness.

Because the development of self-determination is personal and individualized, it lends itself easily to being encouraged and taught within a cultural context. For this to occur, teachers and service providers must be culturally competent and be aware of their own cultural biases. Field et al. (1998) presented cultural perspectives on self-determination. They agreed that general and special educators must listen to students and their family and strive to create "win–win" situations. Listening to Macy and her family was necessary to understand the influence cultural backgrounds and values might have on self-determination. One must not assume that members of specific cultural groups adhere to the same beliefs. Variances between individuals exist just as variances between cultures. Additionally, service providers should seek to understand discrepancies between the student and his or her parents as they relate to cultural backgrounds, and beliefs as they relate to self-determination. Finally, general and special educators should keep in mind how self-determination may be defined within the context of the culture. Insignificant behavioral changes for one culture may represent milestones in self-determination in another. Regarding creating "win–win" situations, educators should aim to develop solutions whereby the needs of both students and parents are met and cultural values are respected.

Although self-determination is often discussed within the context of transition, "acquiring the personal characteristics which lead to self-determination is a developmental process that begins in early childhood and continues throughout adult life" (Ward, 1988, p. 2). This may explain why self-determination is considered both as outcome and intervention (Wood & Test, 2001). Logically, the earlier professionals begin to focus on self-determination, the more likely it is to be an outcome. In fact, they must ensure strong self-determination skills by fostering a culture that supports self-determination. This includes not only teaching new skills, but creating environments in which students of all ages can use the skills in real-life contexts (Sitlington, Clark, & Kolstoe, 2000; Wood & Test, 2001). If students like Macy are to participate fully, they must be assisted in developing skills that help them make decisions across all the domains of their lives. For example, Macy's skills in self-determination may be enhanced if participating in, and eventually directing, her own IEP meeting becomes a personal goal. Several authors have developed materials that assist students in developing appropriate skills (Trogerson, Miner, & Shen, 2004; Van Rusen, Bos, Schumaker, & Deshler, 1994).

BEYOND TRADITION: MULTICULTURAL CONSIDERATIONS IN TRANSITION PLANNING

It is now a well-known fact that the United States is experiencing significant demographic and sociocultural shifts. These shifts have far-reaching implications for various sectors of society. Education in general, and special education transition programming in particular, are intertwined sectors that necessitate culturally appropriate approaches that more fully meet the needs of transitioning students from an array of cultural backgrounds. Presently, more than 280 million persons reside in the United States, of which 13.5% are Latino, 13% are African American,

4% are Asian and Pacific Islander, 1% are American Indian and Alaskan Native, 2.4% are more than one race, and 69% are white (U.S. Census, 2002). Sandefur, Martin, Eggerling-Boeck, Mannon, and Meier (2001) projected that from 2000 to 2050, African Americans will show a slight population increase, while there will be sharp increases in the Latino and Asian populations. American Indians have shown a dramatic population increase over the past 50 years, and their numbers have tended to hover at 1% of the total population. The white population is expected to decline to 53% of the total population by 2050. As a result, transitioning students and those who work with them must reflect a different cultural milieu. Helms and Cook (1999) argued that "the values, beliefs, language, rituals, traditions, and other behaviors that are passed from one generation to another within any social group" (p. 21) will have an impact, in a more diverse manner, on the people and services that are a part of the transitioning process. The worldviews that emanate from culture have the potential to cause intergroup tension if change is perceived as threatening in some form (Parrillo, 1999).

Helms and Cook (1999) explained that mainstream values in U.S. society reflect those of the white culture. Considerable weight, for example, is placed on individualism, which favors the fulfillment of personal needs and goals. Traditional African American, Latino, Asian, and American Indian cultures tend to be more collectivistic, or value the group and its needs above the individual. For example, one transition goal for a white 18-year-old student might include an independent living arrangement away from family, which reflects the values of autonomy in mainstream culture. On the other hand, the value of collectiveness for a traditional Latino student and his or her family might include living with family well past the age of 18, which would require a different transition focus that is no less applicable, but is different. However, it must be remembered that there are individual differences within and between groups that preclude homogeneous classification systems. Helms and Cook reminded professionals to balance their knowledge of common cultural characteristics shared by various ethnic groups with an understanding of individual uniqueness. Logically, for Macy's transition planning to be successful, it needed to focus not just on Macy and her family, but also on the community in which she lived and where she intended to work. For multicultural youth and their families, especially those living in ethnically homogeneous communities, there may already be a natural connection between the school and the community. For example, Ford (1995) argued that regardless of economic status, African American communities have a conglomerate of immediate or at-large resources that can support families. These assets include African American religious institutions, professionals, volunteer grassroots organizations, social and service clubs, businesses, and community-based social agencies. Connection with one's own community may serve as a pathway to the mainstream community.

There are a variety of postsecondary options available to students with disabilities transitioning from high school. Two such options include transition to employment and transition to postsecondary education. Sitlington et al. (2000) noted that the eventual goal of all transition efforts is to transition to employment. The choices Macy and her family would make about transition options vary and would be based on the type and severity of her disability, her personal and professional goals, her readiness for transition, and the availability of support systems and resources. When transition to employment is the immediate goal following high school, the transition planning should take on a work-based, hands-on focus. Although the curriculum for transition to work should span a student's educational career, much of it will be delivered and experienced during the latter years of schooling. Sitlington et al. (2000) proposed the Career Development and Transition Education Model, which offers a framework for transition and transition planning that will facilitate work. The model reflects "critical student outcomes across age/developmental levels, transition exit points for students as they move from one educational level to the next, and the education and service systems needed to deliver transition education and transition services" (p. 26). Nine knowledge and skill domains (i.e., communication and academic performance, self-determination, interpersonal relationships, integrated community participation, health and fitness, independent/interdependent daily living, leisure and recreation, employment, and further education and training) cross the developmental/life phases and exit points. Preparing students for transition to work requires instruction in the knowledge and skills domain, as well as instruction in occupational awareness, employment-related knowledge and skills, and specific vocational knowledge and skills (see Sitlington et al., 2000). In addition to instruction, students need opportunities to put their knowledge and skills to use in real settings. Quality hands-on, work-based experience is a critical predictive factor to success when transitioning to work.

Transition to postsecondary education is increasingly becoming an option for students with disabilities, and a choice that Macy's parents wished for her. Postsecondary education can include vocational and technical programs, community colleges, or four-year colleges and universities. Data on the participation of adolescents and young adults with exceptionalities who choose to transition into postsecondary education varies. However, this group tends to be less likely to participate in postsecondary education when compared to their peers without exceptionalities (HEATH Resource Center, 2001). For instance, in comparison with the 1998 report, freshmen in the 2000 class were more likely to be multicultural students. When preparing multicultural high school students with exceptionalities to transition into postsecondary options, especially two or four-year colleges, the preparation should have a more academic focus. Students need strong content area foundations (i.e., reading, math, and science) to ensure that they are prepared for higher level work in college. Participation in general education is more likely to yield a solid academic foundation; and placement of students in more restrictive environments may lead them to (a) attend fewer general education classes; (b) be more dependent on teachers; (c) have difficulty with test-taking, organizational, and study skills; (d) not participate in extracurricular activities; and (e) know less about career options requiring postsecondary education. These factors have tended to predict college attendance and success. Students may also choose to transition into vocational or technical schools as postsecondary options. Vocational-technical education is geared toward employment that requires specialized education but not a bachelor's degree. Vocational-technical training can be obtained in two-year community or junior colleges or in single specialty schools in a variety of areas including cosmetology, animal health, child care/development, automotive maintenance, and law enforcement/criminal justice. Clearly, multicultural students transitioning into such programs will benefit from hands-on and work-based transition planning and curricula in high school.

A Culturally Responsive Educator

1. Begins transition planning early.
2. Engages in person-centered transition planning.
3. Involves multicultural students in their own transition planning.
4. Understands that multicultural families must be involved in transition planning.
5. Considers a student's cultural orientation in transition planning.
6. Understands that transition planning and activities must be community-focused.
7. Knows that transition curriculum must reflect the transition options available to multicultural students.
8. Needs to be cognizant of his or her thoughts and feelings about working with multicultural students with exceptionalities.
9. Is aware of a variety of transition options available to multicultural learners.
10. Involves multidisciplinary agencies and resources in transition programming.

Conclusion

This chapter addressed the benefits of multicultural transition programming for exceptional learners, especially those with racial and linguistic differences. Effective transition planning for multicultural students like Macy should begin early and involve students and their families. Other critical components to effective transition planning include an assessment and a curriculum that reflect postsecondary goals and options. At all points of the planning process, general and special educators must be mindful of the influences that culture and family expectations have on postsecondary outcomes. Community supports and relationships are also critical in the planning process. Finally, educators must provide optimal transition assistance to multicultural students when they have adequately assessed their own cultural awareness and knowledge.

Discussion Questions

1. Briefly explain one legislative amendment that has significantly affected transition services.
2. Transition planning can be multidimensional. Do you agree? Briefly explain reasons for your answer.

3. Elaborate on two issues to be addressed by transition team members when working with multicultural learners with exceptionalities.
4. Discuss culturally responsive skills needed by transition specialists.
5. Describe postsecondary options available to multicultural learners with exceptionalities.

References

Baer, R., McMahan, R., & Flexer, R. (1999). *Effective transition planning: A guide for parents and professionals*. Kent, OH: Kent State University.

Bullis, M., Yovanoff, P., Mueller, G., & Harvel, E. (2002). Life on the "outs"—Examination of the facility-to-community transition of incarcerated youth. *Exceptional Children, 69*, 7–22.

Clark, G. M., Patton, J. R., & Moulton, L. R. (2000). *Informal assessment for transition planning*. Austin, TX: PRO-ED.

deFur, S. H. (1999). Special education, transition, and school-based services: Are they meant for each other? In S. H. deFur & J. R. Patton (Eds.), *Transition and school-based services: Interdisciplinary perspectives for enhancing the transition process* (pp. 15–50). Austin, TX: PRO-ED.

Egan, G. (2002). *The skilled helper: A problem-management and opportunity-development approach to helping* (7th ed.). Pacific Grove, CA: Brooks/Cole.

Field, S., & Hoffman, A. (1994). Development of a model for self-determination. *Career Development for Exceptional Children, 17*, 159–169.

Field, S., Martin, J., Miller, R., Ward, M., & Wehmeyer, M. (1998). *A practical guide for teaching self-determination*. Reston, VA: Council for Exceptional Children.

Ford, B. A. (1995). African American community involvement processes and special education: Essential networks for effective education. In B. A. Ford, F. E. Obiakor, & J. M. Patton (Eds.), *Effective education of African American exceptional learners: New perspectives* (pp. 235–272). Austin, TX: PRO-ED.

Greenen, S., Powers, L. E., & Lopez-Vasquez, A. (2001). Multicultural aspects of parent involvement in transition planning. *Exceptional Children, 61*, 265–282.

Hanley-Maxwell, C., Pogoloff, S. M., & Whitney-Thomas, J. (1998). Families: The heart of transition. In F. R. Rusch & J. G. Chadsey (Eds.), *Beyond high school: Transition from school to work* (pp. 234–264). Belmont, CA: Wadsworth.

Harry, B., Allen, N., & McLaughlin, M. (1995). Communication versus compliance: African American parents' involvement in special education. *Exceptional Children, 61*, 364–377.

HEATH Resource Center (2001). *College freshmen with disabilities: A biennial statistical profile*. Washington, DC: American Council on Education.

Helms, J. E., & Cook, D. A. (1999). *Using race and culture in counseling and psychotherapy: Theory and practice*. Boston: Allyn & Bacon.

Hoberman, H. M. (1992). Ethnic minority status and adolescent mental health services utilization. *Journal of Mental Health Administration, 19*, 246–267.

Individuals with Disabilities Education Act of 1990, 20 U.S.C. (1400 et seq).

Individuals with Disabilities Education Act Amendments of 1997, 20 U.S.C. (1400 et seq).

IPLAN (1990). Helping students communicate in planning conferences. *Teaching Exceptional Children, 22*(4), 30–32.

Lewis, J. A., Lewis, M. D., Daniels, J. A., & D'Andrea, M. J. (2003). *Community counseling: Empowerment strategies for a diverse society* (3rd ed.). Pacific Grove: CA: Brooks/Cole.

Menchetti, B. M., & Piland, V. C. (1998). The person-centered approach to vocational evaluation and career planning. In F. R. Rusch & J. C. Chadsey (Eds.), *Beyond high school: Transition from school to work* (pp 319–330). Belmont, CA: Wadsworth.

Mullins, E. R., & Irving, J. L. (2000). Transition into middle school. What research says. *Middle School Journal, 31*(3), 57–60.

National Center on Secondary Education and Transition. (2002, June). *IDEA 1997: Implications for secondary education and transition services.* Retrieved October 17, 2003, from www.ncset.org/publications/policy/2002_06.asp

Parrillo, V. N. (1999). *Strangers to these shores.* Boston: Allyn & Bacon.

Sandefur, G. D., Martin, M., Eggerling-Boeck, J., Mannon, S. E., & Meier, A. M. (2001). An overview of racial and ethnic demographic trends. In N. J. Smelser, W. J. Wilson, & F. Mitchell (Eds.), *America becoming: Racial trends and their consequences* (pp. 40–102). Washington, DC: National Academy Press.

Sitlington, P. L., Clark, G. M., & Kolstoe, O. P. (2000). *Transition education & services for adolescents with disabilities.* Boston: Allyn & Bacon.

Sitlington, P. L., Neubert, D. A., & Leconte, P. J. (1997). Transition assessment: The position of the Division on Career Development and Transition. *Career Development for Exceptional Individuals, 20*(1), 69–79.

Stodden, R. (1998). School to work transition: Overview of disability legislation. In F. R. Rusch & J. G. Chadsey (Eds.), *Beyond high school: Transition from school to work* (pp. 60–76). Belmont, CA: Wadsworth.

Sue, D. W., & Sue, D. (2003). *Counseling the culturally diverse: Theory and practice* (4th ed.). New York: Wiley.

Test, D. W., Browder, D. M., Karvonen, M., Wood, W., & Algozzine, B. (2002). Writing lesson plans for promoting self-determination. *Teaching Exceptional Children, 35,* 8–14.

Trogerson, C. W., Miner, C. A., & Shen, H. (2004). Developing student competence in self-directed IEPs. *Intervention in School and Clinic, 39*(3). 162–167.

U.S. Bureau of the Census (2002). *Diversity continues to grow in U.S.* Retrieved on October 17, 2003, from factfinder.census.gov/jsp/sass/SAFFInfo.jsp?geo_id=01000US

Van Rusen, A. K., Bos, C. S., Schumaker, J. B., & Deshler, D. D. (1994). *Self-advocacy strategy for education and transition planning.* Lawrence, KS: Edge.

Ward, M. J. (1988). The many facets of self-determination. *Transition Summary, 5,* 2–3.

Wehman, P. (2002). *Individual transition plans: The teacher's curriculum guide for helping youth with special needs.* Austin, TX: PRO-ED.

Wehmeyer, M. L. (1998). Student involvement in transition-planning and transition-program implementation. In F. R. Rusch & J. C. Chadsey (Eds.), *Beyond high school: Transition from school to work* (pp. 206–233). Belmont, CA: Wadsworth.

Wehmeyer, M. L., & Schwartz, M. (1995). Self-determination and positive adult outcomes: A follow-up study of youth with mental retardation and learning disabilities. *Exceptional Children, 63,* 245–255.

Wischnowski, M. W., Fowler, S. A., & McCollum, J. A. (2000). Supports and barriers to writing an interagency agreement on the preschool transition. *Journal of Early Intervention, 23*(4), 294–307.

Wood, W. M., & Test, D. W. (2001). *Final performance report: Self-determination synthesis project.* Charlotte, NC: University of North Carolina at Charlotte.

Chapter 16

Family Empowerment and Multicultural Special Education

Loretta P. Prater and Shandra R. Terrell

Chapter Outline

Thinking About Multicultural Special Education

Mrs. Smith was a divorced African American mother of two children. She chronicled the years that her son, Ray, had been involved in a school structured setting, from preschool until high school. It was during his preschool experience that Ray was identified as having behavioral problems, although he was labeled as academically talented, especially in math. Subsequently, he was labeled as hyperactive, the leading behavioral diagnosis in American children. Ray also received medication to control seizures. His total school experience was a pattern of misbehavior, being on suspension, or changing school settings in an effort to find the right fit. He would demonstrate brief periods of cooperation, but would digress into disruptive behavioral problems. Additionally, he exhibited uncontrollable anger during these episodes at school.

Interactions with school officials led Mrs. Smith to form perceptions that prompted her to state, "They don't care about the children with problems, only the others." However, Ray's behavior sometimes compromised the safety of faculty and other students at school. For example, in one incident, he attempted to hit a teacher with a chair. Consequently, he spent most of his ninth grade year on suspension and failed most classes, but was promoted to attend another school. In reality, Ray's teachers were not to blame, and his mother was also not to blame even though they both blamed each other for Ray's problems. As a result, they missed some great opportunities to collaborate with each other. The outcome of Ray's school experience was that he dropped out of school. He never completed high school nor even took the G.E.D. test.

- *How can teachers develop collaborative relationships with parents like Mrs. Smith?*
- *Why should schools empower families in general and special education?*

Schools are increasingly serving more racially, culturally, and linguistically diverse populations (Campey, 2002; Villa, 2003). The statement that society is becoming more and more diverse is often used in casual conversations. Few would challenge that belief, especially since the collective multicultural population will represent more than half of the U.S. population by the year 2050 (Walker, 1993). Advancements in technology have increased awareness of cultural diversity through the media and allowed ease of travel to areas very different from the community in which one resides. Through immigration and migration, individuals from diverse cultures reside in common communities. These circumstances have increased the potential for informal interactions and more formal establishments of families among persons from different cultures, ethnic and racial backgrounds, or religious identities. In addition, they add to the complexity of family structures, especially since customs can vary within a general cultural classification (Taylor, 1994).

Recognizing the diversity of cultures and family structures is important to the discussion of multicultural special education, especially as related to family empowerment. Some years ago, Banks (1989) reported that parents of children with special needs tend to be uninvolved in school activities. When this fact is coupled with different cultures and family structures, unique challenges frequently surface.

A primary responsibility of schools is to educate students; but students do not exist apart from their families. In fact, schools occupy only 9% of children's lives (Murphy, 1993). Consequently, families must be accepted as pivotal partners in the education of their children, since such an involvement is positively correlated with students' school achievement (Drummond & Stipek, 2004; Fischer, 2003). A widely accepted assumption is that two entities cannot occupy the same space at the same time. This is absolutely true and provides more justification to prompt parental empowerment. There is a role in the education of children that is occupied only by parents and cannot be replaced by school faculty, administrators and staff, school board members, or legislators. School personnel and others making important decisions about schooling may have undergraduate and graduate degrees from the best colleges and universities, but there is crucial knowledge about children and families that is lacking and must be addressed (Evans, 2002; Gordon, 2002; Hiatt-Michael, 2001; Lee & Manning, 2001; Warner, Duane, Garvan, & Conway, 2002). The impact of this missing information is especially significant when multicultural issues are coupled with a magnitude of expected outcomes for general and special education programming. Ironically, while the world is becoming more diverse, the school's instructional and administrative structure is becoming less diverse. For example, as recently as 1996, African American teachers made up only 7.3% of the teaching force in public schools (Kusimo, 1999). This is a huge disadvantage, especially if practices and regulations of the school environment are structured in a manner resulting in a disengagement of parents in the educational process. In all likelihood, parents share the diverse culture of their children and have an understanding of the child's world that is needed to assist in attaining a successful educational experience and instructional partnership (Geenen, Powers, & Lopez-Vasquez, 2001; Prater, 2002a, 2002b; Prater & Ivarie, 1999). In the case of Mrs. Smith, she had an understanding of Ray's world, but Ray's behaviors, her perceptions, and the lack of empowerment by school officials prevented the formation of collaborative relationships that would have had a positive impact on her son.

Some educators have the mistaken notion that *involvement* and *empowerment* are synonymous terms. They are not the same. Certainly, there is a clear distinction when one considers a wide array of activities (Blasi, 2001; Darch, Miao, & Shippen, 2004; Lawson, 2003). Activities within the purview of parental involvement have little significance in regard to decision making that affects the educational process. Parental involvement could include planning a homeroom party, decorating a bulletin board, or attending a mandated meeting with school personnel to be informed of the child's individualized educational plan (IEP). Conversely, when parents are empowered, they have been afforded resources and control that allow them to actively participate, exhibit competence, and assume a leadership role in the decision-making process regarding the education of their children (Espe-Sherwindt, 1991; Pattnaik, 2003). In other words, they have power that is real, not merely perceived. More than a decade ago, Harry (1992) argued that in order for parents to be empowered in special education programs, they must assume roles as assessors, presenters of reports, policy makers, advocates, and peer supporters. Some teachers generally believe parents must go along with the process because they know what is best for their students. Parents and guardians hope that the work of teachers and service providers will directly benefit their children. These hopes are sometimes unfulfilled when collaborative relationships fail to materialize, as in the case of Mrs. Smith.

FAMILY EMPOWERMENT IN EDUCATION

Parents have always been involved in the education of their children because they are actually the first teachers. Even for children enrolled in preschool, family members are the first to introduce them to their surrounding environment and guide learning opportunities. After the family, the school is likely to be the most profound influence on the course of a child's life. This relationship between the family and the school frequently affects how well the child adjusts to school (Ramey & Ramey, 1994). Concerns about parental participation in schools have surfaced as more children and their families come to school from different cultures and socioeconomic backgrounds. When everyone lived in the "Ozzie and Harriet" household, with the "Father Knows Best" family next door, and in the "Leave It to Beaver" neighborhoods, it was perceived that schools and parents enjoyed a symbiotic relationship. Schoolchildren were academically talented and lived in two-parent households, fathers worked outside the home, and homemaker mothers welcomed children home from school with freshly baked cookies and milk. Viewing those shows on television made people think that most people lived in that world. The reality is that those scenarios represented fantasy for most, because few children lived in those circumstances. Mrs. Smith and her son Ray did not live in that world.

When there were more homogeneous school populations and neighborhood schools, empowerment of parents did not seem to be a concern. The incidence of children in need of special education was also not an issue, because children with special needs were not sent to school. These children were mostly kept at home and shielded from public view. Today, the growing diversity of the population and the forces that are affecting both family life and schools have challenged the belief that children are the only ones who need to be "readied" for school (Pattnaik, 2003; Ramey & Ramey, 1994). Families needed to be readied too.

In most public school settings, and especially in public schools in large urban areas, in comparison to private schools or public schools in rural America, the student population is diverse. One in three students enrolled in schools in the United States has a racial or ethnic minority background, and this number is expected to grow to 46% by the year 2020 (Garrett & Morgan, 2002). This diversity includes racial, ethnic, and cultural differences, but diversity must also include differences in levels of cognitive, emotional, and physical functioning. Because of the diversity of student cultures, there is a natural diverse population of parents and other family members who potentially interact with the school environment. There is constant interaction between schools and the many cultures represented by these students. This occurs because culture is part of a person's very being. When school personnel interact with students, they are interacting with the whole child, including family traditions, beliefs, and experiences. Unlike parents, school personnel are in the position of power and can choose to educate themselves about the multicultural populations present in their school and make accommodations based on those differences. Unfortunately, they also can ignore those multicultural factors, thereby forcing students and their families to completely assimilate into the status quo culture of the school. This forced assimilation frequently leads to conflicts and confusing roles (Colwell, 2002; Voltz, 1998).

Whereas there is endless diversity among multicultural populations of parents, the groups that are more commonly cited in research studies specific to special education programs are African Americans, Latinos, and American Indians (Chinn & Hughes, 1987). Although there is uniqueness among and within these populations, there are also some common themes. For example, poverty based on underemployment or unemployment, family disruption, low levels of educational attainment, perceived lack of school support, and absence of representation among school personnel are among challenges faced by many of these parents (Prater, 2002a, 2002b). More than a decade ago, Bowman (1994) reported that children from low-income families and some minority groups, primarily African Americans, Latinos, American Indians, and some Asians, have higher rates of special education placements than do other children. This is a continuing trend (Artiles, 2003), except in programs designed specifically for gifted students (Ford & Harmon, 2001). Clearly, empowerment in some cultures may be even more challenging than in others, considering the lack of understanding and preparation of educational professionals. For example, Latino children are the fastest growing population in public schools (Castex, 1994). They are a distinctively diverse group, and there is a high level of poverty within approximately 39% of their families (Delgado & Rogers-Adkinson, 1999). Because of the complexity of these issues, empowerment of American Indian parents is also of concern. When poverty and alcoholism are combined with tribal customs and a history of mistrust of public institutions, this is a problem (Sparks, 1999). American Indian families have very strong values and customs, and successful instructional programs must incorporate family values into the academic structure with the understanding that American Indian students are full baskets entering a different environment and not empty glasses entering a classroom to be filled (Lake, 1990). It is important to understand that in blending multicultural education with special education programs in which language is a factor, instructional models must include both home and school languages in these bilingual and literacy situations (Pattnaik, 2003). Another challenge is that children may speak English and parents may not speak the language used in the school setting. However, when parents with limited English proficiency are nurtured to become involved in schooling, their child's school performance is positively affected (Kauffman, Perry, & Prentiss, 2001; Simich-Dudgeon, 1993).

Sometimes families feel powerless and trust educators without question. This can lead to a misdiagnosis. In one southeastern city, an African American child was placed in a special school for children with physical and mental developmental disabilities. It was later discovered that the child had not been screened for auditory functioning and the problem was lack of hearing, rather than mental retardation or defiance, the original labels used to explain the student's behavior. When parents are empowered, this type of situation does not occur. Empowered parents ask questions and insist on accountability. General and special educators frequently make judgments about multicultural parents without knowledge of their circumstances. In their 2003 Annual Conference, the National Urban League called for an "empowerment movement" to benefit African Americans in bridging the gap with white Americans in regards to education, income, wealth, and access to quality housing. These gaps affect many ethnic groups in America. Simply put, if families are unable to deal effectively with individual and household concerns, they will have less time to focus on their children's education. Factors at the individual or household level that cause difficulties for families include poor housing, difficulty managing finances, employability and job sustainability issues, inadequate nutrition, child care, stress management, and parenting skills (Duncan, Dunnagan, Christopher, & Paul, 2003). Racism, gender, and socioeconomic status also present challenges and barriers to parental empowerment (Prater, 2002a, 2002b). Teachers are sometimes defensive when parents visit the school, thus increasing negative communication that presents barriers and nurtures stereotypes. Perceptions based on gender, sexism, and classism reinforce dissonance between parents and teachers. These perceptions also marginalize parents and inhibit parental empowerment (Simpson & Cieslik, 2002).

Roeser, Patrick, Yoon, Anderman, and Eccles (1995) reported that elementary teachers do not go beyond general information and classroom procedures when implementing parent involvement or empowerment strategies and rarely request parent participation in academic tasks or educational activities. In other words, there is little transition from involvement to empowerment, especially when involving minority parents. One way to be involved in academic tasks is to engage in active participation in the parent-teacher organization (PTO), especially by assuming a position of leadership. The importance of clearly defining parental expectations for multicultural populations is vital (Bracey, 2001; Yan, 1999). As parents are afforded a greater role in defining involvement, they gain greater confidence that leads to increased participation in school decision making. Additionally, it is crucial for general and special education teachers to have empathy for the issues that parents confront. Perceived sensitivity from professionals and service providers can increase parental empowerment and aid in guiding parental engagement in meaningful school activities.

MOVING FORWARD WITH FAMILY EMPOWERMENT IN AN ERA OF ACCOUNTABILITY

Family empowerment benefits *all* children, schools, communities, and the entire educational process (Fan, 2001; Obiakor, Grant, & Dooley, 2002; Villa, 2003). It is widely understood that parental empowerment is essential for a child's academic and personal enhancement. In this era of accountability, parental voices are critical for educational success. Positive collaborations between schools and parents strengthen the entire educational process and stimulate a change in the "us versus them" mentality. If parents are viewed as essential partners with schools, an outcome can be an elevation of their status as effective brokers of their child's educational progress. Schools also benefit greatly from parental empowerment because there is less conflict between home and school. Parents may recognize that instead of an adversarial relationship, a cooperative partnership can be developed. When parents are empowered, schools gain and students succeed. For example, Chang, Lai, and Shimizu (1999) reported that exceptional English-language learners from Asian and Pacific American backgrounds progressed when there was intervention utilizing the home in school and community partnerships.

In special education programs within public school settings, federal laws and policies have been established to mandate parental involvement (Prater & Ivarie, 1999). In today's era of accountability, parental empowerment is indispensable. This prompts the question, "If laws can force involvement, can empowerment be mandated?" In the case of Mrs. Smith, laws were in place, but she was definitely not empowered. However, there is good news. Arkansas is an example of a state that is trying to legislate parental involvement. Arkansas recently passed Act 603, a law to require school districts to have a parental involvement plan. This progressive legislation recognizes that if parental involvement is to be effective, schools must first develop a structure to identify the nature and intensity of the involvement. Schools must decide the type of activities that would be most helpful to the educational process, with the outcome of enhanced benefits for students. According to the stipulations of Act 603, each parental involvement plan submitted must include components that will lead to greater parental empowerment. In Act 603, schools must engage parents at all levels, and the parental involvement plan must facilitate two-way communication between parents and schools. Policies or procedures that discourage parents from visiting schools must be avoided. Futhermore, it is the responsibility of school administrators to establish climates conducive to parental empowerment, the accountability component of Act 603. To evaluate the process, the Arkansas Department of Education will review each parental involvement plan, determine if it is in compliance, and send written notification indicating any deficiencies.

A Culturally Responsive Educator

1. Understands that family empowerment is a key factor in successful educational outcomes for students.
2. Knows the burdens confronted by multicultural parents as they navigate complex educational systems.
3. Values cultural differences among parents and community members.
4. Empowers multicultural parents in general and special education.
5. Understands that the traditional structure for parental inclusion is outdated and limits empowerment of multicultural parents.
6. Values parents as resource persons.
7. Treats multicultural parents as partners.
8. Understands societal stereotypes that serve as barriers to parental empowerment.
9. Is realistic in understanding students with exceptionalities and their families.
10. Uses innovative techniques to work with multicultural parents and their children.

Conclusion

Based on the experience of Mrs. Smith in the introductory case, family empowerment is a complex issue, yet it yields many positive outcomes for students. Therefore, it is imperative that all opportunities for parental engagement be explored, even those that have never been used before or those that may seem atypical. First, there must be acceptance of the fact that diversity is here to stay. Second, the term *diversity* must be all-inclusive and not merely limited to physical appearance. And third, future teachers must engage in programs and activities that enhance cultural awareness during their enrollment in teacher education programs and beyond graduation through continuing professional development activities. To make progress toward addressing this problem, it is also important that schools develop projects to target specific groups, such as grandparents raising grandchildren, single fathers, and other groups of identifiable populations parenting children with special needs. As schools look at serving children from diverse backgrounds in this era of accountability, the point of intervention should be the family unit, regardless of the structure of the family grouping. Clearly, attempting to educate children with special needs, in isolation from their families, is a mistake. Collaboration, consultation, and cooperation must be the key.

Discussion Questions

1. Discuss the importance of family empowerment as it relates to the educational achievement of children from multicultural populations.
2. Describe the unique challenges faced by general and special educators as they try to empower families.
3. Discuss ways to lessen the feeling of social dissonance between school professionals and families from diverse cultures.
4. If you were assigned the responsibility of designing a family empowerment program for family members of students with special needs, describe strategies that you would use.
5. Briefly explain methods that school administrators can develop to create a school climate that fosters family empowerment.

References

Artiles, A. J. (2003). Special education's changing identity: Paradoxes and dilemmas in views of culture and space. *Harvard Educational Review, 73,* 164–203.

Banks, C. A. (1989). Parents and teachers: Partners in multicultural education. In J. A. Banks & C. A. Banks (Eds.), *Multicultural education: Issues and perspectives* (pp. 305–322). Boston: Allyn & Bacon.

Blasi, M. J. (2001). [Review of the book *Rethinking family-school relations: A critique of parental involvement in schooling*]. *Childhood Education, 78,* 54.

Bowman, B. T. (1994). The challenge of diversity. *Phi Delta Kappan, 76*(3), 218–224.

Bracey, G. W. (2001). School involvement and the working poor. *Phi Delta Kappan, 82*(10), 795–797.

Campey, J. (2002). Immigrant children in our classrooms: Beyond ESL. *Education Canada, 42,* 44–47.

Castex, G. M. (1994). Providing services to Hispanic/Latino populations: Profiles in diversity. *Social Work, 39,* 288–296.

Chang, J., Lai, A., & Shimizu, W. (1999). Educating the Asian-Pacific American exceptional English-language learners. In F. E. Obiakor, J. O. Schwenn, & A. F. Rotatori (Eds.), *Advances in special education: Multicultural education for learners with exceptionalities* (pp. 33–51). Stamford, CT: JAI Press.

Chinn, P. C., & Hughes, S. (1987). Representation of minority students in special education classes. *Remedial and Special Education, 8,* 41–46.

Colwell, R. (2002). *Opportunities for parent leadership in North Carolina: A resource guide for parents of children with special needs who are leaders and advocates for their children and the larger community.* (ERIC Document Reproduction Service No. ED480176)

Darch, C., Miao, Y., & Shippen, P. (2004). A model for involving parents of children with learning and behavior problems in the schools. *Preventing School Failure, 48,* 24–35.

Delgado, B. M., & Rogers-Adkinson, D. (1999). Educating the Hispanic-American exceptional learner. In F. E. Obiakor, J. O. Schwenn, & A. F. Rotatori (Eds.), *Advances in special education: Multicultural education for learners with exceptionalities* (pp. 53–71). Stamford, CT: JAI Press.

Drummond, K. V., & Stipek, D. (2004). Low-income parents' beliefs about their role in children's academic learning. *The Elementary School Journal, 104,* 197–214.

Duncan, S., Dunnagan, T., Christopher, S., & Paul, L. (2003). Helping families toward the goal of self-support: Montana's EDUFAIM program. *Families in Society: The Journal of Contemporary Human Sciences, 84,* 213–221.

Espe-Sherwindt, M. (1991). The IFSP and parents with special needs/mental retardation. *Topics in Early Childhood Special Education, 11,* 107–120.

Evans, S. (2002). *Preparing urban leaders for special education (PULSE): An integrated doctoral program in research and college teaching for urban and multicultural special education settings, 6/01/97–12/31/02.* (ERIC Document Reproduction Service No. ED478925)

Fan, X. (2001). Parental involvement and students' academic achievement: A growth modeling analysis. *Journal of Experimental Education, 70,* 27–61.

Fischer, R. L. (2003). School-based family support: Evidence from an exploratory field study. *Families in Society, 84,* 339–348.

Ford, D. Y., & Harmon, D. A. (2001). Equity and excellence: Providing access to gifted education for culturally diverse students. *Journal of Secondary Gifted Education, 12,* 141–148.

Garrett, J. E., & Morgan, D. E. (2002). Celebrating diversity by educating all students: Elementary teacher and principal collaboration. *Education, 123,* 268.

Geenen, S., Powers, L. E., & Lopez-Vasquez, A. (2001). Multicultural aspects of parent involvement in transition planning. *Exceptional Children, 67,* 265–283.

Gordon, J. A. (2002). Immigrants and education: Dialogic inquiry as pedagogy. *Teaching Sociology, 30,* 278–290.

Harry, B. (1992). Restructuring the participation of African-American parents in special education. *Exceptional Children, 59,* 123–131.

Hiatt-Michael, D. (2001). *Preparing teachers to work with parents.* (ERIC Document Reproduction Service No. ED460123)

Kauffman, E., Perry, A., & Prentiss, D. (2001). *Reasons for and solutions to lack of parents' involvement of parents of second language learners.* (ERIC Document Reproduction Service No. ED458956)

Kusimo, P. A. (1999). *Rural African-Americans and education: The legacy of the Brown decision.* Washington, DC: Office of Educational Research and Improvement. (ERIC Document Reproduction Service No. ED425050)

Lake, R. (1990, September). An Indian's father's plea. *Teacher Magazine,* pp. 48–53.

Lawson, M. A. (2003). School-family relations in context: Parent and teacher perceptions of parent involvement. *Urban Education, 38,* 77–134.

Lee, G., & Manning, M. L. (2001). Working with Asian parents and families. *Multicultural Education, 9,* 23–26.

Murphy, J. (1993). What's in? What's out? American education in the nineties. *Phi Delta Kappan, 74,* 641–646.

Obiakor, F. E., Grant, P. A., & Dooley, I. A. (2002). *Educating all learners: Refocusing the comprehensive support model.* Springfield, IL: Charles C Thomas.

Pattnaik, J. (2003). Multicultural literacy starts at home: Supporting parental involvement in multicultural education. *Childhood Education, 80,* 18–24.

Prater, L. P. (2002a). African American families: Equal partners in general and special education. In F. E. Obiakor & B. A. Ford (Eds.), *Creating successful learning environments for African American learners with exceptionalities* (pp. 145–157). Thousand Oaks, CA: Corwin Press.

Prater, L. P. (2002b). Family and schooling. In F. E. Obiakor, P. A. Grant, & E. A. Dooley (Eds.), *Educating all learners: Refocusing the comprehensive support model* (pp. 32–48). Springfield, IL: Charles C Thomas.

Prater, L., & Ivarie, J. (1999). Empowering culturally diverse parents in special education programs. In F. E. Obiakor, J. O. Schwenn, & A. F. Rotatori (Eds.), *Advances in special education: Multicultural education for learners with exceptionalities* (pp. 149–166). Stamford, CT: JAI Press.

Ramey, S. L., & Ramey, C. T. (1994). The transition to school: Why the first few years matter for a lifetime. *Phi Delta Kappan, 76*(3), 194–198.

Roeser, R., Patrick, H., Yoon, K., Anderman, E., & Eccles, J. (1995). *A longitudinal study of patterns of parent involvement in school across the elementary years: Teacher and parent reports.* (ERIC Research Document Reproduction Service No. ED385382)

Simich-Dudgeon, C. (1993). Increasing student achievement through teacher knowledge about parent involvement. In N. F. Chavkin (Ed.), *Families and schools in a pluralistic society* (pp. 189–203). New York: State University of New York Press.

Simpson, D., & Cieslik, M. (2002). Education action zones, empowerment and parents. *Educational Research, 44,* 119–128.

Sparks, S. (1999). Educating the Native-American exceptional learner. In F. E. Obiakor, J. O. Schwenn, & A. F. Rotatori (Eds.), *Advances in special education: Multicultural education for learners with exceptionalities* (pp. 73–89). Stamford, CT: JAI Press.

Taylor, R. (1994). Minority families in America: An introduction. In R. L. Taylor (Ed.), *Minority families in the United States: A multicultural perspective* (pp. 1–16). Englewood Cliffs, NJ: Prentice Hall.

Terrell, S. (2002, April). *Parents speak about parental involvement.* Paper presented at the meeting of the American Educational Research Association Conference, New Orleans, LA.

Trueba, H. T. (1989). *Raising silent voices: Educating the linguistic minorities for the 21st century.* New York: Newsbury House.

Villa, C. (2003). Community building to serve all students. *Education, 123,* 777.

Voltz, L. D. (1998). Cultural diversity and special education teacher preparation: Critical issues confronting the field. *Teacher Education Special Education, 21,* 63–70.

Walker, A. J. (1993). Teaching about race, gender, and class diversity in United States families. *Family Relations, 42,* 342–350.

Warner, T. D., Duane, E. D., Garvan, C. W., & Conway, T. W. (2002). One size still does not fit all in specific learning disability assessment across ethnic groups. *Journal of Learning Disabilities, 35,* 500–509.

Yan, W. (1999). Successful African American students: The role of parental involvement. *Journal of Negro Education, 68,* 5–23.

Chapter 17

Culturally Responsive School Leadership for Exceptional Learners

Mark B. Goor, Alice Farling, and Patricia Addison

Chapter Outline

Thinking About Multicultural Special Education

There were particular concerns about Manuel, one of the students of Fenwick School. He was an eighth-grade student whose family immigrated to the United States from El Salvador mid-year when he was old enough to attend fourth grade. Although he had attended school in El Salvador, a Dual Language Assessment revealed that he read on a first-grade level in his native language. Further, a hearing test indicated that he had a moderate hearing loss. He was provided English-language learner (ELL) services and was found eligible for special education services as a student with hearing and speech/language impairments. But Manuel continued to struggle academically and behaviorally, despite support from ELL teachers, the itinerant teacher for deaf/hard of hearing students, and the speech-language clinician.

By sixth grade, Manuel's lack of academic progress and reported social and emotional challenges led to a reevaluation of his individualized education plan (IEP). However, because Fenwick School's board had set targets to reduce disproportionate labeling of multicultural students, the committee hesitated to find Manuel eligible for emotional disability services. In the seventh grade, he was in co-taught classes for all academic subjects. By the end of the year, he had been referred 10 times by three teachers for behavioral disruptions such as showing disrespect to the teacher. Although he received C's and B's in mathematics and science, he failed English and history, for which he had to attend summer school. He began to refuse to wear his hearing aids. At his annual IEP meeting, the team determined that the self-contained setting in English and history would better meet his needs during the eighth grade.

Fenwick School's assistant principal, Mr. Lucas, knew Manuel well and felt he would have strong potential if he were provided with appropriate resources and accommodations to help him monitor and manage his own behavior. As part of Manuel's last IEP team, Mr. Lucas had advocated for him to remain in some co-taught classes; yet his behavioral disruptions did not abate during the first month of eighth grade. Before long, there was a referral for him from his bus driver: There had been a fight at the bus stop, and a student claimed that Manuel had assaulted him. The bus driver was calling for Manuel to lose bus privileges. Teachers of his co-taught classes were telling Mr. Lucas about his consistently poor behaviors across settings and believed he needed to be in all self-contained classes. According to local school district policy, an assault was to result in a 10-day suspension. "Fighting" could be disciplined at the discretion of the principal. Mr. Lucas was aware that suspension of a multicultural student had to be documented. He knew that the atmosphere toward inclusion and the capacity to educate a wide diversity of students at Fenwick School needed additional changes in order to fully support students with diverse needs like Manuel.

- *What leadership abilities are needed to help Manuel to maximize his fullest potential?*
- *What leadership foundation is needed to build a professional learning community that highlights interdisciplinary collaboration?*

In the case presented here, Mr. Lucas was confronted with the immediate dilemma of responding to a discipline referral concerning a special education student who was also a multicultural student. Yet he realized that Manuel's situation brought to light multiple issues in educating a wide range of students from multicultural backgrounds. This case appears to be about a student with an easily identifiable special education condition. However, one must ask whether Manuel's behavior is related to unmet education needs, to discrimination among teachers and peers, or if it is the result of a system that is unprepared for its multicultural population. The President's Commission on Excellence in Special Education (2002) and the National Research Council (2002) agreed that students from multicultural backgrounds are more likely than their majority peers to be labeled as having significantly lower ability and behaviors disruptive to the general education classroom. In addition, once identified, these students are more likely to be educated outside of the general education classroom for more than 60% of their day (Losen & Orfield, 2003; Viadero, 2004). Many general and special educators have assumed that poverty is a significant factor in these special education identification and placement decisions. However, current research has determined that the disparities are more related to subjective decision making and intolerance of culturally different behaviors (Hosp & Reschly, 2004).

Until now, efforts to address the public concern with overrepresentation of multicultural learners in special education have focused on identifying discriminating practices, gathering data, and attempting to educate preservice and inservice teachers and leaders to be more culturally responsive. These efforts are essential, and research and education must continue. However, researchers also know that school leadership is the key variable in special education success (Goor, 1994). This chapter focuses on four dimensions that guide and challenge school leaders in multicultural special education. An understanding of these four dimensions enables these leaders at all levels to be culturally responsive. Based on these dimensions, (a) all educators must be aware of and comply with government requirements for accountability; (b) schools are increasingly aware that they benefit from community partnerships; (c) the most successful school districts provide visionary leadership for all learners; and (d) each school functions best as a professional learning community where all learners maximize their potential.

CULTURAL IMPERATIVES AND GOVERNMENT ACCOUNTABILITY

Interest groups and advocates influence federal and state legislators to create laws that provide guiding principles and focus resources. Based on these laws, government agencies develop policy and procedures that direct school activities. Further, systems are put into place to monitor schools' compliance with these policies and procedures (Cessna, 1994). Effective school leaders analyze the meaning underneath legislation and regulation to construct responses that are multiculturally proactive. An astute leader assesses cultural, linguistic, socioeconomic, and political climates and searches for opportunities for improvement and increased access to resources. Too often, leaders focus on the monitoring function of government, feeling powerless to do anything but comply.

In Manuel's case, the school district had encouraged eligibility teams to be sensitive to decisions regarding students from different language and cultural backgrounds. The current political climate is bringing attention to the overrepresentation of multicultural learners in special education (Hosp & Reschly, 2004). The National Research Council (2002) asked for a broad-based investigation into the characteristics of students found eligible for special services. This council raised concerns about the referral process, culturally biased assessments, differential placement, and discipline. Findings such as these influence legislators, who then amend or create new laws followed by policy and procedure and monitoring. It is critical that special education leaders resist the temptation to comply at a surface level and instead acknowledge the underlying issue: that schools are underprepared to be responsive to the cultural diversity of their student population.

Leaders know that beliefs influence how educators perceive students and make instructional decisions (Goor, 1994). Special education leaders must identify school beliefs that perpetuate inequities and limit educational opportunities. Kozleski, Sobel, and Taylor (2004) stressed the need for a fundamental change in assumptions, practices, and relationships in order to create culturally responsive schools. These schools frequently recognize the impact of culture on behavior, learning, and partnerships; in these schools, leaders arrange for preparing teachers and the system to consider culture when referring, assessing, placing, and disciplining students (Townsend, 2000). A new challenge is currently emerging that could potentially derail efforts to address disproportionality. Viadero (2004) described the pressure school leaders feel to show evidence of improvement in student test scores. This pressure may encourage the identification of students for special education if that label will exclude or justify low test scores. Government leaders must provide guidance to schools in resolving this conflict. Additionally, special education leaders must help schools to understand that the purpose of obtaining test scores is to gather one measure of achievement that should not be expected to reflect all student and school progress.

Special education leaders are aware that the law directs schools to develop policies and procedures that translate government expectations into practice. Cessna (1994) suggested ways that prudent special education leaders could work more proactively with government. First, these leaders must develop relationships with staff or committee members who write laws and policies. Government officials frequently want the phone number or e-mail address of a leader they can contact to ask for input. Second, leaders must check state and federal government Web sites frequently to understand the latest issues and bills for consideration—this information will allow proactive leaders to be prepared when others are surprised by new policies. Further, this knowledge will allow leaders to contact government officials with a perspective from the field. And third, leaders can use the law to improve education for all, including those from multicultural backgrounds.

Many school administrators have learned to use communication systems available through professional organizations. For example, the Council for Exceptional Children (CEC) and their divisions provide many sources of up-to-date legislative information and employ legal experts who have the ear of prominent senators and representatives. Often these professional organizations have weekly Capitol Hill e-mail briefings and invitations to public hearings or panel discussions.

COMMUNITY AND MULTICULTURAL PARTNERSHIPS

The community is a complex web of individuals and groups that have formal and informal power to influence schools. School boards represent the citizens of the community by listening to concerns and making decisions to hire or fire and to allocate resources. Interest and advocacy groups state their case to the school board, school leaders, or media. Parents raise concerns to the school board, principals, and teachers, or the local media. The local media shapes school functioning by raising questions, selectively reporting information, and supporting political agendas. The role of the effective school leader includes actively developing partnerships with all community groups. These partnerships are essential to gain the point of view of community members, share information concerning instructional issues, and form alliances for success. Special education and multicultural issues are particularly sensitive. Individuals and groups in the community have strong beliefs about both populations. Effective special education leaders listen to community voices and respond with new and more successful programs. At the same time, these leaders can inform the community of the reasons for current practices. Together, school and community partners can create the best programs for students and their families. Concerning multicultural learners in special education, leaders must listen and respond to parents' concerns and desires for the most appropriate education.

In Manuel's case, his school district had created policies that encouraged careful reflection on administrative actions regarding discipline and IEP decisions. Similarly, school boards must direct policies and allocate resources to address issues of inequity. Enlightened school boards are sensitive to cultural issues, and they are aware of multiple demands for and complexity of delivering special education services (National School Board Association, 2004). When school boards are less aware, special education leaders can provide information and arrange for community members to rally the support of reluctant board members. School board members often have personal agendas that influence their initiatives and voting practices. Special education leaders must become familiar with each board member, thereby learning who would be willing to champion important conversations and decision making. In addition, these leaders must assemble a group of articulate parents with compelling cases to enlist when critical topics need a personal touch.

In today's changing world, it is imperative for school leaders to work to build interdisciplinary collaborations and partnerships with families, general and special educators, counselors, and other service providers. Ogbu (1992) noted that the major challenge for schools in working with minorities is the difficulty minority cultures have in interfacing with the school's majority culture. That is, one must begin with the assumption that schools reflect the way the majority culture operates. Leaders and teachers must become sensitive to the inherent beliefs and expectations of minority cultures and learn to be open to other ways of reaching out and offering opportunities to parents and community members. Only when multicultural parents feel they are appreciated and truly invited to participate will these collaborations and partnerships work for the good of all.

More than ever, school leaders need to be aware of the power of the media. Newspapers and local TV reporters are always looking for newsworthy activities or situations. Special education leaders must build relationships so that reporters will call to check out leads before going to press or on the air. Effective leaders must be thinking about ways to advance their agendas through media coverage of school events or in interesting interviews. Forward-thinking leaders must build a campaign to advance their work by assembling a committee of principals, teachers, and parents who are familiar with the issues and who can creatively translate school achievements or needs into media events or coverage. Most major newspapers have reporters dedicated to the education beat. They are eager to learn of stories of human or political interest. Special education leaders can increase public awareness by contacting these reporters with a story about the student who succeeded, the program with creative solutions, or the wonderful challenges that emerge with changing populations. For example, a school district could highlight the accomplishments of their English-language learners or new community involvement programs.

DISTRICT-LEVEL VISIONARY LEADERSHIP FOR MULTICULTURAL LEARNERS

Special education leaders at the district level must be visionary in setting a clear direction for excellent services for multicultural learners with exceptionalities. The National Research Council (2002) explained that schools must build capacity to work more effectively with multicultural populations. In a culturally diverse environment, the leader's vision must include essential beliefs about culturally responsive practices. District-level leaders are responsible for the overall compliance of schools with government regulations and higher self-imposed standards. This compliance depends on developing clear policies, communicating effectively, supporting implementation, gathering data, and responding to data with attention to areas of strengths and weaknesses. For special education services to be culturally responsive, attention must focus on district policies regarding referral, assessment, and placement of students from multicultural backgrounds.

Although in Manuel's case, he began with a diagnosed hearing loss, his subsequent teacher referrals were about behavior and learning difficulty. Referrals come primarily from teachers (National Research Council, 2002). Therefore, the district must develop clear guidelines for appropriate referrals and provide inservice professional development that expands teachers' and principals' sensitivity to and strategies for culturally responsive instruction. Assessment practices must be culturally sensitive and result in culturally appropriate placements (President's Commission on Excellence in Special Education, 2002). Data gathering from each school across the district must allow district-level administrators to identify areas for improvement. Statistics concerning referral and placement rates as well as the type of special education services must provide insight into school practices and promote meaningful discussions with school boards, principals, teachers, and parents. Based on these data, leaders can identify schools or systems that need support.

It is imperative that district-level leadership continually support special education teachers in the delivery of services and in identifying schools with challenging situations. Often, special education teachers feel isolated or unsupported (CEC, 1999). District-level leaders must identify ways to provide support through (a) Web sites and Listservs, (b) inservice opportunities that include socializing with peers, (c) publications, (d) collaboration with colleges and universities, (e) resolving individual concerns and conflicts, and (f) visiting schools and making their support felt. Principals must be consistently reminded that their school-level leadership is the key factor in excellent special education, especially in culturally diverse settings (Goor & Porter, 1999). District-level administrators can keep excitement about special education alive by initiating new research-based programs and identifying models of best practices. New programs pump energy into systems that have been lulled into the status quo by difficult daily challenges. New programs promote research-based practice by disseminating the latest best practice into schools in which personnel may not have the time or resources to keep up to date with professional literature. When district-level administrators identify excellent programs, they can spotlight individual teachers, instructional teams, or school-level successes. Publicly recognizing excellence promotes and disseminates good ideas and encourages others to seek higher levels of performance. All these school-level actions must be culturally sensitive and politically astute.

PROFESSIONAL LEARNING COMMUNITIES IN MULTICULTURAL CONTEXTS

The principal is the school's instructional leader and manager for all programs and students (Goor, Schwenn, & Boyer, 1997). In the case of Manuel, the principal knew that this student would be better served in a school community in which all professionals are learning and growing, examining their practices, and continually striving for improvement. Effective principals promote the development of a professional learning community. Dufour and Eaker (1998) presented six characteristics of professional learning communities: (a) they have a shared mission and values, (b) they inquire collectively, (c) they work in collaborative teams, (d) they are action oriented, (e) they continually seek improvement, and (f) they continually assess the results of their efforts. For special education to be successful in culturally diverse settings, the principal must include in the mission the belief in the value of special education and understanding of the impact of culture on school performance. Teachers and administrators must identify challenges, ask questions, and seek answers together. It is critical that teachers and service providers work together in teams such as grade-level groupings, topic-focused committees, and advisory panels. Teams must include members from different backgrounds to reduce feelings of isolation and provide stimulation for attempting new ideas. In fact, professional learning communities with multicultural perspectives must take action whenever there is concern or awareness of a problem.

Schools that have become professional learning communities are always seeking ways to improve through introspection and gathering input from parents and the external community, even when this community is culturally different. Finally, these schools must continually gather data about their efforts and analyze these data to determine where to focus, when to adjust efforts, and when to celebrate positive outcomes in their work. In multicultural schools, this translates to building interdisciplinary collaborations, embracing new ways of looking at instructing, and interacting with children and their families. Teachers and parents can ask questions about the effectiveness of programs or the special education process. Together, the community seeks new solutions and better processes for identifying students who need special attention. These schools could propose new services that support the needs of multicultural students and teachers so that those with special needs do not necessarily have to be labeled and educated apart from others. For example, the prereferral system could be expanded and made a more integral part of the instructional process. Teachers and parents can work together to learn more about each other and obtain insights into preferred methods of communication. The commitment is to consciously experiment and take action. When evaluating data, all members of the community must take responsibility for the outcomes (Fairfax County Public Schools, 2003; Obiakor, Grant, & Dooley, 2002).

For professional learning communities to be successful in challenging multicultural settings, the school leader must identify beliefs that drive school systems, reshape negative beliefs, model positive attitudes, and inspire interdisciplinary collaborations (Goor & Schwenn, 1999; Obiakor & Wilder, 2003; Skrtic, 2003). Beliefs are changed through a three-step process. First, new information is presented in a variety of modes such as literature, inservice training, or mentoring. Second, the leader arranges for more exposure and interaction with peers who have implemented the new knowledge, or visits classes or schools in which new ideas are modeled. And third, learning teams focus on implementation, data gathering, and assessment of outcomes. It is important to remember that parents are an integral part of the professional learning community (Sleeter & Grant, 1999). This gives the opportunity for identifying parents' and educators' beliefs and for working together to change any misperceptions for the benefit of all. Parents are also key decision makers in the special education process and may require education about the process and support in communicating their desires for their children (Fairfax County Public Schools, 2003; Obiakor et al., 2002). When the referral process is collaborative with its goal being to learn about students and their strengths and weaknesses, then no one is to blame; there are just solutions to be discovered. This professional learning community structure also promotes interdisciplinary collaboration, multiple ways to resolve differences through learning approaches, meaningful discussions, and working together to identify mutually agreeable multicultural solutions (Dufour & Eaker, 1998).

Wise school leaders select highly qualified personnel for delivering services in multicultural settings. This means hiring educators who (a) understand the impact of culture on learning and behavior, (b) have a wide range of strategies for instructing and communicating, and (c) can serve as mentors to others in the system. Typically, special educators are treated as experts in their schools in relation to instructional and behavioral issues. Therefore, they must be prepared to take leadership roles, advocate for students with special needs, and participate in the change process in moving to culturally responsive environments. Most importantly, effective leaders in multicultural settings create prereferral-to-placement systems that emphasize building capacity rather than labeling and removing students from the general education classroom (Hosp & Reschly, 2004). This system puts time and resources into the prereferral system. In the most common scenario, the principal designates a committee to consider all teachers' concerns about working with challenging students. Team members listen to teachers to understand the needs of the student, the class, and the teacher. Rather than deciding if the student should be referred for special education, the team must discuss how to enhance the system so the teacher becomes more skilled and knowledgeable, the class or setting gets resources, or the whole school considers a systemic problem (Skrtic, 2003). Only after careful analysis and reflection as well as the implementation of several new instructional or management approaches would the team consider a referral for special education. A logical extension is that effective school leaders build a referral process that ensures a thorough observation of each student's learning situation. These observations must offer critical insights into what is and is not effective with each student, sometimes identifying instructional weaknesses instead of student disabilities. Assessments must be culturally sensitive to ensure that the student can demonstrate true achievement and potential. It is most effective when at least one member of the assessment team has a similar background or can relate to the student's cultural heritage. It is essential to move away from the medical model of identifying the one with the illness toward a holistic problem-solving model that examines all aspects of the situation and proposes a solution that is good for everyone in the system.

The disproportionate labeling of minorities clearly shows a bias against learning styles and behaviors that are different from majority expectations. Assessment teams that are culturally aware carefully consider whether the student should be identified as needing special services, or whether the class or educational setting is in need of more support and resources. Once the determination is made that a student qualifies for special education, decisions must be made through the IEP process about appropriate delivery of services. As previously noted, multicultural students are more likely than majority students to be placed outside the general education classroom for more than 60% of the day (Viadero, 2004). IEP committees must be careful to consider placements in light of this clear evidence that multicultural students receive disproportionately more restrictive special education placements. Clearly, when observing professionals interacting with students, principals must recognize the way a teacher is able to connect with students to motivate and challenge them to do their best. Unfortunately, leaders also observe a mismatch between teacher expectations and student characteristics. Students who feel they are not accepted for who they are often behave in ways that exacerbate the situation. Although the ideal is that *all* teachers learn to appreciate *all* students, the reality is that principals may need to consider carefully the types of students each teacher instructs and manages well and to assign them thoughtfully to classrooms. In addition, school leaders must also consider differential class sizes based on the challenges posed by some students. Smaller classes can be justified for challenging groups of students (Goor & Schwenn, 1999).

In the end, when school leaders are culturally aware, they ensure that schools are safe and productive learning environments for *all* students. Discipline is an integral part of this process. Townsend (2000) reported that multicultural students are more likely to be disciplined, suspended, and expelled from school than their majority peers. Principals and special education leaders in culturally diverse schools must promote reflection regarding attitudes and expectations of individuals and the school culture (Obiakor & Wilder, 2003; Skrtic, 2003). To reduce referrals for discipline, educators must increase their tolerance of interactional patterns that are different from their own culture. Building bridges with the community and enhancing interdisciplinary collaboration will assist in learning the expected modes of interaction that might appear to some educators as unacceptable school behavior. A continual dialogue among teachers, parents, administrators, and other interdisciplinary collaborators is necessary to create a safe but fair environment.

A Culturally Responsive Educator

1. Believes in culturally responsive school leadership.
2. Ensures that prereferral-to-placement systems do not focus on getting rid of students.
3. Values parental inputs when leadership decisions are made.
4. Makes sure that the professional learning community responds to the needs of *all* learners.
5. Acknowledges his or her leadership strengths and weaknesses.
6. Communicates sensitively to educational stakeholders.
7. Condones equity in school policies.

8. Maintains continual dialogue with parents and service providers to promote interdisciplinary collaboration.
9. Is consistently learning new leadership paradigms.
10. Responds to demographic changes in leadership decisions.

Conclusion

Special education in culturally diverse environments requires exceptional leadership and interdisciplinary collaboration. Four dimensions guide and challenge special education leaders. Federal and state governments offer leaders guidance about issues of current concern while at the same time challenging them to demonstrate their accomplishments through monitoring functions. Community partnerships offer critical input and support and yet challenge schools to deliver a wide range of programs and to justify how schools operate. Leaders at the school district level must create visions for excellent services that are responsive to the impact of culture on learning and behavior. In addition, school-level leaders must create effective systems as they facilitate the development of professional learning communities and interdisciplinary collaborations. In the end, these communities must reflect teamwork in their practices and design systems that are sensitive to the delivery of special education in multicultural settings.

Discussion Questions

1. Considering the case of Manuel, analyze issues that an assistant principal must keep in mind as he or she makes a discipline decision.
2. Explain how state and federal governments can encourage schools to be more culturally responsive.
3. Describe how schools can develop partnerships with the community to increase awareness and responsiveness to multicultural students.
4. Discuss multicultural actions that school district leaders can take to promote equity and access for *all* students.
5. Describe the course of action that a principal should consider in building a culturally responsive professional learning community.

References

Cessna, K. K. (1994). Working with government. In M. B. Goor (Ed.), *Leadership for special education administration: A case-based approach* (pp. 61–80). Fort Worth, TX: Harcourt Brace.

Council for Exceptional Children. (1999). *Bright futures for exceptional children: An agenda to achieve quality conditions for teaching and learning.* Arlington, VA: Author.

Dufour, R., & Eaker, R. (1998). *Professional learning communities at work: Best practices for enhancing student achievement.* Alexandria, VA: Association for Supervision and Curriculum Development.

Fairfax County Public Schools. (2003). *Culturally and linguistically diverse exceptional students' handbook.* Fairfax, VA: Author.

Goor, M. B. (1994). *Leadership for special education administration: A case-based approach.* Fort Worth, TX: Harcourt Brace.

Goor, M. B., & Porter, M. (1999). Preparation of teachers and administrators for working effectively with multicultural students. In F. E. Obiakor, J. Schwenn, & J. A. Rotatori (Eds.), *Advances in special education: Multicultural education for learners with exceptionalities* (pp. 183–203). Stamford, CT: JAI Press.

Goor, M. B., & Schwenn, J. O. (1999). Students with behavior problems: An administrative perspective. In F. E. Obiakor & B. Algozzine (Eds.), *Managing problem behaviors: Perspectives for general and special educators* (pp. 240–267). Dubuque, IA: Kendall/Hunt.

Goor, M. B., Schwenn, J. O., & Boyer, L. (1997). Preparing principals for leadership in special education. *Intervention in School and Clinic, 32*(3), 133–141.

Hosp, T. L., & Reschly, D. J. (2004). Disproportionate representation of minority students in special education: Academic, demographic, and economic predictors. *Exceptional Children, 70*(2), 185–199.

Kozleski, E. B., Sobel, D., & Taylor, S. V. (2004). Embracing and building culturally responsive practices. *Multiple Voices, 6*(1), 73–87.

Losen, D. J., & Orfield, G. (2003). *Racial inequities in special education.* Cambridge, MA: Harvard Education Press.

National Research Council. (2002). *Minority students in special and gifted education.* Washington, DC: National Academy Press.

National School Board Association. (2004). *Key work of school boards.* Alexandria, VA: Author.

Obiakor, F. E., Grant, P., & Dooley, E. (2002). *Educating all learners: Refocusing the comprehensive support model.* Springfield, IL: Charles C Thomas.

Obiakor, F. E., & Wilder, L. K. (2003, October). Disproportionate representation in special education. *Principal Leadership, 4,* 17–21.

Ogbu, J. U. (1992). Understanding cultural diversity and learning. *Educational Researcher, 21,* 5–14.

President's Commission on Excellence in Special Education (2002). *A new era: Revitalizing special education for children and their families.* Washington, DC: Author.

Skrtic, T. M. (2003). An organizational analysis of the overrepresentation of poor and minority students in special education. *Multiple Voices, 6*(1), 41–57.

Sleeter, C. E., & Grant, C. A. (1999). *Making choices for multicultural education.* New York: Wiley.

Townsend, B. L. (2000). The disproportionate discipline of African American learners: Reducing school suspensions and expulsions. *Exceptional Children, 66,* 381–391.

Viadero, D. (2004, January 8). Disparately disabled. *Education Week, 12*(17), 22–26.

Part IV

Future Perspectives of Multicultural Special Education

Chapter 18

Transforming Special Education Through Culturally Responsive Practices

James R. Yates and Alba A. Ortiz

Chapter Outline

Thinking About Multicultural Special Education

Espoused Theory Versus Theory in Action in the Education of Multicultural Learners

Prevention and Early Intervention

Accountability

Full and Individual Evaluations

Decision Making

Intervention

Personnel Preparation

A Culturally Responsive Educator

Conclusion

Thinking About Multicultural Special Education

Mario Ramirez, who was born in Mexico, was a third-grade student at Jones Elementary. His father was killed in a car accident when Mario was one year old, and his mother came to the U.S. when he was 4 years old to find work. Mario's mother left him and his other siblings with her mother. Fortunately, the family was reunited when Mario was 7 years old. Records indicated that when Mario entered the school district in second grade, Spanish was the primary language of his home. It was the language he first learned to speak and the one he preferred to use. His mother indicated that he was a quiet child who tended to be a loner, although he had friends in the neighborhood. He got along well with his 11-year-old sister, but did not interact very much with other family members. Mario enrolled at Howard Elementary in December of his second-grade year. His report card did not indicate whether he passed or was socially promoted to third grade. He enrolled at Jones Elementary at the beginning of his third-grade year, and he changed classrooms in October of that year, when the school added a new teacher because of unexpectedly large class sizes.

Results of the English-language learners' (ELLs) assessment conducted at the end of the second grade indicated that Mario was a fluent Spanish speaker, but spoke little English. Mrs. Gonzales, Mario's third-grade teacher, reported that he was a quiet, well-behaved child who could not work independently. With her assistance, however, he successfully completed assignments. He was respectful toward teachers and peers, and they liked him, but he did not seek them out, preferring to work and play alone. Mrs. Gonzales had several conferences with the prereferral team. Based on team recommendations, she provided daily phonics and vocabulary lessons. She reviewed sounds previously taught and introduced new sounds daily. She also worked on two-syllable vocabulary words, but reduced the number Mario had to learn (8 rather than the 10 presented to his peers). She used these same vocabulary words for spelling and sent similar assignments home for practice. Despite these modifications, he continued to exhibit difficulty and his progress was slow.

Mrs. Gonzales said that because of the work schedule of Mario's mother, she was unable to meet with her. However, she communicated with her often through the homework folder she sent home with Mario. His mother never responded to her notes. However, Mrs. Gonzales talked to her by phone to obtain information needed for the referral packet. Mario had no strengths in the area of reading; he had significant problems in both word recognition and comprehension and also had trouble in writing, especially with spelling, sentence structure, capitalization, and punctuation. Mario's handwriting was sometimes illegible, but he did well in math. Assessments conducted by the school psychologist showed he met eligibility criteria under the category of

249

learning disabilities based on the discrepancy between IQ and the writing subtest. Based on the results of the Full and Individual Evaluation (FIE) and evidence that class-room modifications were unsuccessful, the multidisciplinary team determined that he met the criteria for learning disabilities and recommended that he be provided support in the area of reading, one hour per day, in a special education resource setting. Mario's mother did not attend the meeting. She later signed the consent forms agree-ing to the special education placement. She expressed concern that the copy of the IEP she was given indicated that special education instruction would be in English. The principal assured her that Mrs. Gonzales, Mario's bilingual education teacher, would work closely with Mrs. Martin, the resource specialist.

- *If you were a member of the multidisciplinary team, what information do you wish you had about Mario that was not provided?*
- *What should the school do to ensure that Mario's mother understands the decisions and interventions that will be provided to Mario?*

Multicultural learners are no longer invisible in today's schools. For instance, in Texas, "minorities" are already the majority, a demographic shift that occurred much sooner than originally projected (Babineck, 2004; Texas State Data Center, 2004). Multicultural individuals (i.e., culturally and linguistically diverse individuals) are younger than the general population and are therefore more likely to be of school age or to be parents of children of school age. Because of the cultural, lin-guistic, and learning styles that they bring to school, they are less likely to be aca-demically successful than their white peers (Wirt et al., 2004). Concerns about the academic achievement of multicultural students, worries about the adequacy of today's workforce, and, in some instances, simply wanting to be politically cor-rect, have led to attempts to "do the right thing." For example, the Education for All Handicapped Children Act (P.L. 94-142) of 1975 and later, the Individuals with Disabilities Education Act (IDEA, 1997) recognized the disproportionate represen-tation of multicultural learners in special education and called for increased research and culturally responsive teacher preparation programs to address this issue. Even the name of the 2001 legislation, *No Child Left Behind Act* (P.L. 107-110), suggests a concern for the education of *all* students. This act urges states to be ac-countable for the education of *all* students, including ELLs and low-income groups, as well as students with exceptionalities.

Although there has been significant progress, efforts to address the educa-tional needs of multicultural students through public policy have not been en-tirely successful. Half a century after the Supreme Court decision in the 1954 *Brown v. Board of Education* class action suit, segregation has yet to be eliminated (Orfield & Lee, 2004). In fact, the majority of multicultural learners continue to attend racially segregated schools. Moreover, standard measures of educational progress, such as satisfactory academic achievement, normal grade progression, high school graduation, and access to higher education, reveal significant gaps between the achievement of multicultural learners and their white peers (Wirt et al., 2004). Moreover, multicultural learners continue to be disproportionately represented in special education programs (Artiles & Ortiz, 2002; Donovan & Cross, 2002; Heller, Holtzman, & Messick, 1982; Ortiz & Yates, 1983; Utley & Obiakor, 2001). Patterns of representation are often explained as stemming from such factors as intrinsic child characteristics, poor nutrition, lack of medical care, environmental factors (e.g., lead poisoning), or deficit parenting. The contributions of contextual or institutional factors, such as the quality of schools and programs provided these students, and entrenched problems such as racism and prejudice are typically not included in analyses of disproportionality (Artiles & Ortiz, 2002; Kalyanpur & Harry, 1999; Obiakor, 2001; Ortiz & Yates, 2001; Patton, 1998; among others). This chapter suggests a conceptual framework for examining discrepancies between the intent and the actual implementation of educational policies, programs, and services designed to improve educational outcomes for multicultural learners. In addition, it suggests future ways for making special education processes culturally responsive.

ESPOUSED THEORY VERSUS THEORY IN ACTION IN THE EDUCATION OF MULTICULTURAL LEARNERS

More than 30 years ago, Argyris and Schön (1974) developed a framework for distinguishing *espoused theories*, which reflect beliefs, values, and ways of thinking about the world, from *theories in action*, or observed behaviors in daily practice. In other words, an espoused theory is what people say, whereas a theory in action is what people actually do. Conceptually, a perfect match between espoused theories and theories in action produces the highest levels of individual and organizational effectiveness. However, what individuals say they would do under certain circumstances is often different from what they actually do in that situation (Moecker, 1989).

IDEA (1997) established legal requirements for serving individuals with disabilities that are then translated into operational guidelines, rules, and procedures at state levels that govern services provided by school districts. Strict compliance standards and routinized operating procedures are developed to ensure that students with exceptionalities are afforded an appropriate education. However, the intent of policy and law often is not met because observed behaviors are not culturally responsive. For example, IDEA espoused nondiscrimination in the conduct of individual evaluations, but assessors continue to rely on instruments that did not include multicultural students in norming samples. Ortiz and Yates (2001) concluded that "the disproportionate representation of English language learners in special education reflects the general lack of understanding in our school systems of the influence of linguistic, cultural and socioeconomic differences on student learning" (p. 65). This lack of understanding reveals the disconnect between espoused theory and theory in action.

Prevention and Early Intervention

Characteristics of positive school climates include strong administrative leadership, a safe and orderly environment, ongoing systematic evaluation of student

progress, and involvement of administrators in instructional decisions and processes. Ortiz (2002) and others (e.g., Cummins, 1984; Krashen, 1991; Obiakor, 2001,
2003; Thomas & Collier, 1997) have identified other components that must be in
place to prevent school failure for multicultural students. One is establishing
school climates that reflect that educators are responsible for ensuring that all students learn. Ensuring the success of multicultural students also requires that general and special educators have in-depth knowledge of the unique attributes of
these students, including, for example, second language and dialect acquisition,
the relationship between a student's native language or dialect and the development of English as a standard dialect; first and/or second language teaching
methodologies; informal assessment strategies to monitor language development;
and appropriate techniques for working with multicultural parents and communities. Without this knowledge base, multicultural students will continue to experience achievement difficulties, high rates of grade retention, high dropout rates,
and inappropriate referrals to special education.

Strong collaboration between special education, bilingual education, and general education occurs in schools where the school principal publicly and privately
advocates for a strong system of support for multicultural students and provides
the necessary resources to meet the needs of students with special needs, their
families, and the professionals who serve them. With strong collaboration, administrators, teachers, and other school personnel celebrate linguistic and cultural diversities; and special language programs, such as bilingual education and ELL
programs, are viewed as integral to the success of students. Since the majority of
ELLs are in English as a second language (ESL) programs, receiving language support for only a small part of the day, general education teachers must assume major responsibility for ensuring that these students become English proficient.
Students, including struggling learners, must be provided instruction that "nests
basic skill instruction in the context of higher order thinking and problem solving" (Ortiz, 2002, p. 38).

Educators frequently espouse the idea that early intervention programs are
designed to prevent inappropriate special education referrals. In practice,
though, "prereferral" procedures occur too late to be effective and/or are
viewed by general educators as a hurdle they must jump before a student can
be tested to determine eligibility for special education services. Too often, general education alternatives (e.g., modifications or adaptations of instruction,
tutorial or remedial programs, and general education problem-solving teams)
are not made available, are not considered, or are not implemented long
enough for the treatment to have an effect. Some multicultural students are
assessed but do not meet special education eligibility criteria; yet multidisciplinary team members argue that general educators have "given up" on the student and that special education services are better than no services at all.
Although their decision to place a multicultural student without disabilities in
special education may be well intentioned, this action forces the student to
"fit" the system rather than addressing system deficiencies that preclude offering effective services.

Accountability

Despite standards-based reforms, there continues to be a significant gap between the achievement of students with special needs and their middle-class, majority peers. A contributing factor is that educators and policy makers have essentially ignored the changing student demography reflected by an increased diversity in today's classrooms. Under the No Child Left Behind Act, students with special needs must be held to high expectations and provided access to a challenging curriculum. Educators are also accountable for their performance. However, while this is an espoused theory, accountability systems involve high stakes and rewards and sanctions distributed according to outcomes of district- or statewide testing. As a result, students with disabilities are excluded from participation when student outcomes are used to rate teacher effectiveness or to classify schools as low or high performing (Mazzeo, Carlson, Voekl, & Lutkus, 2000). Or these students are referred for special education, presumably because a disability label makes it easier to justify exclusion. Exclusion policies can have far-reaching, negative consequences because if students are not part of the assessment program, they are not targeted to receive resources to improve performance (Ortiz, 2000). On the other hand, inclusion in high-stakes testing does not yield expected results without appropriate accommodations and modifications of performance measures and administration procedures (e.g., alternative assessments, assessments normed on students with disabilities, and tests available in languages other than English). A culturally responsive accountability system deals directly with issues of equity, fairness, and access to resources. Although it is known that certified, experienced teachers produce greater student achievement (Fuller, 1998), multicultural students are more likely than their white peers to be taught by uncertified or alternatively certified teachers or by teachers with the least teaching experience. This is contradictory to the espoused belief that every child should have access to highly qualified teachers.

The lay and business communities are concerned with the development of an appropriately educated workforce and thus support current accountability efforts to improve the educational proficiency of students. This is an appropriate concern, but accountability efforts are too often focused solely on academic achievement. Schools must be responsible for the physical and emotional well-being of students. Few would argue that students can learn academic material if they are hungry, sick, or experiencing physical or emotional trauma. Accountability for multicultural students must then include a restructuring of the power in decision making relative to parents and communities. Currently, the primary stakeholders of schools (i.e., students, parents, and communities) have little influence over decisions that are being made based on accountability information and processes (Obiakor, 2001, 2003). There is a significant discrepancy between informing parents of accountability results for the "espoused" purpose of allowing parent participation and the "action" of developing mechanisms for parents to be equal participants in decisions responding to accountability information.

Full and Individual Evaluations

Another espoused belief is that assessments used for special education eligibility determinations provide the data necessary to determine whether multicultural learners have disabilities and to plan individualized education programs. However, the disproportionate representation of these learners in special education suggests that this is not the case. For example, few ELLs (i.e., students who come from homes and communities where a language other than English is spoken) are tested in their native language and standardized assessment procedures often include inappropriate adaptations such as direct translation of tests (Ortiz et al., 1985) or rely on interpreters who are not trained to serve in this role. Even under the best conditions, when assessments are conducted by bilingual assessment personnel, distinguishing between difference and disability is a complex task (Ortiz & Graves, 2001). Culturally responsive practices require that assessment personnel have knowledge and skills specific to the assessment of multicultural learners. Moreover, they must examine their beliefs and values to ensure that these do not bias their practices or their interpretation of evaluation data. If assessors find they cannot provide a nonbiased assessment, assessors must refer the student to someone who can. If appropriate personnel are not available, the school system should make every effort to contract such expertise. Not to do so is powerful evidence of actions that are discrepant with the intended goals of assessment.

The espoused purposes of assessments are to define problems or issues and develop interventions appropriate to the success of multicultural learners. As indicated, there is often a discrepancy between the intended and actual actions of assessment professionals who work with these learners. According to Ortiz and Yates (2001), culturally responsive practices include, for example, assessing in the native language/dialect, involving parents, using valid and reliable instruments or acceptable adaptations of these (e.g., testing limits), and incorporating curriculum-based assessments to support or refute outcomes of standardized testing. Practices such as these would help achieve the espoused beliefs that assessments provide the data necessary to distinguish cultural and linguistic differences from disabilities and increase the likelihood that assessment outcomes can guide the selection of effective interventions for multicultural learners with exceptionalities.

Decision Making

The multidisciplinary team (MDT) is frequently charged with determining special education eligibility and must by law include representatives from administration, general and special educators involved in instruction and assessment, parents and guardians, and if appropriate, the student. The espoused purpose for including these representatives is to bring information, expertise, personal concern and knowledge of the student, and individuals with the power to implement decisions to these meetings. Yet, although schools ensure that the representatives required by special education law are present at MDT meetings, a person's title or position is insufficient to meet the espoused purposes of team membership. For example, if an

ELL who is being served in an ESL program is being considered for special education placement, the ESL teacher should be present at the meeting. Unfortunately, ESL teachers often are not invited because the student's mainstream teacher fills the role of "general education" representative. If the general education teacher does not have the expertise to participate in discussions of whether limited English proficiency or cultural differences are the cause of the student's problems, the espoused theory that MDTs represent the expertise needed to make appropriate eligibility decisions is unmet.

Parents are required members of the multidisciplinary team, but their presence alone does not satisfy the "espoused" belief that parents should be partners in decision making. MDT meetings may be conducted in English even though the parent does not speak English. Sometimes an interpreter is provided, without first determining whether the interpreter is proficient in the parents' native language and understands special education processes well enough to provide an adequate representation of the discussions. Often the discussion that follows is between the educational representatives, who use educational jargon, further limiting a parent's ability to participate meaningfully. These actions are incongruent with the espoused belief that parents have a right to make informed decisions about their children's education. Beyond concern for meaningful representation, multidisciplinary teams have an obligation to ensure that the student's difficulties are not the result of a lack of academic support, limited English proficiency, cultural differences, or inappropriate assessment processes. Culturally responsive practices in MDT decision making require that members ask questions that will help them rule out factors such as linguistic and cultural differences being the source of difficulties. The information most critical to determining eligibility must include verification that (a) the child is in a positive school climate; (b) the teacher uses effective instructional strategies; (c) neither clinical teaching nor intervention strategies recommended by early intervention or prereferral committees failed to resolve the problem; (d) other general education alternatives proved unsuccessful; (e) results of formal assessments are corroborated by informal measures; and (f) parents are also concerned about the child's performance (Ortiz, 2002). Unless these data are considered, there will be a significant discrepancy in the espoused purpose of the multidisciplinary team, that is, to prevent the inappropriate placement of multicultural learners in special education, and the "actions" of the team may lead to inaccurately labeling differences as disabilities.

Intervention

Multidisciplinary teams have legislated responsibility for developing the individualized education plan (IEP) if a student is eligible for special education services. Although the descriptor "individualized" espouses that the plan will address specific student needs, the IEP formats typically used by school districts address disability-related needs but may not ensure that selected interventions are linguistically and culturally relevant. IEP teams may select interventions from computerized "banks" of goals and objectives or may "check off" options from lists of interventions and placements. Unless the forms and the banks used by committees include linguistically and culturally responsive goals and objectives, IEPs hold less promise of helping students achieve their maximum potential.

Because ELLs with exceptionalities do not lose their right to special language program support once they are determined eligible for special education, IEPs for these learners should indicate whether special education services will be provided in the native language or using ESL strategies. Although the research literature (Krashen, 1982; Thomas & Collier, 1997) is clear on the importance of the native language in producing higher levels of proficiency in English, some educators mistakenly believe that to master the target language of English, the amount and intensity of instruction in English should be increased. For example, Wilkinson and Ortiz (1986) found that IEPs for Latino students rarely indicated native language instruction or ELLs' goals or objectives. This is clearly discrepant with the research literature on second language acquisition. Asking limited English proficient parents to speak only English at home is another example of the lack of understanding of second language development. The irony of this recommendation is that often such a recommendation is given through an interpreter at the meeting. The question then is: How logical is it to expect that a special education teacher who is not bilingual, and who has no training in second language acquisition or ESL techniques, can provide English-language learners an appropriate education? Unless IEPs are linguistically and culturally appropriate, there will be a discrepancy between the intended purposes of special education and the instructional programs provided, precluding the success of interventions.

Personnel Preparation

Professional personnel are the "linchpin" of educational service delivery. Significant conceptual, human, technical and fiscal resources are committed to preservice and continuing professional preparation of teachers, administrators, instructional supervisors, and school psychologists. Educating students in the "least restrictive" environment (IDEA, 1997) requires significant collaboration between general education and special education personnel. Students with mild disabilities spend the majority of the day in the general education classroom (Rea, McLaughlin, & Walther-Thomas, 2002); some students with exceptionalities are the responsibility of general education teachers and administrators 100% of the time.

The espoused theory behind the integration of students with disabilities into the mainstream is that general educators will have the professional competencies needed to serve these students. Given that many of these learners are members of racial/ethnic groups, it is also assumed that both general and special education educators will be able to provide instruction that is culturally and linguistically responsive. For example, analysis of the programs of the annual conferences of professional education organizations shows a paucity of content relative to special education and multicultural populations (Hellriegel & Yates, 1999). In addition, an annual analysis of preparation programs for general education teachers and administrators in central Texas, a state in which for more than 11 years the majority of students in public school have been "minority," reveals that teachers are typically prepared to serve such students by one course (Yates, 2004). This course could be described as having a "disability a week" focus for elementary teachers. *No course work that addresses special education is required for secondary teachers.* Most general and special education teachers do not have training related to the education of multicultural students (Garcia, 1992; Kushner & Ortiz, 2000). Most preparation programs for principals and superintendents do not require formal course work in special education (Yates, 2004). An examination of the preparation of general education personnel relative to multicultural special education reveals discrepancies between "espoused theories" and the "theories in action."

Formal preparation of general education teachers and administrators in content and processes of second language acquisition or stages of language development for second language learners is typically not part of their preparation. For example, teachers in preservice training or continuing education are often provided training in techniques for teaching reading. However, it would be very unusual for training content to include methods of teaching reading using ESL techniques or advancing reading skill by building on the knowledge, vocabulary, or grammar of a child's native language. With regard to general education administrators, the background of training in relation to cultural and linguistic distinction is even less likely than teacher preparation to include knowledge or skill development in addressing the needs of ELLs or appropriate implementation of bilingual education or ESL programs. These skills are critical because local building administrators are typically responsible for being the instructional leader of the school. Yet, without training in the knowledge and skills needed to help these learners to develop English, it is not uncommon for general administrators to encourage or insist that teachers utilize English as the primary language for instructional content with students who are acquiring English. They mistakenly think that since English is the target language, it should be the language of instruction. This, of course, ignores the extensive and consistent research that supports the use of the native language for content instruction as the child acquires English proficiency.

Issues of prevention, early intervention, assessment, placement, instructional intervention, and accountability as they relate to multicultural students with exceptionalities are issues that must be addressed by well-prepared professionals. *No one would advocate that physicians be involved in providing treatments such as surgery if they had no formal surgical training.* Yet today, professional educators with little or no preparation are required by law to be involved in the determination of treatments designed to be life changing or lifelong in terms of effect for students with special needs. There is a significant discrepancy in the "espoused theories" of professional preparation and the "theories in action" relative to special education services for multicultural students. Again, culturally responsive practices require that organizations and individuals responsible for professional educator preparation restructure preparations to meet the needs of multicultural populations. It is no wonder that appropriate professional preparation has continued and will continue to be a burning issue in education (Garcia, Wilkinson, & Ortiz, 1995; Obiakor, 2001, 2003; Ortiz & Yates, 1983; Wang, Reynolds, & Walberg, 1995).

A Culturally Responsive Educator

1. Examines his or her perceptions for bias and prejudice.
2. Is informed of and acknowledges changes in demography.
3. Brings multicultural expertise to his or her decision process.
4. Examines the organization for discrepancies in goals and actions.
5. Recognizes, accepts, and honors cultures different from his or her culture.
6. Does not impose his or her cultural views on other cultures.
7. Recognizes the importance of education in all cultures.
8. Designs and implements processes that ensure access to education for all persons.
9. Recognizes and accepts the value of language differences.
10. Recognizes the primacy of language in educational processes.

Conclusion

The conceptual framework of Argyris and Schön (1974, 1978) provides a helpful means of analyzing agreement between "espoused theories," what people say or believe, and "theories in action," what people actually do or how they behave. Teachers and professionals who can work with students like Mario in the introductory case are needed. Current practices reveal that there is a lack of a match between espoused intents of special education policy or law and actions of educators charged with ensuring compliance with legal mandates. Because discrepancies such as these serve to maintain students' low functioning, it is imperative that general and special educators examine the underlying values and beliefs, policies, procedures, and content of programs and processes with a focus on expected versus actual effects of these programs and services. Otherwise, there will be a proliferation of programs outside the mainstream, aimed at addressing the "deficits" of multicultural populations, but failing to do so because they are not linguistically or culturally responsive. Programs and services must be in consonance with best practices in the education of multicultural students in general and special education. These learners and their parents deserve no less. Given the dramatically changing demography of the United States, the future of the nation depends on it.

Discussion Questions

1. Discuss two discrepancies between "espoused theories" and "theories in action" identified in this chapter.
2. Based on the case of Mario, identify and explain discrepancies between "espoused theories" and "theories in action" related to services given to him.

3. Evaluate two potential explanations for discrepancies identified in your school system.
4. Develop an action plan for you or your group to address accountability problems in your school district.
5. In two short paragraphs, forecast the future of special education for multicultural learners.

References

Argyris, C., & Schön, D. (1974). *Theory in practice: Increasing professional effectiveness.* San Francisco: Jossey-Bass.

Argyris, C., & Schön, D. (1978). *Organizational learning: A theory of action perspective.* New York: McGraw-Hill.

Artiles, A. J., & Ortiz, A. A. (2002). English language learners with special education needs: Contexts and possibilities. In A. J. Artiles & A. A. Ortiz (Eds.), *English language learners with special education needs* (pp. 3–27). McHenry, IL: Center for Applied Linguistics and Delta Systems.

Babineck, M. (2004, August 27). Survey: Latinos regain majority from whites in Texas. *The Daily Texan,* p. 2.

Brown v. Board of Education, 347 U.S. 483 (1954). U.S. Supreme Court. Argued Dec. 9, 1952. Reargued Dec. 8, 1953. Decided May 17, 1954.

Cummins, J. (1984). *Bilingualism and special education: Issues in assessment and pedagogy.* Clevedon, England: Multilingual Matters.

Donovan, S., & Cross, C. (2002). *Minority students in special and gifted education.* Washington, DC: National Academy Press.

Education for All Handicapped Children Act of 1975, P.L. 94-142 (S.6), Nov. 29, 1975.

Fuller, E. (1998). *Do properly certified teachers matter? A comparison of elementary school performance on the TAAS in 1997 between schools with high and low percentages of properly certified general education teachers.* Austin, TX: The Charles A. Dana Center, University of Texas at Austin.

Garcia, E. (1992). Teachers for language minority students: Evaluating professional standards. In *Proceedings of the second national research symposium on limited English proficient students' issues: Focus on evaluation and measurement* (Vol. 1, pp. 383–414). Washington, DC: U.S. Department of Education, Office of Bilingual Education and Minority Language Affairs.

Garcia, S. B., Wilkinson, C. Y., & Ortiz, A. A. (1995). Enhancing achievement for language minority students: Classroom, school, and family contexts. *Education and Urban Society, 27,* 441–462.

Heller, K. A., Holtzman, W. H., & Messick, S. (Eds.). (1982). *Placing children in special education: A strategy for equity.* Washington, DC: National Academy Press.

Hellriegel, K., & Yates, J. R. (1999). *Issues of diversity in education professional organizations.* Unpublished manuscript, The University of Texas at Austin, Austin, Texas.

Individuals with Disabilities Education Act (1997 Amendments), P.L. 105-17, 20 U.S.C. Chapter 33.

Kalyanpur, M., & Harry, B. (1999). *Culture in special education: Building reciprocal family-professional relationships.* Baltimore: Brookes.

Krashen, S. (1982). *Principles and practices in second language acquisition.* Oxford, England: Pergamon.

Krashen, S. (1991). *Bilingual education: A focus on current research* (Occasional Papers in Bilingual Education, No. 3). Washington, DC: National Clearinghouse for Bilingual Education. Retrieved March 26, 2002, from www.ncbe.gwu.edu/ncbepubs/focus/focus3.htm

Kushner, M. I., & Ortiz, A. A. (2000). The preparation of early childhood education teachers for English language learners. In *New teachers for a new century: The future of early childhood professional development* (pp. 124–154). Washington, DC: U.S. Department of Education, National Institute on Early Childhood Development and Education.

Mazzeo, J., Carlson, J. E., Voekl, K. E., & Lutkus, A. D. (2000, March). *Increasing the participation rate of special needs students in NAEP: A report on 1996 NAEP research activities.* Washington, DC: U.S. Department of Education, Office of Educational Research and Improvement.

Moecker, D. L. (1989). *The Argyris/Schon Theoretical Model applied to special education decision processes for Anglo and Latino students.* Unpublished doctoral dissertation, The University of Texas at Austin, Austin, Texas.

No Child Left Behind Act, Reauthorization of the Elementary and Secondary Education Act, P.L. 107-110 §2102(4) (2001).

Obiakor, F. E. (2001). *It even happens in "good" schools: Responding to cultural diversity in today's classrooms.* Thousand Oaks, CA: Corwin Press.

Obiakor, F. E. (2003). *The eight-step approach to multicultural learning and teaching* (2nd ed.). Dubuque, IA: Kendall/Hunt.

Orfield, G., & Lee, C. (2004, January). *Brown at 50: King's dream or Plessy's nightmare.* Boston: The Civil Rights Project, Harvard University.

Ortiz, A. A. (2000). Including students with special needs in standards-based reform: Issues associated with the alignment of standards, curriculum, and instruction. In *Including special needs students in standards-based reform* (pp. 41–64). Aurora, CO: Mid-Continent Research for Education and Learning.

Ortiz, A. A. (2002). Prevention of school failure and early intervention for English language learners. In A. J. Artiles & A. A. Ortiz (Eds.), *English language learners with special education needs* (pp. 31–48). McHenry, IL: Center for Applied Linguistics and Delta Systems.

Ortiz, A. A., Garcia, S. B., Holtzman, W. H., Jr., Polyzoi, E., Snell, W. E., Jr., Wilkinson, C. Y., et al. (1985). *Characteristics of limited English proficient Latino students in programs of learning disabled: Implications for policy, practice, and research.* Austin, TX: University of Texas, Handicapped Minority Research Institute on Language Proficiency.

Ortiz, A. A., & Graves, A. (2001). English language learners with literacy-related disabilities. *International Dyslexia Association commemorative booklet* (pp. 31–35). Baltimore: International Dyslexia Association.

Ortiz, A. A., & Yates, J. R. (1983). Incidence of exceptionality among Latinos: Implications for manpower planning. *National Association for Bilingual Education Journal, 7*(3), 41–53.

Ortiz, A. A., & Yates, J. R. (2001). A framework for serving English language learners with disabilities. *Journal of Special Education Leadership, 14*(2), 72–80.

Patton, J. M. (1998). The disproportionate representation of African-Americans in special education: Looking behind the curtain for understanding and solutions. *Journal of Special Education, 32,* 25–31.

Rea, P. J., McLaughlin, V. L., & Walther-Thomas, C. (2002). Outcomes for students with learning disabilities in inclusive and pullout programs. *Exceptional Children, 68*(2), 203–222.

Texas State Data Center and Office of the State Demographer. (2004, June). *New Texas State Data Center population projections from the University of Texas at San Antonio point to a Texas population that is growing rapidly, increasingly diverse and aging.* San Antonio, TX: Institute for Demographic and Socioeconomic Research (IDSER), College of Business, University of Texas at San Antonio.

Thomas, W. P., & Collier, V. (1997, December). *School effectiveness for language minority students* (Resource Collection Series, No. 9). Washington, DC: National Clearinghouse for Bilingual Education. Retrieved April 20, 2002, from www.ncbe.gwu.edu/ncbepubs/resource/effectiveness/index.htm

Utley, C. A., & Obiakor, F. E. (2001). *Special education, multicultural education, and school reform: Components of quality education for learners with mild disabilities.* Springfield, IL: Charles C Thomas.

Wang, M. C., Reynolds, M. C., & Walberg, H. J. (1995). Serving students at the margins. *Educational Leadership, 52*(4), 12–17.

Wilkinson, C. Y., & Ortiz, A. A. (1986). *Characteristics of limited English proficient and English proficient learning disabled Latino students at initial assessment and at reevaluation.* Austin, TX: University of Texas, Department of Special Education, Handicapped Minority Research Institute on Language Proficiency. (ERIC Document Reproduction Service No. ED283314)

Wirt, J., Choy, S., Rooney, P., Provasnik, S., Sen, A., & Tobin, R. (2004). *The condition of education 2004* (NCES 2004-007). Washington, DC: U.S. Department of Education, National Center for Education Statistics.

Yates, J. R. (2004). *Education professional preparation for serving special populations: Trends and issues in special education administration class reports.* Unpublished raw data, The University of Texas at Austin, Austin, Texas.

Chapter 19

Teacher Preparation and Multicultural Special Education

Angela Stephens McIntosh and Eugene C. Valles

Chapter Outline

Thinking About Multicultural Special Education

Lorenzo Addison always wanted to become a teacher. He became a special educator because of his belief in fairness and equity. When he completed his special education teacher preparation program, he was proud to be entering a system that would ensure a quality and equitable education for all students, regardless of their educational needs. He was eager to begin a career that he believed would allow him to have a positive impact on the lives of many students. Mr. Addison had been hired to teach at an urban middle school in the nation's second largest school district. He had enthusiastically accepted the position and relocated from the small college town in the Midwest where he earned an undergraduate degree in math and his special education teaching credential. But after only one day on the job, he began to wonder if he had been adequately prepared to effectively address the array of educational needs presented by his students.

Mr. Addison was assigned a self-contained class of 22 students from the impoverished urban community surrounding the school. Twelve of his students were English-language learners with varying degrees of proficiency. Four different languages were represented among those 12 students. Three students lived in foster homes and each had changed schools at least twice during the previous year. One student lived in a homeless shelter with her mother and four siblings. Three of the boys in Mr. Addison's class had been involved with the juvenile justice system; one student returned home from the state's juvenile detention center just days before the start of the school year. As Mr. Addison watched his students file out of the classroom at the end of the first week, he sensed that they felt disconnected from the school environment, and he knew that they were not interested in what school had to offer them. As he watched them leave, he contemplated his background, his education, and his preservice preparation. He began to realize that he would need to draw from all of these experiences to address the challenges he now faced.

After reflecting, Mr. Addison realized that his teacher preparation program had included topics related to working with multicultural learners with special needs. His coursework addressed parents' roles in the education of their children, the effects of socioeconomic factors on learning, the issues associated with English-language learning, and the need for culturally relevant pedagogy. Through his preservice preparation, he had acquired a basic understanding of multicultural special education. However, his preservice training had neither provided opportunities to actively engage with these issues in a meaningful way nor fostered the development of skills necessary to use this knowledge effectively. His real-world situation demanded that he integrate what he had learned into his day-to-day practice, and therefore develop a deeper, broader, and more constructive understanding of multicultural special education. Mr. Addison concluded that his own growth and development as a professional were both his responsibility and his obligation.

Although it had been a challenging few weeks, by the second month of school, Mr. Addison's apprehension about his ability to have a positive impact on his students was replaced by his enthusiasm and eagerness. Reflection and review of his preservice teacher preparation program let him see that he had the knowledge necessary to be a successful teacher. He began to view his class as a positive challenge as well as an opportunity to develop the necessary skills to provide a quality and equitable education for all students. His ability to integrate and synthesize knowledge acquired in his preparation into his current setting enhanced his understanding of multicultural special education. He also realized his responsibility to address the individual and collective needs of his students through the implementation of these practices, ideally changing their attitudes about education and potentially changing their life outcomes. Before long, he began to make remarkable differences in his students' schoolwork and life. At the same time, his students they began to feel comfortable around him, and to a large measure, they began to maximize their potential.

- *What would have happened to Mr. Addison's career if he did not have any preservice preparation on multicultural learners with special needs?*
- *Why should teacher preparation programs shift their paradigms today and in the future?*

Any time spent on the grounds of any public school in a large urban U.S. city will clearly reveal the multiplicity of cultures and languages present in schools today. Hodgkinson (1997) stated that every nation in the world is represented among the immigrant population of the United States. Even as diversity increases in the population at large and among schoolchildren in particular, it is predicted that the teaching workforce will remain predominately white, middle-class, female, and monolinguistic (Bartolomé, 2004; Carlson, Brauen, Klein, Schroll, & Willig, 2002; Daunic, Correa, & Reyes-Blanes, 2004; Guyton, 2000; Hodgkinson, 2002; Seidl & Friend, 2002). For instance, Carlson et al. reported in their recent study of personnel needs in special education that the mean age of the personnel is 43 years, and 86% of the personnel are female and white. As a result, institutions of higher education are challenged to recruit and prepare educators who have the necessary skills and dispositions to remain effective as the student body becomes increasingly diverse. Clearly, the frustrations experienced by Mr. Addison in the introductory case reveal sociocultural problems encountered by teachers in today's schools. Fortunately, Mr. Addison possessed an ideology that supported his personal growth and development toward becoming an effective teacher for the diverse group of exceptional students in his class. Many new teachers enter the profession ill prepared or unprepared, lacking core knowledge and skills related to multicultural special education, and without a system of personal values and beliefs that support their growth as effective educators. Although adequate preparation is not a panacea for solving all educational problems facing multicultural learners, it provides multidimensional perspectives for experienced and future teachers. This is the major focus of this chapter.

EDUCATING MULTICULTURAL LEARNERS

As demographic conditions in the United States shift in favor of diversity, the goals of multicultural education will become increasingly relevant to *all* learners. Banks (1992) defined multicultural education as a reform movement designed to bring about equity in education for *all* students, including those from diverse racial, ethnic, social, and economic backgrounds. Institutions of higher education are assigned the responsibility to redefine teacher preparation programs in ways that ameliorate the array of educational deficiencies that result from the ever-widening gap between American teachers and their students. Realization of the goals of multicultural education will rest on the strength and adequacy of teacher preparation programs (Obiakor, 2001, 2003, 2004). In addition to cultural and language-related issues present among students in the general education environment, special education teachers of the future must be prepared to deal with other levels of diversity. These teachers must need skills and strategies in the identification of special educational needs related to disability, individualization of instruction, modification of curriculum, and appropriate assessment. Additionally, they must possess the ability to identify and address cultural variables and to recognize the impact that they may have on any aspect of the teaching and learning process for students with special needs.

The "new age" special education teacher will need preparation to effectively address special educational needs manifested through the interaction of students' disabilities and these students' differing responses to macrocultural perspectives embedded in public education. This interaction of culture and disability creates variables that are likely to influence the ability of multicultural learners to succeed in school. Clearly, institutions of higher education have the responsibility for preparing the special educators of today and those of tomorrow to (a) distinguish between cultural and linguistic differences and disability, (b) recognize the interaction of cultural and linguistic differences with disability, and (c) effectively address educational needs as they occur on any level. Tomorrow's special education teacher preparation programs must include more than training on what to teach and how to teach it. Programs that thoroughly prepare special education teachers to serve the needs of diverse students will engage preservice teachers in a process of analysis and reflection on issues of difference, culture, and diversity. Such programs will provide knowledge and experiences that foster in these new teachers the will to pursue quality and equity for *all* students they serve.

MULTICULTURAL TEACHER PREPARATION

The effective education of students from diverse social, cultural, and linguistic backgrounds is a complex undertaking. The following questions represent issues that confound the design and development of programs to effectively prepare preservice special educators to address multicultural student needs. Definitive answers to these questions continue to plague teacher preparation even though these answers are needed to develop solutions to the challenges presented by diverse exceptional learners to typical educational paradigms.

- Will the use of validated instructional practices equalize the educational environment for diverse students?
- To what extent do intergroup preferences related to learning style, instructional modality, or communication patterns influence the educational environment for multicultural learners with exceptionalities?
- Which educational needs of multicultural learners are related to disability, and which are related to cultural or linguistic difference? Does it matter?
- Will an increase in the number of culturally and linguistically diverse teachers solve the problem?
- To what degree do social variables such as socioeconomic status and the parent's educational level influence outcomes for multicultural students?
- How can the inherent biases generated by the monolingual or monocultural upbringing of most teachers be negated?
- Does American public education represent a level playing field for multicultural students with and without special needs?

Although thoroughly addressing these questions is beyond the scope of this chapter, it is important to recognize challenges these uncertainties pose to the task of educating multicultural students with special needs. The effect becomes increasingly complex for teacher educators as people attempt to disaggregate the inextricable influence of each of the variables represented by these questions in planning effective special education programs for diverse students. Add to this matrix the individual internal differences related to culture, ethnicity, language, or disability that each student brings and that impinge on learning and growth.

Teacher preparation programs generally have specific areas of focus that most likely require at least one course dealing with cultural competency, cultural sensitivity training, or multicultural education. Although such programs are capable of producing new special educators who are highly skilled in the delivery of specialized instructional services, these teachers, like Mr. Addison, may have insufficient knowledge about and experiences with multicultural issues and may be quite naive about the impact of culture on education. The need to prepare special educators to understand and address issues related to student culture is an important component of preservice preparation. Yet a disturbingly low percentage of special education teachers report extensive experience with multicultural students in the field-based aspects of their preservice preparation. As Carlson et al. (2002) noted, only 20% of special education teachers surveyed reported a "great extent" of exposure to culturally and linguistically diverse students in their student teaching experiences. An equal percentage of special education teachers reported that they were "not at all" exposed to cultural and linguistic diversity in their practicum experiences (Westat, 2002). Teacher preparation programs of the future must provide sufficient opportunities for preservice special education teachers to acquire knowledge about culture and to experience working with multicultural groups. These experiences must be accompanied by content integration and guided reflection embedded into the program curriculum. Together, these aspects of preservice preparation will set into motion the ongoing development of personal perspectives and individual ideologies that support the pursuit of quality and equity for multicultural learners with and without exceptionalities.

PROGRAM COMPONENTS FOR MULTICULTURAL TEACHER PREPARATION

Specific components of teacher education programs are determined largely by state certification or licensure requirements and influenced by the perspectives of the faculty and local school districts. However, extensive educational standards for the teaching professions have been developed by national organizations such as the Interstate New Teacher Assessment and Support Consortium (INTASC) and National Council for Accreditation of Teacher Education (NCATE). The Council for Exceptional Children (CEC) (2004) has combined its standards with NCATE to establish parameters for preparing special educators. Major institutions of higher education choose to adhere to these standards to demonstrate a high level of quality in their programs and to ensure that their program graduates are highly qualified and employable. Clearly, attention to the needs of students from multicultural backgrounds is addressed in both the INTASC and NCATE standards. Within the CEC Special Education Content Standards, Standard 3: Individual Learning Differences acknowledges that:

> Special educators understand the effects that an exceptional condition can have on an individual's learning in school and throughout life. Special educators understand that the beliefs, traditions, and values across and within cultures can affect relationships among and between students, their families, and the school community. Moreover, special educators are active and resourceful in seeking to understand how primary language, culture, and familial backgrounds interact with the individual's exceptional condition to impact the individual's academic and social abilities, attitudes, values, interests, and career options. The understanding of these learning differences and their possible interactions provide the foundation upon which special educators individualize instruction to provide meaningful and challenging learning for individuals. (CEC, 2004)

Full accomplishment of the standards stipulated by state agencies and national organizations will be realized only through a comprehensive and multifaceted approach to special education teacher preparation that (a) focuses the attention of preservice special education teachers on diversity in the school population and related issues, and facilitates their understanding of the concept of culture; (b) increases preservice special education teachers' knowledge level about various multicultural groups; (c) facilitates the development of multicultural teaching competencies; and (d) initiates ideological development through the synthesis of knowledge, experience, and reflection. These points represent different levels. The content, meaning, and application of each level of this approach to the preparation of special educators are further discussed below.

Focusing Attention on Diversity and Culture

This first level introduces preservice teachers to the concept of cultural pluralism. At this level, it is important to recognize that many preservice teachers have been raised in middle-class, monolingual communities where their opportunities to become aware of the range of diversity have been limited. This level provides an orientation to the nature of diversity and difference and articulates the impact of cultural and linguistic diversity on the processes and outcomes of education. Preservice teachers are challenged to (a) explore their perceptions about difference, (b) acknowledge the basis for their own worldviews, and (c) explore the foundations of competing worldviews. The concept of bias is introduced and explored. Preservice teachers are guided through the process of introspection, and ideally, they begin to develop a tolerance for difference. Apparently, conversations about difference and diversity must begin as soon as candidates are inducted into a credential or licensure program. Every education course should include discussions about diversity, providing opportunities for open dialogue and feedback. The developing workforce, likely to be white, middle class, and female, must be exposed to the full range of diversity they will likely encounter in their teaching profession. Ultimately, the information and dialogue presented at this level will serve to release preservice special educators from the limitations of their own cultural experiences, fostering acceptance and objectivity regarding others. This level of openness is necessary as a precursor to the exploration of other cultures.

Increasing Knowledge About Multicultural Groups

Once teachers come to understand their own cultural perspectives, worldviews, and the biases created by their individual experiences, they can be open to learning about other cultural and linguistic differences without imposing judgments about good versus bad or right versus wrong. Numerous experiences with students from multicultural backgrounds are a fundamental part of this level. Preservice special educators can begin to learn with understanding about different cultures and their varying ranges of beliefs, attitudes, and behaviors. The social context of attitudes and behaviors particular to certain cultural groups will become more meaningful to the preservice teacher and will become an important consideration in planning and programming for multicultural students with special needs. At this level, preservice special education teachers will gain an appreciation for diversity, and consequently, begin to view diversity as an asset.

Facilitating the Development of Multicultural Teaching Competencies

Programs that prepare special educators usually emphasize methods of individualization of instruction and the modification of curriculum for students with special needs. This level focuses on the processes of multicultural education and addresses the development of methodological competencies related specifically to multicultural students. At this level, the underlying assumption that educational practices validated on nonminority populations will be effective in addressing the needs of diverse students is challenged. According to Valles (1998), teachers are better prepared to address "a broader spectrum of children and their differing abilities" when programs address "diversity, culturally relevant methods and strategies, and knowledge about second language acquisition" (p. 53). Additionally, at this level, preservice teachers learn to apply their understandings about students' cultural and linguistic backgrounds to their teaching practices. They develop expertise in adapting validated practices related to instruction, curriculum modification, and behavior management to specifically address the needs of diverse students. As Daunic et al. (2004) pointed out, "To be effective for culturally diverse learners, teachers must translate these practices as they work with individuals—not through generalized prescriptions, but through a critical awareness of the pervasive influence of language and culture on how teachers teach and how students learn" (p. 106).

Initiating Ideological Development

In this final level, special education teacher candidates begin to synthesize their learning and experiences about diversity and start to develop reformed perspectives about differences and the impact of culture on educational needs. Preservice special educators should begin to embrace their responsibility to educate *all* students, understanding that high-quality education is a right of *all* citizens and not a privilege reserved for those of a particular group. In fact, this level should begin at the preservice stage of teacher preparation, but the transformation set in motion by the preservice teachers' progressions through these four levels should continue throughout their respective teaching careers. This important level is often overlooked. Bartolomé (2004) concluded that

> Increasing teachers' ideological awareness and clarity requires that educators compare and contrast their personal explanations of the wider social order with those propagated by the dominant society. Unfortunately, transforming educators' conscious and unconscious beliefs and attitudes regarding the legitimacy of the dominant social order and of the resulting unequal power relations among cultural groups at the school and classroom level has, by and large, historically not been acknowledged in mainstream teacher education programs as a significant step towards improving the educational processes for and outcomes of low-SES, non-white, and linguistic-minority students. (p. 99)

In the end, when preservice special education teachers are provided with the appropriate experiences and opportunities to explore culture on the levels described above, they frequently experience transformations of their thinking and behaviors. These teachers will become acculturated to the impact of culture on teaching and learning processes and will come to understand that the interaction of disability and difference creates a unique set of educational needs. These special educators will become model teachers and will demonstrate dispositions and behaviors indicative of their transformational experiences provided though the intensive attention to cultural and linguistic diversity provided in the aforementioned four-level approach.

A Culturally Responsive Educator

1. Is aware of his or her own perspectives.
2. Owns the responsibility to teach.
3. Is aware that the overidentification of difference is counterproductive.
4. Does not look for reasons why he or she cannot teach the child; waters down neither the curriculum nor expectations.
5. Believes all children can learn.
6. Communicates with students.
7. Looks at students, not labels or colors.
8. Asks for help.
9. Uses validated methods that work.
10. Analyzes the environment and ventures beyond the boundaries of the school wall for answers.

Conclusion

This chapter addressed multicultural issues in teacher preparation programs. Clearly, special education teacher preparation programs have a responsibility to their graduates, but ultimately they have a greater responsibility to students who are served by their teachers. National and state accreditation reviews are not likely to occur frequently enough nor at a sufficient level of scrutiny to measure a program's quality in terms of the success of its graduates in addressing the needs of multicultural learners with exceptionalities. In order to ensure that general and special education teachers of tomorrow are well equipped to address the needs of an increasingly diverse population of exceptional students, teacher preparation programs must be subjected to an additional level of periodic review measured by the success of its graduates. The success of institutions of higher education in adequately preparing general and special education teachers to address educational issues related to diversity will relate directly to the level of positive outcomes that multicultural learners experience in their educational careers. Programs will have to be diligent in making sure that all preservice teachers have experiences about diversity, and in sustaining the ongoing reflection and evaluation processes that are necessary for the full development of cultural competency in preservice general and special education teachers.

Discussion Questions

1. Discuss two issues that make the identification of special education needs particularly challenging for multicultural learners.
2. Explain two areas in which preservice special educators need preparation to work effectively with multicultural groups.

3. Analyze two issues that complicate the development of culturally sensitive special education teacher preparation programs for multicultural learners.
4. In two sentences, summarize essential components of a teacher preparation program that addresses the needs of multicultural learners.
5. Discuss why culture must be an integral part of teacher preparation programs in this millennium.

References

Banks, J. A. (1992). It's up to us. *Teaching Tolerance, 20,* 20–23.

Bartolomé, L. I. (2004). Critical pedagogy and teacher education: Radicalizing prospective teachers. *Teacher Education Quarterly, 31,* 97–122.

Carlson, E., Brauen, M., Klein, S., Schroll, K., & Willig, S. (2002). *Study of personnel needs in special education (SPeNSE): Key findings.* Retrieved September 4, 2004, from www.spense.org

Council for Exceptional Children. (2004). *Professional standards.* Retrieved September 4, 2004, from www.cec.sped.org/ps/perf_based_stds/standards.html#standards

Daunic, A. P., Correa, V. J., & Reyes-Blanes, M. E. (2004). Teacher preparation for culturally diverse classrooms: Performance-based assessment of beginning teachers. *Teacher Education and Special Education, 27,* 105–118.

Guyton, E. (2000). Social justice in teacher education. *The Educational Forum, 64,* 108–114.

Hodgkinson, H. L. (1997). Diversity comes in all sizes and shapes. *School Business Affairs,* pp. 3–7.

Hodgkinson, H. L. (2002). Demographics and teacher education: An overview. *Journal of Teacher Education, 53,* 102–105.

National Council for Accreditation of Teacher Education. (2002). *Standards for the accreditation of teacher education programs.* Washington, DC: Author.

Obiakor, F. E. (2001). *It even happens in "good" schools: Responding to cultural diversity in today's classrooms.* Thousand Oaks, CA: Corwin Press.

Obiakor, F. E. (2003). *The eight-step approach to multicultural learning and teaching* (2nd ed.). Dubuque, IA: Kendall/Hunt.

Obiakor, F. E. (2004). Impact of changing demographics on public education for culturally diverse learners with behavior problems: Implications for teacher preparation. In L. M. Bullock & R. A. Gable (Eds.), *Quality personnel preparation in emotional/behavioral disorders: Current perspectives and future directions* (pp. 51–63). Denton, TX: University of North Texas, Institute for Behavioral and Learning Differences.

Seidl, B., & Friend, G. (2002). The unification of church and state: Working together to prepare teachers for diverse classrooms. *Journal of Teacher Education, 53,* 142–152.

Valles, E. C. (1998). The disproportionate representation of minority students in special education: Responding to the problem. *The Journal of Special Education, 32,* 52–54.

Westat. (2002). *Extent to which special education teachers had exposure to culturally and linguistically different students in field-based aspects of preservice preparation, by district metropolitan status.* Retrieved August 29, 2004, from www.spense.org

Chapter 20

Using Technology to Advance Multicultural Special Education

Jeffrey P. Bakken and Howard P. Parette

Chapter Outline

Thinking About Multicultural Special Education

Alissa was a 14-year-old Latina student with athetoid cerebral palsy. She was of average intelligence and used a walker at home, school, and in the community. She had good receptive language skills, though her speech was unintelligible. As a result, she received a Dynavox augmentative and alternative communication (AAC) device for communication in her general education classroom settings. The speech-language pathologist (S/LP) who conducted Alissa's evaluation and advocated the importance of getting the Dynavox into her IEP had programmed many phrases into her device to allow her to talk about herself with communication partners. Her parents were not able to attend the AAC evaluation that preceded the IEP team's decision to provide her with the Dynavox, nor were they able to participate in the IEP meeting because her father was working at a local factory and the family did not have transportation to the meeting. Several of Alissa's teachers reported that she demanded a great deal of individualized attention from them and that she did not exhibit the desire to excel in her studies. Each of her teachers valued individual achievement and personal excellence in education.

Alissa came from a very religious family that included her parents and grandparents. Her father was the only adult who spoke English in the family, and Spanish was the primary language spoken in the home. Alissa's teacher and IEP members had emphasized to Alissa the importance of using English in her home and community settings, though the speech-language pathologist reported resistance from Alissa in using her device at home. When asked why she did not like to use the AAC device at home, Alissa answered that her family "did not like it, and it just wasn't working out." Alissa reported that she loved her family, but that she "did not get out much in the community." During a language therapy session with the S/LP, Alissa described a fifteenth birthday party, or quinceanera, that her family was planning for her. The S/LP convinced her to use the Dynavox at this party to demonstrate the potential of the device to her family and community members. The S/LP also agreed to program some Spanish phrases into the Dynavox and worked with Alissa during the intervening weeks to prepare her to use both English and Spanish sentences at the party. Although Alissa's progress in learning to use all the programmed phrases was not as rapid as the S/LP had hoped, she felt that Alissa would make a "good showing" at the birthday party. She contacted Alissa's father at work and urged him to allow Alissa to use the Dynavox at her birthday party. Alissa's father seemed excited about allowing her to use the device to talk to others at the party. But on the Monday morning after Alissa's party, when the S/LP met with her, Alissa said that the Dynavox had embarrassed her family and that they would not allow her to use it again at home.

- *How can teachers and service providers succeed when traditional culture and technology collide?*
- *What can special educators do to motivate multicultural families to value technology in school prsograms?*

Alissa's case reveals a range of issues relevant to practitioners who work with multicultural learners with exceptionalities, particularly when technology solutions are being considered by decision-making teams. For decades, there has been a growing awareness and acceptance of the role of multicultural education in educational settings across the country (D'Andrea, 1995; Gollnick & Chinn, 2002). Teachers and other school professionals are challenged to build on, rather than ignore or minimize, the values and traditions that students bring to school. Bowles and Gintis (1976) noted that many students and families are disadvantaged socially, given that they are required to consume and value the cultural products of others, especially in team decision making and curriculum building. Thus, the cultural products typically presented to children with disabilities and their families are those reflecting white, middle-class values (Kalyanpur & Harry, 1999). As a result, successful school experiences occur to the extent that students, families, and professionals adhere to a primarily white, "prescribed set of cultural content delivered through a narrowly defined curriculum and set of behaviors" (Carolan, 2001, p. 6).

To develop multicultural literacy, school personnel must understand and incorporate cultural, linguistic, and experiential differences, as well as differences in social class, into the learning process for all students (Nieto, 1994). Understanding each student, particularly characteristics of his or her culture and respective value systems, is essential for facilitating, structuring, and validating successful learning for all (Guild, 1994; Parette, Huer, & VanBiervliet, 2005). If classroom expectations are limited or primarily shaped solely by a teacher's own cultural orientation and experiences (e.g., a white perspective), teachers may unintentionally impede successful learning experiences by students from other cultural backgrounds (e.g., African Americans, Latinos, American Indians, and Asian Americans). According to Gorski (2001), multicultural pedagogy should be student centered so that learning is active, interactive, and engaging with emphasis on critical and creative thinking, learning skills, and social awareness as well as facts and figures. Clearly, technology cannot be infused or incorporated properly if students' cultures are undermined. This is the premise of this chapter.

MULTICULTURALISM AND TECHNOLOGY

Developing multicultural literacy requires that school personnel understand the role of technology in working with multicultural learners. There are several categories of technology, each playing different roles for students from diverse cultural and linguistic backgrounds. Two pertinent categories are (a) instructional technology and (b) assistive technology (AT) devices and services.

Instructional Technology

Today, many teachers are committed to the goal of providing their students with active and dynamic learning environments. As they strive to reach this goal, they are discovering that effective classroom-based applications of instructional technology go far beyond simply knowing about technology. In fact, when students possess the knowledge and skills regarding when and how to apply technology strategically, they can solve instructional problems with greater success (Gardner & Wissick, 2002; Jonassen, Howland, Moore, & Marra, 2003). By definition, *instructional technology* may be any technology used to support the process of teaching and learning (Lever-Duffy, McDonald, & Mizell, 2003). Generally, it includes a range of tools that facilitate learning for students or make the learning process faster or more efficient. However, instructional technology tools are not required for such learning to take place. For example, calculators are often used in general education settings to enable students to compute math problems more efficiently when speed of completion is an issue, though these students do not require calculators to use longhand computational processes that have been taught. Similarly, computer software programs are often integrated into classroom settings for drill and practice to teach new skills, though more traditional approaches to teaching those same skills would be equally as effective.

Instructional technologies for all students can be invaluable tools that promote active student involvement in the learning process and assist students in accessing and organizing information (Maccini, Gagnon, & Hughes, 2002). Students use electronic instructional technologies as powerful tools for investigation, problem solving, and creative expression. These technologies have the potential to create highly sophisticated learning environments in which both products and knowledge can be constructed, while being sensitive to each student's needs in an economically acceptable fashion (Fabris, 1992). Of particular importance has been the use of computers in the modern-day classroom. The power of the computer is used for individualizing instruction toward prespecified, fragmented knowledge and skills. In addition, the computer allows students to work at their own speed as well as provides extra support for classroom instruction (Damarin, 1998). General and special education teachers, however, need to be aware of how to use instructional technology applications such as computers appropriately (Roblyer, 2004). For instance, they can select multimedia programs to apply in different learning environments that could include a teaching and demonstration tool, an individual learning station or tutor, or a small-group creation station where multimedia becomes the tutee (Taylor, 1980). The use of multimedia as a tool can increase the teacher's effectiveness at demonstrating subject matter to the whole class or facilitating group interaction. Teachers and students alike can use multimedia presentations to enhance any subject matter demonstration, lecture, or report.

Technology is frequently implemented to make learning situations realistic (Wissick, 1996). The use of multimedia programs with vivid visual representations can be an effective tool for presenting content and assisting transfer of learning to new situations for some students (Dillon & Gabbard, 1998; Swan & Meskill, 1996). However, for students who are at risk, in remedial settings, or who have learning disabilities, teacher-directed multimedia lessons on specific skills will not necessarily assist the transfer of learning to real-life situations without meaningful dialogue and activities related to that context (Wissick). As a result, general and special educators must be cognizant of the fact that technology alone often will not produce the desired transfer of knowledge (Roblyer, 2004). For example, most computer spreadsheet programs have integrated charting and graphing features and can be used to demonstrate mathematical concepts, sort and analyze data, make predictions, and support problem solving (Robyler). The most obvious way to incorporate spreadsheet programs into a lesson is to construct math activities related to the unit's theme that call for students to collect data, enter them into a spreadsheet, create a chart or graph, and make judgments based on interpreting the results. One positive aspect of spreadsheets is that they relieve students of the computational burden of math and help them to concentrate on higher level thinking skills related to math, such as analysis, synthesis, and decision making using numerical information, rather than calculations. In addition, the ease of changing values in a spreadsheet to create new graphs provides students with a tool to make predictions and then test those predictions (Gardner, Wissick, Schweder, & Canter, 2003).

Computer networks are beginning to provide powerful possibilities for student cross-cultural communication. These networks could help students to teach each other about different cultures. Such an education could involve a broadly defined and enriched form of cooperative learning, involving not only groups of students in a single classroom, but groups of students from different geographical locations (Freedman & Liu, 1996). Multimedia in the hands of a resourceful teacher can help create situations that stimulate interest, generate questions, find problems, or motivate investigations (Heinrich, Molenda, Russell, & Smaldino, 2002). Clearly, the integration of multicultural education into educational technology can be integral to closing the digital divide for certain students (e.g., female students; students with disabilities; and students from diverse ethnic, linguistic, and economic backgrounds) (Brown, 2002). In some ways, the infusion of technology into schools can lead to an increased emphasis on including multicultural education as a curriculum topic (see Roblyer, Dozier-Henry, & Burnette, 1996). Another area in which the capabilities of instructional technology have made a contribution is in meeting the unique learning needs of youngsters who are English-language learners (ELL; Roblyer et al., 1996). New developments in multimedia seem to have accelerated the use of multimedia products in multicultural education. Many educators seem to feel that the motivational qualities of multimedia make it the instructional material of choice. These programs make it easier for teachers and other professionals to provide visually compelling examples of people and practices from other cultures. In addition, they provide vivid, concrete examples that are especially important in monocultural classrooms where students may never get to see or meet people from other cultures (see Roblyer et al.). Multimedia products thus provide supportive environments in which multicultural students can practice their writing, reading, and communication skills. In addition, these products (a) allow dialogue and communication, (b) enhance creativity, (c) foster a sense of personal worth, (d) facilitate collaboration among students working together, (e) increase the possibility for interdisciplinary projects, (f) provide rich learning experiences for all students, (g) strengthen students' communication skills, and (h) permit students to express their feelings and opinions (Fabris, 1992).

It is absolutely imperative that educators realize that all students can benefit from instructional technologies such as computers and that inequities in the availability of such technologies exist across the country (Kemp & Parette, 2000; Wilhelm, Carmen, & Reynolds, 2002). For example, family members have noted that greater expenditures have been made on computers in school settings serving middle and upper income children than their lower income peers (Cole & Griffin, 1987; Swain & Pearson, 2003). Milone and Salpeter (1996) observed that just as budgetary constraints have widened the gaps between the haves and have-nots, so too have technologies in the home. Earlier, Piller (1992) found that children and teachers in impoverished school districts are less likely to have computers in their homes. Such disparities have been the focus of discussions pertaining to the *digital divide* (National Telecommunications & Information Administration, 1999; U.S. Department of Education, 2003). The digital divide can be best described as access to computing and information technology by those who are privileged and less access by those who are economically disenfranchised. This phenomenon appears to reflect a recognition by the government and other entities that differences in technology utilization is influenced more by economics than by cultural factors. When individuals from multicultural backgrounds are afforded the opportunity to access and use computers, more often than not, their patterns of usage vary little from patterns exhibited by whites (Pastore, 2000).

Assistive Technology Devices and Services

For students who have disabilities and who are from diverse cultural backgrounds, instructional technologies alone may be inadequate to meet their unique needs. *Assistive technology (AT)* devices and services are often required for them to succeed in classroom settings. AT is defined by the Individuals with Disabilities Education Act of 1990 (IDEA), P.L. 101-476, as "any item, piece of equipment, or product system . . . that is used to increase, maintain, or improve the functional capabilities of children with disabilities" (20 U.S.C. §1401[25]). Sometimes referred to as *adaptive* or *access technology*, AT includes technology devices that address students' needs in such areas as mobility, communication, adaptive toys, positioning, independent living, computers and information technologies, environmental access, leisure/recreation, visual, and listening (Parette, 1998b). AT devices may also be categorized along a continuum, ranging from *no-tech* to *high-tech* in design. No-tech solutions include strategies that do not require devices or equipment (Lindsey, 2000), such as modifying the way that teaching is delivered to accommodate a particular child's unique needs. Low-tech devices include such devices as Velcro fasteners, foam pencil grips, and adapted eating utensils. High-tech devices include more sophisticated devices such as computers and environmental control systems. Factors that may affect whether a particular AT device is deemed to be low tech or high tech include (a) cost, (b) flexibility of use, (c) durability, (d) training required, (e) sophistication, (f) transportability, and (g) maintenance requirements (Parette, 1998b). Examples of no-, low- and high-tech devices are noted in Table 20.1.

TABLE 20.1 *Examples of No-, Low-, and High-Tech Devices*

No Tech	Low Tech	High Tech
Services such as physical therapy, occupational therapy, or services of other specialists	Adaptive switches to allow access to battery-operated toys, electrical systems, or electronic systems	Computers for educational tasks, recreation, communication, and environmental control
Making print larger	Call systems, such as buzzers, or loop tapes to communicate short messages	Augmentative and alternative communication devices that use synthetic or digitized speech
Placing students closer to the teacher to control behavior or provide hands-on instruction	Communication boards, notebooks, folders to communicate a wider variety of messages	Powered mobility devices to enable the individual to independently move about in the environment
Using peers to assist a student who has difficulty performing specific tasks (e.g., reading and writing)	Activity frames or objects stabilized by Velcro, Dycem, elastic, and other materials	Environmental control systems that use infrared, radio frequency, ultrasound, or AC power line control scheme
Increasing test time or decreasing number of test items	Adapted books to facilitate participation in story time or reading	Talking word processors or word prediction software
Positioning students closer to chalkboard or other visual materials	Adapted eating utensils to enable more effective self-feeding	Modified or alternative keyboards and other computer adaptations
Removing distracting sounds and visual stimuli in the child's environment	Jigs, elongated levers for on/off switches, and other adaptations to allow gross or fine motor control, designed for specific work tasks and needs	Braille printers and text-to-speech devices to enable access to information
Teaching mnemonic strategies to remember things	Tactile enhancement such as using raised lines on pictures or to label clothes	Computerized visual amplification systems
	Talking, lighted, or enlarged clocks and calculators to optimize use of these devices	Powered lifts and transfer systems

Equally important in understanding AT are services often needed to support their acquisition and use among students from diverse cultural backgrounds. According to IDEA, an AT service is defined as "any service that directly assists an individual with a disability in the selection, acquisition, or use of an assistive technology device" (20 U.S.C. 1401 §602 [2]). Such services would include (a) evaluation of the child's needs, such as a functional evaluation of the child in his or her customary environment; (b) purchasing, leasing, or otherwise providing for the acquisition of AT devices by the child; (c) selecting, designing, fitting, customizing, adapting, applying, maintaining, repairing, or replacing AT devices; (d) coordinating and using other therapies, interventions, or services with AT devices, such as those associated with existing education and rehabilitation plans and programs; (e) training or technical assistance for the child, or, where appropriate, the child's family; and (f) training or technical assistance (20 U.S.C. 1401 §602 [2] [A-F]). AT devices and services must be considered by team members during any service planning processes for children with disabilities. These devices and services are designed to increase the independence of these children by enabling them to compensate for deficits, enhance self-confidence, and participate more fully in all settings—work, school, home, and leisure. In addition, they enhance the quality of life for a person with a disability by enabling him or her to circumvent specific deficits, while capitalizing on given strengths (Bakken, 1999). Numerous resources are available that describe the continuum of AT devices to assist children with disabilities across both academic, leisure, recreational, self-care, communication, and other important areas of life functions [cf. Abledata, n.d.; Assistive Technology—Strategies, Tools, Accommodations, and Resources (ATSTAR), n.d.; Edyburn, Higgins, & Boone, 2005; Georgia Project for Assistive Technology, 2005; Rehabtool.com, 2004).

Numerous approaches have been advocated to assist teachers in understanding the process of selecting AT devices and services for children with disabilities (see the Institute for Matching Person and Technology, 2004; Reed & Bowser, 1998; Zabala, 1998). As understanding of AT assessment and service delivery processes has evolved, attention has increasingly focused on cultural issues and assistive technology (see Kemp & Parette, 2000; Parette, 1998a; Parette et al., 2005; VanBiervliet & Parette, 1999). Devices and services are student centered, and they include a range of considerations, such as the child's physical, cognitive, and communications skills; preferences; cultural values; and experiences. One goal of AT is to capitalize on the ability of an individual to offset areas in which he or she has difficulties (Kelker & Holt, 2000). It is in this stage that school personnel must compile as much information as possible, including information from family members, to more comprehensively understand exactly what the child brings to the educational setting. The second area in the consideration of assistive technology focuses on environmental factors. Typically, one's ability to perform is greatly dependent on what the environment allows one to do. The third area of AT consideration focuses on the tasks that the student is being asked to accomplish (Bakken & Wojcik, 2004). Finally, tools must be identified that can be of use to the student, across environments, to support the identified tasks. This "phase" occurs in four parts: (a) the identification of possible tools, (b) the evaluation of tool characteristics,

(c) the trial of the tool with the student, and (d) the acquisition of the tool for long-term use (Bowser & Reed, 1995; Edyburn, 2000; Zabala, 1995, 1996).

When an AT device is considered for a student with certain learning characteristics, careful attention must be given to ensure that the recommended device or service will help the student to be successful while also reflecting an appropriate match for him or her (Zabala, 1995, 1996). For example, given that prescription eyeglasses can be considered AT and that a certain degree of visual acuity is generally needed for an individual to visually access print, it is important to ensure that the prescription is indeed required for the student to perform and is appropriately matched to his or her visual needs. If eyeglasses are arbitrarily assigned to an individual, they may serve as an obstacle for the individual to see properly, thus hampering his or her overall performance (Bakken & Wojcik, 2004). When deciding on the appropriateness of the AT device, the characteristics of that device or service are important in determining the best match between the tool and the student. Earlier, King (1999) proposed four dimensions along which AT characteristics should be evaluated. The first dimension deals with cognitive demands placed upon the student by the AT device or service. Cognitive demands refer to the determination of the amount of thinking that is required to use a device or service. This may include remembering, sensing, analyzing, discriminating, and sequencing actions needed to operate the tool. The second dimension refers to the extent to which the AT places physical demands upon the student. Physical demands refer to the amount of muscle strength and movement required to initiate, pursue, and complete the task of using the tool. The third dimension is linguistic, which refers to the amount of symbolic interpretation and processing that the user must invest to operate the particular AT device or service. Finally, the last dimension is time: whether the AT device will aid in the completion of the task within an acceptable amount of time. Other factors related to the characteristics of tools include the tool's durability, dependability, lifespan, and maintenance costs/programs (Parette & Hourcade, 1997).

NEW VISION FOR THE NEW MILLENNIUM

In the case of Alissa presented at the beginning of this chapter, there were a number of cultural issues that contributed to the ultimate abandonment of the AT device recommended for her. It is critical for school personnel to first develop a better understanding of racial, cultural, and linguistic backgrounds of students when considering AT solutions. Characteristics of various cultural groups and their influences on AT decision making have been described in more detail elsewhere (Parette, 1998a), though specific issues that *may* be related to some persons from Latino backgrounds are noted in Table 20.2. Caution should be exercised when examining any listing of characteristics of cultural groups, for there are wide variations across families with regard to the acceptance or presence of these values; and families are, admittedly, changing in response to acculturation effects across time and circumstance (Parette, Huer, & Scherer, 2004; Zuniga, 1998).

TABLE 20.2 *Latino Values That May Affect Successful Assistive Technology Implementation*

Families may

- believe visible disabilities are attributed to external, nonmedical causes,
- view disability as part of a divine plan, or as punishment for wrongdoing,
- have difficulty accepting nonvisible disabilities,
- differ in their acceptance of disabilities,
- tend to keep children with disabilities at home.

Families may

- believe in healing processes involving folk medicines,
- rely on spiritualists to heal their children or dispel evil spirits,
- prefer small clinics/service settings to larger facilities,
- seclude and deprive children of treatment if vitality and health are highly valued,
- have negative perceptions of institutionalization and prefer to treat children at home.

Families may

- view the family unit as the most important institution in Latino society,
- indulge children with disabilities with no expectations for child participation in treatment and care,
- teach children that cooperation is more important than competition and individual achievement,
- teach children to respect adults and not to question authority,
- restrict females and teach them that they should be protected,
- value the wisdom and experiences of grandparents.

Families may

- entrust the education of their children to professionals,
- consider direct disagreement to be disrespectful,
- be hesitant to assume a dominant role in intervention decision making for children,
- encourage children to assume responsibility for learning and only offer support if provided with specific instructions by professionals.

Families may

- prefer direct eye contact except with authority figures,
- use tact and diplomacy to avoid arguments,
- prefer small talk before discussing business,
- believe opinions are not needed concerning education issues; professionals know best and will take care of child's problems,
- view time as being unimportant,
- prefer not to feel hurried by professionals,
- encourage cooperation rather than competition,

(Continued)

TABLE 20.2 *(continued)*

- need information about locations of sites for evaluations and require transportation assistance,
- enjoy refreshments at meetings.

Families may

- prefer electronic speech devices that use the dialect of the culture,
- have high expectations for children to be able to use the AT at important family celebrations,
- desire to have training provided to siblings who may assume responsibility for maintenance of certain AT,
- prefer not to use AT in home setting if children's basic needs are being met,
- prefer AT that allows some degree of independence at home,
- prefer not to have training/support services provided in home settings,
- prefer collaborative implementation of AT.

Source: Adapted from H. P. Parette (1998). Cultural issues and family-centered assistive technology decision-making. In S. L. Judge & H. P. Parette (Eds.), *Assistive technology for young children with disabilities: A guide to providing family-centered services* (pp. 184–210). Cambridge, MA: Brookline. Adapted with permission.

Looking back at Alissa's case, we see some potential areas of concern. Surely, they must be addressed to make the new vision a reality. Following are detailed discussions on the potential areas of concern.

Involving the Family in Decision Making

In Alissa's family, as may be the case in many families from nonwhite backgrounds, grandparents may be important decision makers for the family (Lynch & Hanson, 1998; Roseberry-McKibbin, 2002). In some families, parents may be the initial point of contact with school personnel and openly agree with their recommendations, but may defer implementation of an AT device or service only after seeking the counsel of revered grandparents who might disagree with the recommendations of the school. For technology to work with multicultural learners with exceptionalities in this new millennium, families must be involved very early during decision making, and it is the education team's role to understand who the primary decision maker is in each family unit.

Understanding the Family's Value System

Much has been written about the value systems of individuals from Latino and other multicultural backgrounds (see Battle, 1993; Dodd, Nelson, & Peralez, 1988; Grossman, 1984; Marin & Marin, 1991). The values of these families are often quite different from those of school personnel from white backgrounds. The individualized education plan (IEP) team must obtain family input and understand the

TABLE 20.3 *Family Issues Affecting Assistive Technology Device and Service Selection and Questions for Team Consideration*

Family Issues	Questions for Team to Consider
Understanding resource commitments	Are there reasons why you can't use the AT at home or in the community? How do you think the AT will affect your child? How do you think the AT will affect your home setting? How do you think the AT will affect other children at home? your spouse? other family members? Will the use of the AT result in changes in family routines?
Understanding expectations for independence	Will you use the AT in community settings outside the home? What skills or commitment will be required of others in the community for your child to be able to use the AT successfully? Do you want your child to perform routine daily tasks, or do you or other family members expect to do daily tasks for the child?
Understanding degree of acceptance anticipated	Are there reasons not to use the AT device outside the home? Will AT make you or your child feel self-conscious or cause undue attention if used in public settings? How will people around you and your child feel if the AT is used outside the home?
Family expectations regarding immediacy of benefits	What do you think the AT will do for your child? How will you and your child use the AT? What benefits do you expect? Will they be immediate? Are there special occasions in the future where you would like to "showcase" the AT to family and friends? What training is needed? How will you pay for the AT? How often will your child use the AT? Will your child need assistance? Who will provide the assistance?

Source: Adapted from P. Parette & G. A. McMahan (2002). Team sensitivity to family goals for and expectations of assistive technology. *Teaching Exceptional Children, 35*(1), 56–61. Adapted with permission.

family's value system and preferences—a critical component of family-centered, culturally sensitive practice (Parette, 1998a). Noted in Table 20.3 are questions that might be asked of family members to better understand their needs, preferences, and what they are willing to do when AT devices and services are being considered. In Alissa's case, by not understanding the family's values and preferences, school personnel moved forward in setting an IEP meeting at the school where it was convenient for professionals, but perhaps not for the family given their limited transportation resources. No apparent effort was made to meet the family in an alternative setting that was convenient for them so they could participate in the IEP meeting, a need often expressed by families who might prefer more neutral or accessible meeting sites (Hourcade, Parette, & Huer, 1997). Although Alissa's family may certainly defer educational decision making regarding her education to experts, given that Latino families value the perspectives of educators (Roseberry-McKibbin, 2002), the extension of recommendations into the home setting may be intrusive and overwhelming, and be ignored (Hourcade et al., 1997). Additionally, in Alissa's case, no effort was made to offer or provide training in the use of the Dynavox at home to family members, so it might be expected that the family was ill prepared to support Alissa during her attempts to use the device at the *quinceanera*.

Knowing the Importance of Cooperation Versus Personal Achievement

For many Latinos and other multicultural families, the role of the individual is deemphasized, with greater importance placed on collectivism, or the unity and cooperation of the family (Roseberry-McKibbin, 2002). Unfortunately, school personnel value individual responsibility and achievement, while greater importance is placed on cooperation. If the S/LP had placed greater emphasis on Alissa in setting up her language system (versus an emphasis on cooperative phrases), her communicative efforts might have been disapproved by other individuals within the family. Involving the family in identifying key language for use at home and the social event might have contributed to a more successful outcome for Alissa. The Latino value of *machismo* (Zuniga, 1998), or male dominance and protective feelings toward women, also appeared to be present in her family. Lack of sensitivity to this value by encouraging interactions "in the community" (with other males outside the family) may have become problematic at her *quinceanera*. Understanding such contexts is important for professionals interested in maximizing the fullest potential of multicultural learners in this new millennium.

When families from diverse cultural backgrounds place less importance on the individual (versus the family) and/or also feel obligations to take care of a child with a disability due to religious belief systems (e.g., "God intervened and gave me this special child"), there may be a tendency for families to foster a sense of dependence. School personnel from white backgrounds may place great value on independence (Hanson, 1998), though this value may sometimes conflict with values of families with whom they are working. It is extremely important that professionals understand the relationship between cooperation and personal achievement.

Recognizing Important Holidays

In Latino culture, the *quinceanera* is a fifteenth birthday celebration that is a woman's "coming of age" and more people are invited. Typically, activities surrounding the event occur across an entire day, including attendance at church and recognition by the priest, followed by live music, dancing, and other celebratory activities at the family's home. With proper planning and understanding of the significance of this family event, this ceremony would have been a wonderful time to showcase the power of the Dynavox and achieve family buy-in. Because the S/LP failed to understand its significance and work with family members to identify Spanish language phrases that would be deemed important (e.g., addressing grandparents, aunts, and uncles), the school may have communicated lack of respect to the family and unwittingly contributed to Alissa's unsuccessful experience using the device. Related to this was the failure of the S/LP to use language on Alissa's device that had a Spanish accent, because family members have noted the importance of their children "sounding like" other individuals in their cultural setting (VanBierliet & Parette, 1999). Each student and case is different, but when working with multicultural learners with exceptionalities, educators must be culturally responsive to student and family needs.

A Culturally Responsive Educator

1. Believes students who are economically disadvantaged and culturally different must have access to materials and technology in the classroom.
2. Understands that technological infusion in school curricula will benefit multicultural learners with exceptionalities.
3. Incorporates cultural, linguistic, and experiential differences, as well as differences in social class, into the learning process.
4. Knows that the student's culture is essential in facilitating, structuring, and validating successful learning for all students.
5. Provides supportive multimedia environments in which multicultural students can practice their writing, reading, and communication skills.
6. Understands that failure to address familial/cultural factors may result in the prescription of inappropriate AT devices to children and/or family members.
7. Appreciates technology as a valuable tool that promotes active multicultural student involvement in the learning process.
8. Assists multicultural students in accessing and organizing technological information.
9. Decides on the appropriateness of AT for multicultural learners with exceptionalities.
10. Supports multicultural collaboration and consultation on technological issues.

Conclusion

With all of the technological growth and advancements currently and in the fore-seeable future, it is inevitable that technology will change the way general and special educators teach. Technology will provide students and teachers more resources as well as opportunities in and outside of the classroom to do things they may never have had access to doing before. General and special education teachers must make careful and thoughtful decisions on when and how to use technology and make sure that it is appropriate and not actually hindering multicultural students with exceptionalities. Just like teaching with any method, assessment should be an interwoven component that looks at the effectiveness of the technology in current settings and applications. It is important that all students have accessible and unique opportunities regarding technology regardless of cultural and linguistic backgrounds. To help students in this new millennium, school personnel must teach how to transfer skills from the classroom to the real world and work closely with multicultural families to accomplish this endeavor.

Discussion Questions

1. Briefly explain how technology can aid teachers of multicultural learners with disabilities.
2. Describe how AT tools should be evaluated for multicultural learners with disabilities.
3. Evaluate how teachers can properly facilitate learning for all students.
4. Discuss two examples of ways multimedia can enhance a multicultural classroom.
5. In two short paragraphs, summarize how the family can have an effect on technology for multicultural learners with exceptionalities.

References

Abledata. (n.d.). *Welcome to Abledata.* Retrieved May 4, 2005, from www.abledata.com

Assistive Technology—Strategies, Tools, Accommodations, and Resources (ATSTAR). (n.d.). *AT information.* Retrieved May 4, 2005, from www.atstar.org/information.html

Bakken, J. P. (1999). *Assistive technology. Competencies and skills for teachers. Book 7—Technologies to complete academic tasks.* Normal: Illinois State University.

Bakken, J. P., & Wojcik, B. W. (2004). Technology resources for persons with learning disabilities. In F. E. Obiakor & A. F. Rotatori (Eds.), *Advances in special education: Current perspectives on learning disabilities* (Vol. 16, pp. 113–132). Oxford, England: Elsevier Science/JAI Press.

Battle, D. E. (Ed.). (1993). *Communication disorders in multicultural populations.* Boston: Andover Medical.

Bowles, S., & Gintis, H. (1976). *Schooling in capitalist America: Educational reform and the contradictions of economic life.* New York: Basic Books.

Bowser, G., & Reed, P. (1995). Education TECH points for assistive technology planning. *Journal of Special Education Technology, 12,* 325–338.

Brown, M. (2002). Multicultural education and technology: Perspectives to consider. *Journal of Special Education Technology, 17*(3), 51–55.

Carolan, B. (2001). Technology, schools, and the decentralization of culture. *First Monday, 6*(8), 1–14.

Cole, M., & Griffin, P. (1987). *Contextual factors in education: Improving science and mathematics education for minorities and women.* Madison: Wisconsin Center of Education Research.

Damarin, S. K. (1998). Technology and multicultural education: The question of convergence. *Theory into Practice, 37*(1), 11–19.

D'Andrea, M. (1995). Using computer technology to promote multicultural awareness among elementary school-age students. *Elementary School Guidance & Counseling, 30,* 45–54.

Dillon, A., & Gabbard, R. (1998). Hypermedia as an educational technology: A review of the quantitative research literature on learner comprehension, control, and style. *Review of Educational Research, 68,* 322–349.

Dodd, J. M., Nelson, J. R., & Peralez, E. (1988). Understanding the Hispanic student. *The Rural Educator, 10*(2), 8–13.

Edyburn, D. L. (2000). 1999 in review: A synthesis of the special education technology literature. *Journal of Special Education Technology, 15*(1), 7–18.

Edyburn, D., Higgins, K., & Boone, R. (Eds.). (2005). *Handbook of special education technology research and practice.* Whitefish Bay, WI: Knowledge by Design.

Fabris, M. E. (1992). Using multimedia in the multicultural classroom. *Journal of Educational Technology Systems, 21,* 163–171.

Freedman, K., & Liu, M. (1996). The importance of computer experience, learning processes, and communication patterns in multicultural networking. *Educational Technology Research & Development, 44*(1), 43–59.

Gardner, J. E., & Wissick, C. A. (2002). Enhancing thematic units using the World Wide Web: Tools and strategies for students with mild disabilities. *Journal of Special Education Technology, 17*(1), 27–38.

Gardner, J. E., Wissick, C. A., Schweder, W., & Canter, L. S. (2003). Enhancing interdisciplinary instruction in general and special education. *Remedial and Special Education, 24,* 161–172.

Georgia Project for Assistive Technology. (2005). *Assistive technology resources.* From www.gpat.org/GPAT%20Resource%20Topic%20Pages/GPAT%20Resource%20Main%20Page.htm

Gollnick, D. M., & Chinn, P. C. (2002). *Multicultural education in a pluralistic society* (6th ed.). Upper Saddle River, NJ: Merrill/Prentice Hall.

Gorski, P. (2001). *Multicultural education and the Internet: Intersections and integrations.* Boston: McGraw-Hill.

Grossman, H. (1984). *Educating Hispanic students: Cultural implications in instruction, classroom management, counseling and assessment.* Springfield, IL: Charles C Thomas.

Guild, P. (1994). The culture/learning style connection. *Educational Leadership, 51*(8), 16–21.

Hanson, M. J. (1998). Families with Anglo-European roots. In E. W. Lynch & M. J. Hanson (Eds.), *Developing cross-cultural competence: A guide for working with young children and their families* (pp. 93–126). Baltimore: Brookes.

Heinrich, R., Molenda, M., Russell, J. D., & Smaldino, S. E. (2002). *Instructional media and technologies for learning* (7th ed.). Upper Saddle River, NJ: Merrill/Prentice Hall.

Hourcade, J. J., Parette, H. P., & Huer, M. B. (1997). Family and cultural alert! Considerations in assistive technology assessment. *Teaching Exceptional Children, 30*(1), 40–44.

Individuals with Disabilities Education Act of 1990, Pub. L. No. 101-476. (October 30, 1990). 20 U.S.C. 1400 et seq: *U.S. Statutes at Large, 104,* 1103–1151.

Institute for Matching Person and Technology. (2004). *Matching person and technology.* Retrieved January 22, 2004, from members.aol.com/IMPT97/MPT.html

Jonassen, D. H., Howland, J. L., Moore, J. L., & Marra, R. M. (2003). *Learning to solve problems with technology: A constructivist perspective* (2nd ed.). Upper Saddle River, NJ: Merrill/Prentice Hall.

Kalyanpur, M., & Harry, B. (1999). *Culture in special education. Building reciprocal family-professional relationships.* Baltimore: Brookes.

Kelker, K. A., & Holt, R. (2000). *Family guide to assistive technology.* Cambridge, MA: Brookline Books.

Kemp, C., & Parette, H. P. (2000). Barriers to minority parent involvement in assistive technology (AT) decision-making processes. *Education and Training in Mental Retardation and Developmental Disabilities, 35*(4), 384–392.

King, T. W. (1999). *Assistive technology: Essential human factors.* Needham Heights, MA: Allyn & Bacon.

Lever-Duffy, J., McDonald, J. B., & Mizell, A. P. (2003). *Teaching and learning with technology.* Boston: Allyn & Bacon.

Lindsey, J. D. (2000). *Technology and exceptional individuals* (3rd ed.). Austin, TX: PRO-ED.

Lynch, E. W., & Hanson, M. J. (Eds.). (1998). *Developing cross-cultural competence. A guide for working with young children and their families* (2nd ed.). Baltimore: Brookes.

Maccini, P., Gagnon, J. C., & Hughes, C. A. (2002). Technology-based practices for secondary students with learning disabilities. *Learning Disability Quarterly, 25,* 247–261.

Marin, G., & Marin, B. (1991). Hispanics: Who are they? In G. Marin & B. Marin (Eds.), *Research with Hispanic populations* (pp. 1–17). Beverly Hills, CA: Sage.

Milone, M. N., & Salpeter, J. (1996). Technology and equity issues. *Technology and Learning, 16*(4), 38–47.

National Telecommunications & Information Administration. (1999). *Falling through the net: Defining the digital divide.* Retrieved January 20, 2004, from www.ntia.doc.gov/ntiahome/fttn99/contents.html

Nieto, S. (1994). Lessons from students on creating a chance to dream. *Harvard Educational Review, 64,* 392–425.

Parette, H. P. (1998a). Cultural issues and family-centered assistive technology decision-making. In S. L. Judge & H. P. Parette (Eds.), *Assistive technology for young children with disabilities: A guide to providing family-centered services* (pp. 184–210). Cambridge, MA: Brookline.

Parette, H. P. (1998b). Effective and promising assistive technology practices for students with mental retardation and developmental disabilities. In A. Hilton & R. Ringlaben (Eds.), *Effective and promising practices in developmental disabilities* (pp. 205–224). Austin, TX: PRO-ED.

Parette, H. P., & Hourcade, J. J. (1997). Family issues and assistive technology needs: A sampling of state practices. *Journal of Special Education Technology, 13*(3), 27–43.

Parette, H. P., Huer, M. B., & Scherer, M. (2004). Effects of acculturation on assistive technology service delivery. *Journal of Special Education Technology, 19*(2), 31–41.

Parette, H. P., Huer, M. B., & VanBiervliet, A. (2005). Cultural issues and assistive technology. In D. L. Edyburn, K. Higgins, & R. Boone (Eds.), *Handbook of special education technology research and practice* (pp. 81–103). Whitefish Bay, WI: Knowledge by Design.

Pastore, M. (2000). *Digital divide more economic than ethnic.* Retrieved January 22, 2004, from cyberatlas.internet.com/big_picture/demographics/article/0, 1323, 5901_395581, 00.html

Piller, C. (1992, September). Separate realities. *MacWorld, 9*(9), 218–230.

Reed, P., & Bowser, G. (1998, November). *Education tech points: A framework for assistive technology planning and systems change in schools.* Paper presented at the CSUN Conference on Technology and Persons with Disabilities, Los Angeles, CA.

Rehabtool.com. (2004). *What's assistive technology.* Retrieved May 4, 2005, from www.rehabtool.com/at.html

Roblyer, M. D. (2004). *Integrating educational technology into teaching* (3rd ed.). Upper Saddle River, NJ: Merrill.

Roblyer, M. D., Dozier-Henry, O., & Burnette, A. P. (1996). Technology and multicultural education: The "uneasy alliance." *Educational Technology, 35*(3), 5–12.

Roseberry-McKibbin, C. (2002). *Multicultural students with special language needs* (2nd ed.). Oceanside, CA: Academic Communication.

Swain, C., & Pearson, T. (2003). Educators and technology standards: Influencing the digital divide. *Journal of Research on Technology in Education, 34*, 326–335.

Swan, K., & Meskill, C. (1996). Using hypermedia in response-based literature classrooms: A critical review of commercial applications. *Journal of Research on Computing in Education, 29*, 167–192.

Taylor, R. (Ed.). (1980). *The computer in the school: Tutor, tool, tutee.* New York: Teachers College Press.

U.S. Department of Education. (2003). *Internet access soars in schools, but "digital divide" still exists at home for minority and poor students.* Retrieved January 20, 2003, from www.ed.gov/news/pressreleases/2003/10/10292003a.html

VanBiervliet, A., & Parette, H. P. (1999). *Families, cultures and AAC* (CD-ROM). Little Rock, AR: Southeast Missouri State University and University of Arkansas for Medical Sciences.

Wilhelm, T., Carmen, D., & Reynolds, M. (2002). *Connecting kids to technology: Challenges and opportunities.* Baltimore, MD: Annie E. Casey Foundation. (ERIC Document Reproduction Service No. ED467133)

Wissick, C. A. (1996). Multimedia: Enhancing instruction for students with learning disabilities. *Journal of Learning Disabilities, 29*, 494–503.

Zabala, J. (1995, March). *The SETT framework: Critical areas to consider when making informed assistive technology decisions.* Paper presented at the Florida Assistive Technology Impact Conference and Technology and Media Division of Council for Exceptional Children, Orlando, FL.

Zabala, J. (1996). SETTing the stage for success: Building success though effective selection and use of assistive technology systems. In *Proceedings of the Southeast Augmentative Communication Conference* (pp. 1–11). Birmingham, AL: Southeast AC Conference.

Zabala, J. (1998). *Ready, SETT, go! Online workshop.* Retrieved January 7, 2003, from www2.edc.org/NCIP/Workshops/sett3/index.html

Zuniga, M. E. (1998). Families with Latino roots. In E. W. Lynch & M. J. Hanson (Eds.), *Developing cross-cultural competence: A guide for working with young children and their families* (pp. 209–250). Baltimore: Brookes.

Chapter 21

Multicultural Special Education: Future Perspectives

Robert Rueda

Chapter Outline

Thinking About Multicultural Special Education

Several years ago, a Latino college professor was conducting a research study in a special education classroom in Southern California populated by low-income English-language learners. The school was situated in a neighborhood plagued by poverty, gang problems, and other factors that unfortunately characterize many urban multicultural schools. One aspect of the study was looking at teachers' perceptions of students' academic problems. Teacher interviews pointed to many of the "usual suspects"—visual motor processing problems, low motivation, and low IQ—which reflected the training and labels acquired by them in their teacher education programs. By chance, this professor started a discussion with the paraeducator (a Latina from the surrounding community) in the classroom on the same set of questions, focusing on a particular student he called Armando. Surprisingly, her answers reflected neither the same labels, problem areas, or definition of the problem used by the teacher. In discussing Armando's academic difficulties, she pointed to family problems, (e.g., pending divorce in the family and involvement of an older sibling with a gang) that had nothing to do with presumed psychological deficits within the child. She only knew this because of her familiarity with the community and families in the neighborhood, something not shared by the teacher. Watching this student struggle to write an essay about an abstract person named Abraham Lincoln in preparation for the pending holiday, this professor wondered how the student would ever make some connection between his own experiences and that of President Lincoln from so long ago. How could the issues and problems faced by this far-removed character have some importance or bearing on Armando's own life? Without skillful help that would assist him to make this bridge, it seemed highly unlikely. Unfortunately, the scripted independent writing exercise ("Write two paragraphs about Abraham Lincoln and make sure you have correct spelling and punctuation so that I can check it") fell far short in this regard. Predictably, Armando spent a great deal of time off-task and produced a couple of sentences that were full of mechanical and grammatical errors. As a result, the professor noted to himself that this scene is played out in many classrooms every day, and was left wondering, "What would it take to engage a student such as Armando?"

In that same classroom, the professor noticed something else that struck him. The teacher interacted with the students in a relatively formal "teacher-like" way, as might be expected. The paraeducator, on the other hand, tended to act much more like a grandmother or older relative in terms of language use (using terms of affection in addressing students, switching between Spanish and English similar to students' language patterns, and using locally recognizable words and forms), physical contact (affectionate touching), and general demeanor. In turn, Armando's behavior was different around the paraeducator than it was around the teacher, often more informal and relaxed. What was the connection between these two observations? The professor began to consider that while the teacher had a great deal of pedagogical knowledge as a result of her teacher education program, she did not know a great deal about the lives or interests of the students nor much about the surrounding community. The paraeducator, on the other hand, had a significant amount of knowledge in these areas, but lacked formal training in pedagogy. This unfortunate disconnect highlights a significant issue with a great deal of relevance to the future of special education.

- *How should culture and cultural differences be considered in special education practice and pedagogy?*
- *How can students from all backgrounds be provided a relevant education that builds on their existing skills, knowledge, and interests?*

There are clearly many forces that have served to compel change in special education as a field in the recent past. Some of these forces have included school reform and restructuring efforts, calls for closer collaboration or merger with regular education, an emphasis on inclusion and least restrictive environments, and increased accountability pressures (McLaughlin & Rouse, 1999). Just as significant, however, but perhaps less recognized, is the change in the population served by the system. The population in general has become more diverse along the lines of racial, cultural, language, and immigration backgrounds. Not surprisingly, this has been reflected in the population of students with disabilities (Artiles & Ortiz, 2002). What are the implications of these changes for the special education system? What are the ramifications for instructional practices? How should the field prepare for an increasingly diverse clientele? How can past problems in this area be overcome?

CULTURAL ISSUES IN SPECIAL EDUCATION: FUTURE CHALLENGES

One of the biggest issues having to do with diversity in general and special education in particular has been the tendency to consider differences as deficits (Valencia, 1997). Differences based on race, ethnicity, language, and socioeconomic status (SES) either alone or in combination have a long history of being considered de facto problems to be overcome independent of information directly relating to ability or competence. Given the longstanding but continuing controversy over the issue of overrepresentation of diverse students in special education, the future implications for identification, referral, assessment, and instruction are abundant. What are some of the specific challenges that need to be addressed in the future?

An important challenge for the future will be to remember that *racial, ethnic, cultural, and language differences should not automatically be considered deficits.* Another issue has been the tendency to generalize real or presumed characteristics of a group or subgroup to all members of that group. Yet general overarching cultural values, artifacts, and attributes, even if they are shared by a number of people of a particular group, are mediated by the unique contexts in which these are constructed and expressed. It is more useful to look at what people actually *do* (cultural practices) than to make assumptions about large-scale belief or value systems that they may or may not share (cultural models) (Gallimore & Goldenberg, 2001). Attempting to reduce culture by focusing on visible or invisible attributes is a start at examining cultural factors but it is not a particularly useful one. Another challenge for the field will be to remember that *global labels such as those based on race, ethnicity, or even language are not useful or informative about individuals without other evidence.*

A common error in the educational and psychological literature has been the failure to differentiate SES, ethnicity, race, language, and culture. Sometimes studies group participants by ethnicity and/or race, and they treat these as equivalent to culture. Other times what are thought to be cultural factors may in fact be socioeconomically driven. Crowded living conditions, parents' long working hours, lack of print materials, may all affect an individual student's learning. The field will be challenged to keep in mind that *race, ethnicity, language, and SES can influence learning and development independently as well as interactively.*

Another interesting characteristic of discussions of culture in educational circles has been the appearance that culture and cultural factors are mainly or exclusively characteristics of minority students. Yet culture is a characteristic of every human activity and institution. Every teacher brings unique cultural characteristics to the classroom, and every classroom is characterized by a unique culture and a unique sociocultural organization. In a recent paper I and some of my colleagues examined, for example, how teachers' personal early learning experiences helped shape their current teaching practices (Arzubiaga, MacGillivray, & Rueda, 2002). An additional challenge for the field will be to remember that *teachers, no matter what their background, bring their own unique cultural beliefs and practices into the classroom—culture is not just a characteristic of "minority" students.* It is precisely because much of cultural knowledge is automated and invisible that we are often not aware of how it affects personal behaviors or judgments about others.

ACCOMMODATING CULTURE IN SPECIAL EDUCATION PRACTICE: FUTURE DIRECTIONS

Recent syntheses of research and theory in the area of learning suggest that cultural factors are more important than had been thought in the past (Alexander & Murphy, 1999; Bransford, Brown, & Cocking, 1999; Lambert & McCombs, 1998). Indeed, the store of knowledge that a learner has forms the foundation for future learning. Unfortunately, in special education, there has been a tendency to minimize or ignore such factors in the face of learning difficulties or low achievement, as if an entirely new set of principles were operating. The general rationale seems to be that factors such as cultural considerations should be secondary to more "basic" or fundamental learning. There is little evidence that the learning characteristics of low achievers are regulated by different theories of learning. Although there are some students with disabilities who suffer severe cognitive, affective, and physical impairments, including central nervous system damage that might influence learning, this does not characterize the largest part of the special education population (U.S. Department of Education, 2002). Thus, a major challenge for the field in the 21st century is to consider cultural factors in policy and practice in ways that have not been done thus far. What are promising areas that will guide the field over the next decades? One promising direction for the future is to build on the realization that *the cultural knowledge that a learner brings to a learning situation or task should not be ignored but rather seen as an important resource for learning, and therefore needs to be built on as a tool for learning.*

It is important to note that culture cannot be *trivialized.* It has not been uncommon to see cultural issues being addressed in many classrooms, although it is less common in special education. However, it is often done in ways that focus on trivial cultural artifacts and in ways that are not connected to instructional goals (MacGillivray, Rueda, & Martinez, 2004). An instructional challenge for the future will be to act on the idea that *culturally responsive teaching should not focus on trivial cultural artifacts such as holidays or dress or food in a manner that is unconnected to academic goals, but rather should be strategic and connected to instructional goals that are complex and challenging.*

In the past, interestingly, a common approach to dealing with cultural issues in the classroom has been to incorporate some type of learning styles instruction that seeks to match instructional practice with presumed culturally based learning styles. However, it is important to keep in mind that there are many conceptual and methodological critiques of learning style approaches (Gutierrez & Rogoff, 2003); and moreover, learning theory does not support the view that we learn only through one modality. Most important, there is no research base for the claim that adapting instruction to presumed learning styles makes a difference in achievement. *Culturally responsive teaching does not mean focusing on learning styles in a simplistic way that matches teaching practices with cultural features presumed to characterize entire groups.*

It is critical to know what needs to be accommodated and how far it should go. A common criticism of work in the area of cultural accommodation is that if taken too literally, it would mean transporting all of the features of students' homes and communities into the classroom. However, this is an inappropriate generalization. *Culturally responsive teaching also does not mean trying to recreate children's homes in the classroom. It needs to be selective, strategic, and tied to instructional goals* (MacGillivray et al., 2004). As argued here, culture is a characteristic of every human activity. Every teacher, every classroom, every school, every community—all are surrounded by cultural features and cultural inheritances. It should be kept in mind that *culture is not just a characteristic of minority students. Rather than teaching about students' cultures, teachers should learn to teach culturally.* This means that teachers need to be aware of their own cultural practices and to examine carefully the sociocultural organization of classroom settings they orchestrate, as these can be important mediators of learning.

A current area of much concern in education is opportunity to learn. This is important under the current emphasis in educational policy on accountability, since in a norm-referenced system, valid comparisons about ability and potential can only be made when equal opportunity to learn has been established. *Cultural accommodation may be seen as addressing the issue of opportunity to learn—students can be advantaged or disadvantaged by the way instructional activities are organized and carried out.* Given the history of dissemination practice in education, the temptation might be to design and test a replicable program of culturally responsive instruction for wide-scale dissemination. Indeed, in the current educational landscape, there is a great deal of concern with scientifically validated interventions, replicability, and "scale-up." This current focus on scientific validation of intervention practices is critical (although somewhat methodologically narrow in the insistence on true experimental design as the only way of gaining important information about classroom interventions and processes). The emphasis on better and more systematic investigation and empirical (not necessarily experimental) evidence is a worthy and important target of the field. Yet the hope should not be to design a package that is transportable and "practitioner-proof," equally applicable in all contexts. What is often left out of this discussion is the important mediating influence of context in human behavior. Broad-based principles of practice are extremely valuable, but to think that they can be implemented without considering the features of the local context is to ignore the wealth of research over the last half century that has documented the impact of context. After all, schools are not factories, and students are not products, so there will always be a place for experience, judgment, and local knowledge in deciding the best ways to facilitate learning for any individual student or group of students.

A Culturally Responsive Educator

1. Understands that the future of a student's education is tied to his or her cultural knowledge.
2. Knows that knowledge alone is not enough and that it must be applied to be relevant.
3. Values and infuses culture in skills for identification, assessments, and categorization.
4. Believes disproportionality exists and plans ways to positively deal with it.
5. Sees current demographic changes in the student population as a motivational factor to shift instructional practices in his or her teaching.
6. Understands the importance of multicultural special education in working with students from culturally and linguistically diverse backgrounds.
7. Believes a narrow focus on evidence-based strategies alone will not address pedagogical issues nor foster equitable outcomes for multicultural learners with exceptionalities without attention to sociocultural and policy issues.
8. Shares innovative ideas with parents, colleagues, and students, in spite of their cultural backgrounds.
9. Understands that education is a continuous process of growth for all stakeholders.
10. Understands that the complexity of cultural influences cannot be used as an alibi for not infusing multicultural education in school programs.

Conclusion

The issues raised in this chapter are not new, and as it stands, others have raised similar concerns (Artiles, 2003; Harry, 1992; Kalyanpur & Harry, 1999). Amando's situation in the introductory case supplies significant and important future challenges for the field. What is new is the extent to which the population served by the system has changed. As the field thinks ahead to the next decades, it will be important to deal with the significant variability in the population served and to weave this focus into the extensive knowledge base acquired to this point. The future test lies in the extent to which the field provides equitable instructional and academic outcomes to the entire range of students served.

Discussion Questions

1. Briefly explain cultural characteristics that you as a future teacher bring to the classroom.
2. Discuss salient sociocultural characteristics that you intend to observe in your multicultural classroom.
3. Describe the unique knowledge, skills, and strengths of students in your future classroom and community.
4. Explain how you can build on strengths to create culturally responsive teaching environments and further your instructional opportunities and goals.
5. Evaluate cautions that you should be aware of in thinking about cultural factors in your own teaching and your own classroom.

References

Alexander, P. A., & Murphy, K. P. (1999). The research base for APA's learner-centered psychological principles. In N. M. Lambert & B. L. McCombs (Eds.), *How students learn: Reforming schools through learner-centered education* (p. 26). Alexandria, VA: Association for Supervision and Curriculum Development.

Artiles, A. J. (2003). Special education's changing identity: Paradoxes and dilemmas in views of culture and space. *Harvard Educational Review, 73*(2), 164–202.

Artiles, A. J., & Ortiz, A. A. (Eds.). (2002). *English language learners with special education needs.* Washington, DC: Center for Applied Linguistics and Delta Systems.

Arzubiaga, A., MacGillivray, L., & Rueda, R. (2002). *An ecocultural view of how teachers' early family literacy routines and practices impact current adult routines and practices.* Paper presented at the Annual Meeting of the American Educational Research Association, New Orleans, LA.

Bransford, J. D., Brown, A. L., & Cocking, R. R. (1999). *How people learn: Brain, mind, experience, and school.* Washington, DC: National Academy Press.

Gallimore, R., & Goldenberg, C. (2001). Analyzing cultural models and settings to connect minority achievement and school improvement research. *Educational Psychologist, 36*, 45–56.

Gutierrez, K., & Rogoff, B. (2003). Cultural ways of learning: Individual traits or repertoires of practice. *Educational Researcher, 32*(5), 19–25.

Harry, B. (1992). *Cultural diversity, families, and the special education system: Communication and empowerment.* New York: Teachers College Press.

Kalyanpur, M., & Harry, B. (1999). *Culture in special education: Building reciprocal family-professional relationships.* Baltimore: Brookes.

Lambert, N. M., & McCombs, B. L. (1998). *How students learn: Reforming schools through learner-centered education.* Washington, DC: American Psychological Association.

MacGillivray, L., Rueda, R., & Martinez, A. M. (2004). Listening to inner-city teachers of English language learners: Differentiating literacy instruction. In F. B. Boyd & C. H. Brock (Eds.), *Multicultural and multilingual literacy and language: Contexts and practices* (pp. 144–162). New York: Guilford Press.

McLaughlin, M. J., & Rouse, M. (Eds.). (1999). *Special education and school reform in the United States and Britain.* London, England: Routledge.

U.S. Department of Education. (2002). *Twenty-fourth Annual Report to Congress on the Implementation of the Individuals with Disabilities Education Act.* Washington, DC: U.S. Government Printing Office.

Valencia, R. R. (1997). *The evolution of deficit thinking: Educational thought and practice.* London, England: Falmer Press.

Name Index

Page numbers followed by f indicate figure; those followed by t indicate table.

Subject Index

Page numbers followed by f indicate figure; those followed by t indicate table.